Early praise for

THE OCCUPY HANDBOOK

"More than a scrapbook of the recent Occupy Wall Street movement, *The Occupy Handbook*, a compilation by our best journalists, thinkers, and economists, puts the story of America's revolt against inequality in welcome historical perspective. From the barricades of 1848, to the barrios of modern Chile, to the improbable campgrounds thrown together in the shadows of New York skyscrapers, the *Handbook* examines the budding question of whether democracy can foster a more equal, and also a more prosperous, society. Insightful pieces by Gillian Tett, John Cassidy, Bethany McLean, and many more prepare you to think about the next outbreak of outrage and activism—which is only a matter of time."

—Roger Lowenstein, author of *The End of Wall Street* and *When Genius Failed*

"This fascinating collection explains why *and* how income and wealth inequalities have rightly climbed to the top of the policy agenda in so many countries. With multiple perspectives from both experts and activists, *The Occupy Handbook* contains valuable insights on the historical context, the formation of the popular movements, their impact, and what the future may hold. I suspect it won't be long before this handbook is viewed as the reference guide for understanding how an unstructured gathering of people in Zuccotti Park ended up providing the catalyst redefining policy imperatives around the world."

—Mohamed A. El-Erian, CEO of PIMCO and author of *When Markets Collide*

Also by Janet Byrne

A Genius for Living: The Life of Frieda Lawrence

THE OCCUPY HANDBOOK

EDITED BY JANET BYRNE

GUEST EDITOR
ROBIN WELLS

BACK BAY BOOKS
Little, Brown and Company
New York Boston London

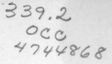

Back Bay Books/Little, Brown and Company
Hachette Book Group
237 Park Avenue, New York, NY 10017
www.hachettebookgroup.com

First Edition: April 2012

Back Bay Books is an imprint of Little, Brown and Company. The Back Bay Books name and logo are trademarks of Hachette Book Group, Inc.

The publisher is not responsible for websites (or their content) that are not owned by the publisher.

The Hachette Speakers Bureau provides a wide range of authors for speaking events. To find out more, go to www.hachettespeakersbureau.com or call (866) 376-6591.

ISBN 978-0-316-22021-7
LCCN 2012933520

10 9 8 7 6 5 4 3 2 1

RRD-C

Printed in the United States of America

To Zack and Daniel,
who heard a lot about the contributors,
and whose own contributions are of another order of magnitude

Contents

CONTENTS

Part II
WHERE WE ARE NOW

Contents

Part III
SOLUTIONS

Contents

Contents

THE OCCUPY HANDBOOK

Introduction

A Tale of Two Taxes

Nobody lies groaning under the yoke of inauthenticity twenty-four hours a day.

—Raoul Vaneigem

One fall morning I stood outside the Princeton Club, on West 43rd Street in Manhattan. Occupy Wall Street, which I had visited several times as a sympathetic outsider, had passed its one-month anniversary, and I thought the movement might usefully be analyzed by economists and financial writers whose pieces I would commission and assemble into a book that was analytical and—this was what really interested me—prescriptive. I'd been invited to breakfast to talk about the idea with a Princeton Club member and had arrived early out of nervousness.

It seemed a strange place to be discussing the book. I tried the idea out on a young bellhop. He said that he took the protests seriously, found himself wondering about the methodology, but was not involved. He didn't have the time: he didn't live in Manhattan and, besides the bellhop job, he was in school. Paying for college was difficult. The protests made sense to him, he said, for one reason: they concerned what mattered to everyone—the economy. I had expected more resistance, some frank skepticism, maybe a comment to the effect that the protests struck him as frivolous. Thirty minutes later, the response of my breakfast companion more or less echoed the bellhop's: the first of many such universal reactions I'd hear to the issues raised by OWS.

Occupy Wall Street has the rare distinction of being a protest movement that even the objects of its attack can find little fault with. According to the Spectrem Group, a consulting firm serving ultra-high-net-worth individuals, 61 percent to 68 percent of millionaires support raising taxes on millionaires. Although every banker I approached to participate in this book, including JPMorgan Chase CEO Jamie Dimon, politely declined, it was impossible not to sense that, behind the scrim, income inequality was a subject that everyone, even bankers, wanted to speak about.

A single exception to the bankers' silence came late in the project, when I received a phone call from Paul Volcker. I had tried to contact him for about two months—two-thirds of this book's entire short gestation period—through such avenues as the Atlantic Salmon Federation: an avid fly fisherman and conservationist, he has served as a director of the organization. Finally, I had sent a letter, by snail mail, to one last address. It was an unconscionably long letter, because by then the roster of contributors, which I included, had grown. I put my phone number under my signature.

Fielding a call from Paul Volcker might have been daunting if he had been all business. I suppose he was, but what I heard on the phone was a disarmingly friendly laugh in a low register. "Tell me," the former chairman of the Federal Reserve said, "did you really get all these people to write something for you?" I remembered a Reuters headline from a few months before: "Paul Volcker Says Volcker Rule Too Complicated." The story was written after the collapse of the brokerage MF Global. MF's filing for bankruptcy was held up as an object lesson in the need for the so-called Volcker rule, which limits the kind of proprietary trading that helped lead to the worldwide financial collapse. Another rumble; one or two more questions. I was being vetted, but there was no hint of challenge. What I detected was more of a we're-all-in-this-together sentiment. One sensed that this was a man who liked the truth and knew how to find it.

His piece came in immediately after our conversation, arriving on the same day as the songwriter Tom Verlaine's interview with *Rolling Stone* journalist Matt Taibbi. Paul Volcker and Matt Taibbi feel basically the same way about certain things.

This is a book about fairness. It came together shockingly fast, in a small laundry room in an old house in the "Pharm Belt": my office. Bucks County, Pennsylvania, was once a "farm belt." With its pharmaceutical and financial corporations grafted onto a largely discarded agricultural landscape, it displays some of the same perversions of income inequality and perks of high-income contagion that are common to much of the country. The median household income is $74,828. Only 4.9 percent live below the poverty level. Infrastructure is superb, people work hard, and there is a firm volunteer ethos and charitableness. A swing state, Pennsylvania is twenty-eighth in so-called entitlement or social safety–net federal expenditure. This is one measure of what some refer to as "red-state socialism," meaning that residents of more heavily Republican, or "red," states, tend to be the greatest beneficiaries of the federal aid they in theory oppose. (They also tend to oppose tax increases.) The top ten state beneficiaries of entitlement spending voted Republican in the 2008 presidential election. Significantly, in a growing nationwide trend, more safety-net spending now goes to the middle class than to the poor.

Thirty miles from Bucks County is Camden, New Jersey,

the poorest city per capita in the nation: median income $27,027, with 31 percent of the population below the poverty level. (New Jersey, a "blue," or Democratic, state, is fiftieth—*last*—in entitlement spending. New Mexico is first.) As the sociologists Kathryn Edin and Maria Kefalas and the writer Chris Hedges have shown, Camden may tell us more about the future than we realize. Its depredations are a source of pain first and most obviously to those who live them; but they are also a source of discomfort to those who witness them. Whether the city represents an end point in the national income-inequality debate or a place from which to begin a discussion, it would be difficult to find many who fail to agree that its position is untenable.

Fanning out from Bucks County in every direction, the pattern of haves and have-nots repeats itself. The train ride into New York reveals a familiar American discordance: high-end condos and junkyards, pristine converted stone farmhouses and old linen mills with smashed windows. The line originates in Trenton, New Jersey, where the median household income is $36,601, and 24.5 percent live below the poverty level, as compared with an overall state average of 9.1 percent. One passes through Princeton—median household $104,234, 6.5 percent living below the poverty level. At the other end is Newark, where I was born: median household income $35,659, with 25 percent living below the poverty level.

The Occupy Handbook is divided into three parts. Part 1, "How We Got Here," takes a look at events that may be considered precursors of OWS: the stories of a brakeman in 1877 who went up against the railroads; of the four men from an all-black college in North Carolina who staged the first lunch counter sit-in of the 1960s; of the out-of-work doctor whose nationwide, bizarrely personal Townsend Club movement led to the passage of Social Security. We go back to the 1930s and the New

Deal and, in Carmen M. Reinhart and Kenneth S. Rogoff's "nutshell" version of their book *This Time Is Different: Eight Centuries of Financial Folly,* even further.

Part 2, "Where We Are Now," which covers the present, both in the United States and abroad, opens with a piece by the anthropologist David Graeber. The world of Madison Avenue is far from the beliefs of Graeber, an anarchist, but it's Graeber who arguably (he says he didn't do it alone) came up with the phrase "We are the 99 percent." As *Bloomberg Businessweek* pointed out in October 2011, during month two of the Occupy encampments that Graeber helped initiate, and three months after the publication of his *Debt: The First 5,000 Years,* "David Graeber likes to say that he had three goals for the year: promote his book, learn to drive, and launch a worldwide revolution. The first is going well, the second has proven challenging, and the third is looking up." Graeber's counterpart in Chile can loosely be said to be Camila Vallejo, the college undergraduate, pictured on page 219, who, at twenty-three, brought the country to a standstill. The novelist and playwright Ariel Dorfman writes about her and about his own self-imposed exile from Chile, and his piece is followed by an entirely different, more quantitative treatment of the subject. This part of the book also covers the *indignados* in Spain, who, before Occupy began, "occupied" the public squares of Madrid and other cities—using, as the basis for their claim that the parks could legally be slept in, a thirteenth-century right granted to shepherds who moved, and still move, their flocks annually.

Part 3 lays out actions. One is disinvestment, on the scale of antiapartheid-level sanctions—see Michael Lewis's interview with himself, "Boycott!," in which he explains his embarrassment at not having stood on a soapbox during two visits to Occupy encampments, and in which he calls for the removal, by universities and other institutions, of endowment funds from the "too big to fail" Wall Street firms. Two other proposals are Felix Salmon's, for reducing the mortgage burden, and Michelle J. White and Wenli Li's, for cutting foreclosures. They address in detail one of the biggest human costs of the crisis: loss of one's house.

Each contributor took a leap of faith in agreeing to participate in this project. Not entirely by design but then more sure-footedly, the project evolved nonhierarchically, as OWS famously has. Contributors initially had no idea what others were writing. Most of them chose their own topics, and agreed generally to avoid overlap, sometimes by being in touch with one another. The contributors were not paid properly for their time, and some of the best technical economists in the country undertook two and sometimes three revisions of their work in order to make their pieces comprehensible to readers who, like myself, are not subject experts.

The question remains: is economics ever a solution to the deep-seated troubles of a city like Camden? If you were trying to think of ways to fix the economy, couldn't you do better than to use economics? The answer is: probably not in this world. What the *Financial Times* journalist Martin Wolf says, in part 3, about capitalism might also be said of economics generally: while imperfect, it is "uniquely flexible, responsive, and innovative." And it's important to distinguish economic practice from—as Paul Krugman and Robin Wells suggest in part 1—politics.

A turning point for me in the book's composition came when Peter Diamond and Emmanuel Saez delivered a complex tax proposal with a simple message: if the marginal tax rate on the income of the top 1 percent were doubled, from 35 percent to 70 percent, any resulting unhappiness experienced by the 1 percent would be socially unimportant; and recall that the majority of millionaires want their taxes raised, as the Spectrem Group's survey demonstrates and as Warren Buffett demonstrated in 2011. Raising the marginal tax rate would cause the 1 percent to work a little less and lead some to find more ways to underreport their income, and might drive some of them from the country; but the response is small enough that revenue still would go up considerably. Yet, as the economist Brad DeLong points out in his commentary on the Diamond-Saez piece, more than half the general population of the United States is against raising the tax rate as the authors suggest.

What are the objections?

You will find some of the answers in this book, but perhaps there is a better question: Is there another, equally persuasive tax proposal? Is there an equally persuasive tax *policy?* The *Washington Post*'s Ezra Klein summarizes Mitt Romney's tax policy as follows:

> Extend the Bush tax cuts and, then on top of that, sharply cut taxes on corporations, the wealthy, and upper-middle-class investors, while letting a set of tax breaks that help the poor expire. The result, according to the Tax Policy Center, would be a $69 tax cut for the average individual in the bottom 20 percent and a $164,000 tax cut for the average individual in the top 1 percent. And Romney would pay for this through unspecified cuts to domestic programs. Since domestic programs mostly go to the poor and seniors, the regressive tax cuts would be regressively financed.

House GOP budget chairman Paul Ryan's 2012 budget plan, not intended to be enacted into law but rather to present, as the congressman's website says, a "roadmap" for the future, would, according to the *New York Times*'s David Leonhardt, *reduce* taxes on the wealthy. Under the Path to Prosperity, as the Ryan plan is called, taxes for the poorest 90 percent would rise, according to the nonprofit Citizens for Tax Justice.

Tax rates are at historic lows. For much of the 1970s, the highest marginal tax rate was in fact 70 percent. In 1950, it was 91 percent. Thus when Diamond and Saez write that they "favor a top tax rate near or in the range of 50 percent to 70 percent," they are proposing simply that we return to something like the rates that were in place before the Bush tax cut for the top earners and earlier.

In choosing between these two broad approaches, which is more in keeping with American policies?

What Paul Volcker expressed astonishment about—that people were willing to contribute to a book like this at all—can be explained, I think, by the unnaturalness of the postures that income inequality has led us to assume. The postures are unsustainable. Income inequality is a form of inauthenticity, and in 2011, from Egypt to Iowa, citizens of the world threw off the yoke.

The Occupy Handbook offers, first, analysis of precedent, then a look at the here and now, and, finally, a view of how we might proceed. Research can never be said to be comprehensive. One has to account for the bias of the researcher; and there is always another alley to go down. But as the proposals on my desk multiplied, I found that none had the quiet power of Diamond and Saez's "Taxing High Earnings." For those who are not convinced, and who will fall into the majority Brad DeLong describes, where is the tax proposal of equal intelligence?

PART I

—⋈⋈—

HOW WE
GOT HERE

Advice from the 1 Percent:
Lever Up, Drop Out

Michael Lewis

Michael Lewis is the bestselling author of *Liar's Poker*, *Moneyball*, *The Blind Side*, *The Big Short*, and *Boomerang*. He lives in Berkeley, California, with his wife and three children.

To: The Upper Ones
From: Strategy Committee
Re: The Counterrevolution

As usual, we have much to celebrate. The rabble has been driven from the public parks. Our adversaries, now defined by the freaks and criminals among them, have demonstrated only that they have no idea what they are doing. They have failed to identify a single achievable goal.

Just weeks ago, in our first memo, we expressed concern that the big Wall Street banks were vulnerable to a mass financial boycott—more vulnerable even than tobacco companies or apartheid-era South African multinationals. A boycott might raise fears of a bank run; and the fears might create the fact.

Now, we'll never know: the Lower 99's notion of an attack on Wall Street is to stand around hollering at the New York Stock Exchange. The stock exchange! We have won a battle, but this war is far from over.

As our chief quant notes, "No matter how well we do for ourselves, there will always be 99 of them for every one of us." Disturbingly, his recent polling data reveal that many of us don't even know who we are: fully half of all Upper Ones believe themselves to belong to the Lower 99. That any human being can earn more than 344 grand a year without having the sense to identify which side in a class war he is on suggests that we should limit membership to actual rich people. But we wish to address this issue in a later memo. For now we remain focused on the problem at hand: how to keep their hands off our money.

We have identified two looming threats: the first is the shifting relationship between ambitious young people and money. There's a reason the Lower 99 currently lack leadership: anyone with the ability to organize large numbers of unsuccessful people has been diverted into Wall Street jobs, mainly in the analyst programs at Morgan Stanley and Goldman Sachs. Those jobs no longer exist, at least not in the quantities sufficient to distract an entire generation from examining the meaning of their lives. Our Wall Street friends, wounded and weakened, can no longer pick up the tab for sucking the idealism out of America's youth. But if not them, who? We on the committee are resigned to all elite universities becoming breeding grounds for insurrection, with the possible exception of Princeton.

The second threat is in the unstable mental pictures used by Lower 99ers to understand their economic lives. (We have found that they think in pictures.) For many years the less viable among us have soothed themselves with metaphors of growth and abundance: rising tides, expanding pies, trickling down. A dollar in our pocket they viewed hopefully, as, perhaps, a few pennies in theirs. They appear to have switched this out of their minds for a new picture, of a life raft with shrinking provisions. A dollar in our pockets they now view as a dollar from theirs. Fearing for their lives, the Lower 99 will surely become ever more desperate and troublesome. Complaints from our membership about their personal behavior are already running at post–French Revolutionary highs.

We on the strategy committee see these developments as inexorable historical forces. The Lower 99 is a ticking bomb that can't be defused. They may be occasionally distracted by, say, a winning lottery ticket. (And we have sent out the word to the hedge fund community to cease their purchases of such tickets.) They may turn their anger on others—immigrants, for instance, or the federal government—and we can encourage them to do so. They may even be frightened into momentary submission. (We're long pepper spray.)

But in the end we believe that any action we take to prevent them from growing better organized, and more aware of our financial status, will only delay the inevitable: the day when they turn, with far greater effect, on us.

Hence our committee's conclusion: we must be able to quit American society altogether, and they must know it. For too long we have simply accepted the idea that we and they are all in something together, subject to the same laws and rituals and cares and concerns. This state of social relations between rich and poor isn't merely unnatural and unsustainable but, in its way, shameful. (Who among us could hold his head high in the presence of Louis XIV or those Russian czars or, for that matter, Croesus?)

The modern Greeks offer the example in the world today that is, the committee has determined, best in class. Ordinary Greeks seldom harass their rich, for the simple reason that they have no idea where to find them. To a member of the Greek Lower 99 a Greek Upper One is as good as invisible. He pays no taxes, lives no place, and bears no relationship to his fellow citizens. As the public expects nothing of him, he always meets, and sometimes even exceeds, their expectations. As a result, the chief concern of the ordinary Greek about the rich Greek is that he will cease to pay the occasional visit.

That is the sort of relationship with the Lower 99 we must cultivate if we are to survive. We must inculcate, in ourselves as much as in them, the understanding that our relationship to each other is provisional, almost accidental, and their claims on us nonexistent.

As a first, small step we propose to bestow, annually, an award to the Upper One who has best exhibited to the wider population his willingness and ability to have nothing at all to do with them. As the recipient of the first Incline Award — so named for the residents of Incline Village, Nevada, many of whom have bravely fled California state taxes — we propose Jeff Bezos.

His private rocket ship may have exploded before it reached outer space. But before it did, it sent back to Earth the message we hope to convey:

We're outta here!

The Widening Gyre:
Inequality, Polarization, and the Crisis

Paul Krugman and Robin Wells

Paul Krugman is a professor at the Woodrow Wilson School, Princeton University, and an op-ed columnist for the *New York Times*. He is the 2008 winner of the Nobel Prize in Economics. He is the author of three *New York Times* bestsellers, *The Great Unraveling* (2005), *The Return of Depression Economics* (1999), and *The Conscience of a Liberal* (2007), and of *End This Depression Now!* (2012). Robin Wells is an economist and a coauthor, with Paul Krugman, of the bestselling textbook *Economics*. She was formerly on the faculty of Princeton University and Stanford University Business School.

America emerged from the Great Depression and the Second World War with a much more equal distribution of income than it had in the 1920s; our society became middle-class in a way it hadn't been before. This new, more equal society persisted for thirty years. But then we began pulling apart, with huge income gains for those with already high incomes. As the Congressional Budget Office has documented, the 1 percent—the group implicitly singled out in the slogan "We are the 99 percent"—saw its real income nearly quadruple between 1979 and 2007, dwarfing the very modest gains of ordinary Americans. Other evidence shows that within the 1 percent, the richest 0.1 percent and the richest 0.01 percent saw even larger gains.

By 2007, America was about as unequal as it had been on the eve of the Great Depression and sure enough, just after hitting this milestone, we plunged into the worst slump since the Depression. This probably wasn't a coincidence, although economists are still working on trying to understand the linkages between inequality and vulnerability to economic crisis.

Here, however, we want to focus on a different question: why has the response to crisis been so inadequate? Before financial crisis struck, we think it's fair to say that most economists imagined that even if such a crisis were to happen, there would be a quick and effective policy response. In 2003 Robert Lucas, the Nobel laureate and then president of the American Economic Association, urged the profession to turn its attention away from recessions to issues of longer-term growth. Why? Because, he declared, the "central problem of depression-prevention has been solved, for all practical purposes, and has in fact been solved for many decades."

Yet when a real depression arrived—and what we are experiencing is indeed a depression, although not as bad as the Great Depression—policy failed to rise to the occasion. Yes, the banking system was bailed out. But job-creation efforts were grossly inadequate from the start—and far from responding to the predictable failure of the initial stimulus to produce a dramatic turnaround with further action, our political system turned its back on the unemployed. Between bitterly divisive politics that blocked just about every initiative from President Obama, and a bizarre shift of focus away from unemployment to budget deficits despite record-low borrowing costs, we have ended up repeating many of the mistakes that perpetuated the Great Depression.

Nor, by the way, were economists much help. Instead of offering a clear consensus, they produced a cacophony of views, with many conservative economists, in our view, allowing their political allegiance to dominate their professional competence. Distinguished economists made arguments against effective action that were evident nonsense to anyone who had taken Econ 101 and understood it. Among those behaving badly, by the way, was none other than Robert Lucas, the same economist who had declared just a few years before that the problem of preventing depressions was solved.

So how did we end up in this state? How did America become a nation that could not rise to the biggest economic challenge in three generations, a nation in which scorched-earth politics and politicized economics created policy paralysis?

We suggest it was the inequality that did it. Soaring inequality is at the root of our polarized politics, which made us unable to act together in the face of crisis. And because rising incomes at the top have also brought rising power to the wealthiest, our nation's intellectual life has been warped, with too many economists co-opted into defending economic doctrines that were convenient for the wealthy despite being indefensible on logical and empirical grounds.

Let's talk first about the link between inequality and polarization.

Our understanding of American political economy has been strongly influenced by the work of the political scientists Keith Poole, Howard Rosenthal, and Nolan McCarty. Poole, Rosenthal, and McCarty use congressional roll-call votes to produce a sort of "map" of political positions, in which both individual bills and individual politicians are assigned locations in an abstract issues space. The details are a bit complex, but the bottom line is that American politics is pretty much one-dimensional: once you've determined where a politician lies on a left–right spectrum, you can predict his or her votes with a high degree of accuracy. You can also see how far apart the two parties' members are on the left–right spectrum—that is, how polarized congressional politics is.

It's not surprising that the parties have moved ever further apart since the 1970s. There used to be substantial overlap: there were moderate and even liberal Republicans, like New York's Jacob Javits, and there were conservative Democrats. Today the parties are totally disjoint, with the most conservative Democrat to the left of the most liberal Republican, and the two parties' centers of gravity very far apart.

What's more surprising is the fact that the relatively nonpolarized politics of the postwar generation is a relatively recent phenomenon—before the war, and especially before the Great Depression, politics was almost as polarized as it is now. And the track of polarization closely follows the track of income inequality, with the degree of polarization closely correlated over time with the share of total income going to the top 1 percent.

Why does higher inequality seem to produce greater political polarization? Crucially, the widening gap between the parties has reflected Republicans moving right, not Democrats moving left. This pops out of the Poole-Rosenthal-McCarty numbers, but it's also obvious from the history of various policy proposals. The Obama health care plan, to take an obvious example, was originally a Republican plan, in fact a plan devised by the Heritage Foundation. Now the GOP denounces it as socialism.

The most likely explanation of the relationship between inequality and polarization is that the increased income and wealth of a small minority has, in effect, bought the allegiance of a major political party. Republicans are encouraged and empowered to take positions far to the right of where they were a generation ago, because the financial power of the beneficiaries of their positions both provides an electoral advantage in terms of campaign funding and provides a sort of safety net for individual politicians, who can count on being supported in various ways even if they lose an election.

Whatever the precise channels of influence, the result is a political environment in which Mitch McConnell, leading Republican in the Senate, felt it was perfectly okay to declare before the 2010 midterm elections that his main goal, if the GOP won control, would be to incapacitate the president of the United States: "The single most important thing we want to achieve is for President Obama to be a one-term president."

Needless to say, this is not an environment conducive to effective antidepression policy, especially given the way Senate rules allow a cohesive minority to block much action. We know that the Obama administration expected to win strong bipartisan support for its stimulus plan, and that it also believed that it could go back for more if events proved this necessary. In fact, it took desperate maneuvering to get sixty votes even in the first round, and there was no question of getting more later.

In sum, extreme income inequality led to extreme political polarization, and this greatly hampered the policy response to the crisis. Even if we had entered the crisis in a state of intellectual clarity—with major political players at least grasping the nature of the crisis and the real policy options—the intensity of political conflict would have made it hard to mount an effective response.

In reality, of course, we did not enter the crisis in a state of clarity. To a remarkable extent, politicians—and, sad to say, many well-known economists—reacted to the crisis as if the Great Depression had never happened. Leading politicians gave speeches that could have come straight out of the mouth of Herbert Hoover; famous economists reinvented fallacies that one thought had been refuted in the mid-1930s. Why?

The answer, we would suggest, also runs back to inequality.

It's clear that the financial crisis of 2008 was made possible in part by the systematic way in which financial regulation had been dismantled over the previous three decades. In retrospect, in fact, the era from the 1970s to 2008 was marked by a series of deregulation-induced crises, including the hugely expensive savings and loan crisis; it's remarkable that the ideology of deregulation nonetheless went from strength to strength.

It seems likely that this persistence despite repeated disaster had a lot to do with rising inequality, with the causation running in both directions. On one side, the explosive growth of the financial sector was a major source of soaring incomes at the very top of the income distribution. On the other side, the fact that the very rich were the prime beneficiaries of deregulation meant that as this group gained power—simply because of its rising wealth—the push for deregulation intensified.

These impacts of inequality on ideology did not end in 2008. In an important sense, the rightward drift of ideas, both driven by and driving rising income concentration at the top, left us incapacitated in the face of crisis.

In 2008 we suddenly found ourselves living in a Keynesian world—that is, a world that very much had the features John Maynard Keynes focused on in his 1936 magnum opus, *The General Theory of Employment, Interest, and Money*. By that we mean that we found ourselves in a world in which lack of sufficient demand had become the key economic problem, and in which narrow technocratic solutions, like cuts in the Federal Reserve's interest rate target, were not adequate to that situation. To deal effectively with the crisis, we needed more activist government policies, in the form both of temporary spending to support employment and efforts to reduce the overhang of mortgage debt.

One might think that these solutions could still be considered technocratic, and separated from the broader question of income distribution. Keynes himself described his theory as "moderately conservative in its implications," consistent with an economy run on the principles of private enterprise. From the beginning, however, political conservatives—and especially those most concerned with defending the position of the wealthy—have fiercely opposed Keynesian ideas.

And we mean fiercely. Although Paul Samuelson's textbook *Economics: An Introductory Analyis* is widely credited with bringing Keynesian economics to American colleges in the 1940s, it was actually the second entry; a previous book, by the Canadian economist Lorie Tarshis, was effectively blackballed by right-wing opposition, including an organized campaign that successfully induced many universities to drop it. Later, in his *God and Man at Yale*, William F. Buckley Jr. would direct much of his ire at the university for allowing the teaching of Keynesian economics.

The tradition continues through the years. In 2005 the right-wing magazine *Human Events* listed Keynes's *General Theory* among the ten most harmful books of the nineteenth and twentieth centuries, right up there with *Mein Kampf* and *Das Kapital*.

Why such animus against a book with a "moderately conservative" message? Part of the answer seems to be that even though the government intervention called for by Keynesian economics is modest and targeted, conservatives have always seen it as the thin edge of the wedge: concede that the government can play a useful role in fighting slumps, and the next thing you know we'll be living under socialism. The rhetorical amalgamation of Keynesianism with central planning and radical redistribution—although explicitly denied by Keynes himself, who declared that "there are valuable human activities which require the motive of money-making and the environment of private wealth-ownership for their full fruition"—is almost universal on the right.

There is also the motive suggested by Keynes's contemporary Michał Kalecki in a classic 1943 essay:

> We shall deal first with the reluctance of the "captains of industry" to accept government intervention in the matter of employment. Every widening of state activity is looked upon by business with suspicion, but the creation of employment by government spending has a special aspect which makes the opposition particularly intense. Under a laissez-faire system the level of employment depends to a great extent on the so-called state of confidence. If this deteriorates, private investment declines, which results in a fall of output and employment (both directly and through the secondary effect of the fall in incomes upon consumption and investment). This gives the capitalists a powerful indirect control over government policy: everything which may shake the state of confidence must be carefully avoided because it would cause an economic crisis. But once the government learns the trick of increasing employment by its own purchases, this powerful controlling device loses its effectiveness. Hence budget deficits necessary to carry out government intervention must be regarded as perilous. The social function of the doctrine of "sound finance" is to make the level of employment dependent on the state of confidence.

This sounded a bit extreme to us the first time we read it, but it now seems all too plausible. These days you can see the "confidence" argument being deployed all the time. For example, here is how Mort Zuckerman began a 2010 op-ed in the *Financial Times*, aimed at dissuading President Obama from taking any kind of populist line:

The growing tension between the Obama administration and business is a cause for national concern. The president has lost the confidence of employers, whose worries over taxes and the increased costs of new regulation are holding back investment and growth. The government must appreciate that confidence is an imperative if business is to invest, take risks and put the millions of unemployed back to productive work.

There was and is, in fact, no evidence that "worries over taxes and the increased costs of new regulation" are playing any significant role in holding the economy back. Kalecki's point, however, was that arguments like this would fall completely flat if there was widespread public acceptance of the notion that Keynesian policies could create jobs. So there is a special animus against direct government job-creation policies, above and beyond the generalized fear that Keynesian ideas might legitimize government intervention in general.

Put these motives together, and you can see why writers and institutions with close ties to the upper tail of the income distribution have been consistently hostile to Keynesian ideas. That has not changed over the seventy-five years since Keynes wrote the *General Theory*. What has changed, however, is the wealth and hence influence of that upper tail. These days, conservatives have moved far to the right even of Milton Friedman, who at least conceded that monetary policy could be an effective tool for stabilizing the economy. Views that were on the political fringe forty years ago are now part of the received doctrine of one of our two major political parties.

A touchier subject is the extent to which the vested interest of the 1 percent, or better yet the 0.1 percent, has colored the discussion among academic economists. But surely that influence must have been there: if nothing else, the preferences of university donors, the availability of fellowships and lucrative consulting contracts, and so on must have encouraged the profession not just to turn away from Keynesian ideas but to forget much that had been learned in the 1930s and '40s.

In the debate over responses to the Great Recession and its aftermath, it has been shocking to see so many highly credentialed economists making not just elementary conceptual errors but *old* elementary conceptual errors—the same errors Keynes took on three generations ago. For example, one thought that nobody in the modern economics profession would repeat the mistakes of the infamous "Treasury view," under which any increase in government spending necessarily crowds out an equal amount of private spending, no matter what the economic conditions might be. Yet in 2009, exactly that fallacy was expounded by distinguished professors at the University of Chicago.

Again, our point is that the dramatic rise in the incomes of the very affluent left us ill prepared to deal with the current crisis. We arrived at a Keynesian crisis demanding a Keynesian solution—but Keynesian ideas had been driven out of the national discourse, in large part because they were politically inconvenient for the increasingly empowered 1 percent.

In summary, then, the role of rising inequality in creating the economic crisis of 2008 is debatable; it probably did play an important role, if nothing else than by encouraging the financial deregulation that set the stage for crisis. What seems very clear to us, however, is that rising inequality played a central role in causing an ineffective response once crisis hit. Inequality bred a polarized political system, in which the right went all out to block any and all efforts by a modestly liberal president to do something about job creation. And rising inequality also gave rise to what we have called a Dark Age of macroeconomics, in which hard-won insights about how depressions happen and what to do about them were driven out of the national discourse, even in academic circles.

This implies, we believe, that the issue of inequality and the problem of economic recovery are not as separate as a purely economic analysis might suggest. We're not going to have a good macroeconomic policy again unless inequality, and its distorting effect on policy debate, can be curbed.

Take a Stand: Sit In

Philip Dray

Philip Dray is the author of several books, including *There Is Power in a Union: The Epic Story of Labor in America* (2010) and *At the Hands of Persons Unknown: The Lynching of Black America* (2002), which won the Robert F. Kennedy Memorial Book Award.

America has often experienced stirrings of unrest that appear inchoate and lacking in direction but which prove enduring and seminal to the country's history. During the Great Upheaval of 1877 the nation learned for the first time the depth of resentment among its starving classes—that there existed many living in not so quiet desperation. The aftermath of the Civil War had seen the rapid expansion of national markets and the related growth of the railroads, symbolized by the driving of the golden spike at Promontory, Utah, in 1869. Organized labor had struggled to keep pace, but its attempts at nationwide union building were uneven. Railroad workers, for instance, had strong guildlike brotherhoods—of engineers, firemen, brakemen—yet lacked a coherent voice.

By 1877 the railroads, overextended logistically and financially, were forced to extract as much labor as possible from their employees for the least amount of money. This resulted in longer shifts, missed payrolls, and impositions such as the lengthened freight trains, known as "double-headers," which demanded twice the work from smaller crews and increased the already unreasonably high risk of on-the-job injury. Early summer found workers on the Baltimore & Ohio once again behind in their pay. On July 16 at Martinsburg, West Virginia, a vital rail junction near the Maryland border, hundreds stopped work. They blocked the tracks, bottling up traffic in all directions, and, using their knowledge of the yard, sabotaged switches and drove locomotives onto sidings. One eastbound train bearing cattle to market was off-loaded, the animals left to graze in a nearby pasture.

Within days the revolt spread to nearby Baltimore, New York, and Pittsburgh, and west to Cleveland, Omaha, and San Francisco. Across the country eighty thousand rail workers walked off the job, stranding freight and passengers and bringing the nation's rail system to a standstill. One Chicago newspaper, unsure what to call the yet unnamed phenomenon, noted its arrival with the simple headline "It Is Here!"

At Pittsburgh an ad hoc Trainmen's Union under the guidance of Robert Ammon, a twenty-five-year-old brakeman, attempted to coordinate the strikers, but generally the uprising was spontaneous and unscripted. It also held a powerful appeal. Almost everywhere, the workers were joined at the barricades by sympathizers—men and women from the mills, domestic workers, children, the jobless, blacks, whites. In St. Louis, rail workers were joined by brewery men, black stevedores, and even the town's newsboys in what was probably America's first general strike. "We're with you. We're in the same boat," a mill worker assured a rally in Pittsburgh. "I heard a reduction of ten percent hinted at in our mill this morning. I won't call employers despots, I won't call them tyrants, but the term 'capitalists' is sort of synonymous and will do as well."

The rail barons, finding no one with whom to negotiate and disinclined to do so anyway, sought to suppress the uprising by force. Telegraphs chattered with urgent requests for troops in governors' offices from West Virginia to Illinois. Crowds blocking train yards confronted units of militia and,

THE FREIGHT-TRAIN BRAKEMAN.—[FROM A DRAWING BY O. V. SCHUBERT.]

Brakemen like Robert Ammon had to hand-stop the cars during blizzards. The mortality rate for rail workers and for laborers generally was a powerful factor in the Great Upheaval of 1877. *(Drawing by O. V. Schubert, 1877. Culver Pictures.)*

after President Rutherford B. Hayes dispatched them, federal soldiers. The official response itself was disordered. In some towns the militia refused to lay hands on the strikers, who were their neighbors and friends, while in Baltimore the governor and other high-ranking officials were trapped in the train station, surrounded by a mob furious that ten men and boys had been shot down by panicked militia. In Pittsburgh a newspaper declared that "The Lexington of the Labor Conflict Is at Hand" after a militia unit opened fire on a crowd. In response the masses descended on local gun shops, buying or looting most of the contents, vandalized trains and tracks, and destroyed the city's central train depot. They then surrounded and set fire to the roundhouse, in which the soldiers had sought refuge, forcing them to flee for their lives. In Chicago, lethal violence occurred at the Halstead Viaduct, where a mob trapped a smaller number of police and a vicious street battle ensued with fists and clubs, bringing the city's death toll to thirty.

As troubling as such scenes were, perhaps more important to the nation was the strike's impact on the flow of goods and commerce. Coal trains were stranded on Pennsylvania mountainsides, and boxcars loaded with rotting produce sat in the sun on sidings just beyond the limits of big-city freight yards. The loading and off-loading of vessels on inland waterways and both the Atlantic and Pacific coasts were interrupted, as was most passenger travel.

Technically, labor failed to win the Great Rail Strike of 1877; the strikers returned to their jobs having secured no formal pact or concessions. Still, rail workers, and all American workers, had gained an invaluable new sense of their collective strength. They had shown that even the vast and powerful railroads were vulnerable. With the weapon of the strike, workers held power; they could shut the railroads—and the country—down. "The Republic had celebrated its Centennial in July, 1876," one historian has noted. "Exactly a year later, the industrial working class of the nation celebrated *its* coming of age."

Nothing would ever be quite the same again; the strike had also opened the country's eyes to its embarrassingly substantial population of poor people. These were the unemployed, the urchins, the homeless "tramps" and "slum-dwellers" who, in desperate times, became what the *Nation*'s E. L. Godkin termed "the mob, ready-made." As events had shown, economic inequality and desperation bred violence, disruption, and radicalism. In the days after the strike, America—from President Hayes to *Harper's Weekly*—paused to reconsider the efficacy of the creed of winner take all. "The *laissez-faire* policy has been knocked out of men's heads for the next generation," one newspaper concluded, while at the White House the president wrote in his diary, "The strikes have been put down by force, but now for the real remedy."

Eighteen seventy-seven was the year the country formally gave up on Reconstruction, withdrawing federal troops from the South and relinquishing the idealistic effort to integrate the more than four million slaves freed by the Civil War into American society. The strike's violence seemed to validate the shift in regional focus; now the troops could quell urban labor strife. The nation's best instincts were also redirected toward the amelioration of economic hardship and social ills in the cities, helping to inspire settlement houses, a liberal intellectual Protestant movement known as the Social Gospel, and an oppositional political consciousness that found expression in the nascent Socialist Party.

Each generation of Americans encounters a political, economic, or social dilemma it may choose to confront with thought and activism. In the early twentieth century the challenge was to introduce fairness and public scrutiny into relations between industry and workers, business and consumers. The 1930s brought the Popular Front and the global crusade against Fascism. When, at 4:30 in the afternoon on February 1, 1960, four black college students occupied stools at the whites-only lunch counter in the F. W. Woolworth's in downtown Greensboro, North Carolina, they secured their generation's role in the nation's struggle for racial justice.

The four young men—David Richmond, Ezell Blair Jr., Franklin McCain, and Joseph McNeil—had become friends at all-black North Carolina Agricultural & Technical College, and in late-night bull sessions had often discussed the predicament haunting their futures; even as educated African Americans they would be unable to enter the front door of a movie theater in the segregated South or eat lunch at a Woolworth's, let alone find meaningful careers. They had planned carefully for that day; all were neatly dressed, and before taking seats at the counter they had purchased school supplies elsewhere in the store and obtained receipts.

Blair cleared his throat and asked the white waitress for a doughnut and a cup of coffee. "I'm sorry, Negroes eat at the other end," she said, directing him to a stand-up snack bar. When Blair and the others showed no sign of leaving, manager C. L. "Curly" Harris was informed. He had worked hard to

February 2, 1960: Day 2 of the Greensboro, North Carolina, Woolworth's sit-in. Left to right: Joseph McNeil, Franklin McCain, Billy Smith, and Clarence Henderson. Smith and Henderson had taken the place of David Richmond and Ezell Blair Jr. (*Photograph by Jack Moebes, News & Record staff photographer*)

maintain his modest corner of the Woolworth's empire, eschewing the term "five and dime" and insisting his emporium be considered a "junior department store." He instructed his employees not to make a fuss over the four young men at the counter. They would leave soon enough, he said, if everyone simply ignored them.

News of what was taking place at Woolworth's spread quickly through the streets of downtown Greensboro, however, and within minutes a crowd had gathered. A lone policeman arrived as well. Although the young men were defying a local segregation law, they were peaceful and had not stolen anything, so he did not arrest them. Finally, Harris announced that the store would close half an hour early. While the crowd exited through the front, the protesters were let out a side door.

Back at the A & T campus, Richmond, Blair, McCain, and McNeil were greeted as heroes. Word of their deed had preceded them, and many of their fellow students wanted to discuss its implications and plan more sit-ins. Greensboro mayor George Roach, meanwhile, had called the school president, Warmoth T. Gibbs Sr. Roach demanded that all A & T students be restricted to campus. Gibbs said that was impossible, as many of them had off-campus part-time jobs. (His first reaction to news of the sit-in at Woolworth's had been to ask, "Why there? The food's supposed to be terrible.")

The next day McCain and McNeil returned to the Greensboro Woolworth's with sixteen other students. McCain, McNeil, Billy Smith, and Clarence Henderson took seats at the lunch counter and remained all day without being served. On February 8 the protest spread to nearby Durham, where students from North Carolina College were joined at a lunch counter by white students from Duke University. Stores in Nashville, Richmond, and Memphis were next, and soon protests challenging Jim Crow segregation were under way all across the South, not only at five-and-dime chain stores but at swimming pools, beaches, libraries, movie theaters, and churches, while sympathy demonstrations occurred at Woolworth's, Kresge's, and W. T. Grant stores in northern cities. A few of the retailers showed signs of capitulation, recognizing that their business relied increasingly on black customers. Many others, however, continued to vow resistance. TV news showed the protesters being jeered at and attacked by hostile whites, and sometimes arrested, but the dominant image was that of nonviolent, decently behaved young people doing something inspiring and good.

"Ella, this is the thing!" Fred Shuttlesworth, a Birmingham, Alabama, minister and a member of the Southern Christian Leadership Conference (SCLC), raved on the phone to Ella Baker, SCLC's executive secretary, after visiting a North Carolina sit-in. "You must tell Martin that we have to get with this right away. This can really shake up the world." Martin Luther King Jr. and his colleagues had led the Montgomery bus boycott in 1955 and '56 and had seen the advances from *Brown v. Board of Education* (1954) and the integration of Central High in Little Rock, Arkansas, in 1957.

Nothing could match what they were witnessing now, a veritable explosion of civil rights activism, one with broad popularity among young people, black and white, in the North and South. It showed no sign of abating and held the promise of reinvigorating the entire movement. Understandably, there was talk of an existing civil rights organization such as SCLC assuming leadership of the student movement. Baker, however, insisted that the young people be allowed to steer their own course. In mid-April she organized a conference at Shaw University, in Raleigh, that gathered sit-in participants from across the country. There were veterans of the North Carolina and Nashville sit-ins, and activists from as far away as Michigan and New York. As a symbol of pride and defiance some wore clothes torn or bloodied in sit-in battles with police or opposing demonstrators. Baker circulated an essay she had written, "More Than a Hamburger," which challenged them to look beyond the integration of lunch counters to the demands of the broader civil rights struggle.

One of the first goals pursued by the Student Nonviolent Coordinating Committee (SNCC), which had been founded at the Raleigh conference with Baker and historian Howard Zinn as adult advisers, was the desegregation of retail businesses in Atlanta and Albany, Georgia. The group had also discussed the need for voter registration projects in parts of the Deep South where the black vote had been all but eliminated for decades by intimidation and legislative fiat, and where the federal government had long ago ceased trying to enforce laws designed to protect African American voting rights.

Many in SNCC felt that sit-ins and other forms of nonviolent public protest, or "direct action," were most needed in the South. Others argued for the urgency of southern blacks regaining the right to vote. The direct action adherents worried that voter registration was too gradual. A central tenet of SCLC's philosophy, voiced by Martin Luther King and James Lawson, one of the young leaders of the successful Nashville sit-ins, was "the beloved community," a society of equality and racial justice attained through nonviolent means. Was nonviolence a faith, as Lawson and others believed, or simply a tactic? And could it be sustained in the face of violent reprisals and arrests?

The questions about direct action were answered in 1961, when SNCC entered "Fortress" Mississippi, the South's most entrenched white supremacist state. "If you went into Mississippi and talked about voter registration, they're going to hit you on the side of the head," one SNCC worker quipped, "and that's as direct as you can get." There had been lonely voter registration efforts in Mississippi for years. In the Delta town of Cleveland, filling station owner Amzie Moore worked with discreet diligence, trying to make inroads without attracting the hostile attention of local whites. His counterpart in Amite County, in the southern part of the state, was E. W. Steptoe, president of the regional NAACP, who kept a loaded gun in every room of his house.

In August 1961 SNCC workers founded the Pike County Nonviolent Movement, which staged a sit-in of local high school students at the Pike County Library; shortly after, the SNCC's Bob Moses, who had taken local residents to the courthouse in Liberty, the seat of Amite County, to register to vote, was roughed up by police and arrested. "I didn't recognize Bob at first, he was so bloody," Steptoe later said. "I just took off his T-shirt and wrung the blood out of it like it had just been washed." After receiving stitches, Moses appeared before a rally that night, his head wrapped in bandages.

"The law down here is law made by white people, enforced by white people, for the benefit of white people," Moses said. "It will be that way until the Negroes begin to vote." He urged his listeners to find the courage to accompany SNCC workers to the voting registrar's office at the courthouse. His colleague Marion Barry, speaking for the direct action group who had staged the library sit-in, told the audience, "The attitude of a lot of people is 'Don't get in trouble.' Let me tell you, Negroes have been in trouble since 1619. How can you get in trouble when you're already in trouble? You're in trouble until you become first-class citizens."

In less than eighteen months, from February 1960 through the fall of 1961, the young people's movement in the civil rights cause had gone from lunch counter sit-ins to a voter registration effort in one of the country's harshest battlegrounds for racial justice. Their example, and the enthusiasm surrounding the sit-in movement, would carry over to the hundreds of young people who came to Mississippi to serve as the movement's nonviolent foot soldiers in the 1963 Freedom Vote and the legendary Freedom Summer of 1964. In August 1964 the Mississippi Freedom Democratic Party, the first coalition of fairly elected, biracial Mississippi voters since Reconstruction, traveled to Atlantic City to demand the right to be seated at the Democratic National Convention.

The Mississippi campaign broke down the walls of official complicity and silence in the state and brought the scrutiny of the U.S. Justice Department, and of the world, to the toughest bastion of the Jim Crow South. As the railroad strike of 1877 had led eventually to expanded workers' rights, so the Greensboro sit-in of February 1, 1960, helped pave the way for passage of the Civil Rights Act of 1964 and the Voting Rights Act of 1965. Both movements remind us that not all successful protests are explicit in their message and purpose; they rely instead on the participants' intuitive sense of justice.

The 5 Percent

Michael Hiltzik

Michael Hiltzik is a Pulitzer Prize–winning business columnist at the *Los Angeles Times* and the author of *The New Deal: A Modern History* (2011), among other books.

Masses of like-minded American citizens gathering together for impromptu protests coast to coast, their theme the concentration of wealth in a privileged class and society's indifference to the neediest, their ultimate goal a nationwide movement. News media awakening slowly to their presence, then blazoning their demands on front pages. A political establishment uncertain about whether to condemn the protesters, embrace them, or co-opt them.

Familiar as these signposts might seem today, the year was 1934. The disaffected segment of society was the 5 percent—seven million Americans aged sixty-five and older, uniquely afflicted by the Great Depression and uniquely underserved by the nascent recovery emerging under Franklin Roosevelt's New Deal.

This 5 percent's protests coalesced as the Townsend movement, launched by a sinewy midwestern farmer's son and farm laborer turned California physician. Francis Townsend was a World War I veteran who had served in the Army Medical Corps. He had an ambitious, and impractical, plan for a federal pension program. Although during its heyday in the 1930s the movement failed to win enactment of its program, it did play a critical role in contemporary politics. Before Townsend, America understood the destitution of its older generations only in abstract terms; Townsend's movement made it tangible. "It is no small achievement to have opened the eyes of even a few million Americans to these facts," Bruce Bliven, editor of the *New Republic*, observed. "If the Townsend Plan were to die tomorrow and be as completely forgotten as miniature golf, mah-jongg, or flinch, it would still have left some sedimented flood marks on the national consciousness." Indeed, the Townsend movement became the catalyst for the New Deal's signal achievement, the old-age program of Social Security. The history of its rise offers a lesson for the Occupy movement in how to convert grassroots enthusiasm into a potent political force—and a warning about the limitations of even a nationwide movement.

Although in technical terms the country touched bottom by the end of 1933, the emergent recovery from the Depression only made conditions on the ground seem that much more dire. Very few groups were left further behind than the aged. The overall unemployment rate had peaked at an estimated 25 percent of the workforce in 1935; but the rate among those sixty-five and older looking for work was 54 percent. The fraying of the nation's economic fabric hit the elderly especially hard: having spent their entire lives in the bosom of the American Dream, working hard and saving, they were thrown out of their jobs, deprived of their homes, and robbed of their bank savings just as they neared the end of their careers and at a point in their lives when the hope of rebuilding the nest egg was dim.

Millions who had been entitled to employer pensions discovered that these, too, were an empty promise—the Depression that wiped out their employers took their pension guarantees down with them. As for public pension programs, twenty-nine states had enacted versions by 1934, but four had run out of money, and the stipend paid by the others averaged $14.34 a month. The Roosevelt White House was inundated with appeals for help, including one letter from a Texas widow

Dr. Francis Townsend, the farmer's son who became a catalyst for Social Security. *(Courtesy Michael Hiltzik)*

on behalf of her aged mother, left blind and delirious from diabetes and with "no place to go unless it be to the poor house."

As the origin narrative of the Townsend movement would have it, one morning in 1933 the sixty-six-year-old physician, himself recently let go from his job in the Long Beach, California, health department, saw from his bathroom window three destitute women rooting for trash in an alleyway. The vision drove him to contrive a program aimed at coaxing workers sixty and older into retirement by granting them a government pension of two hundred dollars a month, financed from a federal "transaction tax." As set forth in a letter published that September in the *Long Beach Press-Telegram*, his plan became the foundation stone of the Townsend movement.

The plan aimed both to succor the elderly and to produce

near-term economic recovery, largely through a mandate that recipients spend their monthly allowances within thirty days, "thereby assuring a brisk state of business, comparable to that we enjoyed during war times." Asked how any recipient's compliance with this requirement could be enforced, Townsend would explain: "The neighbors are going to watch him."

The Townsend campaign would soon take its place as the most important and politically effective mass movement of its time and the first genuine lobby for old-age security. In short order, Townsend Clubs sprang up across the nation. There were newsletters, a national weekly, and a national organization that brought grassroots organizers together and monitored their activities for departures from orthodoxy. The movement became an exemplar of the transformation of a local protest movement into a potent political force. "On Capitol Hill in

Townsend Club members, aged sixty-five and older, in Johnson City, New York. Their power gave politicians pause. *(Courtesy of Timothy Nixon's family collection)*

Washington the politicians are amazed and terrified by it," *Harper's Monthly* reported. In the 1934 and 1936 elections, the movement achieved that nirvana of grassroots protesters—the election to Congress of candidates carrying its banner.

The Townsend movement was not unprecedented in its ambition or even its reach. The thirties were an era of mass movements. The model had been established by the Bonus army of 1932, which, under the disciplined leadership of an unemployed World War I veteran named Walter W. Waters, had advanced peacefully on foot and by rail east from Portland, Oregon, to Washington, D.C. The marchers' quest was for accelerated payment of the veterans' bonus that Congress had enacted in 1924, pegged at $1.25 a day of overseas service but not to be paid until 1945. As the economic slump added urgency to the veterans' demands, Congress tabled almost every proposal for early disbursement. The lone bill to reach President Herbert Hoover's desk earned his chilly veto in 1931 as a "wasteful expenditure."

Reaching the capital in May, the Bonus army camped chiefly in the marshy Anacostia Flats until the afternoon of July 28. Just before 5:00 p.m., army cavalry overran the twenty thousand veterans, firing tear gas, wielding bayonets, and setting the marchers' shacks aflame with torches, all under the command of General Douglas MacArthur while his staff aide, Major Dwight D. Eisenhower, looked on in dismay. The country was appalled by the spectacle of participants in a peaceable gathering being assaulted by government troops, not to mention by Hoover's initial endorsement of MacArthur's attack as a blow against "mob rule." The political import of MacArthur's overzealous offensive and Hoover's stony disdain for Americans seeking help from the government was not lost on the president's electoral challenger. Listening in Albany to reports from the front, Democratic presidential candidate Franklin D. Roosevelt turned to his adviser Felix Frankfurter. "Well, Felix," he said, "this elects me."

With the Capitol in the background, the shacks erected by the Bonus army burn after being torched on July 28, 1932, by General Douglas MacArthur. The raid evicted peaceful protesters led by unemployed World War I veteran Walter W. Waters. *(National Archives)*

The Bonus army's impetus, like that of mass movements following up to the Occupy protesters of the modern day, came less from the absolute harshness of contemporary economic conditions than from the unequal way in which particular segments of society were affected. The Bonus marchers and their supporters lived the phenomenon documented by the economists Thomas Piketty and Emmanuel Saez some seven decades later: while the Depression had impoverished most of the country, the share of income commanded by the top 10 percent of earners had scarcely taken a hit in the downturn. It would keep to a range of 43 to 46 percent from 1929 through the mid-1930s.

The protesters who succeeded the Bonus marchers would themselves speak out for discrete segments of society left stranded by the first emergent shoots of recovery. These movements ranged from the nakedly ideological to the openly partisan. The first category was represented by Rev. Charles Coughlin, the "Radio Priest" of Royal Oak, Michigan. With a liquid brogue that perfectly suited the new broadcast medium, the Canadian-born Coughlin had transformed himself by 1932 from pastor of a wood-frame suburban Detroit church into a Sunday fixture on the Columbia Broadcasting System.

As long as he stuck to castigating the "money powers" of Wall Street and preaching the evils of the gold standard and the virtues of inflation, a message that corresponded reasonably enough to the New Deal's platform, Coughlin was tolerated by the Roosevelt White House—in 1935, at the urging of Joseph P. Kennedy, he was even received by the president at Hyde Park. Coughlin had no specific program to offer. Rather, he was the carrier of undifferentiated alienation among the working class, of anger they aimed equally at bankers and union organizers. By the late thirties, when Coughlin had turned against Roosevelt, formed his own political party, and had begun preaching apocalyptic sermons aimed at the most disaffected and leavened by anti-Semitism, his influence was on the wane, never having been translated into a single piece of legislation.

At the other end of the spectrum was Huey Long's Share Our Wealth movement. The Democratic senator from Louisiana proposed capping any family's wealth at $5 million and its income at $1 million a year, both figures many hundreds of times those of the average family. The guillotine lopping off the excess was federal taxation, with the resulting revenue applied to giving every family a "homestead" allowance of five thousand dollars and a guaranteed annual income of two thousand dollars—a "hillbilly paradise" of wealth without work, as the historian Arthur Schlesinger Jr. uncharitably called it. To Democratic Party leaders, Long's organization of state and local Share Our Wealth clubs looked very much like an assemblage of shock troops for a challenge to FDR's renomination in 1936—a challenge that may have been forestalled only by the assassination of Long in 1935.

Among the other movements that emerged in this period were Howard Scott's utopian technocracy movement and author Upton Sinclair's 1934 campaign for California governor under the banner of his EPIC platform, for "End Poverty in California." His campaign manifesto was a pamphlet entitled *I, Governor of California and How I Ended Poverty—A True Story of the Future.* (He won the Democratic nomination, only to be trampled in the general election by a Republican candidate running with establishment Democratic support.)

But none approached the influence of Townsend and his program, which fell within the extremes represented by Coughlin and Long. One distinction was the character of the leader himself. Thin, erect, and bespectacled, projecting self-effacement and earnestness, Townsend was plainly ill at ease on the rare occasions he shared a stage with the flamboyant Coughlin, Long, or the latter's lectern-pounding chief proselytizer, a Shreveport, Louisiana, minister named Gerald L. K. Smith. Unlike Long, Townsend professed no personal political ambitions; unlike Coughlin, his platform was devoid of febrile conspiracy-mongering. (He was not devoid of egotism, however, especially when his role in his movement was in question.) Reduced to its essentials, the Townsend movement was a quest for justice for an oppressed and abused segment of the population. From this simplicity it drew its political potency.

Economists and newspaper pundits devoted reams of analysis to puncturing Townsend's numbers. Social insurance expert Abraham Epstein observed that, given the challenge of spending two hundred dollars a month when national income per capita was five hundred dollars a year and a new car could be bought for six hundred dollars, the program's guiding principle appeared to be that "everybody wastes his money and everybody gets rich overnight." ("Think of all the old people running into cabarets...trying to drink champagne to spend the money," he added. "It would just ruin them.")

Walter Lippmann, after interviewing the good doctor at length, reported that he had discovered the central financial flaw in the plan: Townsend had calculated his transaction tax on a total value of business transactions he placed at $1.2 trillion; but this was a gross miscalculation, for he did not realize that the sum comprised repeated purchases and sales of a single commodity, as when a farmer sells a bushel of wheat to a miller, who resells it as milled grain to a baker, who resells it as a loaf of bread to a housewife. Taxing every such transaction would bring commerce to a halt, Lippmann reported. "I knew the scheme was fantastic, but in reading about it, it was difficult to fund the particular delusion which had possessed Dr. Townsend," he wrote. "Now that difficulty is cleared up."

Yet the condescension of Epstein and Lippmann missed the point. Townsend's followers were concerned less with the plan's math—except perhaps for the draw of two hundred dollars a month—than with its attention to their welfare when the political establishment seemed to have forgotten them. Indeed, the power of a program that can be simplified into intelligible morsels has been well understood by promoters up to our present day of sound bite–driven politics, as it was by Huey Long himself, who steadfastly turned away press questions about the implausible economics of Share Our Wealth. ("Never explain," he counseled one acolyte. "First you must come into power—POWER—and then you do things.")

Even Townsend's critics recognized the movement's role of political catalyst. The *New Republic*'s Bliven condemned the program as "an economic impossibility"; but in terms that prefigured the rallying cry of Occupy Wall Street, he acknowledged that it had "called public attention most vividly to the fact that the country potentially, and to a large degree actually, the richest on earth[,] gives 80 percent of its people an income not much above the starvation level."

The Townsend movement bolstered the appeal of its leader with effective organizing provided by one Robert E. Clements, who identified himself variously as the movement's "co-founder" and "national secretary," and who insisted on keeping movement leadership centralized. Clements had honed his salesman's instincts as an agent in the Los Angeles real estate market. It would be his talent for organization, abetted by his skill at ballyhoo, that gave the Townsend movement political heft disproportionate to its membership numbers, which were always murky—in the mid-1930s its leaders claimed anywhere from five million to twenty-five million followers. Of the new members of the Seventy-fourth Congress, which convened in January 1935, more than a dozen had run on platforms encompassing the Townsend Plan. But even before the 1934 election, the movement had exerted a gravitational pull on Social Security.

The Committee on Economic Security, created by Roosevelt in mid-June 1934 with Labor Secretary Frances Perkins as its chair, had been given a brief to consider all forms of social insurance. At first, the committee saw as its main goal the creation of a federal system of unemployment insurance, building on a bill that had been introduced in 1933 by two progressive Democrats, Sen. Robert Wagner of New York and Rep. David J. Lewis of Pennsylvania. The Wagner-Lewis bill was a rough draft designed chiefly to soften up Congress to the concept of federal jobless aid—"frankly for educational purposes," Perkins wrote later.

Yet the committee soon recognized that its program would

have to include old-age relief. Politically this was "almost essential," Perkins observed. As the 1934 election approached, "in some districts the Townsend Plan was the chief political issue.... The pressure from its advocates was intense." Roosevelt seemed to have bought into the need for a pension program, "telling people he was in favor of adding old-age insurance clauses to the bill and putting it through as one program," Perkins recalled.

Yet Roosevelt disliked being pressured, and plainly he found the extravagance of the Townsend Plan distasteful. This led to one of his more ill-considered public statements, when he abruptly and publicly pulled the rug out from under his committee's pension proposal. The occasion was a huge gathering of social insurance experts Perkins had convened in Washington in November 1934 to put the finishing touches on the Social Security bill. Delivering the keynote speech, FDR unexpectedly reversed course on pensions. "I do not know whether this is the time for any Federal legislation on old-age security," he said. Without naming the Townsend movement, but leaving no doubt about his target, he continued: "Organizations promoting fantastic schemes have aroused hopes which cannot possibly be fulfilled. Through their activities they have increased the difficulties of getting sound legislation." Security for the aged would remain on his agenda, he said, but would be addressed "in time." The speech marked "the kiss of death" for the old-age program, a crestfallen attendee told a reporter for the *Baltimore Sun*.

Yet the expectations aroused by the Townsendites could not be quelled so easily. Startled by the furor his speech had caused, Roosevelt sent Perkins before the press the following morning to assure them that the audience must have misheard him. Old-age pensions were still in the program, she said, and would very much be part of the bill.

That was true, although the haphazardly drafted old-age provisions of the Social Security bill would reflect the hastiness of the Perkins committee's response to the rising Townsend movement. The unemployment compensation sections, which had an older pedigree and were based on the Wagner-Lewis bill, were much more painstakingly crafted. All the same, when the Social Security bill came to Capitol Hill for hearings beginning in January 1935, it became obvious that the lawmakers were still panicked by the presumed strength of the old-age movement and unsure that the pension provisions in the bill would mollify the Townsendites.

That placed administration officials in a quandary: they had to explain away Townsend's manifestly impractical economics while defending the principle of government old-age pensions. Perkins and Edwin Witte, the bill's chief draftsman, were required to walk this tightrope repeatedly during their long hours of testimony. As Witte explained patiently to the House Ways and Means Committee, to award two hundred dollars a month to everybody over sixty years of age, a population then estimated at ten million, would mean paying out $2 billion a month, or $24 billion a year, when the total annual income of all Americans at the time was $40 billion.

"It is not within the structure of our present economic or governmental system," he said. "I think it is probably not within the structure of any governmental or economic system that is conceivable." Evoking the image of Weimar-period hyperinflation in Germany, he added: "I presume we could start the printing presses and give the people two hundred dollars a month...but within the present structure it is not within the picture."

Perkins was equally blunt when she took her seat before the committee. She assured the lawmakers that the committee on economic security had weighed the Townsend Plan carefully during its deliberations, "because it became a popular newspaper subject of discussion this summer, so that it was looked into sufficiently to make an estimate of what it would cost." She bowed to the "very honest aspiration which is apparently involved in that plan" but observed that the committee's conclusion was that it was "quite impossible, and that we must give our more serious and thorough attention to methods that seem more practical." When Republican Rep. Harold Knutson of Minnesota remarked that the monthly benefits contemplated by the Social Security bill, which averaged about twenty-five dollars, would be "rather disappointing to those who were expecting something like two hundred dollars a month," she snapped, "the government is not responsible for their having assumed that."

By then, Democratic Rep. John S. McGroarty, who had been elected in 1934 from California on a platform solely devoted to the Townsend Plan, won the scramble to be the first to introduce it as legislation in the House of Representatives. Fashioned as an amendment to the Social Security bill, McGroarty's version backed off somewhat from the doctor's original plan—changing the flat two-hundred-dollar monthly benefit to one "not to exceed" that amount, language that contemporary observers noted could accommodate sums as little as a few pennies a month. Even so, it attracted sixty cosponsors and prompted Congress to invite Townsend to testify on its behalf.

At the witness table, Townsend proved to be less than an entirely confident spokesman for his program, acknowledging that it would be so costly that "several years" would be required to register every senior. "Nobody has been fool enough to expect that we could take 10 millions of old folk and put them immediately on a $200 a month basis," he conceded to the Ways and Means Committee, prompting Robert Doughton of North Carolina, its chairman, to complain that the people who had been inundating Congress with letters favoring the plan "had it sold to them on the theory that just as soon as this law is enacted they will immediately go on the payroll." If they realized that they would not get paid for several years, he observed, "the propaganda would cease at once." McGroarty's bill eventually failed on an unrecorded vote without a formal roll call, which spared the members the burden of having either its support or opposition on their records.

Contemporary pundits predicted that once the government's Social Security program was placed fully in operation, the Townsend movement would run out of steam. Yet the movement's momentum carried well beyond the passage of the Social Security Act in mid-1935. A national Townsend convention in Chicago that October attracted seven thousand delegates and nationwide press coverage. In the 1936 election, another congressional candidate, a Michigan Republican, rode a platform based entirely on the Townsend Plan from obscurity to victory in the 1936 election.

That may have been the movement's high-water mark. A congressional investigation in 1936—whether motivated by sincere concern for the movement's members or a desire to undermine a strengthening political threat—raised doubts about whether all the money donated by the members was honestly spent, or whether some of it ended up in Clements's and Townsend's pockets. Clements resigned from the organization just before the hearings commenced, depriving the movement of his indispensable organizing genius.

Toward the end of the thirties, mass movements of all sorts lost their charm. Long was dead and Coughlin had devolved into a crank with narrow appeal. Sinclair did not run for office again after his trouncing, contenting himself with writing a retrospective on the campaign entitled I, Candidate for Governor—And How I Got Licked.

Yet the Townsend movement managed to retain a good portion of its appeal. Its effectiveness as a pressure group waned, as was predicted, with the passage of Social Security. As that bill was imperfect at best—historian William E. Leuchtenburg, though acknowledging the act as a "landmark," described it as "an astonishingly inept and conservative piece of legislation"—the Townsend movement's presence surely played a role in Congress's refinement of the old-age program in 1939, when it accelerated the start of benefits to 1940 from 1942 and pared back a scheduled increase in the payroll tax. Townsend died in 1960 at the age of ninety-three. His program struggled on for two more decades, the last Townsend Club shutting down in 1980. What may be its real legacies, Social Security and the idea that a grassroots movement can truly make a difference, survive to this day.

Hidden in Plain Sight: The Problem of Silos and Silences in Finance

Gillian Tett

Gillian Tett is the U.S. managing editor of the *Financial Times*. She has been named Journalist of the Year (2009) and Business Journalist of the Year (2008) by the British Press Awards and Senior Financial Journalist of the Year (2007) by the Wincott Awards, and she is the author of the *New York Times* bestseller *Fool's Gold: How Unrestrained Greed Corrupted a Dream, Shattered Global Markets and Unleashed a Catastrophe* (2009). Before joining the *Financial Times* in 1993, she was awarded a PhD in social anthropology from Cambridge University.

Late in 2011, Standard & Poor's issued a rating report on the U.S. investment bank Morgan Stanley that made for sobering reading. Buried toward the end was a paragraph saying, in effect, that the agency had decided to award a "moderate" risk profile to the bank because of the "complexity" of its business. In particular, its "exposure to the more volatile capital markets business and to more opaque financial products" was a "weakness to the risk profile that is not reflected in our risk-adjusted capital framework [and] can lead to unanticipated losses despite improved risk controls"—or so the agency solemnly declared.

For 99 percent of the population—for almost anyone working outside a bank—that sentence was meaningless gobbledygook. But what it essentially meant was that Standard & Poor's was unsure what was really going on inside Morgan

Stanley. Never mind all those clever rocket scientists who have been employed to monitor the bank, or those pages of financial regulations that have emerged as a result of the 2010 Dodd-Frank Wall Street Reform and Consumer Protection Act. When it comes to making sense of the risks attached to Morgan Stanley, or other large banks, a group such as Standard & Poor's can still only hazard a reasoned guess about the chance of "unanticipated losses." And for the wider public, it is all but impossible to make sense of that "complexity," since the issues tend to be buried in jargon (if not at the bottom of a ratings report).

Welcome to one of the big paradoxes of twenty-first-century finance. In many senses, it is unfair to single out Morgan Stanley. I cite this report because it happened to cross my desk, but most of the other large banks are equally complex, and thus equally prone to potential risks that the rating agencies are struggling to understand. Precisely because it is so common, however, this report on Morgan Stanley also points to one of the problems in modern finance: the cultural dangers of gobbledygook, silos, and social silences.

The issue at stake concerns how information travels around the system. Four or five long years after the financial crisis first erupted, it is often tempting for the wider public and politicians to blame it on some nefarious banking plot. After all, the assumption goes that during the credit boom—say, from 2003 to 2007—many bankers got extremely rich, engaging in activities that most people barely even knew existed: just think of all those complex collateralized debt obligations (CDOs) made up of mortgage loans that were concocted before 2007. The bankers who engaged in that mysterious activity also created risks that eventually blew the system up. Thus today it seems almost natural to search for villains—surely this disaster happened because bankers were deliberately hiding what they were doing, or concealing it in a cloak of spin. So the popular theory goes.

I think that the reality is more subtle—and unnerving. In general, I did not have the impression that there was any coordinated, *deliberate* plot by bankers to conceal their activities or downplay the risks before 2007. Instead, many of the activities were hidden in plain sight. To be sure, bankers did not always want to talk about these activities; many preferred to keep their deals away from the limelight—and the noses of regulators—because that allowed them to boost their margins (and stop rivals from stealing their ideas). But if more people had been willing to wade through rating agency reports, bank filings, and other data, it would have been possible for outsiders to spot that the system was spinning out of control and becoming prone to excess. Anybody willing to confront the gobbledygook would have been alarmed. The question that citizens and politicians alike need to ask is not why did the bankers "hide" their activities before 2007, but why did so few people actually ask hard questions at all. Why, in other words, did Western society allow finance to spin out of control—in plain sight? And what does that mean for how we treat finance today, on Wall Street or anywhere else?

In my view, there are two key issues that need to be discussed. The first is what might be called the silo trap, or the problem of tunnel vision. When I first started writing about complex finance as a journalist back in 2004, I was struck by the degree to which the modern financial system was marked by a pernicious silo mentality. This played out on many levels. Inside the giant bureaucracies of the modern banks, it seemed that different departments existed almost like warring tribes: although the separate desks, or divisions, of banks were theoretically supposed to collaborate, in practice they competed furiously for scarce resources, knowing that whatever desk earned the greatest profits would wield the most power. As a result, desks tended to hug information. The right hand of the bank rarely knew what the left was doing in any detail—nor was the risk department necessarily better informed.

Across the market as a whole, the silo problem was multiplied many times: different banks competed furiously and were often reluctant to tell competitors (or anybody else) too much detail about their activities. In theory, of course, the regulators were supposed to take an overarching view and look at how markets interacted as a whole. In practice, the regulatory infrastructure was fragmented, too, and marked by tribal rivalries that mirrored (and intensified) those private sector splits. In the United States, for example, the regulatory community was split into different bodies: the Office of the Comptroller of the Currency, the Federal Deposit Insurance Corporation, the Federal Reserve, and so on. The euro-zone financial system was fragmented by numerous different national regulators. Even in Britain, where there was supposed to be a single coordinated regulator (namely, the Financial Services Authority, or FSA), the conduct of regulation was weakened by a sense of tunnel vision: though the FSA looked at micro-level financial activity (that is, checked whether individual banks met the narrow regulatory rules), the Bank of England was supposed to look at overall financial and monetary flows (how the banking system as a whole was operating). Communication between the two bodies was patchy.

This fragmented picture made it hard for anyone to connect the dots, and numerous issues fell between the cracks. Inside the banks and regulatory offices, there were certainly people who understood how small pieces of finance worked; outside the financial system, there were some journalists and economists who could vaguely sense how the overall patterns were playing out. But trying to get a clear vision of how finance was developing as an entire system was hard. A sense of tunnel vision permeated the system—hampering bankers as much as anyone else.

The second key problem that dogged the system before 2007—and which also has implications for the future—is an issue that might be described as "social silences." Before I became a journalist, I trained as a social anthropologist and was influenced by the work of Pierre Bourdieu, a French intellectual who conducted anthropology fieldwork in North Africa. His work has great relevance for finance and many other parts of modern Western society. One of its cornerstones is the idea that societies typically operate with a publicly accepted sense of "discourse" (or *doxa*), which is shaped by the elite and enables them to maintain power. What matters in terms of that discourse is not what is defined as the culturally acceptable form of dialogue but, more crucially, the question of what is not discussed. Social silences, or the parts of everyday life that are typically ignored, are as important as—if not more important than—the issues that are popularly debated, since it is these silences that help to reproduce a system and power structures over time. Sometimes individual actors are aware of these silences and choose to deliberately conceal information (or not discuss it). More commonly, though, there is simply a tacit, half-conscious recognition that it is better simply to avoid discussing an issue, or that there are cultural disincentives to peering into it—because it is considered either taboo or "boring." Either way, a pattern of silence or disinterest often plays a useful function in terms of maintaining social structures, even if it is not *consciously* planned. Or, as Bourdieu says, "The most successful ideological effects are those which have no need of words, and ask no more than complicitous silence." Upton Sinclair, the novelist, expressed broadly the same thing one hundred years ago when he observed, "It is difficult to get a man to understand something, when his salary depends upon his not understanding it!" Finance epitomized this pattern before the financial crash. Back in 2005 and 2006, the topics of credit derivatives and collateralized debt obligations, for instance, were considered to be incredibly boring, if not downright arcane. During that period there were few mainstream media outlets that covered such topics, and even when journalists such as myself wrote about them, it was often tough to get these stories on the front page. That was partly because the subject matter was so unfamiliar; after all, who had heard of CDOs before 2007? But the other problem was that these topics seemed to be wrapped up in technical jargon that few people understood or, more importantly, had much appetite to understand. Faced with financial gobble-dygook, the general populace found it easier to leave the whole field of finance in the hands of technical experts, particularly since those technical experts were insisting, before 2007, that modern finance was a wonderfully beneficial thing. To put it another way, the single biggest reason finance remained hidden in plain sight was that insiders had very little interest in rocking the boat—and outsiders little incentive to peer in. The topic was widely perceived to be boring, at least within Western culture, and that kept the problems buried in a silo, without the need for any banking plot.

This pattern raises big questions about the future. In some senses, thankfully, many lessons have been learned since 2007 and 2008. Banks and regulators are keenly aware of the silo problem and are making efforts to take a more holistic vision of how finance operates. Since the financial crisis, for example, most banks have overhauled their internal risk management departments and are trying to take a more "joined-up" approach to analyzing their own activities. Regulators are now communicating far more intensively with each other, across departments and across borders. A Basel-based body called the Financial Stability Board is promoting a much higher level of international dialogue. One of its tasks, apart from monitoring global banking trends, is to look at "shadow banks," or the non-bank financial institutions that used to be ignored before 2007. Some central banks, such as the Bank of England, are embracing a so-called macro-prudential policy framework, which also seeks to promote a more holistic vision of how financial flows and economies interact. In Washington, the Office of Financial Research is trying to improve the level of data that is being gathered about global financial flow; the hope is that this will also enable regulators to take a more collaborative approach to monitoring the system.

In the aftermath of the 2008 crash, it is also widely recognized that the media and politicians alike need to do a better job of monitoring how modern finance works. No longer are politicians willing to leave banking purely in the hands of bankers, and even the more mainstream elements of the media have tried to unpack these issues in recent years. Ideas that were once near-unimaginable have started to be debated: it is no longer taken for granted, for example, that bankers should naturally get vast bonuses, or considered inevitable that finance should grow faster than the rest of the economy. The concept of state ownership for banks, as well, is no longer taboo—nor is the idea that banks should automatically be allowed to combine businesses as they please. Even the idea of capitalism has come up for more debate, as voices have started to challenge the once-dominant idea that free, globalized markets are always good.

While these signs of progress are certainly welcome, the efforts they represent remain limited in some respects. For one thing, the silo problem has certainly not been eradicated; in spite of all the efforts to embrace joined-up risk management systems and regulatory oversight, many parts of finance remain plagued by tunnel vision. There seems little chance of this disappearing soon. On the contrary, it is almost an inevitable consequence of the sheer size and complexity of many banks: the scale of these operations makes them not simply "too big to fail" but too big to manage—at least in a sensible, collaborative way.

Similarly, the problem of social silences has not disappeared. Instead, it keeps resurfacing in all manner of ways. Take the issue of banking reform. In the last two years, a blizzard of new financial regulations has been created or proposed by parliaments and government bureaucracies in Washington, Brussels, Basel, London, and Paris. Taken together, these regulations could have a significant impact on how finance is conducted in the future, yet their complexity makes them tough to comprehend, let alone monitor. To be sure, there are groups of lawyers who are able to comb through the fine print of the documents, but most of them are employed by banks—since the financial sector is the only player within the system that has enough resources to devote to this analysis. To nonbankers, the task looks as alienating today as making sense of the financial flows that caused the crisis five years ago did.

Put another way, while it was products such as the "CDO squared" or "CDO cubed" that defied public comprehension in 2006, these days the problem is one of "regulatory complexity squared" (or cubed): complex financial products are subject to extremely complex new laws—by governments that have very complex reform goals. And once again a wave of gobbledygook makes it almost impossible for anyone outside the banking world to understand what is going on at banks. *Pace* that report on Morgan Stanley I quoted earlier.

Is there any solution? Some steps might help. One idea

would be to make financial reform dramatically more simple, centering on practical, easy-to-understand principles. (It is worth noting, for example, that the Swiss are driving a wave of radical reform with a mere thirteen-page statement of principles; this compares with hundreds of pages now floating around places such as the United States and the euro zone.) Another sensible step would be to force the banks themselves to simplify their operations—to create companies that can be readily understood by regulators, directors, ratings agencies, and investors alike. Perhaps once a year the directors of the largest banks should be forced to appear in front of a committee of politicians, to explain how their banks make money and where their risks lie. If nothing else, that public grilling might help to concentrate minds.

The other area where there needs to be more debate is in the information business itself. In an ideal world, the best way to deal with the problems of silos and social silences would be to have a lively cadre of institutions and professionals who are committed to silo-busting and shedding light on dark or "boring" places in finance. Journalists are one obvious group who could and should play that role (and speaking as a *Financial Times* journalist, I can say it is a task that we take very seriously). So could academics, political researchers, or even credit rating agencies. Some of these institutions have been trying to fulfill that function in recent years: there has been a host of investigative pieces emanating from the Western media world, and some penetrating reports from academics as well, not to mention some of the credit rating agencies.

Unfortunately, this silo-busting activity is still far too modest and sporadic. Part of the problem is that universities, newspapers, and rating agencies remain riddled with silos themselves. Another related issue is that the resources of silo-busting institutions such as universities and newspapers are being eroded all the time. Most newspapers today, after all, simply do not have enough reporters available to spend days trying to decode Dodd-Frank or comb through the fine details of bank balance sheets—and they are doubly wary of doing this given that many bills, Dodd-Frank included, tend to look distinctly "dull." Thankfully, some academics have more resources and time (the work done by NYU economists that "explains" Dodd-Frank, for example, shows how universities can play that role). As some cash-strapped newspapers have been forced to step back from investigative reporting, other bodies have sprung up to engage in long-form research in finance and other spheres (ProPublica in New York is an excellent example of this). But today, as before, there is still a great deal in finance that remains hidden in plain sight, ignored by the wider public and by politicians because it seems technical, complex—or just boring gobbledygook. That is not a comforting thought, for bankers, journalists, or anyone else.

What Good Is Wall Street?

John Cassidy

John Cassidy is a staff writer at *The New Yorker* and a columnist at *Fortune*. His latest book is *How Markets Fail: The Logic of Economic Calamities* (2009).

In early fall 2010, I came across an announcement that Citigroup, the parent company of Citibank, was to be honored, along with its chief executive, Vikram Pandit, for "Advancing the Field of Asset Building in America." This seemed akin to, say, saluting BP for services to the environment or praising Facebook for its commitment to privacy. During the past decade, Citi has become synonymous with financial misjudgment, reckless lending, and gargantuan losses: what might be termed asset denuding rather than asset building. In late 2008, the sprawling firm might well have collapsed but for a government bailout. Even today the U.S. taxpayer is Citigroup's largest shareholder.

The awards ceremony took place on September 23 in Washington, D.C., where the Corporation for Enterprise Development, a not-for-profit organization dedicated to expanding economic opportunities for low-income families and communities, was holding its biennial conference. A ballroom at the Marriott Wardman Park was full of government officials, lawyers, tax experts, and community workers, two of whom were busy at my table lamenting the impact of budget cuts on financial-education programs in Vermont.

Pandit, a slight, bespectacled fifty-four-year-old native of Nagpur, in western India, was seated near the front of the room. Fred Goldberg, a former commissioner of the Internal Revenue Service who is now a partner at Skadden, Arps, introduced him to the crowd, pointing out that, over the years, Citi has taken many initiatives designed to encourage entrepreneurship and thrift in impoverished areas, setting up lending programs for mom-and-pop stores, for instance, and establishing savings accounts for the children of low-income families. "When the history is written, Citi will be singled out as one of the pioneers of the asset movement," Goldberg said. "They have demonstrated the capacity, the vision, and the will."

Pandit, who moved to the United States at sixteen, is rarely described as a communitarian. A former investment banker and hedge fund manager, he sold his investment firm to Citigroup in 2007 for $800 million, earning about $165 million for himself. Eight months later, after Citi announced billions of dollars in write-offs, Pandit became the company's new CEO. He oversaw its near collapse in 2008 and its moderate recovery since.

Clearly, this wasn't the occasion for Pandit to dwell on his career, or on the role that Citi's irresponsible actions played in bringing on the subprime-mortgage crisis. (In early 2007, his predecessor, Charles Prince, was widely condemned for commenting, "As long as the music is playing, you've got to get up and dance.") Instead, Pandit talked about how well-functioning banks are essential to any modern society, adding, "As President Obama has said, ultimately there is no dividing line between Wall Street and Main Street. We will rise or we will fall together as one nation." In the past couple of years, he went on, Citi had rededicated itself to "responsible finance." Before he and his colleagues approved any transaction, they now asked themselves three questions: Is it in the best interests of the customer? Is it systemically responsible? And does it create economic value? Pandit indicated that other financial firms were doing the same thing. "Banks have learned how to be banks again," he said.

About an hour later, I spoke with Pandit in a sparsely furnished hotel room. Citi's leaders—from Walter Wriston, in the 1970s, to John Reed, in the 1980s, and Sanford Weill, in the late 1990s—have tended to be formidable and forbidding. Pandit affects a down-to-earth demeanor. He offered me a cup of coffee and insisted that I sit on a comfortable upholstered chair while he perched on a cheap plastic one. I asked him if he saw any irony in Citi being commended for asset building. His eyes widened slightly. "Well," he said, "the award we are receiving is for fifteen years of work. It was work that was pioneered by Citi to get more financial inclusion. And it's part of a broader reform effort we are involved in under the heading of 'Responsible Banking.'"

Since Pandit took over, this effort has involved selling or closing down some of Citi's riskier trading businesses, including the hedge fund that he used to run; splitting off the company's most foul-smelling assets into a separate entity, Citi Holdings; and cutting the pay of some senior executives. For 2009 and 2010, Pandit took an annual salary of one dollar and no bonus. (He didn't, however, give back any of the money from the sale of his hedge fund.) "This is an apprenticeship industry," he said to me. "People learn from the people above them, and they copy the actions of the people above them. If you start from the top by acting responsibly, people will see and learn."

Barely two years after Wall Street's recklessness brought the global economy to the brink of collapse, the sight of a senior Wall Street figure talking about responsible finance may well strike you as suspicious. But on one point Pandit cannot be challenged. Since the promulgation of Hammurabi's code, in ancient Babylon, no advanced society has survived without banks and bankers. Banks enable people to borrow money, and, today, by operating electronic-transfer systems, they allow commerce to take place without notes and coins changing hands. They also play a critical role in channeling savings into productive investments. When a depositor places money in a savings account or a CD, the bank lends it out to corporations, small businesses, and families. These days, Bank of America, Citi, JPMorgan Chase, and others also help corporations and municipalities raise money by issuing stocks, bonds, and other securities on their behalf. The business of issuing securities used to be the exclusive preserve of Wall Street firms, such as ' Stanley and Goldman Sachs, but during the past twenty years many of the dividing lines between ordinary banks and invest-ment banks have vanished.

When the banking system behaves the way it is supposed to—as Pandit says Citi is now behaving—it is akin to a power utility, distributing money (power) to where it is needed and keeping an account of how it is used. Just like power utilities, the big banks have a commanding position in the market, which they can use for the benefit of their customers and the economy at large. But when banks seek to exploit their position and make a quick killing, they can cause enormous damage. It's not clear now whether the bankers have really given up their reckless practices, as Pandit claims they have, or whether they are merely lying low. In the past few years, all the surviving big banks have raised more capital and become profitable again. However, the U.S. government was indirectly responsible for much of this turnaround. And in the country at large, where many businesses rely on the banks to fund their day-to-day operations, the power still isn't flowing properly. Overall bank lending to firms and households remains below the level it reached in 2008.

The other important role of the banking industry,

historically, has been to finance the growth of other vital industries, including railroads, pharmaceuticals, automobiles, and entertainment. "Go back and pick any period in time," John Mack, the chairman of Morgan Stanley, said to me recently. "Let's go back to the tech boom. I guess it got on its feet in the late eighties, with Apple Computer and Microsoft, and really started to blossom in the nineteen-nineties, with Cisco, Netscape, Amazon.com, and others. These are companies that created a lot of jobs, a lot of intellectual capital, and Wall Street helped finance that. The first investors were angel investors, then venture capitalists, and to really grow and build they needed Wall Street."

Mack, who is sixty-seven years old, is a plainspoken native of North Carolina. He attended Duke on a football scholarship, and he retains the lean build of an athlete. We were sitting at a conference table in his large, airy office above Times Square, which features floor-to-ceiling windows with views of the Hudson. "Today, it's not just technology—it's clean tech," he went on. "All of these industries need capital—whether it is ethanol, solar, or other alternative-fuel sources. We can give you a list of companies we've done, but it's not just Morgan Stanley. Wall Street has been the source of capital formation."

There is something in what Mack says. Morgan Stanley has raised money for Tesla Motors, a producer of electric cars, and it has invested in Bloom Energy, an innovator in fuel-cell technology. Morgan Stanley's principal rivals, Goldman Sachs and JPMorgan, are also canvassing investors for ethanol producers, wind farms, and other alternative-energy firms. Banks, of course, raise money for less environmentally friendly corporations, too, such as Ford, General Electric, and ExxonMobil, which need cash to fund their operations. It was evidently this business of raising capital (and creating employment) that Lloyd Blankfein, Goldman's chief executive, was referring to last year, when he told an interviewer from a British newspaper that he and his colleagues were "doing God's work."

Yet Wall Street's role in financing new businesses is a small portion of what it does. The market for initial public offerings of stock by U.S. companies never fully recovered from the tech bust. During the third quarter of 2010, just thirty-three U.S. companies went public, and they raised a paltry $5 billion. Most people on Wall Street aren't finding the next Apple or promoting a green rival to Exxon. They are buying and selling securities that are tied to existing firms and capital projects, or to something less concrete, such as the price of a stock or the level of an exchange rate. During the past two decades, trading volumes have risen exponentially across many markets: stocks, bonds, currencies, commodities, and all manner of derivative securities. In the first nine months of 2010, sales and trading accounted for 36 percent of Morgan Stanley's revenues and a much higher proportion of profits. Traditional investment banking—the business of raising money for companies and advising them on deals—contributed less than 15 percent of the firm's revenue. Goldman Sachs is even more reliant on trading. Between July and September 2010, trading accounted for 63 percent of its revenue, and corporate finance just 13 percent.

In effect, many of the big banks have turned themselves from businesses whose profits rose and fell with the capital-raising needs of their clients into immense trading houses whose fortunes depend on their ability to exploit day-to-day movements in the markets. Because trading has become so central to their business, the big banks are forever trying to invent new financial products that they can sell but that their competitors, at least for the moment, cannot. Some recent innovations, such as tradable pollution rights and catastrophe bonds, have provided a public benefit. But it's easy to point to other innovations that serve little purpose or that blew up and caused a lot of collateral damage, such as auction-rate securities and collateralized debt obligations. Testifying in 2010 before the Financial Crisis Inquiry Commission, Ben Bernanke, the chairman of the Federal Reserve, said that financial innovation "isn't always a good thing," adding that some innovations amplify risk and others are used primarily "to take unfair advantage rather than create a more efficient market."

Other regulators have gone further. Lord Adair Turner, the chairman of Britain's top financial watchdog, the Financial Services Authority, has described much of what happens on Wall Street and in other financial centers as "socially useless activity"—a comment that suggests it could be eliminated without doing any damage to the economy. In an article titled "What Do Banks Do?," which appeared in a 2010 collection of essays devoted to the future of finance, Turner pointed out that although certain financial activities were genuinely valuable, others generated revenues and profits without delivering anything of real worth—payments that economists refer to as rents. "It is possible for financial activity to extract rents from the real economy rather than to deliver economic value," Turner wrote. "Financial innovation...may in some ways and under some circumstances foster economic value creation, but that needs to be illustrated at the level of specific effects: it cannot be asserted a priori."

Turner's viewpoint caused consternation in the City of London, the world's largest financial market. A clear implication of his argument is that many people in the City and on Wall Street are the financial equivalent of slumlords or toll collectors in pinstriped suits. If they retired to their beach houses en masse, the rest of the economy would be fine, or perhaps even healthier.

*   *   *

Since 1980, according to the Bureau of Labor Statistics, the number of people employed in finance, broadly defined, has shot up from roughly five million to more than seven and a half million. During the same period, the profitability of the financial sector has increased greatly relative to other industries. Think of all the profits produced by businesses operating in the United States as if they were a cake. Twenty-five years ago, the slice taken by financial firms was about a seventh of the whole. In 2009, it was more than a quarter. (In 2006, at the peak of the boom, it was about a third.) In other words, during a period in which American companies have created iPhones, Home Depot, and Lipitor, the best place to work has been in an industry that doesn't design, build, or sell a single tangible thing.

From the end of the Second World War until 1980 or thereabouts, people working in finance earned about the same, on average and taking into account their qualifications, as people in other industries. By 2006, wages in the financial sector were about 60 percent higher than wages elsewhere. And in the richest segment of the financial industry—on Wall Street, that is—compensation has gone up even more dramatically. In 2009, while many people were facing pay freezes or worse, the average pay of employees at Goldman Sachs, Morgan Stanley, and JPMorgan Chase's investment bank jumped 27 percent, to more than $340,000. This figure includes modestly paid workers at reception desks and in mailrooms, and it thus understates what senior bankers earn. At Goldman, it has been reported, nearly a thousand employees received bonuses of at least a million dollars in 2009.

Not surprisingly, Wall Street has become the preferred destination for the bright young people who used to want to start up their own companies, work for NASA, or join the Peace Corps. At Harvard in spring 2010, about a third of the seniors with secure jobs were heading to work in finance. Ben

Friedman, a professor of economics at Harvard, wrote an article in 2010 lamenting "the direction of such a large fraction of our most-skilled, best-educated, and most highly motivated young citizens to the financial sector."

Most people on Wall Street, not surprisingly, believe that they earn their keep, but at least one influential financier vehemently disagrees: Paul Woolley, a seventy-two-year-old Englishman who has set up an institute at the London School of Economics (LSE) called the Woolley Centre for the Study of Capital Market Dysfunctionality. "Why on earth should finance be the biggest and most highly paid industry when it's just a utility, like sewage or gas?" Woolley said to me when I met with him in London. "It is like a cancer that is growing to infinite size, until it takes over the entire body."

From 1987 to 2006, Woolley, who has a doctorate in economics, ran the London affiliate of GMO, a Boston-based investment firm. Before that, he was an executive director at Barings, the venerable British investment bank that collapsed in 1995 after a rogue-trader scandal, and at the International Monetary Fund. Tall, soft-spoken, and courtly, Woolley moves easily between the City of London, academia, and policymaking circles. With a taste for Savile Row suits and a keen interest in antiquarian books, he doesn't come across as an insurrectionary. But, sitting in an office at LSE, he cheerfully told me that he regarded himself as one. "What we are doing is revolutionary," he said with a smile. "Nobody has done anything like it before."

At GMO, Woolley ran several funds that invested in stocks and bonds from many countries. He also helped to set up one of the first "quant" funds, which rely on mathematical algorithms to find profitable investments. From his perch in Angel Court, in the heart of The City, he watched the rapid expansion all around him. Established international players, such as Citi, Goldman, and UBS, were getting bigger; new entrants, especially hedge funds and buyout (private equity) firms, were proliferating. Woolley's firm did well, too, but a basic economic question niggled at him: Was the financial industry doing what it was supposed to be doing? Was it allocating capital to its most productive uses?

At first, like most economists, he believed that trading drove market prices to levels justified by economic fundamentals. If an energy company struck oil, or an entertainment firm created a new movie franchise, investors would pour money into its stock, but the price would remain tethered to reality. The dot-com bubble of the late 1990s changed his opinion. GMO is a "value investor" that seeks out stocks on the basis of earnings and cash flows. When the Nasdaq took off, Woolley and his colleagues couldn't justify buying high-priced Internet stocks, and their funds lagged behind rivals that shifted more of their money into tech. Between June 1998 and March 2000, Woolley recalled, the clients of GMO—pension funds and charitable endowments, mostly—withdrew 40 percent of their money. During the ensuing five years, the bubble burst, value stocks fared a lot better than tech stocks, and the clients who had left missed more than a 60 percent gain relative to the market as a whole. After going through that experience, Woolley had an epiphany: financial institutions that react to market incentives in a competitive setting often end up making a mess of things. "I realized we were acting rationally and optimally," he said. "The clients were acting rationally and optimally. And the outcome was a complete Horlicks." Financial markets, far from being efficient, as most economists and policymakers at the time believed, were grossly inefficient. "And once you recognize that markets are inefficient, a lot of things change."

One is the role of financial intermediaries, such as banks.

Rather than seeking the most productive outlet for the money that depositors and investors entrust to them, they may follow trends and surf bubbles. These activities shift capital into projects that have little or no long-term value, such as speculative real-estate developments in the swamps of Florida. Rather than acting in their customers' best interests, financial institutions may peddle opaque investment products, like collateralized debt obligations. Privy to superior information, banks can charge hefty fees and drive up their own profits at the expense of clients who are induced to take on risks they don't fully understand—a form of rent seeking. "Mispricing gives incorrect signals for resource allocation, and, at worst, causes stock market booms and busts," Woolley wrote in a 2010 paper. "Rent capture causes the misallocation of labor and capital, transfers substantial wealth to bankers and financiers, and, at worst, induces systemic failure. Both impose social costs on their own, but in combination they create a perfect storm of wealth destruction."

Woolley originally endowed his institute on dysfunctionality with £4 million. (By British standards, that is a significant sum.) The institute opened in 2007—Mervyn King, the governor of the Bank of England, turned up at its launch party—and has published more than a dozen research papers challenging the benefits that financial markets and financial institutions bring to the economy. Dmitri Vayanos, a professor of finance at LSE who runs the Woolley Centre, has presented some of its research at Stanford, Columbia, the University of Chicago, and other leading universities. Woolley has published a ten-point "manifesto" aimed at the mutual funds, pension funds, and charitable endowments that, through payments of fees and commissions, ultimately help finance the salaries of many people on Wall Street and in the City of London. Among Woolley's suggestions: investment funds should limit the turnover in their portfolios, refuse to pay performance fees, and avoid putting money into hedge funds and private equity firms.

Before leaving for lunch at his club, the Reform, Woolley pointed me to a study by the research firm Ibbotson Associates, which shows that during the past decade investors in hedge funds, overall, would have done just as well putting their money straight into the S&P 500. "The amount of rent capture has been huge," Woolley said. "Investment banking, prime broking, mergers and acquisitions, hedge funds, private equity, commodity investment—the whole scale of activity is far too large." I asked Woolley how big he thought the financial sector should be. "About a half or a third of its current size," he replied.

When I got back from London, I spoke with Ralph Schlosstein, the CEO of Evercore, a smallish investment bank of about six hundred employees that advises corporations on mergers and acquisitions but doesn't do much in the way of issuing and trading securities. In the 1970s, Schlosstein worked on Capitol Hill as an economist before joining the Carter administration, in which he served at the Treasury and the White House. In the 1980s, he moved to Wall Street and worked for Lehman with Roger Altman, the chairman and founder of Evercore. Eventually, Schlosstein left to cofound the investment firm Black-Rock, where he made a fortune. After retiring from BlackRock, in 2007, he could have moved to his house on Martha's Vineyard, but he likes Wall Street and believes in it. "There will always be a need for funding from businesses and households," he said. "We saw at the end of 2008 and in early 2009 what happens to an economy when that capital-raising and capital-allocation mechanism breaks down. Part of what has distinguished the U.S. economy from the rest of the world is that we've always had large, transparent pools of capital. Ultimately, that drives down the cost of capital in the U.S. relative to our competitors."

Still Schlosstein agrees with Woolley that Wall Street has problems, many of which derive from its size. In the early 1980s, Goldman and Morgan Stanley were roughly the size of Evercore today. Now they are many times as large. Big doesn't necessarily mean bad, but when the Wall Street firms grew beyond a certain point they faced a set of new challenges. In a private partnership, the people who run the firm, rather than outside shareholders, bear the brunt of losses—a structure that discourages reckless risk taking. In addition, small banks don't employ very much capital, which allows them to make a decent return by acting in the interests of their clients and relying on commissions. Big firms, however, have to take on more risk in order to generate the sorts of profits that their stockholders have come to expect. This inevitably involves building up their trading operations. "The leadership of these firms tends to go toward people who can deploy their vast amounts of capital and earn a decent return on it," Schlosstein said. "That tends to be people from the trading and capital-markets side."

Some kinds of trading serve a useful economic function. One is market making, in which banks accumulate large inventories of securities in order to facilitate buying and selling on the part of their clients. Banks also engage in active trading to meet their clients' wishes either to lay off risk or to take it on. American Airlines might pay Morgan Stanley a fee to guarantee that the price of its jet fuel won't rise above a certain level for three years. The bank would then make a series of trades in the oil futures markets designed to cover what it would have to pay American if the price of fuel rose. However, the mere fact that a certain trade is client-driven doesn't mean it is socially useful. Banks often design complicated trading strategies that help a customer, such as a pension fund or a wealthy individual, circumvent regulatory requirements or reduce tax liabilities. From the client's viewpoint, these types of financial products can create value, but from society's perspective they merely shift money around. "The usual economists' argument for financial innovation is that it adds to the size of the pie," Gerald Epstein, an economist at the University of Massachusetts, said. "But these types of things don't add to the pie. They redistribute it—often from taxpayers to banks and other financial institutions."

Meanwhile, big banks also utilize many kinds of trading that aren't in the service of their traditional clients. One is proprietary trading, in which they bet their own capital on movements in the markets. There's no social defense for this practice, except the argument that the banks exist to make profits for the shareholders. The so-called Volcker rule, an element of the 2010 Dodd-Frank financial reform bill intended to prevent banks from taking too many risks with their depositors' money, was supposed to have proscribed banks from proprietary trading. However, it is not yet clear how the rule will be applied or how it will prevent some types of proprietary trading that are difficult to distinguish from market making. If a firm wants to place a bet on falling interest rates, for example, it can simply have its market-making unit build up its inventory of bonds.

The Dodd-Frank bill also didn't eliminate what Schlosstein describes as "a whole bunch of activities that fell into the category of speculation rather than effectively functioning capital markets." Leading up to the collapse, the banks became heavily involved in facilitating speculation by other traders, particularly hedge funds, which buy and sell at a frenetic pace, generating big fees and commissions for Wall Street firms. Schlosstein picked out the growth of credit default swaps, a type of derivative often used purely for speculative purposes. When an investor or financial institution buys this kind of swap, it doesn't purchase a bond itself; it just places a bet on whether the bond will default. At the height of the boom, for every dollar banks issued in bonds, they might issue twenty dollars in swaps. "If they did a hundred-million-dollar bond issue, two billion dollars of swaps would be created and traded," Schlosstein said. "That's insane." From the banks' perspective, creating this huge market in side bets was very profitable insanity. By late 2007, the notional value of outstanding credit default swaps was about $60 trillion—more than four times the size of the U.S. gross domestic product. Each time a financial institution issued a swap, it charged the customer a commission. But wagers on credit default swaps are zero-sum games. For every winner, there is a loser. In the aggregate, little or no economic value is created.

Since the market collapsed, far fewer credit default swaps have been issued. But the insidious culture that allowed Wall Street firms to peddle securities of dubious value to pension funds and charitable endowments remains largely in place. "Traditionally, the relationship between Wall Street and its big clients has been based on the 'big boy' concept," Schlosstein explained. "You are dealing with sophisticated investors who can do their own due diligence. For example, if CALPERS"—the California Public Employees Retirement System—"wants to buy something that a major bank is selling short, it's not the bank's responsibility to tell them. On Wall Street, this was the accepted way of doing business." Early in 2010, the Securities and Exchange Commission appeared to challenge the big-boy concept, suing Goldman Sachs for failing to disclose material information about some subprime-mortgage securities that it sold, but the case was resolved without Goldman's admitting any wrongdoing. "This issue started to get discussed, then fell to the wayside when Goldman settled their case," Schlosstein said.

*   *   *

The big banks insist that they have to be big in order to provide the services that their corporate clients demand. "We are in one hundred and fifty-nine countries," Vikram Pandit told me. "Companies need us because they are going global, too. They have cash-management needs all around the world. They have capital-market needs all around the world. We can meet those needs." More than two-thirds of Citi's 260,000 employees work outside the United States. In the first nine months of 2010, nearly three-quarters of the firm's profits emanated from Europe, Asia, and Latin America. In Brazil, Citi helped Petrobras, the state-run oil company, to issue stock to the public; in the United Kingdom, it helped raise money for a leveraged buyout of Tomkins, an engineering company.

"It's all about clients," Pandit went on. The biggest mistake Citi and other banks made during the boom, he said, was coming to believe that investing and trading on their own account, rather than on behalf of their clients, was a basic aspect of banking. Even before the Dodd-Frank bill was passed, Pandit was closing down some of Citi's proprietary businesses and trying to sell others. "Proprietary trading is not the core of what banking is about," he said. In place of a business model that was largely dependent on making quick gains, he is trying to revive a banking culture based on cultivating long-term relationships with Citi's customers. "Once you make your business all about relationships, conflicts of interest are not an issue," he said.

Despite Pandit's efforts to remake Citi's culture, the firm remains heavily involved in trading of various kinds. Its investment-banking arm, which has grown rapidly over the past decade, still accounts for about three-tenths of its revenues (close to $20 billion in the first nine months of 2010) and more than two-thirds of its net profits (upward of $6 billion in the same period). And within the investment bank about eighty cents of every dollar in revenues came from buying and selling securities, while just fourteen cents of every dollar came from raising capital for companies and advising them on deals. Between January and September 2010, Citigroup's bond traders alone generated more than $12.5 billion in revenues—more than the bank's entire branch network in North America.

Many banks believe that trading is too lucrative a business to stop, and they are trying to persuade government officials to enforce the Dodd-Frank bill in the loosest possible way. Morgan Stanley and other big firms are also starting to rebuild their securitization business, which pools together auto loans, credit card receivables, and other forms of credit, and then issues bonds backed by them. There have even been some securitizations of prime mortgage loans. I asked John Mack if he could see subprime-mortgage bonds making a comeback. "I think in time they will," he replied. "I hope they do. I say that because it gives tremendous liquidity to the markets."

"Liquidity" refers to how easy or difficult it is to buy and sell. A share of stock in a company on the Nasdaq is a very liquid asset: using a discount brokerage such as Fidelity, you can sell it in seconds for less than ten dollars. A chocolate factory is an illiquid asset: disposing of it is time-consuming and costly. The classic justification for market making and other types of trading is that they endow the market with liquidity, and throughout the financial industry I heard the same argument over and over. "You can't not have banks, and you can't not have trading," an executive at a big private equity firm said to me. "Part of the value in a stock is the knowledge that you can sell it this afternoon. Banks provide liquidity."

But liquidity, or at least the perception of it, has a downside. The liquidity of Internet stocks persuaded investors to buy them in the belief that they would be able to sell out in time. The liquidity of subprime-mortgage securities was at the heart of the credit crisis. Home lenders, thinking they would always be able to sell the loans they made to Wall Street firms for bundling together into mortgage bonds, extended credit to just about anybody. But liquidity is quick to disappear when you need it most. Everybody tries to sell at the same time, and the market seizes up. The problem with modern finance "isn't just about excessive rents and a misallocation of capital," Paul Woolley said. "It is also crashes and bad macroeconomic outcomes. The recent crisis cost about ten per cent of GDP. It made tackling climate change look cheap."

In the upper reaches of Wall Street, talk of another financial crisis is dismissed as alarmism. Last fall, John Mack, to his credit, was one of the first Wall Street CEOs to say publicly that his industry needed stricter regulation. Now that Morgan Stanley and Goldman Sachs, the last two remaining big independent Wall Street firms, have converted to bank holding companies, a legal switch that placed them under the regulatory authority of the Federal Reserve, Mack insists that proper supervision is in place. Fed regulators "have more expertise, and they challenge us," Mack told me. Since the middle of 2007, Morgan Stanley has raised about $20 billion in new capital and cut in half its leverage ratio—the total value of its assets divided by its capital. In addition, it now holds much more of its assets in forms that can be readily converted to cash. Other firms, including Goldman Sachs, have taken similar measures. "It's a much safer system now," Mack insisted. "There's no question."

That's true. But the history of Wall Street is a series of booms and busts. After each blowup, the firms that survive temporarily shy away from risky ventures and cut back on leverage. Over time, the markets recover their losses, memories fade, spirits revive, and the action starts up again, until, eventually, it goes too far. The mere fact that Wall Street poses less of an immediate threat to the rest of us doesn't mean it has permanently mended its ways.

Perhaps the most shocking thing about recent events was not how rapidly the big Wall Street firms got into trouble but how quickly they returned to profitability and lavished big rewards on themselves. In 2009, Goldman Sachs paid more than $16 billion in compensation, and Morgan Stanley paid out more than $14 billion. Neither came up with any spectacular new investments or produced anything of tangible value, which leads to the question: when it comes to pay, is there something unique about the financial industry?

Thomas Philippon, an economist at NYU's Stern School of Business, thinks there is. After studying the large pay differential between financial sector employees and people in other industries with similar levels of education and experience, he and a colleague, Ariell Reshef of the University of Virginia, concluded that some of it could be explained by growing demand for financial services from technology companies and baby boomers. But Philippon and Reshef determined that up to half of the pay premium was due to something much simpler: people in the financial sector are overpaid. "In most industries, when people are paid too much their firms go bankrupt, and they are no longer paid too much," he told me. "The exception is when people are paid too much and their firms don't go broke. That is the finance industry."

On Wall Street dealing desks, profits and losses are evaluated every afternoon when trading ends, and the firms' positions are "marked to market"—valued on the basis of the closing prices. A trader can borrow money and place a leveraged bet on a certain market. As long as the market goes up, he will appear to be making a steady profit. But if the market eventually turns against him, his capital may be wiped out. "You can create a trading strategy that overnight makes lots of money, and it can take months or years to find out whether it is real money or luck or excessive risk taking," Philippon explained. "Sometimes, even then it is hard." Since traders (and their managers) get evaluated on a quarterly basis, they can be paid handsomely for placing bets that ultimately bankrupt their companies. "In most industries, a good idea is rewarded because the company generates profits and real cash flows," Philippon said. "In finance, it is often just a trading gain. The closer you get to financial markets, the easier it is to book funny profits."

During the credit boom of 2005 to 2007, profits and pay reached unprecedented highs. It is now evident that the bankers were being rewarded largely for taking on unacknowledged risks: after the subprime market collapsed, bank shareholders and taxpayers were left to pick up the losses. From an economy-wide perspective, this experience suggests that at least some of the profits that Wall Street bankers claim to generate, and that they use to justify their big pay packages, are illusory. Such a subversive notion has recently received the endorsement of senior officers at the Bank of England. Andrew Haldane, the executive director of financial stability at the Bank, gave a speech in July 2010 titled "The Contribution of the Financial Sector: Miracle or Mirage?" It concluded, "Because banks are in the risk business, it should be no surprise that the run-up to the crisis was hallmarked by imaginative ways of manufacturing this commodity, with a view to boosting returns to labour and capital....It is in bank managers' interest to make mirages look like miracles."

Under pressure from the regulators, the big Wall Street banks have responded to criticisms over executive compensation with something called "clawback." Rather than paying hefty bonuses in cash every January or February, a bank gives its most highly paid employees some sort of deferred compensation designed to decline in value if "profits" turn into losses.

The simplest way of doing this is to issue bonuses in the form of restricted stock that can't be sold for a long period of time. If the firm gets into trouble as a result of decisions taken years earlier, and its stock price declines, those responsible will suffer. Morgan Stanley pays bonuses in cash, but places the cash in a restricted account where it can't be used for a certain number of years. If during this period the investment that generated the bonus turns into a loss, the firm has the right to take back some or all of the cash.

The spread of clawback provisions shows that there has been some change on Wall Street. But it's unclear if the schemes will hold up when inevitably challenged in court—or if they'll deter traders from taking unwarranted risks. On Wall Street and elsewhere in corporate America, insiders generally learn quickly how to game new systems and turn them to their advantage. A key question about clawbacks is how long they remain in effect. At Morgan Stanley the answer is three years, which may not be long enough for hidden risks to materialize. "It's just very easy to create trading strategies that make money for six years and lose money in the seventh," Philippon said. "That's exactly what Lehman did for six years before its collapse."

Given the code of silence that Wall Street firms impose on their employees, it is difficult to get midlevel bankers to speak openly about what they do. There is, however, a blog, The Epicurean Dealmaker, written by an anonymous investment banker who has for several years been providing caustic commentary on his profession. The biography on his site notes, "I facilitate, justify, and advise parties to M&A transactions, when I am not advising against them." In March 2008, when some analysts were suggesting that the demise of Bear Stearns would lead to a change of attitudes on Wall Street, TED—the shorthand appellation the author uses—wrote, "I, for one, think these bankers will be even more motivated to rape and pillage the financial system in order to rebuild their ill-gotten gains." Seven months later, on the eve of the bank bailout, TED opined, "Let hundreds of banks fail. Let tens of thousands of financial workers lose their jobs and their personal wealth.... The financial sector has had a really, really good run for a lot of years. It is time to pay the piper, and I, for one, have little interest in using my taxpayer dollars to cushion the blow. After all, I am just another heartless Wall Street bastard myself."

In September 2010, TED and I met at a diner near my office. He looked like an investment banker: middle-aged, clean-cut, wearing an expensive-looking gray suit. Our conversation started out with some banter about the rivalry between bankers and traders at many Wall Street firms. As the traders came out on top in recent years, TED recalled, "they would say, 'You guys are the real parasites, going to expensive lunches and doing deals on the back of our trading operations.' " He professed to be unaffected by this ribbing, but he said, "In my experience, the proprietary traders are always the clowns who make twenty million dollars a year until they lose a hundred million."

In September 2009, addressing the popular anger about bankers' pay, TED wrote that he wouldn't "attempt to rationalize stratospheric pay in the industry on the basis of some sort of self-aggrandizing claim to the particular socioeconomic utility or virtue of what I and my peers do," and he cautioned his colleagues against making any such claim: "You mean to tell me your work as a [fill in the blank here] is worth more to society than a firefighter? An elementary school teacher? A combat infantryman in Afghanistan? A priest? Good luck with that." The fact was, TED went on, "my pay is set according to one thing and one thing only: the demand in the marketplace for my services....Investment bankers get paid a lot of money because that is what the market will bear."

While not inaccurate, this explanation raises questions about how competition works in the financial industry. If Hertz sees much of its rental fleet lying idle, it will cut its prices to better compete with Avis and Enterprise. Chances are that Avis and Enterprise will respond in kind, and the result will be lower profits all around. On Wall Street, the price of various services has been fixed for decades. If Morgan Stanley issues stock in a new company, it charges the company a commission of around 7 percent. If Evercore or JPMorgan advises a corporation on making an acquisition, the standard fee is about 2 percent of the purchase price. I asked TED why there is so little price competition. He concluded that it was something of a mystery. "It's a commodity business," he said. "I can do what Goldman Sachs does. You can do what I can do. Nobody has a proprietary edge. And if you do have a proprietary edge, you'll only have it for a few weeks before somebody reverse-engineers it."

After thinking it over, the best explanation TED could come up with was based on a theory of relativity: investment banking fees are small compared with the size of the overall transaction. "You are a client, and you are going to do a five-billion-dollar deal," he said. "It's the biggest deal you've ever done. It's going to determine your future, and the future of your firm. Are you really going to fight about whether a certain fee is 2.5 percent or 3.3 percent? No. The old cliché we rely on is this: when you need surgery, do you go to the discount surgeon or to the one you trust and know, who charges more?"

I asked him how he and his coworkers felt about making loads of money when much of the country was struggling. "A lot of people don't care about it or think about it," he replied. "They say, it's a market, it's still open, and I'll sell my labor for as much as I can until nobody wants to buy it." But you, I asked, what do you think? "I tend to think we do create value," he said. "It's not a productive value in a very visible sense, like finding a cure for cancer. We're middlemen. We bring together two sides of a deal. That's not a very elevated thing, but I can't think of any elevated economy that doesn't need middlemen."

The Epicurean Dealmaker is right: Wall Street bankers create some economic value. But do they create enough of it to justify the rewards they reap? In the first nine months of 2010, the big six banks cleared more than $35 billion in profits. "The cataclysmic events took place in the fall of 2008 and the early months of 2009," Roger Altman, the chairman of Evercore, said to me. "In this industry, that's a long time ago."

Despite all the criticism that President Obama has received lately from Wall Street, the administration has largely left the great moneymaking machine intact. A couple of years ago, firms such as Citigroup, JPMorgan Chase, and Goldman Sachs faced the danger that the government would break them up, drive them out of some of their most lucrative business lines— such as dealing in derivatives—or force them to maintain so much capital that their profits would be greatly diminished. "None of these things materialized," Altman noted. "Reforms and changes came in, but they did not have a transformative effect."

In 1940, a former Wall Street trader named Fred Schwed Jr. wrote a charming little book titled *Where Are the Customers' Yachts?*, in which he noted that many members of the public believed that Wall Street was inhabited primarily by "crooks and scoundrels, and very clever ones at that; that they sell for millions what they know is worthless; in short, that they are villains." It was an extreme view, but public antagonism toward bankers and other financiers kept them in check for forty years. Economic historians refer to a period of "financial repression," during which regulators and policymakers, reflecting public suspicion of Wall Street, restrained the growth of the banking sector. They placed limits on interest rates, prohibited deposit-taking institutions from issuing securities, and, by preventing financial institutions from merging with one another, kept most of them relatively small. During this period, major financial crises were conspicuously absent, while capital investment, productivity, and wages grew at rates that lifted tens of millions of working Americans into the middle class.

Since the early 1980s, by contrast, financial blowups have proliferated and living standards have stagnated. Is this coincidence? For a long time, economists and policymakers have accepted the financial industry's appraisal of its own worth, ignoring the market failures and other pathologies that plague it. Even after all that has happened, there is a tendency in Congress and the White House to defer to Wall Street because what happens there, as befuddling as it may be to outsiders, is essential to the country's prosperity. Finally, dissidents like Paul Woolley are questioning this narrative. "There was a presumption that financial innovation is socially valuable," Woolley said to me. "The first thing I discovered was that it wasn't backed by any empirical evidence. There's almost none."

Inequality and Intemperate Policy

Raghuram Rajan

Raghuram Rajan is professor of finance at the University of Chicago's Booth School of Business and the author of *Fault Lines* (2010). In 2005 he delivered a controversial paper, "Has Financial Development Made the World Riskier?," which is widely viewed as having predicted the world economic collapse of 2007–2008. He was chief economist of the International Monetary Fund from September 2003 to December 2006.

The policy responses that income inequality has engendered are a primary factor contributing to the economic crisis—and because we continue to ignore the underlying sources of the problem, the risk that our policies will lead to another calamity, albeit in some other form, will not go away no matter what we do to reform the financial sector.

Deepening income inequality has been brought to the forefront of discussion in the United States. The discussion tends to center on the Croesus-like income of a John Paulson, the hedge fund manager who made a killing in 2008 betting on a financial collapse and netted over $3 billion, about seventy-five-thousand times the average household income. Yet a more worrying, everyday phenomenon that confronts most Americans is the disparity in income growth rates between a manager at the local supermarket and the factory worker or office assistant. Since the 1970s, the wages of the former, typically workers at the ninetieth percentile of the wage distribution in the

United States, have grown much faster than the wages of the latter, the typical median worker.

Economists dispute the reasons for the growing inequality at this level—changes in taxation, globalization, weaker unions, stagnant minimum wages, and growing immigration have all been flagged as possible causes. Perhaps the most important, according to Harvard professors Claudia Goldin and Lawrence Katz, is that although in the United States technological progress requires the labor force to have ever greater skills, the educational system has been unable to turn out enough workers who in fact have the necessary education or skills; a high school diploma was sufficient for our parents, whereas an undergraduate degree is barely sufficient for the office worker today. Yet rates of graduation from high school in the United States have barely budged since the 1970s, and neither have male graduation rates from college.

The real-life consequence for the middle class is a stagnant paycheck as well as growing job insecurity, as the old well-paying, low-skill jobs with good benefits wither away. Politicians feel their constituents' pain. But it is very hard to improve the quality of education. Not only do the causes of indifferent education lie partly in poor nutrition, socialization, and learning in early childhood, which have much to do with the family and community, but the dysfunctional primary and secondary schools that leave too many Americans unprepared for college are hard to reform because of vested interests that favor the status quo. Moreover, any change will require years to take effect and therefore will not address the current anxiety of the electorate. The result is a series of short-term policy fixes that may have done more damage than good.

For example, households ultimately care about their consumption over time—incomes are only a means to obtaining that consumption stream. A smart or cynical politician can see that if somehow the consumption of middle-class householders keeps up, if they can afford a new car every few years and the occasional exotic holiday, they may pay less attention to their stagnant monthly paychecks. And one way to expand consumption, even while incomes stagnate, is to enhance access to credit.

While many oppose an expansion in government welfare transfers, there are few to stand against an expansion of credit to the lower middle class—not the politicians, who want more growth and happy constituents; not the banks, which benefit from expanded lending; not the borrowers, who can now buy the house they had only dreamed of; and not the laissez-faire bank regulators, who are reluctant to oppose credit booms because they mistakenly think they can pick up the pieces easily if the boom collapses.

It is not surprising, then, that a policy response to rising inequality in the United States in the 1990s and 2000s—whether carefully planned or chosen as the path of least resistance—was to encourage lending to households, especially but not exclusively low-income ones, with the government push given to housing credit just the most egregious example. The benefit—higher consumption—was immediate, whereas paying the inevitable bill could be postponed into the future. Indeed, consumption inequality did not grow nearly as much as income inequality before the crisis. The difference was bridged by debt. Cynical as it may seem, easy credit has been used as a palliative by successive administrations that have been unable to address the deeper anxieties of the middle class directly. As I argue in my book *Fault Lines*, "Let them eat credit" could well summarize the mantra of the political establishment in the go-go years before the crisis.

Indebtedness has been aided and abetted by the Federal Reserve. In response to the dot-com bust in 2001, under Alan

Greenspan, the Fed cut short-term interest rates to the bone. Even though overstretched corporations were not interested in investing, artificially low interest rates were a tremendous subsidy to segments of the economy that rely on debt, such as housing or finance. An important benefit of an expansion in housing construction (and related services such as real estate brokerage and mortgage lending) was that it created jobs, especially for the unskilled. Unfortunately, the Fed-supported housing boom proved unsustainable, and many of the unskilled have lost their jobs and are in deeper trouble than before, having also borrowed to buy unaffordable houses.

There are many who advocate borrowing and spending once again—this time by those who still have the capacity to borrow—as a way of speeding up economic growth. More borrowed growth may create the illusion of normalcy and may be useful in the immediate aftermath of a deep crisis to calm a panic, but it isn't the solution to a fundamental growth problem. Even if all government spending is effective, unless it improves the country's long-term innovative and productive capabilities, it will only postpone the day the economy will have to come to terms with its infirmities. And the government, and future generations, will have much more debt to contend with at that point.

More generally, we need to think creatively about how Americans can acquire the skills they need to enhance their incomes, instead of how we can resuscitate spending by those who can ill afford it, through unsustainable bubbles. The central problem is that too much of the U.S. workforce is unqualified for the good knowledge-intensive jobs that are being, and will be, created by its economy. Even though the unemployment rate is high across the workforce, it is much lower among those with degrees. This information is, of course, cold comfort to recent graduates, who face the brunt of unemployment, but they should be heartened by a Georgetown University report titled "Help Wanted: Projections of Jobs and Education Requirements Through 2018," which suggests that the United States may face a shortage of three million college-educated workers by 2018.

Not all education fetches a return in the marketplace, obviously. Some degrees, especially in science, technology, engineering, and mathematics, seem more immediately valuable than others. Similarly, some specialized skills, such as in medical imaging technology, are more in demand as the health care sector grows. Upgrading to the right skills and education is not easy. Retraining programs have a checkered history. Moreover, it is incredibly hard for a forty-year-old single mother of two to go back to school. But the sooner we realize there are no quick fixes, that we should be using resources during this recovery to help people build a bridge to the future rather than simply as Band-Aids, the better.

What is the downside if the United States does little to address the problem? As the country tries to stimulate its way out of trouble repeatedly, government and household finances will get more fragile. Inequality, stemming from large parts of the workforce being unable to take advantage of the opportunities created by the global economy, will cause U.S. politics to become even more fractured and polarized than it already is. And the United States will turn its back on openness and trade, attempting to protect domestic jobs even while hurting growth, domestically and elsewhere. Not just the United States but the entire world will be worse off.

If, instead, the skill base of those falling behind can be improved, the future will be radically different. The United States will be at the forefront of providing the creative and knowledge-based services—the legal services, the consulting services, the entertainment, education, and sophisticated medical services—that growing emerging markets need. As the demand of its teeming millions grows, the dynamic U.S. economy will grow alongside it, and fears about unsustainable debt and unfunded entitlements will diminish. But to reach this future, America needs to accept that it has more than a cyclical problem; significant parts of the workforce have not adapted to changes in technology or global competition. The United States has to tackle the problem at its source by helping more Americans obtain the ability to compete in the global marketplace. This is much harder than doling out credit or keeping interest rates really low, but substantially more effective in the long run.

Your House as an ATM:
The Myth of Homeownership

Bethany McLean

Bethany McLean is a contributing editor to *Vanity Fair* and the coauthor, with Joe Nocera, of *All the Devils Are Here* (2010) and, with Peter Elkind, of *The Smartest Guys in the Room: The Amazing Rise and Scandalous Fall of Enron* (2004).

On December 7, 2006, just as the housing bubble that would metastasize into the worst financial crisis since the Great Crash was beginning to burst, Angelo Mozilo, then the CEO of Countrywide, the nation's biggest mortgage maker, sent an email to the company's board and its top lieutenants. In the memo, he complained about the stunning disintegration of Countrywide's lending standards. He also noted something else: that so-called purchase loans — mortgages used to purchase a home — were just one-third of Countrywide's subprime business in 2006. The other two-thirds were refinancings, which allowed people to replace existing mortgages with new, often bigger, ones.

The ability of consumers to pay off mortgages and replace them with new ones just as, say, the interest rate was about to increase is part of what kept the bubble going. It also points to the fact that, contrary to popular perception, the great machinery of the subprime lending market was not built to enable people to buy homes. Instead, its main purpose was to allow people to borrow against the equity in their homes — the driver of the majority of the risky loans that would have brought down the financial sector without a government bailout. And that tells the more troubling narrative of the will to borrow against the future.

Subprime lending, of course, was sold as a means of enabling homeownership. "I remember the lenders pushing back against regulation of subprime lending by saying that this was how people could qualify for homes," says Kevin Stein, the associate director of the California Reinvestment Coalition. "But I don't think even they believed that." That convenient conflation of homeownership and consumer credit goes all the way back to the genesis of subprime lending, and to the early pioneers in the business.

Subprime lending was given birth through a series of laws passed in the early 1980s. (They were designed to help solve the savings and loan crisis but ended up backfiring dramatically, in more ways than one.) The first law, passed in 1980, was the Depository Institutions Deregulation and Monetary Control Act; among other things, it abolished state usury caps, which had long limited how much financial firms could charge on first-lien mortgages. It also did not distinguish between loans made to buy a house and loans, like home equity loans, that were *secured* by a house. Two years later came the Alternative Mortgage Transaction Parity Act, or AMTPA, which made it legal for lenders to offer more creative mortgages, such as adjustable-rate mortgages or those with balloon payments, rather than plain vanilla thirty-year fixed-rate instruments. It also preempted state laws designed to prevent both these new kinds of mortgages and prepayment penalties.

Around the same time, Congress passed several laws that enabled the creation of mortgage-backed securities — essentially, bonds that were backed by mortgages. This innovation would prove critical in providing the financing for risky mortgages, because Wall Street could package them up into securities and sell them off to investors. The motivation behind all these rule changes? Bolstering homeownership, because everyone feared there wouldn't be enough housing supply to meet the burgeoning demand. "Alternative mortgage transactions are essential...to meet the demand expected during the 1980s," read AMTPA.

Pretty much immediately, lenders saw a different opportunity. So-called hard-money lenders—companies like Associates, Beneficial, and Household, which specialized in offering loans with large down payment requirements, and which had aggressive collection policies that were backed by the merchandise the consumer had purchased—began to move into the mortgage market. Now that savings and loans had more freedom, new, aggressive operators stepped in to run them, too. These new breeds of lenders saw people's homes as just another form of collateral.

One of the first to take advantage of the new opportunities was a thrift called Guardian Savings & Loan, run by a flashy, aggressive couple named Russell and Rebecca Jedinak. Or, as federal thrift examiner Thomas Constantine wrote to a colleague in the fall of 2008, as the world was blowing up: "It started at Guardian. Ground zero, baby."

The Jedinaks' goal was not to help people achieve homeownership. Rather, they offered refinancings to people with bad credit, as long as those people had some equity in their house. "If they have a house, if the owner has a pulse, we'll give them a loan," Russell Jedinak told the *Orange County Register* in Santa Ana, California. Kay Gustafson, a lawyer who briefly worked at Guardian, would later say that the Jedinaks didn't really care if the borrower couldn't pay the loan back because they always assumed they could take over the property and sell it. "They were banking on a model of an ever-rising housing market," she told the *Register.* It was Guardian that, in June 1988, sold the first subprime mortgage–backed securities. Over the next three years, the Jedinaks sold a total of $2.7 billion in securities backed by mortgages made to less-than-creditworthy borrowers, according to the *Register.*

By early 1991, federal regulators had forced the Jedinaks out; the government later fined the couple $8.5 million, accusing them of using Guardian's money to fund their lifestyle, and barred them from the business. Standard & Poor's noted that Guardian's securities were "plagued by staggering delinquencies." The Jedinaks didn't admit or deny the charges, and in the meantime, they'd already started another lender, Quality Mortgage. They sold Quality Mortgage to a company called Amresco. Amresco would itself grow into a major player in making home equity loans to less-than-creditworthy consumers. In 1996, Lehman Brothers bought Amresco.

Right behind the Jedinaks came Roland Arnall. Arnall was a charismatic yet secretive man who started with absolutely nothing and made his fortune from subprime lending. By 2005, he was worth around $3 billion, according to *Forbes.* Arnall got rich by making loans to the borrowers who had long served as the customer base for the hard-money lenders: people who had bad credit, didn't make much money, or both. His first company, a thrift called Long Beach Savings & Loan, grew exponentially; between 1994 and 1998, Long Beach would almost quintuple the volume of mortgages it originated, to $2.6 billion.

Like Guardian, Long Beach's game wasn't homeownership. As the Long Beach financial statements noted, "Many of the Company's borrowers utilize funds from loans to pay off existing debts." Indeed, in 1997 and 1998, roughly two-thirds of Long Beach's loans were used for refinancing; the great majority of those borrowers received cash to pay off other debts. (A cash-out refinancing allows the borrower to get a new mortgage that's bigger than the old one and to take the difference in cash.)

During the late 1990s, house prices increased and interest rates dropped to some of the lowest rates in forty years, thereby increasing people's ability to tap into the equity in their homes. Not coincidentally, start-ups that specialized in helping consumers extract their equity proliferated, and Wall Street firms piled into the business of buying up risky mortgages and turning them into securities. The Money Store, started by Alan Turtletaub in 1967, became a household name after Hall of Famer Phil Rizzuto signed on as its spokesman, telling TV viewers to call 1-800-LOAN-YES. The great majority of its business was home equity loans that were used to refinance existing mortgage loans, consolidate debt, make home improvements, or pay educational expenses. "Management believes that American homeowners have substantial home equity available as security for additional borrowings," noted the company's financial statements. Another major subprime lender, a company called FirstPlus, created a product that enabled consumers to borrow 125 percent of the value of their homes. There was certainly money in this for someone: in 1998, First Union bought the Money Store; Turtletaub's stake was estimated at $710 million.

Many of the executives who founded subprime lending companies had worked at Arnall's Long Beach. "The Long Beach Gang," housing insiders called them. For instance, Steve Holder, who had been an executive at Long Beach, cofounded a company called New Century. Robert Dubrish, another Long Beach alum, founded Option One, which was bought by H&R Block in 1997. Both Option One and New Century had former Guardian executives in key positions.

Mozilo's Countrywide was late to the first subprime lending party. Mozilo, in truth, was horrified by the rise of subprime lending, because he thought it made its business by overcharging unsuspecting customers. The growth was so dramatic, though, that stock analysts started asking why Countrywide wasn't part of it, and by the end of the 1990s, the company had launched its own subprime lending division.

From the beginning, Countrywide was part of the conflation of homeownership and refinancing. No one was a greater advocate for homeownership than Angelo Mozilo. He was an enthusiastic supporter of President Bill Clinton's National Homeownership Strategy program. ("The idea of homeownership is so integral a part of the American Dream that its value for individuals, for families, for communities and for society is scarcely questioned," read a 1995 brief from the Department of Housing and Urban Development announcing the program.) Mozilo pushed hard to remove the old requirement that people getting mortgages make a 20 percent down payment, because he believed it was one of the biggest barriers to homeownership. In speeches to mortgage professionals and academics, he told his audiences that "expanding the American Dream of homeownership must continue to be our mission, not solely for the purpose of benefiting corporate America, but more importantly, to make our country a better place."

Yet much of Countrywide's business, in both prime and subprime mortgages, was built on providing refinancings, not new mortgages. In a March 1998 piece in the *American Banker* about Countrywide's nascent subprime lending operation, Joseph Harvey, then running the business, said that 80 to 85 percent of it was made up of refinancings.

Whether Mozilo deserves blame or not, by the end of the 1990s, the concepts of subprime lending and homeownership were thoroughly intertwined. Economists, including those at the Federal Reserve, credited subprime lending with the increased rate of homeownership, which by 1999 hit a record 66.8 percent.

"[T]he subprime lending market…has expanded considerably, permitting many low-income and minority borrowers to realize their dream of owning a home and to have a chance for acquiring the capital gains that have so increased the wealth of upper-income households," Federal Reserve Board governor Edward Gramlich said in the spring of 2000, in a speech to the Fair Housing Council. This, of course, was actively encouraged by lenders. As one representative told the Federal Reserve at a 2000 hearing, the subprime mortgage market allowed consumers to "fulfill their need for homeownership."

Maybe subprime lending did help homeownership—at least initially—but the numbers make it clear that it was at the margin. According to a joint HUD-Treasury report published in 2000, by 1999 a staggering 82 percent of subprime mortgages were refinancings, and in nearly 60 percent of those cases the borrower pulled out cash, adding to his debt burden. The report noted that "relatively few (16%) subprime mortgages are used for home purchase." "The subprime industry likes to claim credit for increasing homeownership among minorities and low- and moderate-income families," Mike Shea, then the executive director of ACORN Housing, told Congress in 2001. "But the vast majority of their business is in refinancing loans and making second mortgages, not helping people buy homes."

Although consumer advocates like Shea were trying to curtail this lending from the beginning, there were some who celebrated it. The rise of subprime home-based lending unquestionably allowed people with blemished credit to access cash at cheaper rates than they'd been able to do in the past. In 1999, the conservative American Enterprise Institute published a paper about what had come to be known as high loan-to-value (HLTV) mortgage lending, wherein the amount of the mortgage was close to—in some cases, as with the loans offered by FirstPlus, greater than—the value of the home. The paper noted that consumer debt backed by a borrower's home was "effectively a senior claim on his income," and that lenders would benefit, because the consumer's home, which would "otherwise be protected from seizure by creditors if he were to file for bankruptcy," was now at risk. "In essence, HLTV lending provides consumers a means of committing to prevent avoiding debt repayment by filing for bankruptcy under the current permissive bankruptcy laws," the authors wrote. (You have to read that a couple of times.) They also argued that because these loans were funded by being turned into securities by Wall Street, that opened the industry "to constant and detailed market scrutiny and discipline," which would prevent any deterioration in underwriting standards. (It didn't quite work out that way.) They concluded, "HLTV lending is good for the American consumer and for the U.S. economy." The authors said they were distinguishing between high loan-to-value lending to consumers with good credit and lending to those with blemished credit records, but the distinction is a slippery one given that mortgages with a high loan-to-value ratio tend to default at a higher rate than those for which the amount of the mortgage is far less than the value of the home; indeed, some conservatives would later charge that any mortgage with a high loan-to-value ratio was, by definition, a risky loan.

There were also some early warnings. The joint HUD-Treasury report cited data showing that debtors who filed for bankruptcy had often extracted all their home equity before doing so, likely using the subprime lending market. "While this data at best only suggests a link between growing subprime mortgage lending and growing consumer debt and bankruptcy among homeowners, it is important to consider the consequences that many American families ultimately face after borrowing extensively from home equity," the report noted. The consequence, of course, was the loss of a home that may once have been owned debt-free. As University of Minnesota law professor Prentiss Cox, who as an assistant attorney general in Minnesota fought the rise of subprime lending, notes today, it was easy to offer consumers a lower rate than they were getting on their credit card debt when you were converting a loan from being dischargeable in bankruptcy to one that was backed by a house in a rising housing market.

Another skeptic, an independent analyst named Josh Rosner, wrote a piece in early 2001 with a prophetic title: "A Home without Equity Is Just a Rental with Debt." He questioned the boom in housing, in large part based on data he was collecting about refinancings in both the prime and subprime markets. In his report, he noted the following facts: By 1999, 47 percent of homeowners had refinanced their houses at least once, in stark contrast to the 8 percent who had refinanced at least once by 1977. The $3.37 trillion of mortgage refinancing in the 1990s exceeded the $2.93 trillion in *all* mortgage originations in the 1980s. According to a survey by Freddie Mac, more than 75 percent of homeowners who refinanced in the last three months of 2000 took out mortgages that were at least 5 percent higher than the ones that they retired. That was a big change from 1993, in which only 33 percent of homeowners took out bigger mortgages. It worried Rosner, because while refinancing could be a smart financial move that allowed a consumer to take advantage of lower interest rates, it could also allow a consumer who didn't have money to continue to consume. Rosner cited a 2000 study done at the University of Chicago about this second sort of refinancer, which showed that this person typically had "little to no liquid assets" and used 60 percent of the equity extracted for consumption purposes. Wrote Rosner, "We believe that the economic benefit of refinancing will continue to decline and become a detriment to our economic health."

Not surprisingly, the first boom in subprime lending ended

very badly, in part due to the drying up of credit after the crisis in Asia in the late 1990s. When companies began to go bust, there was a wave of lawsuits and complaints from consumer advocates, who accused the subprime industry of engaging in predatory lending. Customers, they said, had been gulled by unscrupulous lenders into taking on expensive mortgages and paying exorbitant fees. Many subprime refinancings had replaced simple, affordable thirty-year fixed-rate mortgages. "We and others were saying to the Fed, state legislators, anyone who would listen in D.C., that lending was getting out of control," says Stein. After conducting extensive interviews with borrowers, the California Reinvestment Coalition concluded that over one-third of consumers who got subprime mortgages weren't even looking for one: they ended up responding to aggressive, targeted marketing by lenders.

The truly remarkable thing is that there was no lesson learned. Almost immediately, another boom in subprime lending started, with much the same cast of characters. New Century, one of the few to survive the bust, went on to become one of the country's biggest subprime lenders. Roland Arnall, who sold Long Beach to Washington Mutual in 1998, built a subprime lending empire called ACC Capital, which consisted of companies like Ameriquest and Argent. At their peak in 2004, Arnall's companies would make more than $80 billion in loans, all of them subprime.

The second boom was different in some ways. Subprime lending was no longer confined to a marginal group of companies and financed by the smaller Wall Street firms. Instead, it entered the mainstream. Countrywide, which had merely dabbled in subprime toward the end of the 1990s, embraced what its executives referred to as a "supermarket" strategy: essentially, if the shoddy mortgage originator down the road offered a certain risky product, Countrywide would, too. That, of course, had the effect of distributing the worst loans across the country. The second boom was also marked by an explosion in so-called Alt-A loans—aggressive products like reduced documentation loans that were made to borrowers with supposedly good credit, at least as reflected by their credit scores.

You didn't have to look very far to see that this time around, risky lending wasn't about homeownership, either. Ameriquest, which by 2004 was the largest subprime lender in the country, offered mostly refinancings, many of them cash-out. In the spring of 2004, a New Century executive named Terry Theologides told Congress that a stunning two-thirds of the company's business in February 2003 consisted of cash-out refinancings "in which our customers tap into their home equity to meet other financial needs such as paying off higher-interest consumer debt, purchasing a car, paying for educational or medical expenses and a host of other personal reasons." New Century had become the second-largest provider of nonprime mortgages. According to the company's financial statements, cash-out refis were 64.2 percent and 59.5 percent of its business in 2003 and 2004, respectively; home purchase loans were only about a quarter of its business. Theologides also told Congress that subprime lenders like New Century were necessary to the economy, because while Fannie Mae and Freddie Mac, which dominated the prime mortgage market at the time, generally wouldn't touch cash-out refinancing loans in which the loan-to-value ratio was over 90 percent, "we and other nonprime lenders allow borrowers to take out more cash."

Overall, from 2000 to 2007, according to a study by Jason Thomas at George Washington University, only one-third of subprime mortgages that were turned into mortgage-backed securities were used to purchase homes. In most of those years, close to 60 percent of the subprime mortgages were used for cash-out refis.

Even Alt-A loans were increasingly used for refinancing. At Golden West, one of the largest purveyors of so-called option ARMs (adjustable mortgages that allowed the borrower to choose how much to pay each month, and whether the payment was principal or interest), the percentage of loans that were used for refinancing increased from 58.6 percent in 2001 to 77.3 percent in 2005. (Golden West didn't disclose what percentage of those were cash-out refis.) This was not unique in the Alt-A market: according to a paper by Rajdeep Sengupta, an economist at the Federal Reserve Bank of St. Louis, in June 2000, 74 percent of Alt-A loans were used for the purchase of a home. By February 2003, that number had shrunk to just 34 percent. Sengupta was particularly struck by the increase in cash-out refinancings. He noted that the percentage of borrowers who were using Alt-A products to extract equity from their homes had almost doubled between 2000 and 2006, to about 40 percent. "In short, the growth in non-prime mortgages since 2000 has been fueled largely by households seeking to extract home equity during a period of appreciating home prices," wrote Sengupta.

An August 2011 paper by Atif Mian, of UC-Berkeley, and Amir Sufi, of the University of Chicago, sums up the twisted reality of subprime lending. The pair studied the growth of subprime lending in microscopic detail by breaking down neighborhoods by zip code into "subprime" zip codes—those with a heavy concentration of subprime loans—and "prime" zip codes. They found that from 2002 to 2005, even in subprime zip codes in which income was declining, mortgage credit grew more than it did in "prime" zip codes in the same area in which income was growing. This was the only time in history, they said, that mortgage origination growth and income growth were negatively correlated. In other words, the areas in which people were struggling financially seemed to be precisely the ones that saw the biggest explosion in subprime lending. This, of course, makes perfect sense once you understand that people weren't using subprime loans to buy houses but rather to pay their bills.

By the peak of the bubble, the percentage of Alt-A loans that were used to purchase homes had grown again from the 2003 lows, and a bigger percentage of subprime loans were used for home purchases. In his December 2006 memo, Angelo Mozilo noted that the percentage of Countrywide's subprime loans that were used to purchase a house grew from 19 percent of the subprime business in 2001 to 33 percent of its business in 2006. Overall, by 2006, subprime and Alt-A loans accounted for a big percentage of home purchases in the country—40 percent, according to Deutsche Bank.

House price appreciation had driven many potential customers out of the market; buyers needed these products so that they could pretend to qualify. Furthermore, cash-out refinancings themselves caused home prices to appreciate. "There is no way to generate the huge price appreciation witnessed without cash-out refinancing activity to liquefy price gains," says Thomas. In other words, it was a virtuous circle until it wasn't: rising house prices led cash-constrained borrowers to extract equity, thereby causing prices to rise even more. Or you could think about it as a giant scam, whereby people were lured into the market until every last penny had been sucked out.

The other reason, though, that more risky loans were used to purchase houses at the peak of the bubble was not that more people were becoming homeowners. It's that more people were speculating. It's very hard to get legitimate numbers on the percentage of risky loans that were used by investors, because everyone lied. But Iowa assistant attorney general Patrick Madigan, using data from a publication called *Inside B&C Lending*, says that in 2006, only 13.5 percent of subprime loans went to first-time homebuyers. The Center for Responsible Lending, using its own proprietary database, estimates that in 2004, 2005, and 2006, only about 10 percent to 11 percent of subprime loans went to such buyers. As for Alt-A loans, according to a paper by Christopher Mayer, Karen Pence, and Shane M. Sherlund in the Winter 2009 *Journal of Economic Perspectives*, 25 percent were used for investment properties.

It wasn't as if any of this was a deep, dark secret. Given that it should have been clear that many risky loans weren't actually being used for the great glory of homeownership—that they might have had the opposite effect of putting homeowners at a serious disadvantage—why didn't Congress or the regulators act to rein them in? A charitable answer is that they didn't want to deprive people of a chance at homeownership, even if only a tiny percentage of these loans were being used for that purpose. A less charitable answer is that it seemed to be in everyone's interest (except, that is, the long-term interest of consumers who stood to lose everything) not to stop the party. Ours is a consumer spending–driven economy; according to the 2011 report by the Financial Crisis Inquiry Commission, from 1998 to 2005, increased consumer spending accounted for between 67 percent and 168 percent of GDP growth in any given year. Overall consumer spending grew faster than the economy, and in some years it grew faster than real disposable income. No one wanted to see what would happen if consumers couldn't spend.

In fairness, in economist circles, there's always been a debate about how much the boom in house prices contributed to consumer spending. The truth is, no one really knows. According to a paper released by the Federal Reserve in 2007 that was coauthored by Alan Greenspan and another Federal Reserve economist, James Kennedy, home-equity extraction accounted for 3.7 percent of consumption in 2005, more than double its share from just five years earlier. Another way of thinking about the impact of rising home prices on consumer spending emerged in 2006. According to a summary of a conference held at the Chicago Fed, Lyle Gramley, a former Federal Reserve governor now at the Stanford Washington Research Group, was the first to address what might happen to consumer spending if house price appreciation stopped. Gramley said that according to one theory, "mortgage equity withdrawal," spending increased during the bubble not because consumers felt wealthier but because they in fact had more cash—due to the equity they took out of their homes. Under this model, every dollar of equity extracted created sixty-six cents of consumer spending. Gramley noted that a 10 percent drop in home prices could have "blockbuster" negative effects.

In many circles, the financial crisis has come to be seen as a referendum on the notion of homeownership. How many times have you heard someone say, "Well, this is what happens when the government says everyone should have a home"? It's true that the worship of homeownership provided cover for a lot of practices that had nothing to do with putting people in homes. Encouraging slightly riskier loans for the purpose of putting people into homes may or may not be good policy. But the crisis doesn't prove it one way or the other, because if subprime and Alt-A loans had been limited to first-time homebuyers, there never would have been a crisis.

What the crisis *is* a referendum on is precisely what so many are protesting today: the growing income inequality in America. If a great number of people could spend only because they were drawing on an unsustainable source of wealth, one that isn't coming back any time soon, then we all have a problem. Because ultimately, all of us—consumers, job seekers, job creators, businesses, and even banks—are in this economy together.

Against Political Capture: Occupiers, Muckrakers, Progressives

Daron Acemoglu and James A. Robinson

Daron Acemoglu is the Elizabeth and James Killian Professor of Economics at MIT. He received the John Bates Clark Medal in 2005. James A. Robinson is a political scientist and an economist, the David Florence Professor of Government at Harvard University, and a world-renowned expert on Latin America and Africa. Acemoglu and Robinson are the authors of *Why Nations Fail: The Origins of Power, Prosperity, and Poverty* (2012).

For the past hundred years the United States has been one of the most prosperous and egalitarian societies in the world. Racial discrimination notwithstanding, in a comparative context the United States has been an inclusive society, with economic opportunities open to most and property rights secure. The inclusiveness of economic institutions has harnessed talent and driven growth. Thomas Edison, the inventor of the phonograph and the first commercially viable lightbulb and the founder of General Electric, still one of the world's largest companies, was the youngest of seven children. His father, Samuel Edison, split roof shingles, was a tailor, and kept a tavern. Thomas was homeschooled by his mother. The economic institutions of the United States—and patent law—allowed him to thrive, to his own and society's benefit.

Political institutions have also been inclusive in the sense that, by world standards, power has been relatively evenly distributed. It was the distribution of political power that forced open economic institutions, breaking down monopolies (for example, in banking) and opening up the frontier to allow land to be equally distributed. This system came about not because of enlightened elites either in the British Colonial Office or in Philadelphia in 1787 but through conflict and struggle. From as early as the founding of the Jamestown colony in 1607, there were efforts to create an elitist oligarchy. The Virginia Company tried, after it realized it could not make money by exploiting indigenous peoples (too thin on the ground) or precious minerals (there were none). Instead it propagated its Lawes Divine, Morall and Martiall (1611). These laws included clauses that specified various actions punishable by death. They included escape from the colony "to the Indians"; robbing a garden, field, or vineyard; and selling or giving goods made inside the colony to anyone outside the colony.

Private property was all but abolished, and settlers were forced into barracks and a draconian regime. It didn't work. The settlers ran away to the frontier, and they organized to demand rights, a process that culminated in the creation of the headright system in 1618, giving settlers access to land. The headright system couldn't exist in a vacuum, however, and needed to be supported by inclusive political institutions that gave the settlers power to defend it. This was achieved by the introduction of a legislative assembly in 1619, making the colony self-governing. Aspiring oligarchs didn't give up. The Fundamental Constitutions of Carolina, like the Charter of Maryland before it, provided a blueprint for an elitist, hierarchical society based on control by a landed elite. The Fundamental Constitutions laid out a rigid social structure. At the bottom were the "leet-men," who were supposed to do the work for the benefit of the elite. Hence the Fundamental Constitutions decreed: "All the children of leet-men shall be leet-men, and so to all generations." Not exactly the American Dream.

U.S. economic and political institutions were forged out of these conflicts between settlers and chartered companies and, eventually, the British state. The U.S. Constitution was simply the culmination of the struggle. It came about because the nature of political institutions and economic institutions fed on each other. Broadly distributed political power led to inclusive economic institutions, which spread opportunities, income, and wealth more equitably. This, in turn, helped sustain the broad distribution of political power, as economic resources and power begat political power.

The system faced continual challenges, most obviously from the southern states. The federal system allowed for institutional divergence within the United States, and the southern economy was built on slavery—the canonical example of an extractive economic institution. The children of slaves were also slaves; slaves could not own property; it was illegal to teach slaves to read and write in most southern states prior to the Civil War. As a consequence of its economic institutions, the South was considerably poorer and less innovative than the North. The system was held in place by a distribution of political power that was much narrower in the South than in the North.

The potential for extractive southern institutions to undermine the inclusive nature of U.S. institutions was defeated by the Civil War. Still, the rapid economic success of the country in the second half of the nineteenth century created fresh challenges. Even as inclusive institutions generated equality and progress, efforts to create barriers to entry and monopolies continued, most notably by the robber barons during the Gilded Age, in the second half of the nineteenth century. The robber barons derived their political power from their wealth and tried to use it to create more wealth for themselves. Cornelius Vanderbilt famously remarked, "What do I care about the Law? Hain't I got the power?" John D. Rockefeller started the

Standard Oil Company in 1870, quickly eliminating rivals in Cleveland and monopolizing the transportation and retailing of oil and oil products. By 1882, he had created a massive monopoly—in the language of the day, a "trust." By 1890, Standard Oil controlled 88 percent of the refined oil flow in the United States, and Rockefeller became possibly the first billionaire. A turn-of-the-century cartoon depicted Standard Oil as an octopus wrapping itself around not just the oil industry but Capitol Hill. One can almost draw a straight line to Matt Taibbi's description of Goldman Sachs as a "great vampire squid wrapped around the face of humanity, relentlessly jamming its blood funnel into anything that smells like money."

The accumulation of wealth accompanied rapid economic growth, but it was in the political realm that inequality created huge potential problems. The Senate was indirectly elected by state legislatures, and the robber barons effectively monopolized this process. In a series of articles in *Cosmopolitan*

One nation, two cephalopods. This cartoon depicting Standard Oil's reach found an echo in Matt Taibbi's iconic description, in 2009, of Goldman Sachs as a "great vampire squid." *(By artist Udo J. Keppler, in* Puck, *September 7, 1904. Source: Library of Congress Prints and Photographs Division, Washington, D.C.)*

magazine in 1906, the novelist and investigative journalist David Graham Phillips went state by state showing how the robber barons had captured the Senate. First up was New York senator Chauncey Depew, a lawyer for the Vanderbilt family and their chief lobbyist in Albany. Phillips moved on to Rhode Island senator Nelson W. Aldrich, whose daughter, Abby, was married to John D. Rockefeller Jr. "Thus, the chief exploiter of the American people is closely allied by marriage with the chief schemer in the service of their exploiters," Phillips wrote. "It is a political fact; it is an economic fact."

This undermining of inclusive political institutions created a societal backlash in the form of the Populist and, subsequently, Progressive movements. The Populist movement emerged out of a long-running midwestern agrarian crisis that began in the late 1860s. The National Grange of the Order of Patrons of Husbandry, known as the Grangers, was founded in 1867 and began to mobilize farmers against unfair and discriminatory business practices. In 1873 and 1874, the Grangers won control of eleven midwestern state legislatures. Rural discontent found common ground with organized labor, and the People's Party was formed, in 1892, on a platform that declared, "From the same prolific womb of governmental injustice we breed the two great classes — tramps and millionaires."

The People's Party demanded the introduction of an income tax, until then deemed unconstitutional, and direct election of senators. It got 8.5 percent of the popular vote in the 1892 presidential election. In the next two elections, the Populists fell in behind the two unsuccessful Democratic campaigns by William Jennings Bryan, who made many of their issues his own.

These political movements slowly began to have an impact on political attitudes and then on legislation, particularly concerning the role of the state in the regulation of monopoly. The

Interstate Commerce Act of 1887, which initiated federal regulation of industry, was followed by the Sherman Antitrust Act of 1890, whose passage was driven by the farm vote. The Sherman Act, still a major part of U.S. antitrust regulation, was to become the basis for attacks on the robber barons' trusts during the presidencies of Theodore (Teddy) Roosevelt (1901–1909), William Taft (1909–1913), and Woodrow Wilson (1913–1921).

From the ashes of the Populists, whose influence declined after they threw their weight behind the Democrats, came the Progressives, a reform movement concerned with many of the same issues, though its members tended to be intellectuals rather than farmers. The Progressive movement initially gelled around the figure of Teddy Roosevelt, who was William McKinley's vice president and who assumed the presidency following McKinley's assassination in 1901. In his first address to Congress, Roosevelt turned his attention to the trusts. He argued that the prosperity of the United States was based on a market economy and the ingenuity of businessmen, but at the same time he cited the "real and grave evils" of "combination and concentration," which "should be, not prohibited, but supervised and within reasonable limits controlled."

Key to the success of the Progressive agenda was the coalition that formed around it, which included the farmers who had spearheaded the Populist movement, organized labor, middle-class urban groups dissatisfied with the political domination of the robber barons and their political allies, and, crucially, parts of the media. Muckrackers, among them David Graham Phillips, publicized abuse by politicians, trusts, and robber barons, and contributed to the widespread sentiment that political reform was necessary. Equally transformative, however, was that this coalition directly influenced political parties and recruited leading politicians to its cause. Its influence came in part because politicians such as Presidents

Roosevelt (initially a Republican) and Wilson (a Democrat) made the Progressive cause their own, and in part because the threat raised by a third-party candidate forced Democrats and Republicans to converge on programs with key Progressive elements. The Democrat Wilson reiterated key Progressive messages in his 1913 book *The New Freedom:* "If monopoly persists, monopoly will always sit at the helm of government. I do not expect to see monopoly restrain itself. If there are men in this country big enough to own the government of the United States, they are going to own it."

It was more than rhetoric. Roosevelt had proposed that Congress establish a federal agency with power to investigate the affairs of the great corporations. In 1902, he used the Sherman Act to break up the Northern Securities Company, partly owned and controlled by J. P. Morgan, and subsequent suits were brought against DuPont, the American Tobacco Company, and the Standard Oil Company. Taft prosecuted trusts even more assiduously, with a series of actions culminating in the breakup of Standard Oil in 1910. Taft also promoted the introduction of a federal income tax, which finally came during Wilson's presidency with the ratification, in 1913, of the Sixteenth Amendment. Because Progressives understood that the problems of the Gilded Age had their roots in politics, reforms also tackled vestiges of the system that allowed political power to be captured by the wealthy. Key steps among these were direct elections of senators to stack the cards against the "capture of the Senate" that Phillips had vividly documented and, in 1920, extension of voting rights to women.

These reforms meant to preserve the inclusive nature of U.S. political and economic institutions were effective at reversing the massive increase in inequality and the concentration of wealth that had built up in the previous half century. One way to see this is by looking at the number of billionaires in relation to the working population. In 1900, it is estimated that there were twenty-two billionaires in the United States, including most of the famous robber barons. This represented about 0.00008 percent of the labor force. By 1957, even though being a billionaire meant much less than before because of inflation in the intervening decades, there were only sixteen, about 0.00002 percent of the labor force. In 1982 there were twenty-three billionaires, still about 0.00002 percent of the labor force. The Populist/Progressive-era reforms left a long-lasting impact on the number of billionaires and, more generally, on inequality in the United States.

The U.S. experience generates some robust lessons for world economic history. Countries that have succeeded in creating egalitarian, economically dynamic societies have done so because they have forged inclusive political institutions. This is precisely what happened in 1688 after England's Glorious Revolution and in much of Western Europe after the French Revolution. Yet history is full of examples of societies that seemed to be on the path to the establishment of inclusive institutions but then got derailed. In the Middle Ages, Venice became arguably the most prosperous city in the world, based on a set of political institutions that spread power quite broadly and economic institutions that allowed for free entry into trade and created a comparably inclusive society. Yet toward the end of the thirteenth century, the political elites of the Republic were able to increase their power and block others from contesting it. As political power became more unequal, these elites were also able to abolish the economic institutions that had made Venice rich. These same institutions, by creating social mobility and new economic elites, threatened the power of the older elites. The process was institutionalized in 1315 with the *Libro d'Oro*, the Golden Book, an official registry of the Venetian nobility — a sort of Italian version of the Fundamental Constitutions of

Carolina. Now there were elites and non-elites and no social mobility. Soon Venice stagnated and tipped into decline.

More than a century after the Gilded Age, a new era of opportunity has again coincided with a huge increase in economic inequality in the United States. Part of the rise of inequality can be explained by the fact that the technological developments that have swept the U.S. labor market since the 1970s have increased the demand for high-skilled workers, particularly those with greater than high school education, and this has increased their wages and incomes relative to other workers'. Yet this effect is much too small to plausibly account for why the top 1 percent of Americans, a small subset of those with college-level education, received 23.5 percent of national income in 2007, up from 9 percent in 1970. For the 0.1 percent, this has gone from 3 percent to 12 percent of national income. We can track in a simple way how this reflects the unraveling of the changes wrought by the Progressives by returning to the number of billionaires in the United States. By 1996 there were 132 billionaires, 0.0001 percent of the labor force; by 2010, *Forbes* claimed that there were 403 billionaires in the United States.

To understand why inequality has surged since the 1970s, we have to turn to politics — and to the increasing influence of a narrow and wealthy segment of society over the U.S. political system. The roots of this development appear to lie in the backlash by business interests against the Great Society programs of the 1960s and early 1970s; in the reaction of certain conservative segments of the U.S. population to the civil rights movement; in the decline of organized labor as an economic and political force; in the rise of an electorate (particularly fundamentalist Christian voters) who care more about normative issues than the value of the tax rate; and particularly in the increasing power of money in politics, possibly as a result of the rise of television and other forms of mass media. Though there are many aspects of this transformation we do not understand, several pieces of evidence suggest that political institutions in the United States have become less inclusive, less responsive to what most citizens want, and more responsive to the wishes of those able and prepared to pay for political influence.

Nothing like the political coalitions that gave rise to the Populist and Progressive movements are likely to form again, but the political and economic dynamics of the past thirty years are beginning to create another backlash from outside the traditional political parties in the form of the Occupy Wall Street movement. OWS styled itself as speaking for the 99 percent, those excluded from the 1 percent of the population who have snapped up the economic gains the U.S. economy has generated over three decades. They protest against rising inequality, falling social mobility, the decline in the social safety net, and the increased influence of the wealthy, the financial industry, and large corporations in Washington, D.C. As they put it on their webpage, they organized themselves to fight "back against the corrosive power of major banks and multinational corporations over the democratic process."

The interests underpinning this group are different from those of the Populists and the Progressives, and so are their tactics. For example, Progressives did not react to the control of the Senate by occupying the front lawn of the Breakers, Vanderbilt's mansion in Newport, Rhode Island. However, the Progressives did found organizations that they themselves could control democratically, just as OWS did through its General Assemblies, a form of direct democracy. Moreover, it is not surprising that the specific tactics of OWS differ from those of the Populists and the Progressives. If one looks at the evolution of social protest over the past few centuries, one sees that there is continual change; social movements must alter their strategies in response to changes in the structure of the economy and society, in technology, and in the nature of political institutions. An obvious reason for the form that OWS protests took is the successful model of revolt in Egypt. If occupying Tahrir Square was effective, then so might occupying Liberty Square be effective. The Progressives had no such model. The technology of protest is also radically different. The spread of newspapers and literacy allowed modern mass protests to emerge in the eighteenth century, and we have seen the positive role that newspapers and independent muckrakers played in pushing forward the Progressive agenda. Today, the Internet and the emergence of Twitter and other social media are important in facilitating the protest and shaping the form it takes.

Nevertheless, the aims are, generally speaking, the same: to roll back the increasing threats to the inclusive nature of economic institutions in the United States. To do this the OWS protesters recognize, as the Populists and the Progressives did, that political institutions must be changed to remove the control that the wealthy have over the agendas and policies of the main political parties. History also suggests that it is indeed mobilization of people outside a political system that has the potential to stop the slide of inclusive institutions toward becoming extractive ones.

Will they succeed in their aims? Of course it is far too early to know the answer, but the parallels with the Populists and the Progressives are instructive—and not just because they, like Occupy, understood that inequality was largely about politics, and that inequality would have its most deleterious effects on how truly inclusive the political system was. There are several ways in which the experience of these earlier movements might inform Occupy. First, although the Populists and the Progressives mobilized outside of traditional political parties, their agendas had an enduring impact on political and economic institutions in the United States because they were able to force traditional political parties to take up many of their reforms. Although they did this partially by threatening the entry of an effective third party, this is probably not a necessary condition for such influence. Ultimately OWS may want to build bridges to sympathetic politicians in the mainstream political parties, many of whom object to the power that money has over politics. From this perspective, the statement on the OWS webpage that "we don't need politicians to build a better society" may be shortsighted.

Second, Populists and Progressives were successful because they formed a broad coalition. The Populist Party brought organized labor together with farmers, and the Progressives added middle-class groups and intellectuals. OWS reached out to organized labor and to environmentalists and extended onto university campuses. The details of the coalition are less important than its breadth, which makes it politically powerful and keeps it focused on national issues of general interest.

Third, the role of the media will be critical in determining the success of the movement. The muckrakers had considerable influence, but it's not a given that the media will play a reformist role in society, as the impact of the Fox News Channel today illustrates. Moreover, as we have seen, one theory of the stranglehold that money has on U.S. politics is precisely that television since the 1970s has served as a primary source of political information. It is not just the existence of media that matters but who owns it and what it is trying to achieve. In light of this, the use of the Internet, owned by nobody, is probably critical.

Finally, the lesson from the Populists and the Progressives is that to succeed, OWS may have to come up with a list of specific institutional and policy changes that will help to counterbalance the trends they are fighting against. These will not be the same as those proposed a hundred years ago, but they will be important for maintaining focus and for institutionalizing the movement's successes. A cautionary tale comes from the French student protests and occupations of May 1968. These were initially successful in putting politicians on the defensive and in making them more responsive than they had otherwise been to demands for educational and social change. However, the French students did not come up with specific proposals about how, for example, the educational system might change. The government responded first with large wage increases for trade union members to try to isolate the students and then with a proposed *loi d'orientation* concerning university reform. The students were effective on the streets, but once the lawmaking got under way they were squeezed between interest groups and party politics. With their influence waning, they ended up with emasculated reform.

There is still room for optimism about the resilience of U.S. institutions, which have withstood huge challenges in the past. This optimism should not lead to complacency, however, because the root of resilience lies in activism.

A Nation of Business Junkies

Arjun Appadurai

Arjun Appadurai is an anthropologist and a professor of media, culture, and communication at New York University's Steinhardt School of Culture, Education, and Human Development. He is the author of, among other books, *Worship and Conflict Under Colonial Rule: A South Indian Case* (2007), *Fear of Small Numbers: An Essay on the Geography of Anger* (2006), and *Globalization* (2001).

I first came to this country in 1967. I have been either a crypto-anthropologist or professional anthropologist for most of the intervening years. Still, because I came here with an interest in India and took the path of least resistance in choosing to maintain India as my principal ethnographic refer- ent, I have always been reluctant to offer opinions about life in these United States. I have begun to do so recently, but mainly in occasional blogs, Twitter posts, and the like. Now seems to be a good time to ponder whether I have anything to add to the public debate about the media in this country. Since I have been teaching for a few years in a distinguished department of media studies, I feel emboldened to put my thoughts forward.

My examination of changes in the media over the past few decades is not based on a scientific study. I read the *New York Times* every day and the *Wall Street Journal* occasionally, and I subscribe to the *Atlantic*, *Harper's*, the *New York Review of Books*, the *Economist*, and a variety of academic journals in anthropol- ogy and area studies. I get a smattering of other useful media pieces from friends on Facebook and other social media sites. I also use the Internet to keep up with as much as I can from the press in and about India. At various times in the past, I have subscribed to the *Nation*, *Money* magazine, *Foreign Policy*, the *Times Literary Supplement*, and a few other periodicals.

I have long been interested in how culture and economy interact. I want to make an observation about the single biggest change I have seen over my four decades in the United States, which is a growing and now hegemonic domination of the news and of a great deal of opinion, both in print and on television, by business news. Business news was a specialized affair in the late 1960s, confined to a few magazines such as *Money* and *Fortune*, and to newspapers and TV reporters (not channels). Now it is hard to find anything but business as the topic of news in all media. Consider television: if you spend even three hours surfing between CNN and BBC on any given day (surfing for news about Libya or about soccer, for example), you will find yourself regularly assaulted by business news, not just from London, New York, and Washington but from Singapore, Hong Kong, Mumbai, and many other places. Look at the serious talk shows, and chances are that you will find a CEO describing what's good about his company, what's bad about the government, and how to read his company's stock prices. Channels like MSNBC are like an endless, mind-numbing Jerry Lewis telethon about the economy, with more than a hint of the desperation of the Depression movie *They Shoot Horses, Don't They?* (1969), as they bid the viewer to make insane bets and to mourn the fallen heroes of failed companies and fired CEOs.

Turn to the newspapers and things get worse. Any reader of the *New York Times* will find it hard to get away from the business machine. Start with the lead section, and stories about Obama's economic plans, mad Republican proposals about taxes, the euro crisis, and the latest bank scandal will assault you. Some relief is provided by more corporate news: the op-ed piece about the responsibilities of the superrich by Warren Buffett, Donald Trump advertising his new line of housewares to go along with his ugly homes and buildings. Turn to the sports section: it is littered with talk of franchises, salaries, trades, owner antics, stadium projects, and more. I need hardly say anything about the Business section itself, which has now virtually become redundant. And if you are still thirsty for more business news, check out the Home, Lifestyle, and Real Estate sections for news on houses you can't afford and mortgage-financing gimmicks you have never heard of. Some measure of relief is to be found in the occasional Science Times piece and in the *Book Review*, which do have some pieces not primarily about profit, corporate politics, or the recession.

The *New York Times* is not to blame for this. They are the "newspaper of record," and that means that they reflect broader trends and cannot be blamed for their compliance with them. Go through the magazines when you take a flight to Detroit or Mumbai, and there is again a feast of news geared to the "business traveler." This is when I catch up on how to negotiate the best deal, why this is the time to buy gold, and what software and hardware to use when I make my next presentation to General Electric. These examples could be multiplied in any number of bookstores, newspaper kiosks, airport lounges, and dentists' offices.

What does all this reflect? Well, we were always told that the business of America is business. But now we are gradually moving toward a society in which the business of American *life* is also business. Who are we now? We have become (in our fantasies) entrepreneurs, start-up heroes, small investors, consumers, homeowners, day traders, and a gallery of supporting business types, and no longer fathers, mothers, friends, or neighbors. Our very citizenship is now defined by business, whether we are winners or losers. Everyone is an expert on pensions, stocks, retirement packages, vacation deals, credit card scams, and more. Meanwhile, as Paul Krugman has written, this discipline, especially macroeconomics, has lost much of its capacity to analyze, define, or repair the huge mess we are in.

The gradual transformation of the imagined reader or viewer into a business junkie is a relatively new disease of advanced capitalism in the United States. The avalanche of business knowledge and information dropping on the American middle class ought to have helped us predict—or avoid—the recent economic meltdown, based on crazy credit schemes, vulgar scams, and lousy regulation. Instead it has made us business junkies, ready to be led like sheep to our own slaughter by Wall Street, the big banks, and corrupt politicians. The growing hegemony of business news and knowledge in the popular media over the past few decades has produced a collective silence of the lambs. It is time for a bleat or two.

Causes of Financial Crises Past and Present: The Role of the This-Time-Is-Different Syndrome

Carmen M. Reinhart and Kenneth S. Rogoff

Carmen M. Reinhart is the Dennis Weatherstone Senior Fellow at the Peterson Institute for International Economics and a research associate at the National Bureau of Economic Research and the Centre for Economic Policy Research. Kenneth S. Rogoff is the Thomas D. Cabot Professor of Public Policy and professor of economics at Harvard University and a research associate at the National Bureau of Economic Research. They are the authors of *This Time Is Different: Eight Centuries of Financial Folly* (2009).

> *There is nothing new except what is forgotten.*
>
> —Rose Bertin

The financial press has often characterized the 2007–2008 United States subprime mess as a new breed of crisis. Indeed, this view often points to the international repercussions of the U.S.-based crisis as evidence that the globalization of financial portfolios has introduced new channels for spillovers that were never present before. In light of the unfolding Greek tragedy, there is also considerable confusion in academic and policy circles as to whether the shaky predicament of the global economy stems from new forms of contagion channels or shared (common) economic fundamentals.

In this essay, we attempt to place the question of "how we got here" in the context of an international and historical comparative setting. It is of some poignancy that the "we" here refers to the wealthiest economies in the world, which, as late as 2006, had been enjoying the benefits of the so-called Great Moderation. The Great Moderation was a term used to describe (and extrapolate from) the drop in macroeconomic volatility that the advanced economies experienced starting in the late 1980s. A considerable majority of economists and policymakers held that the business cycle had been "tamed" thanks to better monetary and fiscal policy, deeper and more sophisticated financial markets, and a laundry list of other factors, including greater geopolitical stability. Few macroeconomists took seriously the possibility that a deep financial crisis might soon slam the United States and Europe, at least not without an unforeseen catastrophe of biblical proportions. As for a sovereign default in a euro-zone country, "orderly" or not, that was simply inconceivable. Never mind the glaring imbalances in the global economy that a small number of worrywart economists emphasized. "This time is different" yet again. And of course it was not.

Our approach does not dwell on (no doubt) important idiosyncratic features of the unfolding crisis in each of the advanced economies. Instead, we will focus on those factors that are common to great crises across time and geography; there is little doubt the recent and still ongoing crisis will be considered one of the greatest. In what follows, we will discriminate between root causes of the crisis, its symptoms, and features such as financial regulation, which serve as amplifiers of the boom-bust cycle. Pertinent to the financial globalization era that has unfolded since the 1980s, our discussion begins with the link between financial liberalization (internal and external), the financial innovation and credit booms these spawn, and banking crises. This is a "nutshell" version of the analysis of banking crises found in our book *This Time Is Different: Eight Centuries of Financial Folly.*

The setting. Across countries and over the centuries, economic crises of all types follow a similar pattern. An innovation emerges. Sometimes it is a new tool of science and industry, such as the diving bell, the steam engine, or the radio. Sometimes it is a tool of financial engineering, such as the joint-stock company, junk bonds, or collateralized debt obligations. Financial innovations in particular often accompany, or are a direct result of, financial liberalization. Investors may be wary at first, but once they see that these new instruments appear to offer extraordinary returns, they rush in. Financial intermediaries — banks and investment companies — stretch their balance sheets so as not to be left out. As borrowing swells, the upward surge in asset prices continues, and a new generation of financial market participants concludes that rules have been rewritten: risk has been tamed, and leverage (borrowing to buy assets such as houses and stocks) is always rewarded. All too often, policymakers assert that the asset-price boom is a vote of confidence for their regime — that "this time is different." Only seldom, to our knowledge, do they protest that perhaps the world has not changed, that the old rules of valuation still apply, and that investors should be far more cautious about debt.

But, eventually, the old rules *do* apply, and with a vengeance. The asset price rise peters out, sometimes from exhaustion on its own or sometimes because of a real shock to the economy. This exposes the weaknesses of the balance sheets of those who justified high leverage by the expectation of outsized capital gains. Many financial firms admit losses, and some ultimately fail. All those financial firms hunker down, constricting credit availability in an effort to slim their balance sheets. With wealth lower and credit harder to get, economic activity typically contracts. Only after the losses are flushed out of the financial system, often with the encouragement of lagging monetary and fiscal ease, does the economy recover.

BOX 1. THE THIS-TIME-IS-DIFFERENT SYNDROME

The essence of the this-time-is-different syndrome is simple. It is rooted in the firmly held belief that financial crises are something that happen to other people in other countries at other times; crises do not happen here and now to us. We are doing things better, we are smarter, we have learned from past mistakes. The old rules of valuation no longer apply. The current boom, unlike the many booms that preceded catastrophic collapses in the past (even in our country), is built on sound fundamentals, structural reforms, technological innovation, and good policy. Or so the story goes.

For anyone needing an example of the timelessness of the collective self-delusion encapsulated in the this-time-is-different syndrome, please consult box 2.

The roots of financial crises. There is a striking correlation between freer capital mobility and the incidence of banking crises, as shown in figure 1. Periods of high international capital mobility have repeatedly produced international banking crises, not only famously, as they did in the 1990s, but historically. The figure plots a three-year moving average of the share of all countries experiencing banking crises on the right scale. On the left scale, we graph the index of capital mobility, following Maurice Obstfeld and Alan Taylor's *Global Capital Markets,*

Box 2. THE *THIS-TIME-IS-DIFFERENT SYNDROME* ON THE EVE OF THE CRASH OF 1929

FAMOUS WRONG GUESSES
IN HISTORY
when all Europe guessed wrong

The date—October 3rd, 1719. The scene—*Hotel de Nevers*, Paris. A wild mob—fighting to be heard. "Fifty shares!" "I'll take two hundred!" "Five hundred!" "A thousand here!" "Ten thousand!" Shrill cries of women. Hoarse shouts of men. Speculators all—exchanging their gold and jewels or a lifetime's meager savings for magic shares in John Law's Mississippi Company. Shares that were to make them rich overnight.

Then the bubble burst. Down—down went the shares. Facing utter ruin, the frenzied populace tried to "sell". Panic-stricken mobs stormed the *Banque Royale*. No use! The bank's coffers were empty. John Law had fled. The great Mississippi Company and its promise of wealth had become but a wretched memory.

Today you need not guess.

HISTORY sometimes repeats itself—but not invariably. In 1719 there was practically no way of finding out the *facts* about the Mississippi venture. How different the position of the investor in 1929!

Today, it is inexcusable to buy a "bubble"—inexcusable because unnecessary. For now every investor—whether his capital consists of a few thousands or mounts into the millions—has at his disposal facilities for obtaining the *facts*. Facts which—as far as is humanly possible—eliminate the hazards of speculation and substitute in their place sound principles of investment.

STANDARD STATISTICS
200 VARICK ST.
New York, New York (now the home of Chipotle Mexican Grill)

Saturday Evening Post, September 14, 1929

This advertisement was kindly sent to the authors by Professor Peter Lindert.

Source: Reinhart and Rogoff (2009).

updated and backcast using their same design principle, to cover our full sample period. While the Obstfeld–Taylor index may have its limitations, we feel it nevertheless provides a concise summary of complicated forces by emphasizing de facto capital mobility based on actual flows.

For the post-1970 period, Graciela L. Kaminsky and Rein-hart's "The Twin Crises" presents formal evidence of the links of crises with financial liberalization. In eighteen of the twenty-six banking crises they study, the financial sector had been lib-eralized within the preceding five years, usually less. In the 1980s and 1990s most liberalization episodes were associated with financial crises of varying severity. Only in a handful of countries (for instance, Canada) did financial sector liberaliza-tion proceed smoothly. Specifically, the paper presents evi-dence that the probability of a banking crisis conditional on financial liberalization having taken place is higher than the unconditional probability of a banking crisis. Americans may remember the savings and loan crisis of the early 1980s, which followed on the heels of a massive liberalization of financial markets in the late 1970s and early 1980s, some elements of

Figure 1. Capital Mobility and the Incidence of Banking Crises: All Countries, 1800–2010

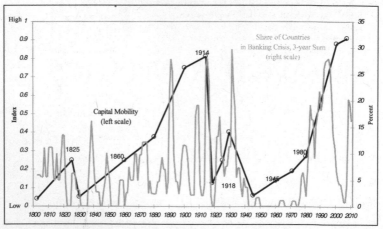

Sources: Updated from Reinhart and Rogoff (2009) and sources cited therein.

Notes: This sample includes all countries. On the left scale, we updated our favorite index of capital mobility, admittedly arbitrary, but a concise summary of complicated forces. The smooth dark line shows the judgmental index of the extent of capital mobility given by Obstfeld and Taylor (2004), backcast from 1800 to 1859.

which were driven more by political expediency than economic logic.

The symptoms of financial crises. The recurring historical pattern described above is associated with some well-defined symptoms. In table 1, we focus on a few quantitative parallels that have been widely present during the current crisis and that were seen systematically in numerous earlier crises in advanced and emerging market economies alike. Specifically, large capital inflows and sharp housing and equity price run-ups top the "leading indicator" group. So do surges in private domestic and external debts. Although it can be very difficult to call the exact timing of a crisis—partly because so much depends on fragile confidence and partly because key vulnerabilities are often hidden by creative accounting—countries experiencing these quantifiable symptoms over a sufficiently long period are highly vulnerable.

Table 1. Quantitative Antecedents of Financial Crises: The "Lead" of the Leading Indicators

Large capital inflows
Sharp run-ups in equity prices
Sharp run-ups in housing prices
Inverted V-shaped growth trajectory
Marked rise in indebtedness

If we were to quantify periods of capital flow bonanzas—periods during which capital inflows are unusually large—who comes up on the radar screen before the 2007–2009 crisis? As Carmen M. Reinhart and Vincent R. Reinhart document in "Capital Flow Bonanzas," in addition to the United States and the United Kingdom, the other countries listed there—Spain, Italy, Iceland, Ireland—are all countries that have undergone a period during which the large capital inflows ended badly.

Capital inflows facilitate domestic lending and fuel asset price inflation and in most instances increase the indebtedness of the private sector, the public sector (if the government behaves procyclically), or both.

Table 2. Capital Inflows Typically Surge Ahead of Financial Crisis

Countries with recent notable capital inflows	2006	2007	2008
Bulgaria	√	√	√
Iceland	√	√	√
Italy	√	√	√
Jamaica	√	√	√
Latvia	√	√	√
New Zealand	√	√	√
Pakistan	√	√	√
Romania	√	√	√
Slovenia	√	√	√
South Africa	√	√	√
Spain	√	√	√
Turkey	√	√	√
United Kingdom	√	√	√
United States	√	√	√

Source: Reinhart and Reinhart (2009).

Capital inflows (see table 2) are, of course, the mirror image of sustained current account deficits that rightly concerned many economists from the early 2000s onward, including Obstfeld and Rogoff, and Nouriel Roubini and Brad Setser, among others. But the idea that capital inflows might be problematic was dismissed by many analysts and policymakers, particularly in the United States, because "this time is different." After all, booming emerging-markets countries required someplace safe to park their savings, and what could be the harm in that? The idea that these huge capital surges might distort asset prices and encourage dangerously lax regulation, even in a relatively well-managed economy like the United States, was dismissed as hysterical. "This time is different."

Similarly, it is surprising how many contemporary observers believed the U.S. housing price bubble of 2000–2006 to be both unique and unprecedented. The magnitude of the bubble was certainly unprecedented for the United States—at least during the past century for which we have comparable data. However, in a broader global context, the subprime housing bubble experience is not unique to the United States (as figure 2 highlights); nor is it magnitudes out of line with other real estate bubbles that have ended, equally lamentably, in financial crises (dark bars in figure 2). Taken together, our remarks on capital flows and housing bubbles suggest that the simultaneous timing of the recent crises owes a great deal to common vulnerabilities in the fundamentals rather than contagion.

The boom in real housing prices (or real estate, and other asset prices, more broadly) is fueled by ample domestic credit availability, large capital inflows, and the easy liquidity environment that facilitates the boom. Couple the ample liquidity environment with the presumptions that this time is different and that the old rules of valuation do not apply, and you've got the makings of or the ingredients for a crisis.

As to growth, investors and policymakers typically become inebriated with the boom that precedes the crisis, not fully appreciating how much it is amplified by easy credit and growing wealth as asset prices. Unfortunately, once growth begins to fall, as it eventually must, the whole dynamic implodes on itself. We have described the "inverted V" pattern of growth that characterizes a crisis (listed in table 1), a cruel parody of the famous V-shape recoveries that characterize normal business cycles, where the deeper the fall in output, the sharper the postrecession recovery.

Figure 2. Percent Change in Real Housing Prices (2002–2006) and Banking Crisis

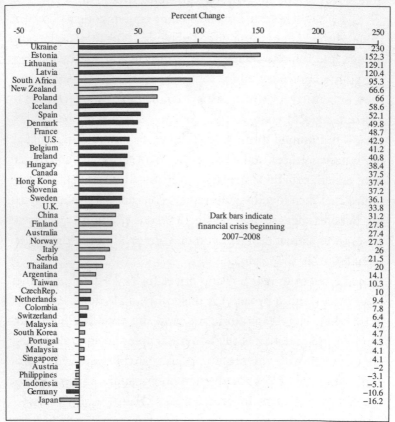

Source: Reinhart and Rogoff (2009).

The importance of the last entry in table 1, a marked rise in indebtedness, cannot be stressed enough. Rising indebtedness can be domestic, external, or both. It can be private, public, or both. Any combination of these forms of rising indebtedness has been a hallmark of the pre-crisis period as far back as our data can take us. Perhaps Iceland illustrates this point in its most extreme form, as external debts rose from about 90 percent of gross domestic product in 2000 to well over 900 percent of GDP in 2009. The overall debt matters greatly also, of course, but sharp, sustained borrowing booms are particularly worrisome because the rapid changes are so often accompanied by softer regulation and ever-weaker bank lending standards in a dynamic that is all too familiar to those who have just lived through the recent crisis.

The "amplifiers" of financial crises. In table 3, we list a variety of "usual suspects" that amplify crises, often making them far worse than they have to be, even given other vulnerabilities. These range from procyclical macroeconomic policies to over-valued currencies to myopic rating agencies. Despite its breadth, the list is not meant to be exhaustive. Nevertheless, it has withstood the test of time. Countless case studies of banking crises across countries and time list these same factors on a recurring basis, and these amplifiers are sometimes blamed as underlying causes of the crises. However, it is our view that these factors are better viewed as exacerbating both the boom and bust phases of the crisis cycle. For example, Gerald Caprio Jr. and Daniela Klingebiel's evidence in "Bank Insolvency" suggests that inadequate regulation and lack of supervision at the time of the liberalization may play a key role in explaining why deregulation and banking crises are so closely entwined. But it is difficult to explain a cycle with a structural flaw that is a constant. In a great many countries, especially emerging markets, supervision has always been lacking and regulations perennially ill-defined. But such deficiencies may have limited consequences when credit conditions are tight (or, in the case of emerging markets, when access to international capital markets is extremely limited). If, on the other hand, financial liberalization (domestic and/or external) creates lending possibilities that did not exist before, then inadequate supervision can make a bad lending scenario worse. Outright fraud (often through connected lending), which crops up as another hardy perennial in studies of the run-up to crises, works the same way.

The procyclicality of credit ratings, both at the sovereign and corporate levels, also acts to amplify the cycle of lending and subsequent default and crash. Credit agencies all too often are as blinded by the boom as regulators and investors, keeping countries on pedestals even as risks peak. Overvalued currencies are another magnet for capital inflows, while procyclical fiscal policies add to the surge in borrowing during the boom phase of the cycle. Governments all too often believe the boom will go on forever and sharply raise spending instead of using surging tax coffers to reduce public debt burdens.

Far from being mutually exclusive, many, if not most, of the items listed in table 3 are present simultaneously in the most severe financial crises throughout history.

Table 3. Amplifiers of Boom-Bust Cycles: The Usual Suspects

Procyclical macroeconomic policies
Hidden debts (implicit guarantees)
Overvalued currencies
Poor regulation
Even worse supervision
Outright fraud
Myopic credit rating agencies

Where we are: the sequencing of crises. Just as financial crises have common macroeconomic antecedents in asset prices, economic activity, external indicators, and so on, so common patterns appear in the sequencing (temporal order) in which crises unfold. Obviously not all crises escalate to the extreme outcome of a sovereign default. Yet advanced economies have not been exempt from their share of currency crashes, bouts of inflation, severe banking crises, and, in an earlier era, sovereign default. The long debt cycle we have discussed does not necessarily come to an end with a banking crisis. Unfortunately, more bad news usually follows—a stylized fact that should be kept in mind when trying to make sense of the current conjuncture.

Investigating what came first, banking or currency crises, was a central theme of Kaminsky and Reinhart's "Twin Crises"; they also concluded that financial liberalization often preceded banking crises and, indeed, helped predict them. Asli Demirgüç-Kunt and Enrica Detragiache, who employed a different approach and a larger sample, arrived at the same conclusion in "The Determinants of Banking Crises in Developing and Developed Countries." In 2002 Reinhart examined the currency crash–external default link. Our work here has investigated the connections between domestic and external debt crises, inflation crises and default (domestic or external), and banking crises and external default. Figure 3 maps out a "prototypical" sequence of events yielded by this literature.

As Carlos Diaz-Alejandro recounts in his classic paper about the Chilean experience of the late 1970s and early 1980s, "Good-bye Financial Repression, Hello Financial Crash," financial liberalization simultaneously facilitates banks' access to external credit and more risky lending practices at home. After a while, following a boom in lending and asset prices, weaknesses in bank balance sheets appear and problems in the banking sector begin. Often these problems are more advanced in the shakier institutions (such as finance companies) than in the major banks.

The next stage in the crisis sees the central bank beginning to provide support for these institutions by extending credit to them. If the exchange rate is heavily managed (it does not need to be explicitly pegged), a policy inconsistency arises between supporting the exchange rate and acting as lender of last resort to troubled institutions. Experience suggests that, more often than not, the exchange rate objective is subjugated to the

Figure 3. The Sequencing of Crises: A Prototype

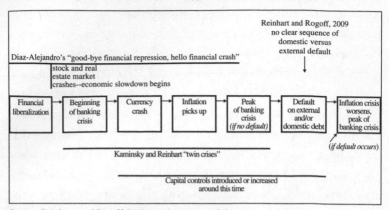

Source: Reinhart and Rogoff (2009) and sources cited therein.

lender-of-last-resort role of the central bank. Even if central bank lending to the troubled financial industry is limited in scope, the central bank may be more reluctant to engage in an "interest rate defense" policy to defend the currency than would be the case if the financial sector were sound. This brings the sequence illustrated in figure 3 to the box labeled "Currency crash."

The depreciation or devaluation, as the case may be, complicates the situation in at least three dimensions: (a) it exacerbates the problem of the banks that have borrowed in a foreign currency, worsening currency mismatches; (b) inflation usually worsens (the extent to which the currency crisis translates into higher inflation is highly uneven across countries, since those with a history of very high and chronic inflation usually have a much higher and faster pass-through from exchange rates to prices); and (c) if the government has foreign currency denominated debt, the currency depreciation increases the odds of an external and domestic default.

At this stage, the banking crisis either peaks following the currency crash, if there is no sovereign credit crisis, or keeps getting worse as the crisis mounts and the economy marches toward a sovereign default (as in figure 3).

Of course, the alert reader will recognize one departure from the pattern in figure 3 in the current crisis. At the peak of the crisis, the U.S. dollar actually appreciated rather than depreciated. The answer, of course, is that figure 3 describes a typical country or regional crisis. But the recent financial crisis was global in nature; the U.S. subprime crisis infected the entire global economy. It is not mathematically possible for *all* currencies to depreciate at the same time. One currency's fall has to be reflected in a corresponding *rise* in the value of at least some other currencies. In the recent episode, many countries at the epicenter of the crisis, including the United Kingdom and Iceland, experienced large depreciations. And a euro-zone country such as Spain could not see its currency collapse despite a severe banking crisis and housing price collapse because the value of its currency was tied to larger neighbors, such as Germany, that were in less dire straits.

Despite not being a perfect parallel because currency depreciation is a zero-sum game in a global crisis, there is no reason to assume that the other features of the pattern in figure 3 will not hold true. Notice especially in figure 3 that sovereign debt defaults typically unfold in the latter stages of the crisis. The series of events that began to play out in the summer of 2007 with the onset of the subprime crisis are still unfolding as the crisis morphs. This episode is not yet over.

Government as Tough Love:
Sitting Down with Robert Shiller

Brandon Adams

Yale University's Robert Shiller is a bestselling author and one of the world's leading economists. The Chicago Mercantile Exchange maintains futures markets based on the repeat-sales home price indices he developed originally with Karl E. Case. He writes a regular column, "Finance in the 21st Century," for Project Syndicate, which publishes around the world, and "Economic View" for the *New York Times.* His most recent book is *Finance and the Good Society* (2012).

Brandon Adams taught undergraduate economics courses at Harvard University for eight years.

When we observe people fall from grace, we tend to get a dopamine jolt that can be picked up on brain scans. This schadenfreude is especially strong if the person who falls is similar to us but objectively superior in some key characteristics. It explains, among other things, the overwhelming popularity of tabloid news coverage. Robert Shiller drops kernels of this type at an astounding rate, making our hour-and-a-half discussion at Yale both a fascinating and an intellectually taxing endeavor.

In conversation, one gets the impression that Shiller has fifty thoughts for every one he airs. His mind seems to move too fast for speech; you get the impression that he'd rather be reading. Yet he had graciously arranged to meet on a day in December 2011 when most of Yale had decamped for winter break. A messy office often suggests, in my experience, extreme breadth of intellectual interest, and on this count Shiller did not disappoint. Before our discussion got under way, he offered me an espresso, which, as a caffeine addict, I eagerly accepted. He then surprised me by making himself a Nestlé hot chocolate. That pretty much summed up Shiller in a moment: a sixty-something millionaire academic, holed up in his office on a late Friday afternoon and drinking Nestlé hot chocolate. This was, I thought, the academic's academic.

Shiller has always been ahead of the curve. In 1981, he wrote a cornerstone paper in behavioral finance at a time when the field was in its embryonic stages. In the early 1990s, he noticed that insufficient attention was paid to real estate values, despite their overwhelming importance to personal wealth levels; this led him to create, along with Karl E. Case, the Case-Shiller index—now the Case-Shiller Home Prices Indices. In March 2000, Shiller published *Irrational Exuberance*, arguing that U.S. stocks were substantially overvalued and due for a tumble. In 2008, he published *The Subprime Solution*, which detailed the origins of the housing crisis and suggested innovative policy responses for dealing with the fallout. These days, one of his primary interests is neuroeconomics, a field that relates economic decision making to brain function as measured by fMRIs.

Shiller is unique among academics in that he has a deep level of trust for both markets and government. It is fair to say that he is comfortable with the idea of a large and active government sector, but he's long been an advocate of expanding the scope of financial markets, and some of his most important work (covered in *Macro Markets* and *The New Financial Order*) concerns the creation of tradable markets in entirely new areas. He believes, for example, that there should be indices of professional earnings, such that one could go short or long expected future salaries of doctors, lawyers, or computer engineers. Much of the motivation for the creation of the Case-Shiller index stemmed from Shiller's belief that there should be a reliable index of local real estate prices, such that individuals could potentially hedge the value of their homes. Shiller suggests of free markets that "the rare brilliance outweighs the nonsense."

Today's world is one in which financial markets are extremely loud, but they don't do much. There is a lot of stir and fizzle, with personal trading accounts and twenty-four-hour news, but there is also a general sense that financial markets are not doing a great job with the fundamentals—allocating capital to businesses that can profitably deploy it, helping people save for retirement and hedge risk in intelligent ways. In Shiller's ideal world, financial markets would be extremely quiet, but they would do quite a lot. He prefers markets that are boring and highly functional, and he thinks that such markets are possible.

Shiller believes that one of the dangers of our highly juiced markets is that, to some extent, the louder and more visible they get, the more irrational they become. "Most people don't think about the real determinants of market prices," he noted. "They tell themselves a story about market prices." Shiller believes that today's world of minute-by-minute market updates interacts with the dopamine reward system in the human brain. The stories we tell ourselves to support our financial decision making are "hijacked by our dopamine system," which is "notably irrational."

I asked Shiller about Twitter, and he said, "I think it might be fundamental, in that it connects our thoughts at a much higher frequency." He suggested that the higher frequency creates an echo-chamber effect during times of protest, as people speed up their use of social media. In a sense, more action is demanded at such times for consumption value via social media, and so more happens.

Echoing Daniel Bell, Shiller believes that Americans are conflicted over our Protestant ethic and our frenetic form of market capitalism. During boom times, this tension becomes especially severe. During bubbles, the growth in value of financial assets (which represent claims on real goods and services) far exceeds the growth rate in the economy's ability to produce goods and services. The maintenance of a bubble requires that a strictly limited number of people attempt to convert their newfound financial wealth into real wealth. There is, in Shiller's terminology, a "moral anchor" to extreme financial bubbles; bubbles cannot persist without a behavioral standard that one not cash in one's gains from a bubble too quickly. The Protestant ethic encourages Americans to "behave like good capitalists" and not, in essence, cash out their financial holdings to go live on a beach somewhere. This societal tendency makes financial bubbles in the United States somewhat more common and more extreme than those elsewhere in the world.

Shiller is strongly sympathetic to Occupy Wall Street. His policy views are infinitely nuanced; one could say they are situational. He'd be a terrible talk show guest, because one could never be sure of his policy opinions *ex ante*. If I had to pin him down, I'd say that his views in macroeconomics are New Keynesian, and his political views are strongly liberal. But it gets quite complicated from there. Shiller has great faith in free markets, but he is not afraid of suggesting heavy-handed government intervention and regulation, and he believes that government should at times step in to protect individuals from their own terrible decision making. His view seems to be that government should act something like a benevolent grandfather.

He approvingly cites David Moss's 2004 *When All Else Fails: Government as the Ultimate Risk Manager*. Although Shiller is strongly pro-market, he believes that governments are essential for setting the rules of society and (to a lesser extent) for redistributing wealth and facilitating intelligent risk sharing. He eschews simple solutions; he believes that in a fast-moving and largely unpredictable world, the relationship among individuals, business, and government is likely to be highly complex.

He believes that much of the populace was duped during the long housing bubble that ended in 2007. Shiller suggests that maintaining a free market, with broad investor participation and reasonably accurate and stable prices, is no easy matter—that it involves a comprehensive system of investor education, along with a strong regulatory structure that deters fraud and misrepresentation.

People know less about finance than they think they do, in Shiller's view, in part because "almost all financial advice people receive is biased," as it tends to be paid for in one way or another by people trying to sell financial products. Shiller thinks that it might be beneficial for the government to subsidize financial education. He gives the example of civil notaries in Germany, where government-trained legal professionals go over important financial contracts with citizens and ensure that they are fair and properly understood; he remains agnostic on whether such a system is beneficial, but he suggests that we should be open to such solutions because our own system is more flawed than is generally realized.

Shiller believes that most Americans' perception of the country as a level playing field has changed. He cites bailouts, which he believes have poisoned the atmosphere. A common sentiment, he said, is "I don't even have a lawyer. All the rich people have lawyers and lobbyists." Indeed, he noted that much of the so-called 99 percent not only have no lawyers, no lobbyists, and no financial education—they also have no money. What is needed is not so much education about stocks and bonds but rather education about, as Shiller put it, "Suze

Orman–type stuff." Most people are ill informed about simple matters of personal finance and personal spending behavior, and they are up against a business sector that carefully crafts products that cater to their every impulse. "The democratization of finance has a long way to go," he said.

Shiller is a student of what he terms "the morale of the American populace." He believes that Americans' patriotism and sense of purpose have contributed to the country's economic strength. Morale has wavered lately, he said, but remains relatively strong. At times, positive morale can have a perverse impact. "During a bubble, there's a sense that the confidence has to be maintained. People are reluctant to express skepticism. They self-censor. An atmosphere of hypocrisy reigns."

Shiller describes Federal Reserve chairman Ben Bernanke as "well-meaning" but says that Bernanke was a strong apologist for the boom, arguing that it was driven by fundamentals. As late as May 2007, Bernanke said, "We believe the effect of the troubles in the subprime sector on the broader housing market will likely be limited, and we do not expect significant spillovers from the subprime market to the rest of the economy or to the financial system." Shiller said that not only Bernanke but opinion makers generally feel strong pressure during bubbles to keep to "the general chorus of optimism."

"Contracts are not inviolable," he noted, pointing out that governments often step in to change them when they are no longer in the general interest. In the early phases of the subprime crisis, Shiller favored a bailout of both homeowners and banks. Both had made severe mistakes, in his view, and although he found a bailout of either offensive, he recognized early on that the scale of the crisis was such that a bailout was overwhelmingly in the general interest.

Shiller was disappointed but not surprised when governments bailed out banks in extreme fashion while leaving the contracts between banks and homeowners unchanged. He said, of Hank Paulson, "As Treasury secretary, he presented himself in a very sober and collected way.... He did some bailouts that benefited Goldman Sachs, among others. And I can imagine that they were well-meaning, but I don't know that they were totally well-meaning, because the sense of self-interest is hard to clean out of your mind."

PART II

——⋈⋈——

WHERE WE
ARE NOW

Occupy Wall Street's Anarchist Roots

David Graeber

David Graeber is a Reader in Social Anthropology at Goldsmiths, University of London. He is widely credited with having come up with the slogan "We are the 99 percent," based on the income-inequality research of Thomas Piketty and Emmanuel Saez. He is the author or editor of more than half a dozen books.

Almost every time I'm interviewed by a mainstream journalist about Occupy Wall Street, I get some variation of the same lecture: "How are you going to get anywhere if you refuse to create a leadership structure or make a practical list of demands? And what's with all this anarchist nonsense—the consensus, the sparkly fingers? Don't you realize all this radical language is going to alienate people? You're never going to be able to reach regular, mainstream Americans with this sort of thing!"

If one were compiling a scrapbook of worst advice ever given, this might well merit an honorable place. After all, since the financial crash of 2007, there have been dozens of attempts to kick off a national movement against the depredations of the United States' financial elites taking the approach such journalists recommend. All failed. It was only on August 2, 2011, when a small group of anarchists and other anti-authoritarians showed up at a meeting called by one such group and effectively wooed everyone away from the planned march and rally to create a genuine democratic assembly, on basically anarchist principles, that the stage was set for a movement that Americans from Portland to Tuscaloosa were willing to embrace.

I should be clear what I mean here by "anarchist principles." The easiest way to explain anarchism is to say that it is a political movement that aims to bring about a genuinely free society—that is, one in which humans only enter those kinds of relations with one another that would not have to be enforced by the constant threat of violence. History has shown that vast inequalities of wealth and institutions like slavery, debt peonage, or wage labor can only exist if backed up by armies, prisons, and police. Anarchists wish to see human relations that would not have to be backed up by armies, prisons, and police. Anarchism envisions a society based on equality and solidarity, which could exist solely on the free consent of participants.

Traditional Marxism, of course, aspired to the same ultimate goal, but there was a key difference. Most Marxists insisted that it was necessary first to seize state power, and all the mechanisms of bureaucratic violence that come with it, and use them to transform society—to the point where, they argued, such mechanisms would ultimately become redundant and fade away. Even back in the nineteenth century, anarchists insisted that this was a pipe dream. One cannot create peace by training for war, equality by creating top-down chains of command, or, for that matter, human happiness by becoming grim, joyless revolutionaries who sacrifice all personal self-realization or self-fulfillment to the cause.

It's not just that the ends do not justify the means (though they don't); you will never achieve the ends at all unless the means are themselves a model for the world you wish to create. Hence the famous anarchist call to begin "building the new society in the shell of the old" with egalitarian experiments ranging from free schools to radical labor unions to rural communes. There has always been a wide range of views among anarchists of the larger mechanisms that would exist in a free society—from those in favor of mutualist banking, for instance, to those in favor of eliminating currency systems altogether; from those who favored decision making by popular assemblies on a neighborhood-by-neighborhood level, to those who emphasized workplace democracy through confederations of radical labor unions. The most sophisticated approaches usually conceded that a truly free society would be endlessly complex, with a constant proliferation of new social experiments, facing problems that most of us couldn't imagine. The one thing almost everyone agreed on was that we had to begin by learning what it would mean to behave as genuinely free men and women, coming together in voluntary association, making decisions democratically, eschewing relations of exploitation for the practice of solidarity and mutual aid.

Anarchism was also a revolutionary ideology, and its emphasis on individual conscience and individual initiative meant that during the first heyday of revolutionary anarchism, between roughly 1875 and 1914, many took the fight directly to heads of state and capitalists, with bombings and assassinations. Hence the popular image of the anarchist bomb-thrower. It's worthy of note that anarchists were perhaps the first political movement to realize that terrorism, even if not directed at innocents, doesn't work. For nearly a century now, in fact, anarchism has been one of the very few political philosophies whose exponents never blow anyone up (indeed, the twentieth-century political leader who drew most from the anarchist tradition was Mohandas K. Gandhi).

Yet for the period of roughly 1914 to 1989, a period during which the world was continually either fighting or preparing for world wars, anarchism went into something of an eclipse for precisely that reason: to seem "realistic," in such violent times, a political movement had to be capable of organizing armies, navies, and ballistic missile systems, and that was one thing at which Marxists could often excel. But everyone recognized that anarchists—rather to their credit—would never be able to pull it off. It was only after 1989, when the age of great war mobilizations seemed to have ended, that a global revolutionary movement based on anarchist principles—the global justice movement—promptly reappeared.

How, then, does OWS embody anarchist principles? It might be helpful to go over this point by point.

The first principle OWS shares with anarchists is the refusal to recognize the legitimacy of existing political institutions. A reason for the much-discussed refusal to issue demands is that issuing demands means recognizing the legitimacy—or at least the power—of those of whom the demands are made. Anarchists often note that this is the difference between protest and direct action: protest, however militant, is an appeal to the authorities to behave differently; direct action, whether it takes the form of a community building a well or making salt in defiance of the law (Gandhi's example again), trying to shut down a meeting or occupy a factory, is a matter of acting as if the existing structure of power does not even exist. Direct action is ultimately the defiant insistence on acting as if one is already free.

Second is the refusal to accept the legitimacy of the existing legal order. This principle, obviously, follows from the first. From the very beginning, when we first started holding planning meetings in Tompkins Square Park in New York, organizers knowingly ignored local ordinances that insisted that any gathering of more than twelve people in a public park is illegal without police permission—simply on the grounds that such laws should not exist. On the same grounds, of course, we chose to occupy a park, inspired by examples from the Middle East and southern Europe, on the principle that as the public, we should not need permission to occupy public space. This might have been a very minor form of civil disobedience, but it was crucial that we began with a commitment to answer only to a moral order, not a legal one.

The third principle is the refusal to create an internal hierarchy and the decision instead to create a form of consensus-based direct democracy. From the very beginning, too, organizers made the audacious decision to operate not only by direct democracy, without leaders, but by consensus. The first decision ensured that there would be no formal leadership structure that could be co-opted or coerced; the second, that no majority could bend a minority to its will, and that all crucial decisions had to be made by general consent. American anarchists have long considered consensus process (a tradition that emerged from a confluence of feminism, anarchism, and spiritual traditions like Quakerism) crucial because it is the only form of decision making that can operate without coercive enforcement—since if a majority does not have the means to compel a minority to obey its dictates, all decisions will of necessity have to be made by general consent.

Fourth is the embrace of prefigurative politics. As a result, Zuccotti Park, and all subsequent encampments, became spaces of experiment with creating the institutions of a new society—not only democratic General Assemblies but kitchens, libraries, clinics, media centers, and a host of other institutions, all operating on anarchist principles of mutual aid and self-organization: a genuine attempt to create the institutions of a new society in the shell of the old.

Why did it work? Why did it catch on? One reason is, clearly, because most Americans are far more willing to embrace radical ideas than anyone in the established media is willing to admit. The basic message—that the American political order is absolutely and irredeemably corrupt, that both parties have been bought and sold by the wealthiest 1 percent of the population, and that if we are to live in any sort of genuinely democratic society, we're going to have to start from scratch—clearly struck a profound chord in the American psyche.

Perhaps this is not surprising: we are facing conditions that rival those of the 1930s, the main difference being that the media seem stubbornly unwilling to acknowledge it. It raises intriguing questions about the role of the media itself in American society. Radical critics usually assume that the "corporate media," as they call it, mainly functions to convince the public that existing institutions are healthy, legitimate, and just. It is becoming increasingly apparent that those running the media do not really see that this is possible; rather, their role is simply to convince members of an increasingly angry public that no one else has come to the same conclusions they have. The result is an ideology that no one really believes but most people at least suspect everybody else does.

Nowhere is this disjunction between what ordinary Americans really think and what the media and political establishment tell them they think more clear than when we talk about democracy.

According to the official version, of course, "democracy" is a system created by the Founding Fathers, based on checks and balances among president, Congress, and judiciary. In fact, nowhere in the Declaration of Independence or the Constitution does it say anything about the United States being a democracy. The authors of those documents, almost to a man, defined democracy as a matter of collective self-governance by popular assemblies, and as such they were dead-set against it.

Democracy meant the madness of crowds: bloody, tumultuous, and untenable. "There was never a democracy that didn't commit suicide," wrote John Adams; Alexander Hamilton justified the system of checks and balances by insisting that it was necessary to create a permanent body of the "rich and well-born" to check the "imprudence" of democracy, or even that limited form that would be allowed in the lower house of representatives.

The result was a republic—modeled not on Athens but on Rome. It only came to be redefined as a democracy in the early nineteenth century because ordinary Americans had very different views and persistently tended to vote—those who were allowed to vote—for candidates who called themselves democrats. But what did—and what do—ordinary Americans mean by the word? Did they really just mean a system where they get to weigh in on which politicians will run the government? It seems implausible. After all, most Americans loathe politicians and tend to be skeptical about the very idea of government. If they universally hold out democracy as their political ideal, it can only be because they still see it, however vaguely, as self-governance—as what the Founding Fathers tended to denounce as either democracy or, as they sometimes also put it, "anarchy." If nothing else, this would help explain the enthusiasm with which Americans have embraced a movement based on directly democratic principles, despite the almost uniformly contemptuous dismissal by the United States' media and political class.

In fact, this is not the first time a movement based on fundamentally anarchist principles—direct action, direct democracy, a rejection of existing political institutions and an attempt to create alternative ones—has cropped up in the United States. The civil rights movement (at least its more radical branches), the antinuclear movement, and the global justice movement all took similar directions. Never, however, did one grow so startlingly quickly. In part, this is because this time around, the organizers went straight for the central contradiction. They directly challenged the pretenses of the ruling elite that they are presiding over a democracy.

When it comes to their most basic political sensibilities,

most Americans are deeply conflicted. Most combine a profound reverence for individual freedom with a near-worshipful identification with institutions like the army and the police force. Most combine an enthusiasm for markets with a hatred of capitalists. Most are simultaneously profoundly egalitarian and deeply racist. Few are actual anarchists; few even know what anarchism means; it's not clear how many, if they did learn, would ultimately wish to discard the state and capitalism entirely. Anarchism is much more than simply grassroots democracy: it ultimately aims to eliminate all social relations, from wage labor to patriarchy, that can be maintained only by the systematic threat of force.

But one thing overwhelming numbers of Americans do feel is that something is terribly wrong with their country, that its key institutions are controlled by an arrogant elite, that radical change of some kind is long since overdue. They're right. It's hard to imagine a political system so systematically corrupt—one in which bribery, on every level, has not only been made legal, but soliciting and dispensing bribes has become the full-time occupation of every American politician. The outrage is appropriate. The problem is that up until September 17, 2011, the only side of the spectrum willing to propose radical solutions of any sort was the right.

As the history of past movements makes clear, nothing terrifies those running the United States more than the danger of democracy breaking out. The immediate response to even a modest spark of democratically organized civil disobedience is a panicked combination of concessions and brutality. How else can one explain the national mobilization, in the fall of 2011, of thousands of riot cops; the beatings, chemical attacks, and mass arrests of citizens engaged in precisely the kind of democratic assemblies the Bill of Rights was designed to protect and whose only crime—if any—was the violation of local camping regulations?

Our media pundits might insist that if average Americans ever realized the anarchist role in Occupy Wall Street, they would turn away in shock and horror; but our rulers seem, rather, to labor under a lingering fear that if any significant number of Americans do find out what anarchism really is, they might well decide that rulers of any sort are unnecessary.

Economic Insecurity and Inequality Breed Political Instability

Nouriel Roubini

Nouriel Roubini is professor of economics at New York University's Stern School of Business and chairman of Roubini Global Economics (www.roubini.com). He served in the White House and in the U.S. Treasury from 1998 to 2000 and is the author, with Stephen Mihm, of *Crisis Economics* (2010) and, with Brad Setser, of *Bailouts or Bail-Ins?* (2004).

The year 2011 was characterized by social and political turmoil and instability throughout the world, with masses of people in the real and virtual streets protesting. There were the Arab uprising and revolts; the riots in England as well as earlier protests against pension cuts and higher tuition fees; the Israeli middle class protesting high housing prices and the squeeze from high inflation; Chilean students concerned about education and jobs; vandalism of the expensive cars of fat cats in Germany; Greeks demonstrating against fiscal austerity; India's movement against corruption; mass demonstrations by the Russian middle class against the authoritarian Putin regime; riots in China in reaction to corruption, inequality, and illegal land seizures, as well as similar complaints in the blogosphere, where the Chinese can more freely express their dissatisfaction with government policies; and then the Occupy Wall Street movement in New York and across the United States. While these protests don't have a single unified theme, they express — in different ways — the concerns of the working and middle classes about their economic future, challenges in access to economic opportunity, and the concentration of power among economic, financial, and political elites.

Some of the common causes of these protests are serious economic and financial insecurity and malaise among blue- and white-collar workers, with the global financial crisis leading to a very weak recovery in advanced economies; high rates of unemployment and underemployment in advanced and emerging economies; a lack of skills and a skills-mismatch preventing young people and workers from competing in a more globalized world economy; resentment against corruption, including legalized forms such as interest groups using the financial power of lobbying to pursue their narrow interests; poverty, insecurity, anger, and hopelessness about the future and a desire for greater social justice; and a sharp rise in income and wealth inequality (figure 1) in advanced economies and even fast-growing emerging markets (EMs), as well as across economies.

The concept of a squeezed and sinking 99 percent and a thriving top 1 percent (as the Occupy Wall Street protesters have it) may be a simplification of a highly complex situation. But it resonates with a deeper truth that unfettered free markets, deregulation, and globalization have not benefited everyone and that some of their pernicious consequences are associated with massive job losses, mediocre income growth, and rising inequality. To save globalization and its power to increase productivity and economic growth, we need to start seriously addressing its consequences, including the rise in inequality and the stagnating real incomes of most households and workers.

Of course, the causes of this social, economic, and financial malaise are complex and cannot be attributed to one single factor. The addition of about 2.5 billion "Chindians," the population of

Figure 1: Income Inequality Worsens in the United States

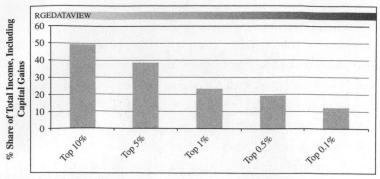

Source: *Paris School of Economics.*

China and India, and about another billion EM workers to the global labor force is reducing the number of jobs and the level of wages available to unskilled blue-collar workers and to white-collar workers in advanced economies whose jobs are offshorable. Other causes include skill-biased technological change; winner-take-all effects; the nascent rise of inequality in rapidly growing, previously low-income economies (as shown in the Kuznets curve or inverted U inequality-income relationship); the growth of less competitive and margin-increasing oligopolies; some effects of economic and financial globalization; and less progressive taxation.

In the United States, for example, by 2007, income inequality reached levels not seen since 1928, before the onset of the Great Depression (figure 2). The share of income of the top 1 percent was 23 percent, having risen from 10 percent two decades earlier. The top 5 percent control about 75 percent of the financial wealth. The Gini coefficient, which measures inequality on a scale of zero to one, shows a sharp rise to over 0.45 (see figure 3), close to or worse than that of highly unequal economies in poorer EMs. At the same time, real median

Figure 2: Top 1% Share of U.S. Total Income at Highest Level Since the Great Depression

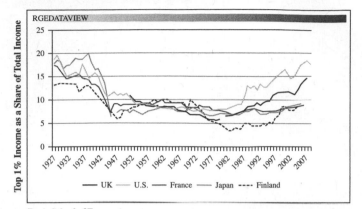

Source: Paris School of Economics.

incomes for U.S. households are back to 1999 levels. The working and middle classes are seriously squeezed, both income-wise and wealth-wise—stock prices have moved sideways for over a decade, and home prices have fallen by over one-third from their peak in 2006.

The rise in income and wealth inequality is a complex phenomenon that is driven by a series of factors and changes in the global economy. First, technological change is always initially labor-shedding, but over time it leads to income increases and rising demand that in turn increases labor demand. Thus "Luddites" in every generation—dating from the Industrial Revolution, when the original Luddites destroyed machines that in their view reduced the demand for labor—have been wrong in arguing that technological progress destroys jobs: it actually creates greater per capita income and more jobs over time. Still, the nature of technological change in recent decades has been more labor-saving than labor-increasing, and biased toward skilled labor and against unskilled and low-skilled labor.

Figure 3: Income Gini Coefficient, 2006–2008

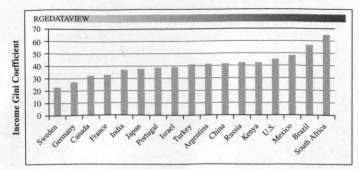

Source: Central Intelligence Agency, World Bank.

Workers with fewer skills have lost jobs and incomes, while skilled workers have done much better in terms of the growth of their real wages and job opportunities.

Second, a basic principle of international trade theory is that greater trade with a labor-abundant economy will reduce the wages of workers in a capital-abundant economy. The fact that workers in EMs are joining the global economy reduces, over time, the wages of unskilled workers in advanced economies. But adding billions of people to the global labor supply—workers from "Chindia" and other EMs—is a much more disruptive factor (in a long transition) than the rise of Germany in the 1960s or Japan in the 1970s. In the latter situations, it was thought that Germany first and Japan next would monopolize jobs, but over time the rise in these nations' wages and policy mistakes assuaged any worries that either country would take over the world economy. Similarly, present-day concerns that China will take over all manufacturing jobs and the global economy are misplaced; some of the increased costs of moving to China are, in fact, prompting "reshoring," and the production of the lower-value-added labor-intensive goods produced by China is moving to some poorer countries in Asia, such as

Bangladesh and Vietnam. Still, adding billions of workers to the global economy is a problem that is several orders of magnitude larger than the integration of Germany or Japan into the global economy. The production of cheaper goods and services by these workers increases the purchasing power of consumers all over the world, including those in advanced economies, but it hurts the real wages and jobs of unskilled blue-collar workers and white-collar workers in advanced economies.

There are winners and losers from international trade and globalization. For globalization to be Pareto-efficient—that is, beneficial to all—policy needs to redistribute income to losers or, better, to retrain them to do other jobs and to acquire new skills, which would allow them to compete and regain their lost jobs and incomes. It takes much longer to provide greater skills to such workers than it took for the displacement of such jobs to occur. The rise of EMs is a much larger phenomenon than the reintegration of Germany, the rest of Western Europe, and Japan into the global economy.

Third, because of the information technology revolution, services—which were, traditionally, internationally nontraded goods—have increasingly become international tradable products. Thus, while the rise of China and other low-income EMs has been threatening the jobs of low-skilled blue-collar workers in advanced economies, the tradability of services (think of Indian call centers, software developers, and so on) implies that even the jobs of low-skilled (and even some higher-skilled) white-collar workers are subject to international competition. A study by Alan S. Blinder suggests that up to 22 percent to 29 percent of U.S. jobs could be—in principle—offshorable. In the 1980s and even part of the 1990s, most jobs in manufacturing and traded sectors lost to foreign competition could be substituted for with the growth of jobs in nontraded sectors (professional services, health care, education, government, and so forth). Now that a larger number of previously nontraded sectors are tradable, given the new information technologies, jobs can be offshored even in the services sector, leaving even fewer opportunities for income and job creation for workers so displaced.

Fourth, as recently documented in a study by Nobel Prize winner Michael Spence, globalization may be associated with the increase in inequality: globalization does not benefit all but leads to winners and losers, both within countries and across countries, as skills-biased technological change and rising competition in traded labor-intensive low-value-added sectors from labor-abundant EMs have squeezed jobs and real wages. Little job creation has occurred in the traded sectors of advanced economies, while most of the benefits of the sharp increase in the productivity of sectors able to adapt and thrive in international competition have gone to capital and to skilled labor, not to unskilled workers. At the same time, job creation in service sectors sheltered by trade competition—education, health care, government—has been stronger than in traded sectors, but real wage growth in such nontraded sectors has stagnated, since productivity growth there has been mediocre. In recent decades, competitive traded sectors have created few jobs, while nontraded sectors have created more jobs but very little wage growth. According to Spence, we need to find new and better policy trade-offs that achieve a balance between the efficiency and economic growth that globalization provides and the inequality of incomes, wealth, and job opportunities that globalization causes.

The rise in inequality and the related weak growth of working-class and middle-class incomes have many causes; they are also problematic even if one ignores the issue of "fairness."

First, the increase in private and public leverage and the

related asset and credit bubbles are partly consequences of inequality: the mediocre growth in incomes of the past few decades—driven by the factors causing an increase in inequality, as discussed above—created a gap between incomes and spending aspirations ("keeping up with the Joneses"). In Anglo-Saxon countries (not just the United States and the United Kingdom but also others that followed the Anglo-Saxon economic model, such as Iceland, Ireland, Spain, and Australia in recent years), the response was a democratization of credit. Financial liberalization allowed struggling households to borrow to make up the difference between spending and income, leading to a rise in private debt. In the social welfare state economies of continental Europe, the gap was filled by the provision of public services (free education, health care, and so forth) although not fully paid for with taxes, thus leading to the rise of public deficits and debt.

In both cases, such growing private and public debts eventually became unsustainable, leading to financial crisis. So, while originally there was a surge of private debt in the laissez-faire Anglo-Saxon economies and of public debt in the continental European social welfare state economies, both ended up with massive—and at times unsustainable—levels of public debt. When the private debt bubbles burst as asset prices collapsed, public deficits and debts surged even in the Anglo-Saxon economies while private losses were socialized, automatic stabilizers kicked in, and countercyclical fiscal policies were implemented to prevent the Great Recession of 2007–9 from turning into the Great Depression 2.0.

Second, corporate firms in advanced economies are cutting jobs because they say that there is uncertainty, excess capacity, and not enough final demand. But cutting jobs reduces labor income, increases inequality, and reduces final demand. Thus, what is individually rational (firms need to survive and thrive, be profitable, and achieve Wall Street's or The City's earnings targets) is destructive in the macro-aggregate, as a firm's labor costs are an individual's labor income and demand. We end up with a catch-22: free markets don't create enough final demand as firms shed jobs due to insufficient demand, and those actions further reduce labor income and demand. The sharp worsening in the distribution of income that comes from this labor-cost slashing—from labor to capital, from wages to profits, from poor to rich, from households to corporate firms—then reduces aggregate demand, as the marginal propensity of households, workers, and the poor to spend (save) is higher (lower) than that of firms, capital owners, and the rich. It's also important to note that the share of labor income in gross domestic product is sharply down and falling in the United States. It is down to about 58 percent, from an average closer to 64 percent in the decades before 2000.

In a previous era, Henry Ford was willing to increase the wages of his own workers as he realized that higher spending, including spending to purchase the cars that he produced, was dependent on higher wages. But the Ford Motor Company was large enough in the early part of the twentieth century to internalize the effect that its own wage policy would have on the overall economy. In the United States today, the belief that markets always work if unfettered by regulation has led to a destructive decrease in jobs. The past few recessions have been followed by job-loss recoveries, then jobless recoveries, and then weak job-creating recoveries. Even labor markets don't work properly if countries don't invest enough in the skills and human capital of their labor force. In this regard, the labor market policies of some continental European economies—such as Germany—have proven better at maintaining and restoring job growth. In Germany, during the recent financial crisis, as working hours were reduced we saw labor-hoarding—

unlike the massive labor-shedding by U.S. corporations. Still, the Germans avoided substantial outright slashing of jobs; as a result, labor income did not fall as much, workers' skills were not damaged as much by a long spell of unemployment, and, once the economic recovery started in earnest, the unemployment rate decreased rapidly, while it has been stagnating at high chronic levels in the United States.

Karl Marx was partly right in arguing that globalization, unfettered financial capitalism, and the redistribution of income and wealth from labor to capital could lead capitalism to self-destruct (even if many of his views were wrong and his view that socialism would be a better system has proven totally mistaken). As he reasoned, unregulated capitalism could lead to a regular excess of capacity and production, to underconsumption, and to repeated and destructive financial crises, fueled by booms and busts of asset prices and credit bubbles.

These excesses of laissez-faire capitalism were clear even before the Great Depression as workers began to organize to ensure that their wages and benefits increased with productivity growth. Enlightened bourgeois classes in liberal democracies in Europe realized that, to avoid socialist revolutions, workers' rights needed to be protected, wage and labor conditions improved, and a welfare state created to redistribute wealth and to provide the financing of public goods—education, health care, a social safety net—for the working masses. That push toward a modern welfare state accelerated after the Great Depression, when the state took on the role of macrostabilization, with the development of more advanced welfare state institutions, such as social safety nets and the provision of opportunity to all via public education, health care, old-age pensions, and progressive income and wealth taxation. Thus, the rise of the social welfare state was a response of market-oriented liberal democracies to the threat of popular revolutions, social-ism, and communism as the frequency and severity of eco-nomic and financial crises increased. Three decades of relative social and economic stability ensued, from the 1940s until the early 1970s, during which period inequality sharply fell, median incomes grew rapidly, and the working and middle classes experienced a sharp rise in their living standards.

Classical economists from Thomas Malthus (1766–1834) to David Ricardo (1772–1823) and Marx believed—based on hun-dreds of years of economic history—that the working classes would always be stuck at close to subsistence wages, since an unlimited supply of labor would prevent real wages from rising above such a level. In fact, real wages and economic conditions sharply improved in the second half of the nineteenth century. The technological innovations of the Industrial Revolution led to an increase in productivity growth that was shared by both labor and capital. Indeed, the major intellectual revolution of thinkers such as Alfred Marshall (1842–1924)—compared with classical economists—was the novel idea that wages could grow over time alongside the increase in labor productivity growth, driven by technological innovation and spurred by investment in physical capital that makes workers more pro-ductive. The massive rise in incomes of many societies in the past 150 years that has vastly improved the living conditions of a large fraction of humanity has been driven by market-oriented economic regimes and the progressive application of techno-logical progress to the production of goods and services, thus leading to a huge increase in the productivity of labor.

But that relationship between rising productivity and increas-ing working- and middle-class incomes was never mechanical; it required workers to obtain the opportunity and skills—via education, training, proper health care—to boost their own productivity and thus partake of the added income deriving from the growth that new technologies provided. It also required the existence of a welfare state that provided such public goods, as well as a social safety net and old-age income security. All those government policies were key to preventing an increase in inequality that in laissez-faire markets is often the result of the excessive concentration of economic, financial, and political power within small elites.

While policies that purely redistribute income from capital to labor and from rich to poor do not work if the economic pie is small and not growing quickly enough, proper taxation policies (effectively progressive) to fund the provision of public goods that increase the skills, productivity, and economic opportunities of lower-income and lower-skill individuals in turn allow the economic pie to grow faster so that its benefits are shared by both labor and capital. The ability of workers to organize themselves into unions and thus demand better wages, benefits, and working conditions also helped to sustain the share of labor income in GDP and prevent a sharper rise in inequality.

The rise of the middle class and the rising living standards of the working class were thus not mechanical results of economic growth but the active outcome of many economic policies— such as universal publicly provided education financed by progressive taxation, to give just one example. These policies improved the skills, knowledge, and economic opportunities even of individuals born in disadvantaged circumstances. Social mobility in any society was never the result of market forces but rather the outcome of progressive economic, fiscal, taxation, and other social policies.

Some of the lessons about the need for prudent regulation of the financial system, for limiting the excesses of unregulated laissez-faire markets and the inequality effects of unfettered competition, were lost in the cycle of deregulation that accelerated

in the Reagan-Thatcher era of unfettered market capitalism—
the Anglo-Saxon model. The drive to massive deregulation was
also fed by the extremes of the social welfare model, the deficits
of which were illustrated in fiscal crises, excesses of regulation,
and a lack of economic dynamism, leading first to "euro-sclero-
sis" and then to the euro-zone crisis. But that laissez-faire
Anglo-Saxon model has also failed miserably, as the economic
and financial crisis has shown.

To enable market-oriented economies to operate in more
stable and balanced ways, we need to return to the right balance between markets and the provision of public goods. That
means moving away from both the Anglo-Saxon model of
unregulated laissez-faire capitalism and voodoo economics and
the continental European model of deficit-driven welfare
states. Even an alternative "Asian growth" model—if there
really is one—has not prevented a rise in inequality in China,
India, and many other parts of the continent. EMs—from Asia
to Latin America—need to further develop some of the key
institutions of a modern social welfare state to prevent sociopo-
litical instability and to promote the growth of consumption-
based economies.

For example, China will not become a consumer society
until wages start to grow more quickly than productivity to
reverse the opposite trend of the past few decades, and until
other policies are implemented to shift income from capital,
corporations, and state-owned enterprises to workers and
households. Latin America was a region cursed for decades by
political instability driven by massive inequality, with repeated
cycles of authoritarian regimes followed by radical populist
regimes and a return to dictatorships. This vicious cycle was
broken in the last two decades. Market-oriented reforms were
combined with economic policies—introduced both by moderate center-left and center-right governments—aimed at

reducing inequality and providing economic opportunities to the working class.

Any economic model that doesn't properly address inequality by providing public goods and opportunity to all will eventually face a crisis of legitimacy. Many academic research studies, including a 2011 International Monetary Fund study, show that widening inequality leads to lower economic growth. Even aside from the issue of fairness, inequality is bad according to traditional economic "efficiency" criteria. The frequency, severity, and consequences of the economic and financial crises of the past decades, themselves partly caused by rising inequality and income insecurity, are damaging and risk creating a backlash against globalization and market-oriented reforms. A third way that balances the role of markets and states in the economy needs to be found. Otherwise, the protests that began in 2011 will become more severe and cause disruptive social and political instability that will eventually harm long-term economic growth and welfare—by leading to a backlash against globalization and against market-oriented economies in advanced economies and EMs alike.

A Master Class in Occupation
Chris Hedges

Chris Hedges spent nearly two decades as a foreign correspondent and was part of the team of reporters at the *New York Times* awarded a Pulitzer Prize in 2002 for the paper's coverage of global terrorism. He is a Senior Fellow at The Nation Institute and teaches inmates at a correctional facility in New Jersey. He has written eleven books, including *Days of Destruction, Days of Revolt*, with illustrations by Joe Sacco (2012), and *War Is a Force That Gives Us Meaning* (2003), a finalist for the National Book Critics Circle Award for Nonfiction. The following profile was written in October 2011.

Jon Friesen, twenty-seven, tall and lanky with a long dirty-blond ponytail, a purple scarf, and an old green fleece, is sitting on concrete at the edge of Zuccotti Park leading a coordination meeting, a gathering that takes place every morning with representatives of each of Occupy Wall Street's roughly forty working groups.

"Our conversation is about what it means to be a movement and what it means to be an organization," he says to the circle. A heated discussion follows, including a debate over whether the movement should make specific demands.

I find him afterward on a low stone wall surrounding a flower bed in the park. He decided to come to New York City, he said, from the West Coast for the tenth anniversary of 9/11. He found a ride on Craigslist while staying at his brother's home in Champaign, Illinois.

"It was a television event when I was seventeen," he says of the 2001 attacks. "I wanted to make it real to myself. I'd never been to New York. I'd never been to the East Coast."

Once he reached New York City he connected with local street people to find "assets." He slept in the parks and on the street. He arrived on the first day of the occupation in Zuccotti Park. He found other "traveler types" whose survival skills and political consciousness were as developed as his own.

In those first few days, he says, "it was the radicals and the self-identifying anarchists" who set up the encampment. Those who would come later, usually people with little experience in Dumpster diving, sleeping on concrete, or depending on a McDonald's restroom, would turn to revolutionists like Friesen for survival. Zuccotti Park, like most Occupied sites, schooled the uninitiated.

"The structure and process carried out by those initial radicals," he says with delight of the first days in the park, now have "a wide appeal."

The Occupy movements that have swept across the country fuse the elements vital for revolt. They draw groups of veteran revolutionists whose isolated struggles, whether in the form of squatter communities or acts of defiance such as the 2006–2008 tree-sit in Berkeley to save an oak grove on the University of California campus, are often unheeded by the wider culture. The Occupy movements were nurtured in small dissident enclaves in New York, Oakland, Chicago, Denver, Boston, San Francisco, Los Angeles, and Atlanta. Bands of revolutionists in these cities severed themselves from the mainstream, joined with other marginalized communities, and mastered the physical techniques of surviving on the streets and in jails.

"It's about paying attention to exactly what you need and figuring out where I can get food and water, what time do the parks close, where I can get a shower," Friesen says.

Friesen grew up in an apolitical middle-class home in Fullerton in Southern California's Orange County, where systems of power were obeyed and rarely questioned. His window into political consciousness began inauspiciously enough when he was a teenager, with the Beatles, the Doors, and Crosby, Stills, Nash & Young. He found in the older music "a creative energy" and "authenticity" that he did not hear often in contemporary culture. He finished high school and got a job in a LensCrafters lab and "experienced what it's like to slave away trying to make glasses in an hour." He worked at a few other nine-to-five jobs but found them "restrictive and unfulfilling." And then he started to drift, working his way up to Berkeley, where he lived in a squatter encampment behind the UC-Berkeley football stadium. He used the campus gym to take showers. By the time he reached Berkeley he had left mainstream society. He has lived outside the formal economy since 2005, the last year he filed income taxes. He was involved in the tree-sit protest and took part in the occupations of university buildings and demonstration outside the Berkeley chancellor's campus residence to protest fee hikes and budget cuts, activities that saw him arrested and jailed. He spent time with the Navajos on Black Mesa in Arizona and two months with the Zapatistas in Mexico.

"What I saw in the Zapatistas was a people pushed to the brink of extinction and forgetting," he says. "Their phrases ring true: Liberty! Dignity! Democracy! Everything for Everyone! Nothing for Ourselves! The masks the Zapatistas wear check egos. People should be united in their facelessness. This prevents cults of personality.

"I have no interest in participating in the traditional political process," he says. "It's bureaucratic. It's vertical. It's exclusive. It's ruled by money. It's cumbersome. This is cumbersome, too, what we're doing here, but the principles that I'm pushing and that many people are pushing to uphold here are in direct opposition to the existing structure. This is a counterpoint. This is an acknowledgment of all those things that we hate, or that I hate, which are closed and exclusive. It is about defying status and power, certification and legitimacy, institutional validation to participate. This process has infected our consciousness as far as people being allowed [to participate] or even being given credibility. The wider society creates a situation where people are excluded, people feel like they're not worth anything. They're not accepted. The principles here are horizontal in terms of decision making, transparency, openness, inclusiveness, accessibility. There are people doing sign language at the General Assembly now. There are clusters of deaf people that come together and do sign language together. This is an example of the inclusive nature that we want to create here. And as far as redefining participation and the democratic process, my understanding of American history is that it was a bunch of white males in power, mostly. This is radically different. If you're a homeless person, if you're a street person, you can be here. There's a radical inclusion that's going on. And if it's not that, then I'm not going to participate."

The park, especially at night, is a magnet for the city's street population. The movement provides food along with basic security, overseen by designated "peacekeepers" and a "de-escalation team" that defuses conflicts. Those like Friesen who span the two cultures serve as the intermediaries.

"It draws everyone, except maybe the superrich," he says of the park. "You're dealing with everyone's conditioning, everyone's fucked-up conditioning, the kind of I'm-out-for-me-and-myself, that kind of instinct. People are unruly. People are violent. People make threats.

"We are trying to sort this out, how to work together in a more holistic approach versus just security-checking someone—you know, like, tackling them," he says. "Where else do these

A fixture at Zuccotti Park in the fall of 2011: This chalkboard announced meetings and activities such as teach-ins and marches that were open to all. *(Photograph copyright © Alice Mairs. Used with permission.)*

people have to go, these street people? They're going to come to a place where they feel cared for, especially in immediate needs like food and shelter. We have a comfort committee. I've never been to a place where there's a comfort committee. This is where you can get a blanket and a sleeping bag, if we have them. We don't always have the resources. But everyone is being taken care of here. As long as you're nonviolent, you're taken care of. And when you do that you draw all sorts of people, including those people who have problematic behavior. If we scale up big enough we might be able to take care of the whole street population of Manhattan."

The park, like other occupied sites across the country, is a point of integration, a place where middle-class men and women, many highly educated but unschooled in the techniques of resistance, are taught by those who have been carrying out acts of rebellion for the past few years. These revolutionists bridge the world of the streets and the world of the middle class.

"They're like foreign countries almost, the street culture and the suburban culture," Friesen says. "They don't understand each other. They don't share their experiences. They're isolated from each other. It's like Irvine and Orange County [home of the city of Irvine]; the hearsay is that they deport the homeless. They pick them up and move them out. There's no trying to engage. And it speaks to the larger issue, I feel, of the isolation of the individual. The individual going after their individual pursuits, and this facade of individuality, of consumeristic materialism. This materialism is about an individuality that is surface deep. It has no depth. That's translated into communities throughout the country that don't want anything to do with each other, that are so foreign to each other that there is hardly a drop of empathy between them.

"This is a demand to be heard," he says of the movement. "It's a demand to have a voice. People feel voiceless. They want a voice and participation, a renewed sense of self-determination, but not self-determination in the individualistic need of just-for-me-self. But as in 'I recognize that my actions have effects on the people around me.' I acknowledge that, so let's work together so that we can accommodate everyone."

Friesen says that digital systems of communication helped inform new structures of communication and new systems of self-governance.

"Open source started out in the fifties and sixties over how software is used and what rights the user has over the programs and tools they use," he says. "What freedoms do you have to use, modify, and share software? That's translated into things like Wikipedia. We're moving even more visibly and more tangibly into a real, tangible, human organization. We modify techniques. We use them. We share them. We decentralize them. You see the decentralization of a movement like this."

Revolutions need their theorists, but upheavals are impossible without hardened revolutionists like Friesen who haul theory out of books and shove it into the face of reality. The anarchist Mikhail Bakunin by the end of the nineteenth century was as revered among radicals as Karl Marx. Bakunin, however, unlike Marx, was a revolutionist. He did not, like Marx, retreat into the British Library to write voluminous texts on preordained revolutions. Bakunin's entire adult life was one of fierce physical struggle, from his role in the uprisings of 1848, where, with his massive physical bulk and iron determination, he manned barricades in Paris, Austria, and Germany, to his years in the prisons of czarist Russia and his dramatic escape from exile in Siberia.

Bakunin had little time for Marx's disdain for the peasantry and the lumpenproletariat of the urban slums. Marx, for all his insight into the self-destructive machine of unfettered capitalism, viewed the poor as counterrevolutionaries, those least capable of revolutionary action. Bakunin, however, saw in the "uncivilized, disinherited, and illiterate" a pool of revolutionists who would join the working class and turn on the elites who profited from their misery and enslavement. Bakunin proved to be the more prophetic. The successful revolutions that swept through the Slavic republics and later Russia, Spain, and China, and finally those movements that battled colonialism in Africa and the Middle East as well as military regimes in Latin America, were largely spontaneous uprisings fueled by the rage of a disenfranchised rural and urban working class, and that of dispossessed intellectuals. Revolutionary activity, Bakunin correctly observed, was best entrusted to those who had no property, no regular employment, and no stake in the status quo. Finally, Bakunin's vision of revolution, which challenged Marx's rigid bifurcation between the proletariat and the bourgeoisie, carved out a vital role for these rootless intellectuals, the talented sons and daughters of the middle class who had been educated to serve within elitist institutions, or expected a place in the middle class, but who had been cast aside by society. The discarded intellectuals—unemployed journalists, social workers, teachers, artists, lawyers, and students—were for Bakunin a valuable revolutionary force: "fervent, energetic youths, totally déclassé, with no career or way out." These déclassé intellectuals, like the dispossessed working class, had no stake in the system and no possibility for advancement. The alliance of an estranged class of intellectuals with dispossessed masses creates the tinder, Bakunin argued, for successful revolt. This alliance allows a revolutionary movement to skillfully articulate grievances while exposing and exploiting, because of a familiarity with privilege and power, the weaknesses of autocratic, tyrannical rule.

The Occupy movement is constantly evolving as it finds what works and discards what does not. At any point in the day, knots of impassioned protesters can be found in discussions that involve self-criticism and self-reflection. This makes the movement radically different from liberal reformist movements that work within the confines of established systems of corporate power, something Marx understood very well. It means that the movement's war of attrition will be long and difficult, that it will face reverses and setbacks but will, if successful, ultimately tear down the decayed edifices of the corporate state.

Marx wrote:

Bourgeois revolutions, like those of the eighteenth century, storm more swiftly from success to success, their dramatic effects outdo each other, men and things seem set in sparkling diamonds, ecstasy is the order of the day—but they are short-lived, soon they have reached their zenith, and a long *Katzenjammer* [hangover] takes hold of society before it learns to assimilate the results of its storm-and-stress period soberly. On the other hand, proletarian revolutions, like those of the nineteenth century, constantly criticize themselves, constantly interrupt themselves in their own course, return to the apparently accomplished, in order to begin anew; they deride with cruel thoroughness the half-measures, weaknesses, and paltriness of their first attempts, seem to throw down their opponents only so the latter may draw new strength from the earth and rise before them again more gigantic than ever, recoil constantly from the indefinite colossalness of their own goals—until a situation is created which makes all turning back impossible, and the conditions themselves call out: *"Hier ist die Rose, hier tanze"* [Here is the rose, dance here].

Is Democracy Still in the Streets?

James Miller

James Miller, professor of politics at the New School
for Social Research and formerly the editor of *Daeda-
lus*, is the author of six books, including *"Democracy Is
in the Streets": From Port Huron to the Siege of Chicago*
(1994), *The Passion of Michel Foucault* (1993), and *Examined Lives: From Socrates to Nietzsche* (2011).

On the afternoon of August 2, 2011, a group of self-selected
activists, about sixty in all, met at Bowling Green, a park
in downtown Manhattan with the famous bronze statue of a
snorting bull, installed in 1989 as a tribute to the financial
power of nearby Wall Street.

The people had gathered by the bull in response to a call
for a General Assembly to organize an occupation of Wall
Street, set to start on September 17. They came from a variety
of political backgrounds. Some were students, others were
union organizers. There were socialists, but a surprising number were conservatives, libertarians committed to "leaderless
resistance," and also conservatives allied with Ron Paul. Still
more were avowed anarchists, including David Graeber, a fifty-
year-old professor of anthropology and a veteran activist.

Expecting an open assembly, Graeber and some friends
from 16 Beaver, a downtown arts collective, discovered instead
a group of conventional organizers with megaphones and plac-
ards, trying to rally participants for a conventional march that
would make conventional demands. In response, Graeber and

his group retreated to a corner of the park to discuss alternative next steps. Sitting in a circle, they debated how they might better organize a Wall Street occupation. Graeber proposed implementing one of the most radical forms of direct democracy conceivable: a daily General Assembly where virtually all decisions would be made without voting, by consensus—and formally subject to veto by a single "block," if anyone felt a proposed decision violated an ethical principle.

It seemed quixotic. But Graeber's vision prevailed. Against all odds, the movement that he helped to launch—Occupy Wall Street—has been a stunning success.

It has transformed the political conversation in America. It has compelled the media to pay fresh attention to voices on the left. Despite a lack of explicit demands, the movement has "reignited hope in the possibility of a free society," in part by exemplifying, in the words of one participant, a new world that is "participatory and democratic to the core." Occupy Wall Street has resurrected a defining aspect of the New Left of the 1960s: an overriding commitment to participatory democracy, understood as the making of decisions in a face-to-face community of friends and not through elected representatives.

The ongoing experiment of Occupy movements around the world with the General Assembly process suggests that democracy is *still* "in the streets": a welcome reminder that politics isn't just about elections and voting, and proof, if proof were needed, that the Port Huron Statement—the 1962 manifesto of Students for a Democratic Society (SDS), which first popularized the ideal of participatory democracy—has left a living legacy, however paradoxical.

As I wrote a quarter century ago in my book *"Democracy Is in the Streets": From Port Huron to the Siege of Chicago*, perhaps the most important result of the sixties experiment with participatory democracy, at least in my view, was to demonstrate "the incompatibility of rule-by-consensus with accountable, responsible government in a large organization—or even in a small group of people with divergent interests and a limited patience for endless meetings." Even this modest lesson has proved hard to learn, perhaps because, as I also wrote, "for anyone who joined in the search for a democracy of individual participation—and certainly for anyone who remembers the happiness and holds to the hopes that the quest itself aroused the sense of what politics can mean will never be quite the same again."

The result, for many subsequent groups on the global left, has been an unstable political idealism, an amalgam of direct action and direct democracy, with many of the virtues of a utopian and romantic revolt—passion, moral conviction, a shared joy in the joining of battle—but also some of the vices: above all, an obsession with directly democratic processes and an addiction to creating ever more intense situations of felt personal liberation, regardless of the wider political ramifications.

Take, for example, the case of the Movement for a New Society—an important model for contemporary anarchists like David Graeber. An offshoot of a Quaker direct-action group, the organization, founded in the early seventies, was inspired by the direct democratic experiments of the Student Nonviolent Coordinating Committee and Students for a Democratic Society in the sixties, and also by Gandhi's pacifist injunction to "be the change you want to see." A strict adherence to rule by consensus became perhaps the group's most distinctive feature, its preferred means of acting, and also an end in itself, because organizing direct actions via consensus was *the* way to show that direct democracy, individual freedom, and a society based on principles of solidarity are possible in practice.

The problem, as George Lakey, the tutelary spirit of Movement for a New Society, ruefully acknowledged in retrospect (the group dissolved itself in 1988), was that rule by consensus had some perverse consequences. "While an organization is new and vital," Lakey remarked years later, "consensus decision making can be valuable for encouraging unity. In the longer run, however, consensus can be a conservative influence, stifling the prospects of organizational change"—not least because any one person can "block" any change that is proposed. At the same time, an obsession with the purity of the process of participation slowly but surely began to erode the group's capacity to engage constructively with the larger social and economic world, in part by crippling its capacity to exploit the full range of political tactics in a democracy, from protests to the mechanics of electioneering.

Veterans of the Movement for a New Society, and activists inspired by its example, played key roles in organizing the anti–World Trade Organization demonstrations in Seattle in 1999—and have played key roles in the Occupy Wall Street movement. Though the General Assemblies that have become a hallmark of the Occupy movement have not been uniformly organized in every single city, most of them have followed characteristic rules that are meant, in part, to solve some of the problems that have arisen in previous direct democratic experiments.

Avowedly antiauthoritarian, nonhierarchical, and leaderless, the OWS assemblies have generally adhered to rule by consensus as an end in itself and as the best way to show that direct democracy is really workable. The assemblies are explicitly free associations: they are formally open to everyone, no matter his or her political, ethnic, or religious affiliation. Anyone may join and participate, just as anyone may exit at any time. The assemblies thus enshrine, in a radical form, the autonomy of each individual in the association: "Every person is free to do as they wish."

While the freedom of the individual is in principle inviolable in the assemblies, the goal is to forge, through consensus, a new form of collective freedom. Naturally, the assemblies cannot hope to realize this without some help. Since leaders are not formally acknowledged, help takes the form of "facilitators," individuals who are trained to foster what one guide to the process calls "collective thinking," a form of thinking

> diametrically opposed to the kind of thinking propounded by the present system. When faced with a decision, the normal response of two people with differing opinions tends to be confrontational. They each defend their opinions with the aim of convincing their opponent, until their opinion has won or, at most, a compromise has been reached.
>
> The aim of collective thinking, on the other hand, is to construct. That is to say, two people with differing ideas work together to build something new. The onus is therefore not on my idea or yours; rather it is the notion that two ideas together will produce something new, something that neither of us envisaged beforehand. This focus requires of us that we actively listen.

If a single person blocks consensus, the group must listen even more carefully and seek to find common ground in a way that wins over the individual who has objections. "Prejudice and ideology must be left at home" — the goal is to forge a "new subjectivity," expressed in a new form of political speech.

*   *   *

At first, the New York City General Assembly seemed to succeed in some of its most utopian objectives: as supporters of OWS chanted in the street, *"This is what democracy looks like!"*

The joy of collectively creating a new political space is palpable in the earliest firsthand accounts of those who occupied Zuccotti Park on September 17: "If you want to see what real democracy, run horizontally, with full participation, looks like, you should be here," wrote one Occupier the next day. Here was a real, and striking, alternative to simply pulling levers to choose between candidates selected in advance by others, and often selected precisely in order to defend the interests of an oligarchic elite. "There is an energy and an amazing consensus process working with 50+ people in general assembly several times a day," wrote another participant a few days later, marveling at how the group was successfully "making decisions about how to run the occupation—from when to do marches, to how to communicate, to ideas about food, art, entertainment, and all kinds of issues that anyone can bring up."

The first surge of enthusiasm gradually waned. As time passed and the Occupiers dug in for the duration, the assembly in New York became bogged down in logistical details. A great deal of time and energy was devoted to making sure the Occupiers had sleeping bags and food and were able to clear garbage from the site. Meetings often lasted for hours. To keep the assembly moving, the facilitators became ever more forceful in setting an agenda and limiting the scope of debate.

Effective decision making on many matters, both logistical and political, simultaneously devolved to a number of "working groups" that met separately and fell under the control of various individuals who assumed de facto power within the movement. The groups working on direct action naturally put a premium on solidarity and discretion, not an open airing of doubts and disagreements. (At the New School in November, for example, the direct-action working group that planned an occupation of a school building worked largely in secret and functioned as a cadre controlled by vanguard activists, with no formal accountability to the school's General Assembly.)

In an effort to acknowledge such problems, the General Assembly in Zuccotti Park voted to institute an Operational Spokes Council, which began to meet regularly in November 2011, on nights when the General Assembly was not in session. In this way, among others, the occupation in New York City slowly turned from "experiences of visionary inspiration," in the words of David Graeber, to "a much slower, painstaking struggle of creating alternative institutions."

It is too soon to say if America's experiment with participatory politics can elaborate new forms that can solve some of the problems encountered in previous experiments. I don't think it is too soon to make a few observations about some obvious limits to the experiment, if one takes the General Assembly and Spokes Council seriously as a preview (or "prefiguration") of alternative institutions—as well as a demonstration that a direct democracy based on individual freedom, combined with a newly formed capacity for collective thinking, is feasible in practice.

The first and perhaps most obvious problem is scale. It is one thing to create a participatory community of 500 or 1,000—or even a democracy of 40,000 direct participants, as the Athenians did in the fifth and fourth centuries BC. It is quite another thing to imagine direct, participatory interaction in large and complex societies on the scale of the United States. Perhaps one can envision a federation of nested assemblies, but any serious effort to implement such a structure will require a delegation of authority and the selection of representatives—in short, the creation of an *indirect* democracy, much more intricate and extensive than the Spokes Council, and at some distance from most participants.

Even more challenging is the fact that many of the protesters' concerns—for example, systemic debt, structural unemployment, the unfettered power of finance capital, global warming—involve dilemmas that can be addressed best by new forms of global and transnational regulation and governance, not by local assemblies.

It is also true that the self-selected participants in these General Assemblies represent but a tiny fraction of the 99 percent they claim to embody, if only symbolically. Working people and parents with small children are unlikely and often unable to commit to spending hours on weekday evenings at a General Assembly. The most active participants in the movement tend to be white and well educated, which has predictably produced collective hand-wringing over the lack of racial and economic diversity.

In any case, the very conditions of the General Assembly's existence—it is, after all, a free association of self-selected participants—means that these experiments in participatory democracy never have to confront the toughest challenge to democratic ideals in a complex and large modern society. That challenge is one of coping with participants who hold radical, often incommensurable differences of opinion, including different views on whether or not social justice requires less income inequality, never mind the abolition of capitalism.

One glance at the world we actually live in should suffice to remind us of the many other things people do *not* share: notably moral beliefs and religious convictions, but also a passion for political participation. (As Hannah Arendt once remarked, one of "the most important negative liberties we have enjoyed since the end of the ancient world" is "freedom from politics, which was unknown to Rome or Athens and which is politically the most relevant part of our Christian heritage.")

The larger a group, the more ineradicable such diversity will be, unless the group is willing to resort to coercion in an effort to force unity and political participation (as has happened routinely in a great many avowedly democratic and socialist organizations and states over the years). In other words, I seriously doubt that experiments like the General Assembly and Spokes Council can ever generate the kinds of alternative institutions that are needed to meet the challenges of our current situation. Instead of single-mindedly pursuing a new form of "collective thinking" through endless meetings meant to forge consensus, I think we would do better to explore as well new ways to institute viable forms of modus vivendi—and this will entail fostering a tolerant ethos that accepts, and can acknowledge, that there are many incompatible forms of life, not always democratic or participatory, in which humans can flourish.

Unfortunately, negotiating a modus vivendi with people whose beliefs you deplore, or devising new forms of international cooperation, may well seem boring and dull, certainly in comparison with the pleasures of direct action.

As David Graeber has observed, so-called Black Bloc tactics, including vandalism and street fighting with police, can be heady, even transporting: "It is a way to create one, fleeting moment when autonomy is real and immediate, a space of liberated territory, in which the laws and arbitrary power of the state no longer apply, in which we draw the lines of force ourselves." After the "whole world is watching" showdown between police and protesters in Chicago in August 1968, the most militant partisans of participatory democracy, similarly electrified by the feeling of liberation through direct action, heaped scorn on the dreary compromises involved in electoral politics.

This brings me to perhaps the most insidious paradox of participatory democracy, when a movement that pursues its aims through polarizing protests simultaneously demands consensus in its organs of self-government. The paradox unfolds as follows. The success of a polarizing movement hinges on obtaining publicity and sympathetic attention from outsiders. The surest way to obtain such publicity is through demonstrations that prompt a disproportionate and unjust response from the authorities. Meanwhile, back in the General Assembly, the demand for consensus willy-nilly puts the most uncompromising militants—including many of those who in fact have spurred the growth of the movement and have become militant activists by taste as well as political conviction—in a position in which they can veto the tactics and strategy proposed by more cautious comrades. The group becomes polarized, but consensus remains the holy grail of the assembly meetings, and the moderates in the group are by definition inclined to compromise. So they silence their reservations—and in some cases simply choose to drop out of the movement. As a result, the consensus view that prevails is generally the most radical alternative on offer (an extreme illustration of what Cass Sunstein has called "the law of group polarization").

Disagreements disappear, at least for public consumption. Indeed, in the General Assemblies of Occupy Wall Street, "ideological" disputes are formally discouraged, since any open debate—for example, over the value of Black Bloc tactics or the meaning of the group's ostensible commitment to nonviolent civil disobedience—might undermine the group's solidarity and also, potentially, infringe on the autonomy of the most militant individuals in the association. Although everyone on the inside knows who the most articulate leaders of the different factions and working groups are, none of these de facto leaders can be held accountable, since, according to the group's professed principles, there are no leaders.

Still, these are early days. Around the world, the injustices that have given rise to the Occupy movement remain unaddressed, and in New York City, at least, Occupy Wall Street shows no sign of disappearing anytime soon. Since the many different General Assemblies affiliated with the movement are works in progress, meant to provoke an ongoing conversation, it is impossible to predict how this latest experiment in participatory democracy will unfold.

And who knows? If today's radical Democrats can avoid fetishizing the demand for consensus, and instead deploy rule by consensus only in situations where it may be both useful and feasible, young activists may yet prove able to forge a movement that is broader and open to a greater diversity of opinion: one that is able to welcome advocates of moderation, pragmatism, and tolerance, and not just the voluptuaries of unrestrained direct action and "collective thinking."

In any case, that is the sort of movement toward a more participatory democracy that I'd like to see in 2012—a half century after Port Huron.

The Arc of Communism:
Lessons for Occupy Wall Street?

Robert M. Buckley

Robert M. Buckley is a Senior Fellow at the New School for Public Engagement. He was an adviser and lead economist at the World Bank and managing director at the Rockefeller Foundation. His most recent book is *Urbanization and Growth*, which he coedited with Patricia Clarke Annez and Michael Spence.

Many talk about Occupy Wall Street's lack of a coherent program to address the concerns and anxieties that prompted the protests. What is reasonable to expect from such a spontaneous and seemingly heartfelt movement? Does history offer any insights into what might be expected—or suggestions as to how the movement might try to turn the protests into action? Perhaps one place to look for answers is at the rise and fall of the largest social revolution of the twentieth century, a revolution that grew out of a similarly simultaneous eruption that effectively went viral across many cities through greater connectivity. It also, unfortunately, turned out to be one of the most costly social innovations ever. The communist revolution, viewed through a filter of black humor in the former Soviet Union, has come to be known as the longest road taken on the path from capitalism to capitalism.

Both communism's seemingly inexorable rise and its precipitous demise have been extensively examined, and while there are many interpretations of what happened and why, the basic narrative is largely well accepted. In the case of its rise in the early years of the twentieth century, a key is generally purported to be the steely resolve and actions of extremely clever and ruthless revolutionaries such as Lenin and Trotsky at a particularly auspicious moment in history. The shock of communism's sudden dénouement makes interpretations of that event a bit less straightforward. Some attribute it to the collapse of the Soviet economy, others to Ronald Reagan's raising of the stakes in the arms race, while still others point to the moral bankruptcy of a rotting political system. All, in one way or another, point to a system that after seventy years had simply run out of gas.

Yet in discussions of communism's arc, little has been said about exactly how the recent end point was reached. What was the event that finally overturned the cart? Why, for example, did one of the most powerful military states ever within one year unwind into fifteen separate countries? And not much has been said about the dress rehearsals for the communist revolution that took place seventy years earlier across Europe— rehearsals that, in their spontaneous ubiquity, are precursors of the Occupy movement. Shortly after the publication of *The Communist Manifesto*, in February 1848, Paris, Berlin, Vienna, Milan, Prague, and Budapest erupted in often violent protests. Within weeks of the *Manifesto*'s publication, the French monarchy fell, and the new "social media" of the day—the telegraph—led to widespread calls for greater democracy and social justice across Europe. Communism had provided an alternative to the view that the results of laissez-faire produced the best of all possible worlds. However, the fact that this movement, like the 2010–12 Arab uprisings, was referred to as "the springtime of the peoples" is in many ways not encouraging, as almost everywhere it was brutally suppressed. Nevertheless, even though the movement soon vaporized, ultimately it was to have far-reaching consequences, particularly in addressing

Vilnius, Lithuania, 1991: A statue of Lenin is dismantled and carted away on August 23. *(Wojtek Druszcz/AFP/Getty Images)*

increasingly skewed income distribution, which was a key catalyst for the uprisings and, similarly, helped to initiate the "We are the 99 percent" movement.

While tomes have been written about the fall of communism, little attention has been given to details of exactly how it unwound and, in particular, to the role that the extraordinarily heroic actions of Lithuanians played in communism's breakup. In January 1991 tens of thousands of them poured onto the streets of Vilnius as the world watched Gorbachev at the last minute reverse course and back down on brutally suppressing the freedom movement—after hundreds had been wounded and fourteen had died, some crushed by tanks. The unflinching and nonviolent reaction to the killings by the commandos who had been sent to restore Soviet authority put the final nail in the coffin of the Union of Soviet Socialist Republics. By the end of the year, the thirteen other states of the Soviet Union followed Lithuania out of Soviet entanglement. Only Russia remained to replace the Soviet Union in the international community.

The pan-European uprisings of 1848 were prompted by a combination of factors: the increasingly concentrated distribution of income brought about by the Industrial Revolution, the lack of any sort of social assistance, and a severe economic downturn, which intensified the plight of the poor. An international group, many of them German, the communists clearly saw the moment as a golden opportunity for revolution, and hurried Marx and Engels to produce the *Manifesto*, under threat of expulsion from the party if it wasn't rapidly completed. At Engels's suggestion, Marx rewrote his colleague's didactic question-and-answer approach to dialectical materialism. Engels may have been many things—brilliant, lighthearted, a horse lover—but he did not have Marx's rhetorical flair.

The *Manifesto* was published days before the Second Empire folded, and the news of the protests and fighting that had ensued in Paris spread throughout Europe. While brief, the disorder was sufficiently threatening to the empire that it led Baron Haussmann a few years later to redesign Paris in a way that would include wide boulevards, "which would eviscerate old Paris neighborhoods of riots and barricades," and which would allow his cavalry faster deployment. Many died on those barricades, and many more were to die twenty-three years later in the suppression of similar protests by the Paris Commune. In fact, more died in the 1871 event—as many as thirty thousand—than all those executed in the French Revolution. The unrest was to continue, but the moment had passed.

As Marx would say, in 1851, "[T]he obligation to share in public with all these asses in the general absurdity of the party—we're done with that for now." Never one to suffer those who did not share his views, he had by then moved to London, where he was to spend the rest of his life, much of it in the British Museum, studying political economy and writing his masterwork, *Das Kapital*. However, while the moment may have passed, a study by Daron Acemoglu and James A. Robinson indicates that the effects of the protests did not. They argue that the threats implied by the uprisings provided the basis for the extension of voting rights, which led to the development of sustained redistributive policies and social safety nets across Germany, France, and England. The result of this enfranchisement was that after inequality continued a steady rise until around 1870—as calculated, for example, by the traditional measure of inequality, the Gini coefficient—the trend reversed. (The Gini coefficient ranges from a measure of zero, for complete equality of income, to one, for complete inequality.) By 1901 inequality had significantly declined, by about 25 percent, to a level well below that in the United States today (about 0.46). Similar trends occurred across Europe, and the "specter" of communism that Marx and Engels warned was haunting the continent slowly dissipated, except in the autocratic and unreformed tsarist Russia.

The obvious question in all this is: what did communism have to do with this outcome? If anything, Marx and Engels might appear more as opportunists who wished to implement their views than as theorists who had successfully anticipated the crushing of the bourgeoisie in a deterministic historical process. Nor is there much evidence that the *Manifesto* actually induced action by the protesters. Unlike Trotsky and Lenin, who were to use the call to arms of the *Manifesto* to successfully prosecute the communist revolution seventy years later in Russia, Marx had to settle for saying of the events of 1848, "What succumbed in these defeats was not the revolution.... Success would have been a disaster in disguise.... it was only by a series of rebuffs that the revolutionary party could free itself of... opportunistic leaders." The answer to the question of communism's effect on the outcomes of the events of 1848 lies in reviewing the demands made in *The Communist Manifesto*. Within sixty years many of the basic demands that it had articulated had at least partially been fulfilled in the core European countries—those that Donald Rumsfeld might refer to as "Old Europe."

In all wealthy countries in the world today, many of the basic demands of the *Manifesto* have long since become part of the social infrastructure: progressive income taxes, freely available education, restrictions on inheritances, national banks (that is, counterparts to the Federal Reserve), and a large public sector role in transport and communication are now the rule rather than the exception. While neither Old Europe nor North America did away with private property or created workers' paradises, a twelvefold increase in average per capita income since the writing of the *Manifesto*, along with a much more egalitarian distribution of income—realized largely through *Manifesto*-like reforms—is not a bad deal.

Thus, in the 160 years since it was written, the *Manifesto* has certainly inflamed passions and enkindled revolutions, and is rightly referred to as one of the most influential books ever published. But, perhaps even more importantly, it also focused on the elements of reform that are the touchstones of whether a society is fair—education, taxation, and finance. In short, even if in the end Marx and his disciples believed that the post-1848 reforms were not sufficient to overcome the exploitation of the working classes, and even if the *Manifesto* reflected rather than created a movement, its arguments nonetheless helped keep attention focused on what was important.

*   *   *

Perhaps the main lesson that emerges from this experience is that the same policy levers that obtained then—education, taxes, and finance—remain the central determinants of social welfare and cohesion today. While these instruments may be designed or implemented differently in different cultures, they are and always will be the mainstays of social balance. For example, while the United States, Japan, and Germany have similar pretax income distributions, the post-tax distributions are much lighter on higher-income earners in the United States, so that U.S. after-tax income distribution is significantly more regressive. Similarly, not only has the United States' undercapitalized financial sector grown to more than twice the size it was twenty years ago (as a share of GDP); it has also induced many of our nimblest young to shift their career focus so that they, too, can realize the gains from the risks afforded by excessive indebtedness. In 2011 almost one-third of Harvard's graduating seniors bet their human capital on becoming Gordon Gekko. Finally, it is no accident that a significant portion of the increase in income inequality observed in the United States is due to a growing gap in pay between those who have earned a college degree and those who haven't. Widely available education has always been and will remain a key to equitable growth.

New theories about what is going on in our more globalized world aren't needed. The ways to address the problems are well known, and there is an infinite number of no doubt clever ways to implement them. The problem, in brief, is not in understanding what is going on but in acting upon what is known, much as was true in mid-nineteenth-century Europe. Before the focus shifts to too much emphasis on the details of What Is to Be Done, more attention should be given to why what needs to be done isn't getting done.

What is needed, as Occupy's People's Assembly suggests, is much stronger enfranchisement of those who are affected by the changes in economic opportunities and the threats provided by changes in the real costs of economic activity—such as, to bring up another elephant in the room, climate change. Of course, this implies that stronger enforcement of the regulations that ensure financial transactions is made fairly, and by those who both understand and cover the risks involved. Unfortunately, this is much easier said than done. It is difficult because greater enfranchisement of the 99 percent implies a corresponding reduction in the access of the 1 percent to policymakers.

To get a sense of just how disproportionate the access of the rich to policymakers has been, consider the behavior of the financial institutions bailed out at taxpayer expense. Even after evidence has been presented that these same institutions successfully "bought" the kinds of weaker regulation that created the subprime crisis, their lobbying expenses, which were the most of any industry, have more than doubled between 2000 and 2010—with funds particularly targeted on watering down the Dodd-Frank financial legislation, which would increase regulatory oversight. It is no wonder that over the decade 2001–2011, outside of Greece and Italy, the United States has had one of the largest increases in corruption among Organisation for Economic Co-operation and Development countries, as judged by Transparency International's Corruption Perceptions Index.

Rather than going into the details of what is implied by the disproportionate access of the rich to policymakers—a topic much more effectively dealt with by the movement itself—let's consider some questions about the process of reform from the other side of communism's arc: what might be inferred from the endgame of communism?

First, do the sorts of basic changes in policy that are required take time to realize, as they did in nineteenth-century Europe? It is on this count that the Lithuanian example is important. In this instance, one of the world's strongest military regimes collapsed quickly and irreversibly, pushed over the edge by one of Europe's smallest countries, which was essentially unarmed. Moreover, the Soviet Union fell after its tiny opponent acted in what can be seen as an irrational manner. That is, instead of assuming that the Soviet Union simply couldn't afford to let independence stand, as would have been perfectly rational because of the likelihood that such a position would lead to the dissolution of the Soviet empire, thousands of Lithuanians, and a week later most of the Latvian population, took to the streets to continue to protest the efforts to suppress their claims to independence. They went to the locations that the Soviets had attacked, and broadcast the suppression to the outside world. The point is that not only can basic change happen quickly, but that it can happen outside the cold calculus of rational decision making.

Second, why did Lithuania, one of the richest of the Soviet republics, as well as a country that had the extraordinarily egalitarian distribution of income typical of former Soviet republics, act against the Soviet empire? At a minimum, the intensity of the efforts to dismantle communism were of course motivated by a very different set of concerns than the distributional issues that motivated the revolutionaries who sought to establish communism. The passion of the Lithuanian effort to destroy communism can be explained by the animosity toward the Soviets that was generated by Stalin and Hitler's having anschlussed many small European countries out of existence during World War II. The Soviets treated Lithuania as a plaything that could be managed by genocide of nearly 80 percent of the country's Jews and the shipping of thousands of others to the Siberian gulag. Certainly this legacy played a major role. But so, too, were distributional factors involved. At the end of World War II, Lithuania had a per capita income level similar to Finland's. By 1991 its income had fallen to one-seventh the Finnish level. In other words, all Lithuanians, not just those at the top of the income pyramid, paid an enormous "tax" that involved transfers to the rest of the Soviet republics. All had been punished, so even without the historical legacy there were strong distributional rationales for seeking to overthrow the economic system.

Third, won't the establishment of a capitalist democracy with such an egalitarian distribution of income ultimately kill the growth engine? Won't establishing a democratic system of governance in a country with such an even distribution of income assure that voters will redistribute from those who are most productive to the more numerous voters who are least productive?

So far, such populist redistribution has not happened. Between 1991 and the 2008 financial crisis, Lithuania has been both one of the most rapidly growing economies in the world — at a rate of 9 percent per annum between 2000 and 2009 — and one with a still egalitarian distribution of income, with a Gini coefficient 25 percent lower than that of the United States. And while twenty years is certainly too soon to say, the Lithuanian experience suggests, and evidence from other countries confirms, that while higher rates of economic growth tend to create inequality, growth and equity are by no means mutually exclusive.

Finally, does the threat of revolt have to carry a threat of violence, as might be inferred from Acemoglu and Robinson's work about the prime motivator of the European reforms of the nineteenth century? On this, the Lithuanian experience speaks forcefully, if inconclusively. Perhaps the hallmark of the

Lithuanian independence movement was that it succeeded in achieving independence and enfranchisement through nonviolent resistance. While we do not yet know why Lithuania was allowed to become an independent state in light of the high losses that the Soviets incurred for tolerating their rebellion, the results are clearly encouraging. Even if the Lithuanian experience only provides an example of how seemingly improbable demands can be realized without violence on the part of the protesters, it nevertheless is a hopeful result, one worth pursuing.

Ultimately, there are certainly many reforms that could lead to a much fairer, more equitable society. In the past fifteen years, Latin America, particularly Brazil, has shown that a range of policies could be pursued that are not only not expensive, but which can also have major implications for creating a sense that rewards, effort, and luck are dealt with in a way that is in keeping with a culture's sense of fairness. Certainly since the U.S. financial sector has been the leveraged epicenter of the deep sense of unfairness about the U.S. economy, this is a sector worthy of increased attention. The truism that the rich can live comfortably on the interest from their capital has been replaced by a newer truth: the rich are now so wealthy that they can live on the interest they earn on the interest on their capital. Without attention to much greater transparency and accountability for financial-sector risk taking, fairness will be impossible to realize.

Finally, even though the frequency of the claim almost makes it not worth repeating, it is impossible not to comment on how extreme the changes in income inequality have been. As many studies have shown, the disparities between the very top portion of income earners and the rest of society are simply incredible. The share of income going to the top 1 percent of the income distribution in the United States is almost four times that of Japan's, and larger than that of South Africa, a country with one of the world's most unequal income distributions and a long legacy of apartheid. Attention needs to be given to adjusting all three of the policy instruments I've mentioned—education, finance, and taxes. More important than a focus on particular reforms is the need to focus on the process by which reforms are made and sustained. The political process in the United States now is as broken as those of various countries in mid-nineteenth-century Europe or that of the late-twentieth-century Soviet Union. In both cases, the countries that demonstrated a sense of outrage at the vestiges of privilege became dynamic, culturally rich countries. Those that did not, like Russia, have, unfortunately, been placed on what Trotsky called the ash heap of history. A practical agenda of actions is needed, but for such reforms to take hold it is essential that action be taken on the ways the rules are made. One hopes the Occupy Wall Street movement can have the courage of the Lithuanians and the foresight of the *Manifesto*.

Globalization and the Perils of Democracy

Pankaj Mishra

Pankaj Mishra, the author of several books of literary fiction and nonfiction, including the forthcoming *From the Ruins of Empire: The Revolt against the West and the Remaking of Asia* (2012), writes for the *New York Review of Books, The New Yorker,* and the *Financial Times.* He is also a columnist at Bloomberg View.

The 2011 Occupy Wall Street protests in New York found sympathetic echoes in nearly all of the world's major cities. From Santiago to Johannesburg, London to Manila, demonstrators poured into the streets to express their frustration with what they see as the built-in inequities of global capitalism. In India, tens of thousands of middle-class people joined an anticorruption movement led by the quasi-Gandhian figure of Anna Hazare. Middle-class Israelis demanding "social justice" turned out for their country's first major demonstrations in years. In China, the state broadcaster CCTV unprecedentedly joined millions of cybercritics in blaming a government that placed economic growth above social welfare for the fatal high-speed train crash in Wenzhou in July 2011. Add to this the uprisings against kleptocracies in Egypt and Tunisia, the street protests in Greece and Spain, and the spate of self-immolations in Tibet and you are looking at a fresh political awakening.

The specific contexts may seem very different from each other, and the grievances may be phrased differently from place to place. Nonetheless, public anger derives from a single source: a form of economic progress that, geared toward private wealth creation, is indifferent to, if not contemptuous of, ideas of collective welfare, social justice, and environmental protection. The phenomenon, which raises profound questions about the prospects of democracy and political stability, seems especially striking when viewed from Asia, where I have been traveling these past few years, and where political frustration has been intensifying all through the last decade despite—some might even say because of—record-breaking economic growth. In Thailand in 2006, the urban middle class revolted against a populist prime minister and received the support of the country's military, leading to chaotic violence on the streets in Bangkok. China, too, has had its moments of middle-class disaffection. In the month following the collision of two trains on China's high-speed-rail network, tens of thousands of well-to-do protesters in Dalian, known as the "Bangalore" of China, succeeded in closing down a chemical plant.

Such incidents, which reveal the frustrations of articulate and largely well-connected people, have been widely covered in the international media. Economic growth in poor countries, it is widely believed, inevitably creates a progressive-minded middle class—one that is eager to affirm its rights and to extend them to its underprivileged compatriots, bringing about democratic and accountable governments. This is at least how it seems within the information ecosystem of the global middle class, with its many echo chambers in the national and international media, which are attuned to the fears and preoccupations of people like us—those, for instance, who might be reading this essay. In the past decade, billionaires, billionaire-friendly legislators, and CEO-worshiping writers and journalists have together constituted what the political economist Ha-Joon Chang calls a "powerful propaganda machine, a financial-intellectual complex backed by money and power"—and they have constructed their own powerful version of reality.

In heavily populated countries such as India, even a small number of people moving into the middle class made for an awe-inspiring spectacle, leading *Foreign Affairs* to declare the country, where the world's poorest people live, a "roaring capitalist success story." It was possible, until very recently, to ignore the bad news—the suicides, for instance, of hundreds of thousands of Indian farmers in the past decade. The success narrative of global capitalism could also exclude the wide range of forceful dissent among the real toilers of globalization in Asia. It is clear, however, that these undercurrents always point to larger conflicts and tensions within Asian societies, which will shape the political future of many parts of the continent—further imperiling the prospect of justice and dignity for hundreds of millions of people who have yet to enter the cycle of steady socioeconomic growth that in the West is coming to an end.

In postcolonial India and China, where billions are being coerced into a transition from agrarian to urban-industrial economies, this cycle had barely begun before it started to splutter. A secure and dignified life seems even more remote for most as a tiny minority hives off the fruits of "economic growth." Worried by the prospect of social unrest, China's communist leaders frankly describe their nation's apparently booming economy as, in Chinese premier Wen Jiabao's words, "unstable, unbalanced, uncoordinated, and ultimately unsustainable."

Agricultural and factory labor still constitutes the vast majority of the workforce in populous countries such as India and China. These laborers are also the people who shape political life more enduringly than the smooth-tongued tweeters and Facebookers, such as those in the Anna Hazare movement, whose revolution, however evanescent, will always be televised. Watching India's main news channels, you would not have realized—probably because the protesters don't carry many banners in English, post videos of themselves on YouTube, or receive endorsements from Bollywood stars—that rolling strikes disrupted production for months at Maruti Suzuki India Ltd., which makes nearly half the cars sold in India.

You would have no sense of the strong backlash against globalization among the Indian poor or of the gravity of the civil war in central and eastern India, where indigenous peoples led by armed Maoist militants across a broad swath of commodities-rich forests are fighting their dispossession by mining companies that are backed by the Indian government. Early last year, India's Supreme Court censured the government for creating an informal militia against communist militants. Claiming that "the poor are being pushed to the wall," the court blamed increasing violence in the country on "predatory forms of capitalism, supported by the state."

China, too, manifests all the symptoms of a highly unequal society on the boil. In late 2011 and early 2012, workers demanding better wages led strikes across Guangdong province. In one of a series of similar incidents, migrant workers in Guangdong rioted for days in June 2011 after a wage dispute, smashing cars and setting fire to police cruisers. Sun Liping, a professor of sociology at Beijing's Tsinghua University, estimates that China had 180,000 "mass incidents" in 2010, double the number from 2006. Certainly, the communist regime's wager that continued growth will keep the masses content seems lost.

This is visible most dramatically in the province of Tibet, where riots erupted in March 2008 and where, since March 2011, more than a score of Tibetan protesters have immolated themselves. Many Western commentators scrambling to interpret the protests find that they don't need to work especially hard. Surely the Tibetans are the latest of many brave peoples to rebel against communist totalitarianism? The rhetorical templates of the cold war are still close at hand, shaping Western discussions of Islam and Asia.

Dusting off the hoary oppositions between the free and unfree worlds, the *Wall Street Journal* declared that religious freedom was the main issue. "On the streets of Lhasa, China has again had a vivid demonstration of the power of conscience to move people to action against a soulless, and brittle, state." This is stirring stuff. Never mind that the Tibetans have had more religious freedom in recent years than at any time since the Cultural Revolution. Eager to draw tourists to Tibet, Chinese authorities have helped to rebuild many of the monasteries destroyed by Red Guards in the 1960s and 1970s, turning them into Disneylands of Buddhism. Tibet and Tibetan Buddhism have even inspired a counterculture among Chinese jaded by their new affluence.

Indeed, Tibet's economy has surpassed China's average growth rate, helped by generous subsidies from Beijing and more than a million tourists a year. The vast rural hinterland shows few signs of this growth, but Lhasa, with its shopping malls, glass-and-steel office buildings, massage parlors, and hair salons, resembles a Chinese provincial city on the make. Tibet has been enlisted into what is arguably the biggest and swiftest modernization in history: China's development on the model of consumer capitalism, cheered by the Western financial media, which found in China the corporate holy grail of low-priced goods and high profits. Tibetans—whose biggest problem, according to Rupert Murdoch, is believing that the Dalai Lama "is the son of God"—have the chance to be on the right side of history; they could discard their superstitions and embrace, like Murdoch, China's brave new world.

So why do they want independence? According to a recent

edition of the *Economist*, in the prefecture of Ganzi, the setting
for several self-immolations in 2012, rural incomes rose by an
average of 30 percent in 2011 and are expected to rise just as
much in 2012. So how is it that, as the magazine put it in 2008,
"years of rapid economic growth, which China had hoped would
dampen separatist demands, have achieved the opposite"?

For one, the Chinese failed to consult Tibetans about the
kind of economic growth they wanted. In this sense, at least,
Tibetans are not much more politically impotent than the hundreds of millions of hapless Chinese uprooted by China's Faus-
tian pact with consumer capitalism. The Tibetans share their
frustration with farmers and tribal peoples in the Indian states
of West Bengal and Orissa—who, although apparently inhab-
iting the world's largest democracy, are confronting a murderous axis of politicians, businessmen, and militias determined to
corral their ancestral lands into a global network of profit. The
usual simpleminded oppositions between authoritarianism and
democracy deployed in discussions of India and China are not
of much use here.

Chinese-style development, which heavily favors urban
areas over rural ones, could only exacerbate economic inequality and threaten traditions such as nomadic lifestyles. The
unavailability of jobs, together with the undermining of the
Tibetan language, has led to a general feeling of disempower-
ment among the population. Not surprisingly, Deng Xiaoping's
post-Tiananmen gamble—that people intoxicated with prosperity will not demand political change—failed in Tibet. Like
predominantly rural ethnic minorities elsewhere, Tibetans
lack the temperament or training needed for a fervent belief in
the utopia of modernity—a consumer lifestyle in urban
centers—promised by China.

A Tibetan interviewed by researchers from Gongmeng
Law Research Centre (a Beijing-based NGO that was shut

down by the Chinese authorities after it published a report on Tibetan protests in 2008) spelled out the radical difference of worldview: "A Tibetan's prosperity is more about freedoms such as religious belief, a respect for people, a respect for life, the kind of prosperity you get from extending charity to others." Chinese-style modernization has imposed alien values on Tibetans, forcing them to accept "development" and "consumption" as the last word. Far from losing his aura during his long exile, the Dalai Lama has come to symbolize more urgently than ever to Tibetans their cherished and threatened identity. It has also become clear to Tibetans that they pay a high price for other people's enhanced lifestyles. Global warming has caused the glaciers of the Tibetan plateau, which regulate the water supply to the Ganges, Indus, Brahmaputra, Mekong, Thanlwin, Yangtze, and Yellow rivers, to melt at an alarming rate, threatening the livelihoods of hundreds of millions in Asia.

Woeser, a Tibetan poet and essayist, told me when I met her in Beijing in 2007 that not even the Cultural Revolution undermined Tibet as much as the feckless modernization of recent years. The new rail link from Beijing to Lhasa, which started operating in 2007, has further deepened the Tibetan sense of siege. No Tibetan I met in Lhasa that year had any doubt that the railway was devised by and for the Han Chinese, thousands of whom had already begun to pour into the city every day, monopolizing jobs and causing severe inflation.

In the past two decades, new railways have economically integrated China's remote provinces of Qinghai and Xinjiang, making them available for large-scale resettlement by the surplus population. China, its leaders insist, will rise "peacefully," and they may be right insofar as China refrains from the invasions and occupations that Japan resorted to in its attempt to modernize and catch up with Western imperial powers. But it is not hard to see that China has employed in Xinjiang and now Tibet some of the same means of internal colonialism that the United States used during its own westward expansion. Propelled by an insatiable global thirst for consumer markets and natural resources, China has done little to allay the fear that Tibetans could soon meet the fate of Native Americans first confined to reservations—reduced, in the words of the Tibetan novelist Jamyang Norbu, to a "sort of broken third-rate people" who, some years from now, will be "begging from tourists."

Western commentators may continue to rail at the straw man of communism in China. Tibetans, however, seem to have sensed that they confront a capitalist modernity more destructive of tradition, and more ruthlessly exploitative of the sacred land they walk on, than any adversary they have known in their tormented history.

There were, of course, some specific conditions that triggered the recent protests in Tibet. In *The Force of Obedience*, ostensibly about Tunisia, the sociologist Béatrice Hibou offers some insights into the psychologies of many other semiglobalized and unequal societies. Hibou describes how it wasn't so much top-down coercion by a one-party state as the promise and practices of inclusion into global modernity—the visible bonanza of growth in gross domestic product, the creation and co-optation of local elites, and the myth of an ever-imminent "economic miracle" that would lift all boats—that generated a kind of "obedience" among the majority of the population.

For a long time, things seemed appealingly "stable" to foreign governments and investors. Tunisia had achieved a satisfactory macroeconomic equilibrium. It was slowly integrating into the world market. The widely advertised possibility that anyone could join the conspicuously consuming new middle class seemed to be defusing political anger among the disenfranchised. And then a poor vegetable vendor named Mohamed Bouazizi broke the spell, burning himself to death and igniting mini-revolutions across West Asia and North Africa.

What, then, you might ask, is the fate of democratic rights in much of Asia, where they have always existed precariously, frequently undermined by military coups and authoritarian governments? Here, too, there is more than meets the eye of the Western media. Early in 2012, I found myself wandering through the strange but distinctive arena of one of Asia's latest conflicts: CentralWorld, allegedly the biggest shopping mall in Southeast Asia. Protesters supporting Thaksin Shinawatra—Thailand's populist ex–prime minister and a self-made, extremely rich businessman—had set up base camp in the mall's big plaza in May 2010. During a widely covered clash with security forces, they had set the building on fire, destroying much of it.

The newly renovated mall—and the traffic outside, restored to Bangkok gridlock—can project, again, an image of uninterrupted prosperity and consumption. However, Thailand itself—remote-controlled by Thaksin from Dubai—looks no more stable, or closer to being a functional democracy, than at any other time since the Asian financial crisis of 1997.

Since the late 1950s, most Western commentators reflecting on the fate of democracy in the developing and mostly nondemocratic world have shared a broad assumption: that middle and other aspiring classes created by industrial capitalism would bring about accountable and democratic governments. This was an axiom of the "modernization" theory. First proposed during the cold war as a gradualist and peaceful alternative to communist-style revolution, it was revived in the 1990s to explain events in South Korea, Thailand, and Taiwan, where educated and politicized populations emerged to demand elected governments from their longstanding authoritarian-minded rulers.

The theory always had some strong critics, most notably Samuel Huntington, who, in *Political Order in Changing Societies* (1968), questioned whether social and economic transformation in developing societies is always benign or leads to democracy. Failing to take into account the profound isolation and insecurity experienced by many in largely poor and extremely unequal countries, the theory also naively assumed that the rising middle class would form a progressive political avant-garde.

Modernization theorists, resident in a simple world defined by the ideological binaries of communism and capitalism, were hardly in a position to anticipate the vast, complex, and unpredictable forces of economic globalization we live with today: how they would weaken national sovereignty, and turn electoral democracy itself into another source of the seemingly permanent political conflict and instability in large parts of the world. This is true of Thailand, among many other nation-states. Much like Vladimir Putin in Russia, Thaksin emerged after a devastating economic crisis in the late 1990s, promising to restore the pride of a country that felt itself scorned and humiliated by foreigners. Thailand seemed to need a politician who could cope with external pressures and also deal with the internal challenges posed by increasingly politicized masses, restless ethnic minorities, and rising economic inequality; and Thaksin seemed to fit the bill.

With his social-welfarist schemes and aggressive rhetoric, he soon alienated the urban middle class and—an important constituency in Thailand—the royalist elites in the military and bureaucracy. Like many successful populists, he had sighted an electorally underrepresented majority among Thailand's rural and urban poor. As it turned out, securing their votes was as far as he was willing to go in the direction of democracy.

Even as he instituted universal health care and consolidated his base among a large population left behind by economic growth, Thaksin cracked down on press freedoms, undermined the judiciary, and launched a bloody assault on the Malay Muslim population of South Thailand. Projecting an image of brute machismo—again, like Putin in, for example, Chechnya—he became at the same time East Asia's leading exemplar of crony capitalism, installing his friends and relatives in strategic positions in the state and the private sector. Finally, Thailand's older, paternalistic elites revolted against his attempt to create a one-man democracy. Confronted with an invincibly popular politician, the elites were forced to resort in 2006 to an old-fashioned military coup, endowing Thaksin with the aura of a martyred democrat. Successive elections, most recently in 2011, have proved that a majority of Thais still back Thaksin in spite of his contempt for civil liberties. But then the middle class that originally supported him before turning against him has even weaker credentials as democrats.

Certainly, the cold war prejudice that middle-class beneficiaries of capitalism are programmed for democracy looks ready for the trash heap of history. In Russia, the small middle class created during the long reign of Vladimir Putin coexisted well, until very recently, with an oligarchical dictatorship that impoverished a majority of Russians. And our distaste for Putin should not blind us to the fact that the middle-class opposition to him is led by an extreme nationalist, who would deny democratic rights to many of Russia's ethnic and religious minorities.

The lack of progressive political choices is evident even in India, where a middle-class campaign against corruption last year was led by a man—Anna Hazare—with a Taliban-like faith in the virtues of hanging, flogging, and amputation. Last month a survey in the country's bestselling newsweekly, *India Today*, revealed that Narendra Modi, a Hindu nationalist implicated in a pogrom that killed two thousand Muslims in 2002, was the middle class's top choice as prime minister.

But then our many soothing illusions about enlightened middle classes are best maintained by an indifference to recent history, which is replete with examples of how contemporary global capitalism, unleashing severe inequalities and empowering small elites everywhere, can prove incompatible with fledgling democracies in poor countries. Middle classes in Singapore and Malaysia complained little about their undemocratic governments. The conservative nationalism of China's middle-class beneficiaries of post-Mao economic growth is a well-documented phenomenon. Until the Asian financial crisis, the Suharto regime in Indonesia enjoyed broad and eager support among the country's middle class.

In many countries where despotic regimes were finally unseated in the 1980s and '90s—Thailand, South Korea, Taiwan—regular elections have hardly amounted to democracy. Freely and fairly elected, Thaksin was no less a ruthless demagogue than Putin and Venezuela's Hugo Chávez, who also received unequivocal endorsement at the ballot box.

In some countries, elections—usually the means to the end of democracy—have become an end in themselves. Thailand has had its *nak leuaktang,* or "electocrats"—professional politicians primarily devoted to self-enrichment. India's leading public intellectual, Ashis Nandy, believes that his country's much-battered democracy, too, is dwindling into "psephocracy."

What is the prospect for democracy? It is not the question we should be asking now, even if it was piously and frequently raised during the heyday of modernization theory. Today, a political inquiry about any country should start with this question: which figure or political formation looks likely to manage the social, political, and economic conflicts unleashed by uneven globalization, and on whose behalf?

Certainly, as the differing cases of Russia, China, India, and Thailand reveal, authoritarian figures offering quick technocratic solutions to political and economic problems are here to stay, and they will seek support among the beneficiaries of globalization even as they try to keep the masses passively committed to, or distracted by, the larger project of national greatness.

Of course, once the masses have been awakened, they will demand a larger share of the political and economic goods, bringing them inevitably into conflict with already privileged classes. The days of "obedience" are long gone. It would be absurd to predict a repeat of the 1930s, when freshly politicized mass societies, angered by internal chaos and humiliations abroad, and frustrated with the weaknesses of bourgeois democracy, eagerly embraced authoritarian rulers. No pivotal event like the burning of the Reichstag seems to have occurred yet. Yet, walking through Southeast Asia's biggest mall, I couldn't help but wonder if its immolation in 2010 might one day possess the same iconic significance.

"15M": The *Indignados*

Salvador Martí Puig

Salvador Martí Puig is a permanent lecturer at the University of Salamanca, where he is director of the master's and PhD programs in political science.

> *Madrid's iconic central square, La Puerta del Sol, was the site of a strange convergence of the cyber age and the Middle Ages....As the Madrid police prepared to eject the first "indignados"...legally savvy bloggers tweeted: "Puerta del Sol is on the Cañada Real grazing paths; we have the right to sleep there."*
>
> *The fledgling protest movement was...claiming protection under a...decree...that protects the rights of shepherds to camp out with their flocks...on...hundreds of ancient grazing routes.*
>
> —Andy Robinson, reporter for the Barcelona
> daily *La Vanguardia*, June 8, 2011, *The Nation*

The expansion and growth of Spain's economy that began in the late 1970s produced a strong feeling that the country had won a place in the club of wealthy nations. Nevertheless, not everything was in order. Two elements formed a painful Achilles' heel: huge private debt and an unemployment rate that was double the European average and whose main victims were young people.

Without a doubt, Spain's economy offered very few employment opportunities for the young. Many chose not to work for low wages, staying in their hometowns, living with their parents, and enjoying the country's boom. Their interest in conventional politics was weak, following the general pattern in southern Europe: the level of electoral abstention was over 60 percent, and the numbers of those registered for political parties and trade unions were relatively low. Trust in politicians, the government, parliament, and the justice system was virtually nil.

In 2007 the word "crisis" began to appear, destroying the "Spanish miracle" in one fell swoop. In 2011, the economy ground to a halt, budgets and salaries were cut, unemployment (according to Organisation for Economic Co-operation and Development data) reached 22 percent, and youth unemployment rose to over 47 percent. Of course, Spain was not an

Transhumant and human traffic: Sheep pass through Madrid's Puerta del Sol on October 30, 2011. The *indignados'* right to camp out in Madrid derived from a decree issued in 1273 by the Castilian monarch Alfonso X (1221–1284). Transhumance, or the movement of livestock, continues in Spain to this day. *(Associated Press)*

isolated case. Iceland, Ireland, Greece, and Portugal had suffered the effects of the crisis, and their citizens had taken to the streets. In Lisbon, on March 12, 2011, three hundred thousand young people protested, using the slogan *Geração à Rasca* — Portugal's desperate generation. Madrid erupted on May 15. The date was later shortened to "15M," giving the *indignados* movement its name. *Indignados* means "the outraged." It was a week before local elections, and the movement soon began to redefine politics. Within five months, the *Guardian* called the 15M movement "the most interesting political development since the death of Franco in 1975."

In fact, several groups had preceded the 15M: *V de Vivienda* and the *Plataforma de Afectados por la Hipoteca*, which fought for affordable housing; *Juventud sin future*, young people who protested against the precariousness and commercialization of education; and the *No les votes* and *Democracia Real YA* movements, which rejected the main political parties. Active neighborhood and municipal assemblies had also had a strong presence.

It was in the context of these earlier groups that the events of May 15 gained the country's, and then the world's, attention. *Democracia Real YA* had organized a protest. The protest was met by repression on the part of the authorities. Police brutality was in itself nothing new in Madrid, but within a few hours, some fifty thousand had gathered in the Puerta del Sol.

Researchers who aim to find out why people rebel also aim to find out why power is challenged and confronted at a particular time. The answer is never simple, but Cornell University's Sidney Tarrow, a political scientist and sociologist, maintains that the "when" can explain to a large extent the "why" and the "how." Theorists call the context that facilitates the appearance of social movements the political opportunity structure, or POS. The basic idea is that a set of circumstances makes collective action more or less likely. In this formulation, various factors reduce the costs and consequences of collective action, the disaffected discover potential allies, and the authorities show themselves to be vulnerable. Following this argument, we could say that the right climate for the 15M movement existed because on May 22, local elections were to be held throughout Spain, and there were regional elections scheduled for thirteen of the seventeen Autonomous Regions.

What was the relationship between the upcoming elections and the mobilizing dynamic of the 15M movement? Possibly, the authorities were less likely to use repression to move the protesters, and people saw that it was possible, worthwhile, and low-risk to go out into the streets to express their frustration and discontent. The police gave assurances that they would not intervene if there were acts of provocation. In addition, in the context of the international media glare in which the movement found itself, the violent eviction from public spaces would have been a public relations nightmare for a democratic country—particularly given that a large part of Spain's economy is based on tourism. Spain's international image was at risk and the authorities knew it. So did the protesters.

The 15M organizers were able not only to attract attention and gain sympathy for the movement but also to find points of agreement among a large and heterogeneous group of people on several issues. The considerable and expressive protest that emerged was more a denouncement than a proposal, and it was for this reason that the protesters called themselves the *indignados*. Although it is not easy to synthesize their grievances, Carlos Taibo, of the Universidad Autónoma de Madrid, cites three main issues: (1) a rejection of establishment political parties, on the grounds that their representatives could be bought and sold and that there was a disconnect between the parties and the demands of ordinary citizens; (2) a denouncement of the degree to which financial markets and institutions dictated government policies; and (3) unemployment, layoffs, and large firms moving their factories out of the country and gloating about profits.

According to sociologists Kerman Calvo, Teresa Gómez-Pastrana, and Luis Mena, the principal motives of the protesters were: anger at the banks, corruption, and the electoral system, and frustration and disgust with the press. The slogans that the protesters chanted expressed their demands in fairly cutting and ingenious ways:

> There's not enough bread for all this chorizo.
> They call it democracy but it isn't.
> I think, therefore I get in the way.
> Money's not the problem, it's the thieves.
> If you don't let us dream, we won't let you sleep.
> France and Greece fight, Spain wins at football.
> Politicians and bankers, wake up!
> Focused on robbing you.
> I think of Iceland.
> Yes We Campo.

Like the Arab Spring, the 15M movement was a 2.0 mobilization. News of the *indignados* spread immediately across the Web, initially on the movement's various websites and later from the Twitter accounts of those camping out: acampadasol@ in Madrid, acampadacatalunya@ in Barcelona. Indeed, those who participated were mainly "digital natives" of university age and older. Surveys show that 65.3 percent of the participants found out about the call to protest via Facebook/Tuenti, 34.7 percent from a friend, 17.8 percent via email, 17.7 percent via the Internet, 13.9 percent via the press, 11.9 percent via an organization, and 9.9 percent via Twitter. Protests spread to almost all of the fifty provincial capitals in Spain and to various cities abroad, including Berlin, London, Paris, and Buenos Aires, eventually reaching Mexico.

The most striking thing about the protest was its staying power and its capacity to spread. According to Calvo, Gómez-Pastrana, and Mena, some of the reasons for the movement's longevity and reach were, in order of importance: a desire to occupy public spaces and to protest openly; discontent with the attitude of the media; the lack of understanding on the part of the Central Electoral Board, which prohibited the protests; the support and sympathy of locals; the sense of belonging to a group; and, last, the motivation of the movement's leaders.

The call to protest without mediation by activists is something new in Spain; above all, it's a pattern of mobilization that is specific to new generations. (Eventually, both younger and older people who had never before been part of a protest movement joined the protesters in the streets.) While the phenomenon of virtual mobilization gave the movement a fresh, new, and spontaneous face, it also resulted in weak cohesion. Consequently, the threat it posed to the authorities was smaller than it might have been.

With regard to internal organization, the movement worked via assemblies, without leaders, and on a decentralizing principle. Thus each city was in charge of its own priorities, demands, and manifestos. In this sense, the movement was similar to a confederation of sovereign and symbiotic local movements: each city's template was the same, in essence, but there were different agendas and interests, and what happened in one place had an impact on what happened in others. Public assemblies took place mainly in public squares, and, as was the case later in Zuccotti Park and elsewhere in the United States, there were working groups that concentrated on legal issues, communication, action, activities, neighborhood issues, the dissemination of information, and so forth. Of central importance was the occupation of public spaces, including squares and avenues, and the use of unconventional, peaceful forms of protest. In this sense, one sees economist Albert O. Hirschman's point that for many people collective action is attractive not only because it can be exciting and risky but also because of the opportunity it offers for self-expression.

Up to a point, what happened in the days following May 15 influenced the outcome of both the May 22 elections and elections held on November 20. The impact of the movement also goes beyond what happened in those elections and may be felt long-term in Spanish society and politics. May 22 saw an increase in the protest vote: a 48 percent increase in null votes and a 37 percent increase in blank votes compared to the 2007 elections. At the same time, if we take a closer look at the results of these elections at the local level, it is clear that in the larger municipalities—where the incidence of the movement was more significant—the protest vote was even greater, according to the political scientist and sociologist Manuel Jiménez Sánchez.

It is worth pointing out the progress made by the conservative party—in the hands of the Partido Popular (the People's Party, or PP)—which saw an increase of 7.05 percent compared to 2007. At the same time, the center-left governing party, the Spanish Socialist Workers' Party (PSOE), lost 1.5

million votes—or 19.3 percent of votes in relation to the 2007 elections (from 7,760,865 to 6,276,087). A similar trend occurred in the general elections of November 20: the PP achieved a comfortable victory, with 44.62 percent of the vote, compared to 28.73 percent for the PSOE and 6.92 percent for Izquierda Unida, or the United Left.

Whether a causal relationship exists between this considerable loss of PSOE votes and the 15M mobilization is uncertain, but it does seem that progressives have punished the government for introducing austerity measures (many of which were dictated by the European Union) and for failing to prevent the massive destruction of jobs that occurred from 2009 to 2011. We could argue that, as is often the case, the voters who are most sensitive to issues of equality, justice, and transparency are those who stop voting when they feel let down, deserting the political groups that claim to be center-left.

It remains to be seen how the proposals of the 15M movement will enter into the political agenda in the more immediate future. Some issues, such as electoral reform, may be debated, whereas others, such as the control of politics by finance, are less likely to be raised unless the mobilizations continue. Nevertheless, the movement has not disappeared and is still active in some public spaces, generating activities and appearing in different forums. What isn't yet clear is if this mobilization will mark the beginning of a more critical, demanding, and vigilant citizen political culture or if, on the contrary, it was just an explosion of antipolitical populism. This is one of the most relevant issues. How can the movement evolve? Will there be a repoliticization of a sector of society or will the distance between citizens and politicians widen? If a sector retains its defiant attitude, will it become more radical now that the conservatives are in power? It is still very early to offer a satisfactory answer, but we can conclude that the 15M movement is a call to attention for the existing democracy in Spain. It is a call for politicians to move closer to citizens, for greater transparency in public affairs, and for a type of politics that is not subordinated to the markets but rather to the interests of citizens.

In the Footsteps of Salvador Allende: Chile and the Occupy Movement

Ariel Dorfman

Ariel Dorfman, the Chilean American writer and human rights activist, holds the Walter Hines Page Chair at Duke University. His books, written both in Spanish and English, have been translated into more than forty languages and his plays staged in over one hundred countries. He has received numerous international awards, including the Laurence Olivier Award (for *Death and the Maiden*, which Roman Polanski made into a feature film). His latest book is the memoir *Feeding on Dreams: Confessions of an Unrepentant Exile*. He contributes regularly to major newspapers worldwide.

If, twenty-two years ago, Camila Vallejo had been in the streets of Santiago leading a student uprising against injustice and inequality as she did throughout 2011, I might well be writing these words in Chile rather than from the distance of Durham, North Carolina. I might have decided not to leave my country and become an expatriate.

Democracy had returned to Chile in that year of 1990 and so had I, coming back with my wife, Angélica, and our two boys to participate in a new dawn for our land after seventeen years of General Augusto Pinochet's dictatorship. Back then, of course, Camila Vallejo was a two-year-old toddler and not yet the charismatic undergraduate who would become a worldwide celebrity (one of *Time*'s Persons of 2011, and *the* Person of the Year, according to the readers of the London *Guardian*). And

Camila Vallejo, surrounded by photographers. *(Photograph by Roberto Candia, Associated Press)*

yet, I met plenty of youngsters like her during that 1990 resettlement journey. Like me, they were full of hope that our people would be able to overcome the terrorist legacy of Pinochet and the glaring abyss that separated—the term had not been popularized yet, but Chile was a country that obscenely exemplified the trend—the 99 percent from the small group that owned our wealth and controlled power. But in postdictatorial Chile there was no space for those young rebels to breathe or find major popular support, no space for a Camila Vallejo to flourish. The land was too deeply wounded, too filled with fear. Those who had headed the Resistance and were governing the country felt that it was imprudent, indeed even dangerous, to rock the boat, to risk another coup—the sort of violence that the military (and those who had benefited financially from its rule) kept on threatening. Hampered by a series of roadblocks that Pinochet had left behind, the democratic forces of the Concertación were unable to undo much of the damage that lingered from the past. Among the many authoritarian institutions and projects that remained deeply tainted was the educational system, rife with privilege and greed, and sorely lacking the resources to fulfill the promise to the young of a better life.

The student revolt of 2011 did not merely question that aspect of a broken-down policy but—and here is where it overlaps and reverberates with the worldwide Occupy movement and the Arab Spring—it mistrusted the whole model behind that policy; it cast doubt on the way in which Chile had dreamt itself, had excluded radical change from the agenda. Camila Vallejo (and when I pinpoint her name, I am, of course, really referring to the movement that she embodies) understood that an era was ending, that there could be no solution to education at all levels in Chile without creating a different land, where the inhabitants, and not the profits, were the priority.

Sound familiar?

Yes, except that there is one (at least) remarkable difference between this and other current rebellions.

What has characterized so many of these insurgent global movements is the gap between the protesters and the political parties. One of the strengths (and possible weaknesses) of the Occupy Wall Street activists, for instance, is that they will not allow themselves to be absorbed into any preexisting structures, that they have no "theory" or long-term strategy for how change can really occur. And one of the surprises of the elections in the Arab countries freed from autocratic oppression is how poorly those who had fought the battles in the streets fared in the electoral clashes that followed.

A similar wariness and disgust with the political elite pervades the Chilean protests, composed as well of environmentalists and those who struggle for the rights of women and gays and native populations. Yet Camila Vallejo is a member (she has been since 1988) of the Communist Party, and as such she has been criticized for not being revolutionary enough, for working within the framework of democracy and believing that change needs to happen through parliamentary means. In fact, in December 2011 she was ousted as president of the Student Unión of the Universidad de Chile by a more extreme extraparliamentary group to her left. And so, the incredibly young and fiery Camila is a member of an organization that was founded in the north of Chile ninety years ago, an old, even ancient, party by the country's standards. Indeed, she may soon be a candidate for Congress.

In that sense, she follows in the footsteps of Salvador Allende, the first Socialist in history to be elected president through the popular ballot. She believes, as he did, that popular mobilization needs to be accompanied by organized, organic participation in the system in order to alter it radically.

And just in case readers think Vallejo is a fluke, it's enough to turn to Giorgio Jackson, another major student leader of the 2011 protests — less well known outside Chile but just as influential and lucid. He appeared before a group of senators and they made the mistake of televising the proceedings — he made intellectual mincemeat of them. Giorgio has announced that, along with a vast cohort of others, he is founding a new political movement, Revolución Democrática, that will build an alternative to the present parties and which may eventually participate in elections. He has not ruled out running for Congress in 2013, once he has graduated as a civil engineer from the Universidad Católica.

Camila and Giorgio are the future of Chile.

If they had been around when I settled in Santiago in 1990, I would have tried to walk by their side — or as close as possible or maybe a few steps behind their young, exalted figures. I would have found in their rebellion reasons to stay in my country. Instead, disappointed that the dream of justice I had for

Chile, nurtured during my endless exile, seemed no longer possible, I left for the United States.

Where, twenty years later, the Occupiers of Wall Street made me feel at home in my adopted homeland, made me feel that I was not alien or apart, that there was hope anywhere, that there are many Camilas and everlasting Giorgios awaiting their moment in history.

¡Basta YA! Chilean Students Say "Enough"

Nora Lustig, Alejandra Mizala, and G. Eduardo Silva

Nora Lustig is Samuel Z. Stone Professor of Latin American Economics at Tulane University and non-resident fellow at the Center for Global Development and the Inter-American Dialogue. Alejandra Mizala is professor of economics at the Center for Applied Economics, University of Chile. Eduardo Silva is Lydian Professor of Political Science at Tulane University.

When Occupy Wall Street burst on the political scene in lower Manhattan's Zuccotti Park in the summer of 2011, it energized flagging public debate about socioeconomic fairness in a nation in which inequality has risen to embarrassing levels for an advanced democracy. The kernel of a social movement that aims to articulate the demands of those left behind or let down, OWS is a refreshing and long-overdue response to the Great Recession and the concentration of wealth in the United States. In a way, OWS can be seen to represent those who have lost and who are systematically exploited and excluded, as opposed to those who do not want to pay for bailouts or a social safety net—that is, the Tea Party and its supporters. OWS activists are the *indignados*, or the outraged, of the United States. Perhaps the people who lost homes and jobs, whose incomes did not rise even in times of prosperity, who do not have access to quality education, who are denied health insurance, and who continue to face discrimination will finally carve themselves a space for transformational social dissent. But is OWS a vehicle for them to do that, and why were the inroads it made in the fall of 2011 not more significant? How does OWS compare to similar contemporary social movements that have succeeded in garnering widespread support and placing their issues at the forefront of the political and policy agenda in their countries? One place to look to is the 2011 Chilean student movement, which has several key characteristics in common with OWS.

The Chilean student movement began in May–June 2011 with marches and the occupation of school buildings. It was able to quickly rally public opinion (70 percent of the public supports the movement), it kept the conservative government of billionaire president Sebastián Piñera on the defensive for six months, and it forced the political establishment to deal with its grievances. Although many observers and the Chilean government itself were taken by surprise—high-growth Chile is considered a model of economic success—the students' complaints are legitimate. Because education is a major gateway to social mobility, students want not only access to a college education but assurances that what they get is affordable and of high quality. The members of the new middle class created by Chile's strong economic growth over the past twenty years do not want to lose their status either because they cannot afford to pay back their loans when the economy is failing or because of inferior training. Students essentially protested because the Chilean educational system—in spite of its undeniable progress—had failed to reduce entrenched inequality of opportunity in one of the most unequal countries in the world.

Although access to higher education, including among the poorest segments of the population, rose steadily between 1990 and 2011 (among those eighteen to twenty-four years old, enrollment increased from 16 percent to 50 percent), the gap in access between the rich and the poor remains large. The difference in enrollment rates between the poorest and the richest 10 percent is seventy percentage points: 20 percent and over 90 percent, respectively. To a large extent the expansion in access was possible due to the mushrooming of expensive private universities under the regime of Augusto Pinochet, president of Chile from 1974 to 1990.

There are three types of universities in Chile: public; traditional, pre-1981 private universities; and Pinochet-era private universities. None of them are open to all, and all of them charge tuition. Although by law not-for-profit, the Pinochet-era private universities turned into highly profitable ventures through a dubious arrangement involving payments from the universities themselves to the owners of the land on which the universities are built. The quality of these institutions is uneven, and there is no reliable system to help prospective students choose the right place. Tuition (even at public universities) is relatively high and is paid by the nonwealthy with student loans, some at a subsidized interest rate but many not. (Beginning in 2006, the nonsubsidized rate was set at 5.9 percent. In early 2012, a bill was introduced to reduce the interest rate to 2 percent, but at this writing it had not passed.)

On average, the cost of sending a child to college is around 40 percent of the family income for those in the bottom 60 percent of the population. Many young people who hope to use education as a vehicle to move up the socioeconomic ladder find themselves unable to complete their degrees because of the cost and mounting debt. Even when students are able to graduate, they end up without access to the higher-paying jobs that go to those who have attended elite universities. Saddled with low-paying jobs, young graduates and their families struggle or default. Crushed hopes of upward mobility—the failure to gain entry to the burgeoning middle class—is cause for deep-seated frustration and understandable anger. Effort does not really lead to economic success.

In response to these difficult conditions, the Confederation of Chilean Students (Confederación de Estudiantes de Chile, or CONFECH) drafted a proposal for reform—the Social Agreement for Chilean Education—that included university and high school student demands. These centered on free public education, quality education across all tiers of the system, an end to loopholes that allow nonprofit colleges to turn a profit, creation of a state agency to ensure quality of education and closure of said loopholes, and a more affordable and accessible university system as a whole.

Throughout the ensuing cycle of protest that culminated in a legislative battle over the 2012 budget in December 2011, students never achieved their maximum demand: to change the market-driven education model for a state-funded and state-administered system. They had consistently rejected all government overtures that limited negotiation largely to the issue of student loans, and they declared themselves dissatisfied with the results of the politicians' wrangling over the education budget. Nevertheless, the protesters achieved far more than had been accomplished in previous protests over education policy, such as the "revolution of the penguins" in 2006. Those protests were led by high school students who wore blue blazers, white shirts, and gray pants (hence the penguin moniker); university students later joined in. The protests culminated in a government-appointed blue-ribbon commission that left the students feeling sidelined. They felt that their demands for a more centralized and state-financed system were not addressed. However, the commission did recommend regulations to improve the educational system that later became law. Unlike the 2006 episode, the university-led student protests of 2011 placed the issue of inequality front and center in the national political debate, where it is likely to stay until at least the December 2013 presidential election.

The 2012 budget substantially increased funds for education in general, established new merit- and income-based scholarship programs for the bottom 60 percent of the population, and increased funds for student loans to levels the state would not have contemplated otherwise. These are to be offered at significantly lower interest rates than before, making education more accessible and affordable. A separate bill created a new state oversight agency, the Education Superintendency, whose purpose is to ensure quality education and strict adherence to not-for-profit rules. Significantly for OWS, legislative support for tax increases has surged, including from Piñera and his party. Temporary corporate tax increases to help pay for the 2010 earthquake recovery will probably be made permanent, among other measures.

Does the Chilean experience hold positive lessons for OWS? The student movement and OWS share several significant characteristics; strangely, it is precisely these characteristics that have been cited by media analysts as reasons for OWS's relative lack of traction. Members of both movements are rebelling against complex problems that potentially divide the public, such as the injustice of high levels of socioeconomic inequality in market societies. Tired of neglect and ineffectual politics as usual, their repertoire emphasizes disruptive direct action that transgresses norms of public order to focus public attention on the problems. Both movements consciously reject links to establishment politics, especially political parties and complicit insider organizations—and particularly those that might be in these political parties' pockets. They also refuse to be drawn into the policy process, claiming that as a social movement their responsibility is to force the establishment to engage with pressing issues it ignores, not to formulate policy.

Since the Chilean student movement had significant political impact, in and of themselves these characteristics cannot explain OWS's difficulty in amplifying its message. What did the Chilean students do differently? What does the Chilean experience offer as points of reflection for OWS regarding its positions? Issue framing is critical. Chilean students tackled the broad and diffuse issues of socioeconomic injustice through the prism of their educational system. Everyone had experience with this more tightly focused issue, which offered the perfect frame for the larger problem and resonated with people in many different social situations, drawing them in. Education had been turned into a commodity in a largely private system that replicated the inequalities of Chilean market society. The existing educational system could not be the vehicle by which citizens could universally aspire to social mobility. This was a frame that successfully challenged the official discourse to legitimate the market-based model. It was then extended to other issues, such as labor rights, environmental justice, and identity politics.

By doing precisely this, the Chilean student movement served as a fulcrum for coalition building with other movements—a key to increasing the power of the movement. Throughout, it maintained its autonomy, demonstrating that cooptation is not necessarily the outcome of working with others. The student movement was secure in its identity, its goals (taking the market out of education), and its targets (school administrations and the state). Members did not engage in conflicts over representation with other movements, which left a broad swath of potential allies weary of market orthodoxy free to join in.

The Chilean students had great organizational capacity, from the department or lower school levels up through colleges, university-wide, and among national confederations. At each level students voted on whether to mobilize and on the type of direct action they would employ. While rejecting in principle involvement in institutionalized politics, the Chilean student movement was very political. It sought to effect change in national education policy without getting embroiled in policy debates. It employed highly ritualized mass marches and rallies with deep roots in the history of social protest in Chile. The students obtained permits for the marches, which generally followed the same route and were limited to a timetable by the authorities. Riot police were deployed in numbers, at a distance but still visible and sufficiently menacing. The marches ended in rallies in front of government offices and the presidential palace, La Moneda. The implication was clear: problems could be solved in these buildings.

Not all was seriousness and anger; the marches had a strongly festive feeling, too. There were samba bands, dancing, huge puppets symbolizing the continuity of education policy from Pinochet to Michelle Batchelet to Piñera, banners made

Santiago: This mass kissing event, in July 2011, was both an effort on the part of Chilean students to call attention to grievances and a comment on establishment prudishness. *(Photograph by Fernando Nahuel, European Pressphoto Agency)*

by art school students, humorous drama school skits, and the famous mass-kissing events. When the official time for a march was up, the police would start to disperse the crowd. There were some violent skirmishes, and property was attacked; this was played up by national media in news reporting of the events. Students also occupied schools and universities for months to pressure administration officials. The government's attempts to divide and break the movement failed. The Chilean student movement achieved its objective of bringing the limits of market-oriented approaches to education—and to social policy more broadly—to the forefront of political discourse. By placing the issue on the agenda and by galvanizing the public's support, the students forced more established and institutionalized political actors to deal with it. This did not happen by accident. The students leveraged a critical political opportunity. The government had declared 2011 the year of higher education and had proclaimed education as the vehicle for social mobility in a market society. True to a campaign pledge, it had initiated a review of the education law inherited from the Pinochet dictatorship.

Might OWS activists think a little more politically about objectives, targets, opportunities, and actions without compromising their core values? OWS is more diverse and diffuse, but it could work at this nonetheless. "Unity in Diversity"—the watchword of the global justice movement, which successfully dealt with the problem of heterogeneous agendas, ideologies, social values, and perspectives—could be a useful guide to action. OWS activists could work on framing the issues differently. For instance, reducing income inequality requires taxation of higher-income groups. Highlighting this or some other issue as a means of understanding social inequality, particularly in ways that resonate with American political culture, could be a fruitful exercise. Whatever the frame, the exercise does not require coming up with policy position papers, or making a list of demands, or giving up on inclusiveness of issues. It does imply a more strategic approach to explaining the roots of the problem through a narrative that members of a broader public can comprehend and recognize themselves in. One of the aims of such an approach would be to rouse the public to undertake action in its own way.

In just a few months, OWS started a national conversation about inequality. With the closing of many of its encampments, the movement entered a new phase. Some said the change would ensure success. Others think the movement will fail without political partners and compromise. More than forty years ago, the victims of racial and gender discrimination, young adults who repudiated conscription and the Vietnam War, students who wanted to protect their basic rights, and the disenfranchised organized themselves in distinct but overlapping movements. The civil rights movement, the antiwar movement, and women's lib and the broader free speech and counterculture movements of the 1960s and 1970s led to fundamental changes in social norms, practices, and the law. However, as we know, the work in each case was left unfinished, and some of the gains were reversed with the ascent of conservative politics. Can OWS and its sister movements across the country seize the opportunity to move the progressive agenda forward?

Occupying the Israeli Street:
The Tents Protest Movement and
Social Justice in the Holy Land

Neri Zilber

Neri Zilber is an Institute of Current World Affairs writing fellow based in Israel. He has contributed articles on international politics, particularly the Middle East, to publications including the *Guardian*, the *Jerusalem Post*, and *Dissent*, and to PBS's *Frontline*. He holds degrees from the School of Foreign Service, Georgetown University, and the Department of War Studies, King's College London.

Before nearly half a million people took to the streets of Israel in the summer of 2011 demanding economic and social justice, before tent cities began sprouting up in cities and towns across the country, before the vast, dormant Israeli political center finally found its voice, there was cottage cheese.

Yitzhak Alrov, a twenty-five-year-old cantor and father of one from the ultra-Orthodox Jewish town of Bnei Brak, outside Tel Aviv, had finally had enough. In the early summer of 2011 he started a Facebook group calling for a boycott of the soft cheese Israelis consider a staple. Due to the elimination of government price controls three years before, the cost of cottage cheese had risen by over 40 percent. Yet the biggest outrage was that this Israeli-made product—actively marketed as a little taste of home—cost less in real terms after export, outside the country, than on a local supermarket shelf.

"There is no reason for us to be so disproportionally

screwed," Alrov was quoted as saying. His Facebook group drew over one hundred thousand supporters, and the boycott proved to be a massive success—sales of cottage cheese plummeted, with the small white containers piling up in markets untouched. The three giant dairy companies—Tnuva, Strauss, and Tara—and the domestic supermarket chains eventually lowered their prices.

The "cottage boycott" set a precedent. Faced with a politics unresponsive to its needs, the Israeli public began thinking and working outside the system. A few weeks later, another twenty-five-year-old, Dafni Leef, a freelance filmmaker, started her own Facebook group. On July 14, she moved to a tent on Tel Aviv's Rothschild Boulevard, a wide, leafy thoroughfare usually host to the city's trendy and affluent. It would be an act of rebellion, Leef said, against the high cost of housing in Israel generally and the raising of her own already substantial rent. She invited people to join her, and by the first weekend a few dozen tents and several hundred people were visible on Rothschild's central pedestrian promenade. The following week the national student union joined, giving the fledgling movement additional bodies and geographic reach. Tent cities began popping up in towns across Israel, from Kiryat Shmona in the northern Galilee hills to Jerusalem to Be'er Sheva in the southern Negev desert. "It shouldn't be this hard to make a living and support myself in this country," Leef said. "I have no family, I'm young, I work seven days a week, I'm willing to work on the Sabbath." Like most others in the country, she could not make ends meet; could not, as Israelis say, "close the month."

By the end of its first full week, the tents protest Leef had started with just a handful of other core organizers drew thirty thousand people to a Saturday-night mass demonstration through central Tel Aviv. Subsequent days saw the country's venerable trade union, the Histadrut, join the protest movement, as well as young parents decrying the cost of raising a family in Israel (a "baby carriage protest," ten thousand strong, was organized). Cabdrivers blocked a major highway in solidarity, and Israeli Arabs began setting up tent cities in predominantly Arab towns like Nazareth and Jaffa.

The following Saturday night, July 30, 2011, one hundred fifty thousand people took to the streets of Tel Aviv and other major cities. The tents protest was just over two weeks old. The numbers were remarkable—it was by far the largest protest ever held for a strictly social issue. The demonstrators yelled slogans in Hebrew: "Welfare State," "A whole generation demands a future." By far the most popular: "The people demand social justice." It became the rallying cry of the movement.

Polls indicated that 87 percent of the population supported the cause, an unprecedented number for a country normally thought of as fractious, for a citizenry seen as apathetic. Almost overnight, a youth-led, Internet-fueled grassroots phenomenon had captured the imagination of the nation.

Israel has arguably weathered the global financial crisis better than any other advanced Western economy, with high growth rates, historically low unemployment, and manageable government debt. Yet the average Israeli believes that this prosperity has failed to trickle down.

The middle class is frustrated with an economic system in which the gulf between average citizens and a superrich elite has only widened. From 2000 to 2010, CEO pay among Israel's twenty-five largest companies (according to market capitalization) increased from a measure of 49 times the average market salary in 2000 to 114 in 2010; as of 2011, only four countries in the Organisation for Economic Co-operation and Development had an income disparity between rich and poor greater than Israel's. A 2011 OECD report noted that Israel was the only member country aside from Japan that saw the real income of the bottom 10 percent of households decrease since the mid-1980s.

Income disparity, however, is only part of the story. Well before the start of the social protests, the media increasingly highlighted the rising cost of basic services like water and electricity, as well as the higher average cost of living in Israel compared to other industrialized countries. The price of automobiles,

Tel Aviv: A tents protester in Israel holding a handmade Israeli flag with the image of a house—expensive and unattainable—where the Star of David would normally be. *(Courtesy Neri Zilber)*

gasoline, cell phones, and, yes, food (including the homely cottage cheese) is higher in Israel than in many other OECD states.

Above all, buying a home in Israel is no longer a realistic possibility for many people, even for those in the middle class. Only New York City, out of the 175 largest American cities, has higher average housing prices than Israel. According to the Taub Center for Social Policy Studies in Israel, a Jerusalem-based think tank, it takes an average of 7.7 years of salary to purchase a home in Israel—compared to 2.9 in the United States, 5 in England, and 6.8 in Australia.

It's not a coincidence, therefore, that a full-blown social protest movement was initially launched as a direct revolt against the high cost of housing. The unique nature of the Israeli protests, however, resides in the fact that they took place in a prosperous economic environment. The government and the people had ostensibly done everything right—no subprime mortgage crisis as in America, no tax dereliction as in Greece, no hefty budget deficits as in Italy. Still, the average working person could not eke out a reasonable life. "[The tents protest] is the first uprising, anywhere in the world, against a successful neoliberal regime," the political philosopher Michael Walzer, visiting Israel, observed in 2011. Or, as one local columnist put it, "This is the time for 'political economy' in the sense of economics for human beings," and not just numbers.

From the Tel Aviv hipsters of Rothschild Boulevard to the religious family in Jerusalem ten people strong; from the segregated Arab encampment in Jaffa to the farmers of the Jezreel Valley north of the West Bank—all of Israel, it seemed, was now living outside in tents.

A mass demonstration in early August 2011 comprising three hundred thousand people was followed a month later, in September, by the largest protest in Israeli history. Another

Saturday night and more than four hundred thousand people—a fifteenth of the entire population—took to the streets. The equivalent, in American terms, would have been twenty million people. Mobilizing these kinds of numbers, anywhere in the world, is the biggest challenge for any fledgling political movement. In Israel, the tents protest succeeded by actively eschewing politics. From the first, the organizers emphasized repeatedly that theirs was an "apolitical" social movement that cut across age, ethnicity, geography, and party politics. Unity was paramount, so any talk about divisive issues such as the peace process or West Bank settlements was strictly avoided. The old definitions of Right and Left were no longer operative: "Everyone should come, even the far-right parties," a dovish protest leader told me.

Ultimately, the tent cities themselves—even the 1,200-tent, kilometer-long Rothschild shantytown—could not remain forever. Real-life obligations and the changing weather caused some to dwindle; municipal authorities deployed local police and city inspectors to take down those that remained.

In a democratic system such as Israel's, as in many other places, change is brought at the ballot box, incrementally. It might not be as spiritually satisfying or as sexy as occupying public spaces and marching in the streets, but there is likely no other mechanism to effect lasting change. Israelis are still waiting for this change, yet the protests did usher in a genuine public debate over increased social spending and welfare provisions in areas such as education, housing, and taxation. New government regulations were tabled, with public figures seeking to raise competitiveness in the market and lower prices; to, in effect, curtail the power of the dozen or so corporate (and often family-owned) conglomerates that dominate an estimated 30 to 40 percent of the economy.

Structural challenges remain. The massive government subsidies to the ultra-Orthodox and settler communities, the third rail of national politics, were left untouched. Efforts to curtail the defense budget and shift some of the money to social programs were quickly defeated. Stanley Fischer, the governor of the Bank of Israel, publicly fought efforts to increase government spending.

"Changing the entire order of priorities for the State of Israel," as many of the protesters demanded, will have to await the results of future elections. Still, Israel's social protests have to be understood as a consciousness-raising watershed. "The goal [of the movement] is...to teach the nation and the citizens that they have power," Yigal Rambam, a protest leader, told the daily *Haaretz* in the summer of 2011. "Not everything is a commandment from up high that we need to bend to....It's not natural law."

From Tahrir to Zuccotti: Justice but No Peace in Egypt

Chris Stanton

Between November 2011 and May 2012, Chris Stanton was the Egypt correspondent for *The National*, an English-language daily newspaper based in Abu Dhabi. Most of the information for this article came from interviews conducted with the help of a translator, Dr. Seham Abd el-Salam. Before arriving in Cairo, Stanton covered oil and gas for three years for *The National* in the Persian Gulf. He is pursuing an MBA in energy finance at the University of Texas at Austin.

The ashen-faced man who was once the fourth most powerful official in Egypt clearly wasn't going to get the benefit of the doubt from this crowd. Imprisoned within the steel cage of the defendant's cell in a Cairo courtroom, his usually dapper attire exchanged for a white jumpsuit, former interior minister Habib el-Adly gazed out at a mob of journalists and lawyers who shouted accusations that he was alternately a thief, a torturer, and a murderer. El-Adly wasn't indicted for the violence committed by his security forces—he would answer for those charges at a later hearing. Instead, he appeared on March 5, 2011, to defend himself in the first of a series of high-level corruption trials brought by prosecutors against some of the robber barons of Egypt's business and political elite.

If anger at former president Hosni Mubarak's autocratic tactics sparked the initial rally by dedicated youth activists in Tahrir Square on January 25, 2011, it was rage about corruption, cronyism, and economic stagnation among middle-class residents that carried the revolt through to his resignation on February 11. In a society in which at least a quarter of the workforce was unemployed, double-digit inflation was pushing up the cost of living each week, and even hardworking, educated Cairo professionals were earning less than $150 a month, a small band of tycoons surrounding Mubarak and his family became the most reviled people in the Arab world's most populous state. In the months after the dictator's fall, prosecutors answered the revolutionaries' call for justice against men like el-Adly and Ahmed Ezz, the Egyptian steel monopolist, with a series of convictions. Yet one year later, the protesters' fantastic hope of fixing Egypt's massive economic inequalities in one fell swoop by jailing the men in charge confronted a painful reality.

A career policeman, el-Adly, seventy-four, was brought in by Mubarak to wield an iron fist as interior minister in 1997 after Islamist militants killed sixty-two tourists and Egyptians in Luxor. Somewhere along the way, he got involved in illegal real estate deals, according to the court that found him guilty of corruption and sentenced him to twelve years in prison in May of 2011. In one instance cited by prosecutors, el-Adly netted about eight hundred thousand dollars when his staff at the interior ministry arranged for the sale of a plot of his own personal property to a contractor hired by the ministry.

To a large extent, el-Adly was a small-time player in a much larger, very public plunder of the government's resources that took place against the backdrop of a drive to deregulate and privatize an anachronistic, state-owned economy. Ahmed Ezz, a billionaire who at one point cornered as much as 65 percent of Egypt's steel market through three of his companies, jump-started his empire by illegally acquiring an export license, a court ruled in 2011. Zuhair Garana, the former minister of tourism, and Ahmed el-Maghrabi, the housing minister, each gave away or sold valuable parcels of state-owned land for a pittance to friends and family, the courts also ruled. Even the Sawiris family, the billionaire telecom and construction clan that has not been accused of any wrongdoing, built its fortune in part through snapping up newly privatized state resources.

Beginning in the mid-1990s, technocrats under Mubarak implemented an economic reform program to stabilize the Egyptian currency, reduce state interference in the economy, and privatize state-owned companies and assets. In response, the economy grew at over 5 percent most years for a decade, improving the government's fiscal position and creating a new class of ultrawealthy who built villas and shopping malls on the edges of Cairo that rival the richest suburbs of America in their glitz and luxury-brand offerings. Very little of that prosperity was passed on to the growing population, who continued to send their children to overcrowded schools with outdated curricula, sit through nightmarish traffic jams, and suffer medicine shortages at hospitals. Approximately 44 percent of Egyptians were living on less than two dollars a day, and at least half of the population depended—and still depends—on government-subsidized bread to survive. The desperation of the middle classes was laid bare in November 2010 on Eid al-Adha, the holiest day of the Muslim calendar, traditionally marked by the killing of a lamb or goat—a rare chance for a working-class Egyptian to eat meat. The 2010 holiday was called the most miserable in decades, as a spike in the price of meat and other foodstuffs put a festive meal out of reach for many families. A week later the regime stuffed ballot boxes and deployed thugs in polling stations in perhaps the most fraudulent parliamentary vote in Egyptian history. The two-day process, which effectively stripped opposition parties of their seats in the already powerless body, saw less than 10 percent of voters turn out in many districts, according to independent counts. In a cynical rationale echoed by others that day, a civil servant emerging from a polling station in a poor part of Cairo said that he knew voting would achieve nothing, but that he could not countenance the very real possibility that his name and vote would be stolen by Mubarak's ruling party.

Into this combustible mix of economic desperation and overt disenfranchisement was added a spark of inspiration from the Tunisian revolution, coaxed and fanned by the meticulous planning of a group of Egyptian activists in Cairo. In years of small-scale protests that were inevitably broken up by police, the largely university-educated organizers had learned that they would grow powerful enough to confront the regime only by uniting with the working class, said Rasha Ramzy, thirty-eight, a graduate student and veteran political activist: "I've been a protester for fourteen to fifteen years, but back then the protests were made by the elite people so they weren't effective." In the weeks leading up to the January 25 protest, a group of young activists set in motion a secret plan to bring the poor and hungry to their side. That morning, as a few hundred protesters responded to Facebook calls to gather at points across Cairo and confront lines of policemen, a small group of activists entered a slum west of the capital and gathered several thousand people with chants about wages and food prices. Swelling in size, the group entered the city's main thoroughfares and attracted enough protesters to march on Tahrir Square, the city's center. Over the next eighteen days, as the demonstrators braved violent attacks from both uniformed officers and plainclothes government thugs, men from the working class played a central role in recapturing and then holding the square. In scores of interviews about their personal reasons for participating, these men stressed the need for economic improvement and justice against the hated police force over the need for freedom and democracy.

In the ensuing year, the protesters got much of what they asked for in economic terms. The tycoons were put on trial, along with Mubarak and his sons. Workers in the public sector and many large private companies received significant wage increases. Bread and fuel subsidies have stayed in place. Yet the economy remains at a standstill—the situation is so bad that in December of 2011 Prime Minister Kamal el-Ganzouri tearfully described it to reporters as "worse than you can imagine." Foreign investors have fled in the face of political uncertainty, tourism has slowed dramatically, prices for gas exports have fallen, and major Egyptian companies have had their operations disrupted by strikes, a poorer domestic market, and regulatory uncertainty.

In the immediate term, the country needs stability and security. In the longer term, both leftist and right-leaning economists will say, it needs a drastic reform of its education system, institutionalized respect for the rule of law, and, most basically, the development of a viable private-sector economy that competes on its own without financial support from the indebted, dysfunctional government. To the newly elected Muslim Brotherhood majority, it has become clear that reversing the worst abuses of the military-led regime will not by itself fix the country's deep-seated economic challenges. The Brotherhood has so far avoided populist talk on economic policy: it's strongly supportive of the stock market, private investment, tax cuts, and a smaller government budget deficit.

The protests continue. The Egyptian people want an end to the rule of the military council that replaced Mubarak, and the country's economic woes seem to be worsening daily—the protests themselves, and the widespread shutdown of Egypt's cities that they cause, is no small part of this. The old regime's rich men are no longer stockpiling the wealth that belongs to the people, as many Egyptians had believed they were, but their fabled coffers of gold have not spilled onto the streets for all to gather up as many had imagined.

From Resistance to Revolution
à la française

Robert Zaretsky

Robert Zaretsky is author or coauthor of several books, including, with Alice L. Conklin and Sarah Fishman, *France and Its Empire Since 1870* (2010). He is a contributing editor to *Tablet* magazine and is completing a book on Albert Camus for Harvard University Press titled *A Life Worth Living*.

On March 15, 1944, a document titled "Program of the CNL" began to circulate in Nazi-occupied France. It was the work of the National Council of Liberation, a grouping of representatives from the nation's resistance movements and political parties whose immediate task was to coordinate the liberation of France with the Allies and General de Gaulle's Free French. Yet France's liberation would only begin, not end, with the crushing of the Nazis. An even greater future, based on a more generous understanding of liberation, was in store. Albert Camus, editor of the resistance newspaper *Combat*, was characteristically blunt when he made "From Resistance to Revolution" the motto of his paper.

In effect, by "revolution," these men and women understood 1789. The Charter, as the document came to be called, was a heroic effort to link France's imminent liberation to the chain of events first begun with the taking of the Bastille. As another underground paper, *Les Cahiers politiques*, declared, the postwar resistance would "take up the broken thread of 1789." This meant nothing less than "a true democracy, freed from the reign of money, a power derived from the people but strong and stable, the equitable disposition, by the nation, of our common riches, a dignified life for free workers, the sharing of economic responsibilities by all and no longer only by a few."

The Charter both echoed and codified this idealism. In its preamble, the authors affirmed that the struggle that had begun against the Nazis would continue against the oppressive social and political forces that had been entrenched in France before the war. Only then, declared the Charter, could the nation reclaim its "moral and social balance and again reveal its greatness and unity to the world." In order to reach this end, the Charter proposed a host of economic, political, and social laws. Several demands, such as "respect for the human person" and "absolute equality for all citizens before the law," referred most immediately to the bloody reality of the occupation.

Other demands, however, looked further back to an era fraught with searing economic inequalities and polarized politics. Interwar France had been an arena for repeated clashes, often murderous, between the Third Republic and forces at both ends of the ideological spectrum that refused its legitimacy. There was little reason for workers to rally to a republic that seemed indifferent, if not hostile, to their lives. In fact, as Simone Weil revealed in her *Factory Journal*, working-class life was entirely absorbed in the struggle of everyday existence. The philosopher and activist worked at several factories during the 1930s, and she discovered that the rhythm and nature of the labor, the quest for productivity, and the indifference to the well-being of workers made for an earthly hell. As she raced to meet her daily quota, Weil found that she was emptied of all thoughts and feelings; assembly-line work had reduced her to a "thing," and she simply submitted, leaving the factory at the end of the day with just one hope: "that they will allow me to spend yet another such day." As she told a friend, "They make a favor, you see, of allowing us to kill ourselves, and we have to say thank you."

The year 1789 was thus viewed through the prism of two competing memories: the hopeful memory of the factory occupations that accompanied the victory of the Popular Front in 1936 and the grim memory of the Nazi occupation of 1940–44. The Charter called for the "setting up of a true economic and social democracy, entailing the conviction of the great economic and financial feudalities." The use of the term "feudalities" conjured an image of the Old Regime on the eve of 1789, yet the specific measures went far beyond the ambitions of that earlier revolution. The Charter called for "the return to the nation of the great monopolies," the "rational organization of the economy assuring that particular interests obey the general interest," and the "participation of employees in the management of their companies." Moreover, it demanded the creation of full social security, including health insurance and retirement pensions, along with the establishment of fair wages.

What may seem utopian to our eyes was eminently practical to the French in the summer of 1944. With the collapse of the political right, compromised by its collaboration with the Vichy regime, and the ascendancy of the political left, fueled by its role in the resistance, the Charter's legitimacy was beyond question. The resistance, in effect, made Charles de Gaulle, the leader of the Provisional Government, an offer he could not refuse. De Gaulle was well aware of the popular sentiment behind Camus's warning that "we will have accomplished only an infinitesimal part of our task if the French Republic of tomorrow were to find itself, like the Third Republic, under the strict control of Money." De Gaulle, no friend to France's financial and industrial magnates, hardly needed such prodding. Moreover, he placed himself in a long line of French statesmen, stretching back to King Louis IV's minister of finance, Jean-Baptiste Colbert, who insisted upon the ascendancy of the state over private interests.

As a result, the short-lived Provisional Government ushered in a New Deal with a pronounced French accent. The government nationalized the major banks and insurance companies, airlines and automobile manufacturers, energy and transportation sectors. Although these actions were debated bitterly for the next forty years, far less controversial was the enactment of laws that made a reality of the Charter's demand for "a complete plan of social security...with control over it assured for representatives of beneficiaries and of the state." Generous retirement pensions and medical insurance were implemented, as was disability insurance. In short, the experience of war, occupation, and liberation had been necessary in order to insure all citizens against illness and support them in old age. It was with the attainment of such *droits acquis*, legal rights, that "respect of the human person" became the law of the land.

In the same month that the CNR issued its Charter, a recently naturalized Frenchman of German birth parachuted into France. Sent on a mission by the Free French, Stéphane Hessel had the task of organizing communication lines among the resistance movements. He had little time to do so: the Gestapo soon captured and tortured Hessel, and packed him off first to Buchenwald, then Dora, the camp where tens of thousands of slave laborers assembled V-1 and V-2 rockets. Hessel escaped during the transfer of prisoners to Bergen-Belsen and found his way to an American army regiment near Hanover. Joining their ranks, he entered a liberated Paris on May 8, 1945.

The experience of resistance and imprisonment forever fixed Hessel's worldview. Though he had been a student at France's most prestigious university, the École Normale Supérieure, prior to the war, and steeped in the works of Jean-

Paul Sartre and Martin Heidegger, he decided he could best engage the world as a diplomat. In 1946, the French government assigned him to the newly created United Nations, where he participated in the writing of the Universal Declaration of Human Rights. There followed a long career in government, most notably as a close adviser to Pierre Mendès-France, who served as prime minister from 1954 to 1955. Hessel's deep and enduring identification with Mendès-France is telling. The ministry's short time in power was long enough to pull France from its imperial nightmare in Indochina. Mendès-France's effort to preempt the gathering tragedy in Algeria failed, however, and brought down his government. Though Mendès-France would never again serve as prime minister, this shining moment of enlightened and honorable political leadership left an indelible mark on Hessel.

After a series of diplomatic appointments, including ambassador to the UN, Hessel retired from active public service, but for the past half century and more, he has dedicated himself to the ideals of the Charter. In 1996, he assumed a national role in France as mediator between the government and three hundred African *sans-papiers* (undocumented aliens) squatting in a Parisian church to protest the state's refusal to grant them work visas. The affair ended abruptly when the police broke down the church door with axes and, despite Hessel's protestations, removed the squatters, many of whom were then deported to their home countries. He has also been a prominent defender of the Roma in France and of the Palestinians living in Gaza and the occupied territories in Israel.

"Being myself an immigrant," Hessel observed, "I cannot help but take an interest in other immigrants." Having been a *résistant* and concentration camp inmate, Hessel also cannot help but take an interest in the disempowered and disenfranchised, as have other former *résistants* and *résistantes*. In 2004, a dozen celebrated members of the Resistance marked the sixtieth anniversary of the Charter's birth, among them the anthropologist Germaine Tillion, the historian Daniel Cordier, the classicist Jean-Pierre Vernant, and Raymond and Lucie Aubrac. The group announced that while Nazism had been defeated, other kinds of barbarism still existed. Their "anger at injustice still intact," these men and women whose lives had spanned most of a century called for a "peaceful insurrection against the means of mass communication which offer today's youth nothing more than mass consumption, collective amnesia, scorn for the weak, and a world of brutal competition that pits all against all."

Hessel was a signatory to this manifesto. With his colleagues, he feared that "the social advances made after the Liberation" were threatened by the conservative government of Jacques Chirac, but more importantly by the "international dictatorship of financial markets." Since the publication of the manifesto, Tillion, Vernant, and Lucie Aubrac, among others, have died. This relentless attrition makes it impossible not to reflect, as does Hessel, that at the age of ninety-three one has arrived "at the final stage where the end is not far."

To reach the age of ninety-three remains an exploit; to be regarded at that age as the author of France's bestselling book is an *exploit sans pareil*. Stéphane Hessel's pamphlet *Indignez-vous!* reflects the remarkable qualities of its author. The work's unprecedented success also speaks to the particularities of our era, one in which a deepening sense of disappointment and disenchantment—indeed, of moral indignation—was suddenly and unexpectedly catalyzed into a movement anticipated and perhaps hastened by a thirty-page pamphlet.

Since the small publishing house Indigène Editions released *Indignez-vous!* in late 2010, it has sold more than two million copies in France. Beyond France, the pamphlet's success has been no less stunning. More than a million copies of the work, translated into nearly three dozen languages, have been sold across the globe. *Time for Outrage*, the American edition of the work, was released in August 2011—scarcely a month before OWS first took to the streets. As with so much else in Hessel's life, the timing was both fortuitous and fateful.

Indignez-vous! was born in 2009 on the Alpine plateau of Glières. Citoyens Resistants d'Hier et Aujourd'hui, an organization inspired by the call to arms made by Hessel and his comrades in 2004, had invited him to speak at their reunion that summer. The choice of Glières was deliberate: in January 1944, five hundred *maquis* had climbed to the icy plateau to coordinate their activities with the Allies. They were crushed two months later by the Germans, yet the uprising showed the

Maquis: Four members of the French underground resistance depart a small coastal town in 1944 for service behind the German lines, backs to the camera to shield their identities. *(Corbis)*

world that the spirit of resistance still burned in France. Glières has become a central *lieu de mémoire*, or site of memory, for France.

Standing under a warm sun in a three-piece suit, Hessel spoke without notes to a great throng of militants and activists in shorts and T-shirts. Following a bracing litany of French president Nicolas Sarkozy's sins of commission and omission against the values of the resistance, Hessel affirmed the "indignation" that he said all French must feel. Not only did the word resonate, as the philosopher and sociologist Edgar Morin has observed, but it catalyzed public opinion in France. Then, as now, France confronted several crises. Along with the economic crisis that had mobilized labor and student unions against a government determined to pare down the social advances heralded by the Charter, there were also the institutional failures reflected in the burgeoning crisis over the euro. No less significant were the social and political crises exploited by Sarkozy's government, whose punitive laws concerning national identity pandered to a base it wished to prevent from straying to the radical right-wing National Front. At the same time, however, Sarkozy draped himself in the mantle of Gaullism. In a 2007 speech to the UMP (Union for a Popular Movement), the neo-Gaullist party he leads, Sarkozy recalled "those who made me dream of another destiny, of a larger life and more bracing future"—in short, the "heroes of the Resistance and Free French" who were prepared to "break with received ideas and traditional order when they lead France toward decline."

The indignation that courses through Hessel upon hearing such claims echoes the outrage that spurred the birth of the resistance more than a half century ago, as well as the outrage that has led more than two million Frenchmen and -women to purchase the pamphlet.

*   *   *

But to what end? The French cultural critic Éric Aeschimann has observed that the mere purchase of *Indignez-vous!* is a "militant act, a communal gesture, a way of participating in a collective emotion." But a glance at history suggests it might be more than that. Slightly more than 250 years ago, Jean d'Alembert, coeditor of the Enlightenment *Encyclopédie*, opened a letter from his old friend Voltaire. Big books, Voltaire predicted, would never lead to change, much less revolution: "It is, instead, small books that cost 30 sous which are to be feared. Had the Gospels cost 1200 sesterces, Christianity would never have seen the light of day."

Not only was Voltaire the most prestigious contributor to the *Encyclopedia*, but he was also the author of hundreds of mostly anonymous pamphlets in which he railed against the enemies of reason and tolerance. And while historians may debate the ties between Voltaire's words and the revolutionary events that followed soon after his death, his remark about the impact of books—large and small, expensive and cheap, scholarly and polemical—raises important questions about the role of today's inheritors of his mantle. France is witnessing the rise of the *livre à bas prix*, the modern equivalent of the "30-sous book."

Enter a French bookstore today and you will see the *livre à bas prix* sprouting in the vicinity of the cash registers. It moves easily between the political and the personal; it subverts, or pretends to subvert, the established order of things; it is cheap and easily passed from one reader to the next; and most important, it taps into deep reserves of popular anxiety about, and hostility toward, traditional political and economic institutions.

This has been the model not just for *Indignez-vous!* but for a number of other works also seeking to mobilize public opinion in France. The *Manifeste d'économistes atterrés* (*Manifesto of Concerned Economists*), signed by more than seven hundred European economists, challenges the ascendancy of neoliberal economic theory. The signatories affirm that these neoliberal economists serve as apologists for international financial markets and domestic austerity policies that cripple not just national economies but the lives of countless citizens. Perhaps their most potent criticism concerns the European Union, whose raison d'être was to promote enlightened social policies and thus serve as a "rampart" against globalization. Instead, it has become an administrative Trojan horse, turning the EU into a mechanism "to adapt European nations to the demands of the global market." In *Voter pour la démondialisation (Vote for Deglobalization)*, the Socialist firebrand Arnaud de Montebourg takes up the same argument. While Montebourg plays fast and loose with statistics, and ignores the complexity of globalization, his crusade—in which he qualifies globalization as a "swindle" and "disaster for those whose sole resource is their labor"—has clearly struck a chord. In the first round of the 2011 Socialist primary for the presidential election, Montebourg stunned the party by placing a strong third. Another candidate in the same primary, Ségolène Royal—who had been the Socialist presidential candidate in 2007—also published, early in 2011, a short work with a long title: *Lettre à tous les résignés et aux indignés qui veulent des solutions (An Open Letter to the Resigned and Indignant Who Demand Solutions)*.

Not only was Royal deliberately echoing Hessel, but her open letter also underscored what many perceived as the great weakness of the ur-pamphlet, *Indignez-vous!*—namely, that outrage is not an agenda for political action. In a particularly cruel caricature, the philosopher Luc Ferry, who had been minister of National Education in an earlier conservative government, ridiculed the pamphlet, dismissing its "cheap moralizing" and insisting that "indignation" was the last thing the French needed. No doubt Ferry felt even more strongly about this when, in June 2011, it was reported that he had been collecting a university salary although he had not taught courses in several years.

Hessel has never pretended, of course, that indignation alone suffices. Instead, in echoing Camus's attitude toward the absurd, he has always recognized that outrage is nothing more than a starting point. Hessel has thus followed *Indignez-vous!* with *Engagez-vous!* (*Get Engaged!*), a hundred-page conversation with a young militant, Gilles Vanderpooten, in which he emphasizes the defense of the environment and support of the Green movement in Europe. Hessel has also published *Le Chemin de l'espérance* (*Path of Hope*), an eloquent manifesto he coauthored with Edgar Morin, which calls for global regulation of both the financial markets and the environment.

In an interview in 2011, Hessel noted that expressing outrage does not mean a great deal if "one doesn't then act to construct something else." For this reason, he declared, "I feel closer to the *indignés* of Wall Street than those in Spain or Greece. In the U.S., indignation is the response—a healthy and just one—to serious flaws in global finance." While the enemy today is far less obvious than it was in occupied France, "we know who it is: financial speculation. Come tomorrow, political engagement will be the same as in 1944: to regulate the markets and introduce a true social democracy." When asked by the interviewer for his advice to today's protesters, Hessel replied, "[T]hey need to read books more substantial than my own and find how to implement real economic, social and educational reforms." Most important, he concluded with a smile, they need to lead us to a world "where we are not simply obsessed by money but also capable of play and poetry."

Occupy the Media: Journalism for (and by) the 99 Percent

Amy Goodman and Denis Moynihan

The host and executive producer of *Democracy Now!*, Amy Goodman is a broadcast journalist and reporter, a columnist, the bestselling author of *Breaking the Sound Barrier* (2009), and the coauthor, with David Goodman, of several best sellers, including *Standing Up to the Madness: Ordinary Heroes in Extraordinary Times*. Denis Moynihan met the *Democracy Now!* team at the World Trade Organization protests in Seattle in 1999 and has coordinated live broadcasts from all continents except Antarctica. He lives in Denver and founded a noncommercial community radio station in Colorado's high country.

> *The media conglomerates are not the only industry whose owners have become monopolistic in the American economy. But media products are unique in one vital respect. They do not manufacture nuts and bolts: they manufacture a social and political world.*
>
> —Ben Bagdikian, *The New Media Monopoly*

Coverage of the Occupy Wall Street movement and of the Arab Spring challenged much of the traditional corporate media around the world. Whether broadcasting from Tahrir Square under a U.S.-backed military dictatorship or from Liberty Square (Zuccotti Park), where reporters were beaten and harassed by the NYPD, a vibrant media emerged, a media that let people speak for themselves.

We need a media that covers grassroots movements, that seeks to understand and explain the complex forces that shape our society, a media that provides information and empowers people to make sound decisions on the most vital issues of the day: war and peace, life and death. Instead, the media system in the United States, increasingly concentrated in the hands of fewer and fewer multinational corporations, spews a relentless stream of base "reality" shows (which depict anything but reality), hollow excuses for local news that are larded with ads and highlight car accidents and convenience store robberies, and an obsessive coverage of traffic, sports, and extreme weather (which is never linked to another two words: *climate change*). Perhaps most harmful of all, we get the same small circle of pundits, who know so little about so much, explaining the world to us and getting it so wrong.

The corporate media came late to Occupy Wall Street, offered superficial, often derogatory coverage, and, with a few exceptions, still haven't gotten it right. *Democracy Now!* was on the story before it began. Justin Wedes, one of the OWS organizers, told our team the day before the protests started, "More than having any specific demand per se, I think the purpose of September seventeenth, for many of us who are helping to organize it and people who are coming out, is to begin a conversation—as citizens, as people affected by this financial system in collapse—as to how we're going to fix it, as to what we're going to do in order to make it work for us again."

While the protest unfolded on its first day, organizer Lorenzo Serna told *Democracy Now!*, "The idea is to have an encampment...this isn't a one-day event. We're hoping that people come prepared to stay as long as they can and that we're there to support each other." Another participant explained, "I came because I'm upset with the fact that the bailout of Wall Street didn't help any of the people holding mortgages. All of the money went to Wall Street, and none of it went to Main Street."

The gross disparity in coverage between independent, noncommercial news organizations such as *Democracy Now!* and most of the corporate entities was, in part, one of the problems that drove the OWS movement in the first place. Among the grievances against corporations detailed in the first major statement of OWS—the Sepember 29, 2011, Declaration of the Occupation of New York City—was that "they purposefully keep people misinformed and fearful through their control of the media."

True to OWS's accusations, corporate media descended on Zuccotti Park, complaining that the movement had no identifiable leaders and no clear, concise list of demands. Freshly hired by CNN, Erin Burnett, known for her fawning interviews with corporate CEOs at her prior position on the financial channel CNBC, produced, for her first show on CNN, a mocking segment called "Seriously?!" She opened with a clichéd video montage that mischaracterized protesters as dirty, unemployed layabouts seeking handouts—and universally ignorant of the very financial industry they were protesting:

ERIN BURNETT: Seriously, it's a mixed bag. But they were happy to take some time from their books, banjos, bongos, sports drinks, catered lunch—yes, there was catered lunch, designer yoga clothing—that's a lululemon logo—computers, lots of MacBooks, and phones to help us get to the bottom of it. This is unemployed software developer Dan...

So do you know that taxpayers actually made money on the Wall Street bailout?

DAN MOYNIHAN: I was unaware of that.

EB: They did. They made—not on GM—but they did on the Wall Street part of the bailout.

DM: Okay.

EB: Does that make you feel any differently?

DM: Well, (inaudible)—

EB: If I were right it might?

DM: Oh, sure.

(*END VIDEO CLIP*)

EB: Seriously?! That's all it would take to put an end to the unrest? Well, as promised, we did go double-check the numbers on the bank bailout and this is what we found. Yes, the bank bailouts made money for American taxpayers, right now to the tune of ten billion dollars, [and it's] anticipated that it will be twenty billion dollars. Those are seriously the numbers. This was the big issue, so we solved it.

Burnett ambushed one person, asking about what is likely the largest and most complex emergency financial program in the history of money, claiming that the purported revenue from the U.S. Treasury's Troubled Asset Relief Program (TARP) should mollify the OWS protesters. Jump over to nonprofit investigative news organization ProPublica's detailed reportage on the bailout, and you see that the $10–20 billion in reported revenue from TARP is dwarfed by the hundreds of billions still outstanding, likely never to be recovered. Burnett's coverage was sadly typical.

Skeptical of the corporate media, people have developed their own. The decade that preceded OWS saw the rapid maturation of the digital media sector. In late 1999, media activists set up an independent media center and website to cover the World Trade Organization protest in Seattle, Washington.

Days after going live, indymedia.org was getting more hits than CNN.com, exposing police violence denied by the mainstream news. In the lead-up to the invasion of Iraq in 2002–3, when the public was being force-fed pro-war propaganda through the mainstream media (*Weapons of mass destruction? Mushroom clouds?*), millions turned to the Internet as an alternative source of information, and people around the globe used it to organize the largest antiwar protests in history. On February 15, 2003, millions rocked the globe for peace. During major protests in New York City in 2004, against President George W. Bush and the Republican National Convention, technology activists deployed a program, TXTMob, that allowed protesters to coordinate actions, which later evolved into Twitter.

Justin Wedes explained media strategy as we walked through Liberty Square: "Throughout this process, we understood the importance of having an independent media center — in other words, of creating our own media. We could never rely on the mainstream media to depict us fairly. And we wanted to be the most go-to, responsible, accurate depictors of what is happening in this space. So, from day one, we set up an indy media center, which includes a live stream."

The live video streams of OWS advanced independent media strategy by making the unfiltered activity of the occupation available in real time to a global audience. The way the protest was organized, how the General Assembly operated, and how working groups were established were all streamed live, serving as an organizing template for solidarity occupations that began sprouting around the world. A group formed at OWS to video-stream the events there and to aggregate live video feeds from around the world, GlobalRevolution TV, was cofounded by Vlad Teichberg, a Muscovite whose parents were forced out of the Soviet Union in the early 1980s. Teichberg was a derivatives trader on Wall Street until 2001, when he saw both the negative effects of globalization pushed by his industry and the rightward political shift in the United States following 9/11. He quit and became an activist opposing corporate power.

Teichberg told *Democracy Now!* that the OWS independent media center "allows many people to work together to push out the message of what is being done, why it's being done.... About a week or a week and a half into the protests, we finally broke through the mainstream media wall. At least the event was no longer boycotted or blocked. And, you know, the rest was history."

The live video stream, along with the increased interest in the story from mainstream journalists and the near ubiquity of cell-phone cameras and social media, allowed for another aspect of the protests to become widely and instantly publicized: the police crackdown. Thousands of arrests have been made since OWS started, in New York and around the country, including those of an extraordinary number of journalists. Josh Stearns, of the media policy group Free Press, started documenting these stories and amassed a list of close to sixty journalists arrested at the time of this writing.

In New York City, the volume of the arrests, and the police harassment and intimidation of journalists, led a consortium of news outlets and professional organizations, including the *New York Times*, the Associated Press, Reuters, and Dow Jones, to appeal for action from Mayor Michael Bloomberg and Police Commissioner Raymond Kelly.

During the November 15, 2011, early-morning raid on Zuccotti Park, BuzzFeed's Rosie Gray told the police she was press and was told back, "Not tonight." In mid-December, police raided the Brooklyn building to which Global Revolution TV moved after the shutdown of Liberty Square, arresting Teichberg and five other volunteers. Other occupants of the building, which the city's Department of Buildings abruptly deemed "imminently perilous to life," were not arrested.

Arrests of reporters, as Stearns's data shows, are not limited to New York City, and they present a serious threat to journalism. Targeting of journalists is by no means a new phenomenon. What seems to be accelerating, along with the technological ease with which both the press and the public can record, stream, post, and otherwise publish events as they occur, is police interference—through intimidation, forced relocation away from sites of newsworthy events, assault, destruction of equipment or the erasure of digital media, and arrest.

Three years earlier, two colleagues and one of us (Amy) were violently arrested while covering the 2008 Republican National Convention in St. Paul, Minnesota. The police pulled the battery from our coworker Nicole Salazar's video camera as they pinned her to the ground, bloodying her face. After producer Sharif Abdel Kouddous and Amy were handcuffed, a U.S. Secret Service agent tore our press credentials from our necks, declaring, "You won't be needing these anymore." More than forty journalists were arrested there that week. St. Paul police chief John Harrington offered no apologies. Rather, he suggested we could "embed" with the mobile field force. He was referring to the Pentagon system of embedding reporters with the troops in Iraq and Afghanistan, which has brought the media to an all-time low.

Embed with the police? Rather than do that, we sued and, after three years, won a settlement, which included, in addition to a monetary penalty, the requirement that the St. Paul police receive training in how to conduct themselves while being covered by the press. The court ordered that the course curriculum meet the approval of the three journalists who had been arrested, along with that of the American Civil Liberties Union and the Center for Constitutional Rights. While enormously time-consuming, the lawsuit was one of the only available means by which to hold the authorities accountable.

At the heart of the Occupy Wall Street movement is the critique that wealth and opportunity are not equitably distributed, and our media system, largely controlled by corporations, contributes to that status quo. But the Internet has created a seismic disruption to the balance of power in the media. It is getting easier and easier to post your thoughts, photos, or videos. Yet the Wild West of the Web is being tamed. Small Internet service providers are being driven out of business, with corporations like Comcast, Time Warner, Verizon, and AT&T dominating the market. Privacy, security, and the freedom to publish without fear of censorship are dwindling with each merger, with each effort by corporate lobbyists to further restrict the open Internet in favor of a narrow profit advantage.

While fighting to preserve a free Internet, journalists, press organizations, and the public must not give up on the older legacy media institutions. Television is still how most Americans get their news. We have a public television system in the United States that is a shadow of public broadcasting abroad, forever hobbled by congressional threats to "zero out" its budget. Groups like the Prometheus Radio Project fought for over a decade to win an opening for potentially thousands of new, low-power FM community radio stations to open. To take advantage of that, groups will still have to organize and do the hard legwork to submit applications to the Federal Communications Commission. Public access television stations around the country are under attack from cable companies, who want to defund and shutter them, which will require time and organizing to combat.

The "crisis in journalism," which has been blamed on the Internet's disruption of traditional advertising business models, is also traceable to the very corporate behavior that many of the Occupiers are protesting. Leveraged buyouts of media properties have left newspapers with massive debt, forcing layoffs of journalists and support staff. By stripping away the profit motive—by removing the Wall Street bankers from the picture—solid, disciplined nonprofit journalism is possible.

When the police raided Zuccotti Park on November 15, 2011, and evicted the entire occupation, they destroyed most of the OWS People's Library, which contained five thousand-plus books, along with the tent that housed it, a tent donated by legendary rocker and National Book Award winner Patti Smith. The *Democracy Now!* team managed to get behind police lines to document the raid. Amid the rubble, we found one tattered book that escaped the library's destruction: Aldous Huxley's *Brave New World Revisited*, published in 1958.

Huxley writes, citing the American sociologist Charles Wright Mills:

> Big Business, made possible by advancing technology and the consequent ruin of Little Business, is controlled by the State—that is to say, by a small group of party leaders and the soldiers, policemen and civil servants who carry out their orders. In a capitalist democracy, such as the United States, it is controlled by what Professor C. Wright Mills has called the Power Elite. This Power Elite directly employs several millions of the country's working force in its factories, offices and stores, controls many millions more by lending them the money to buy its products, and, through its ownership of the media of mass communication, influences the thoughts, the feelings and the actions of virtually everybody.

To avoid Huxley's grim vision, to turn the tide against it, we need a strong, independent media, a media that serves the interest of the silenced majority.

On the Meaning of Occupation
Michael Greenberg

Michael Greenberg is the author of *Hurry Down Sunshine* (2008) and *Beg, Borrow, Steal: A Writer's Life* (2009). From 2003 to 2010 he wrote the "Freelance" column for the *London Times Literary Supplement*. He writes "The Accidentalist" column for *Bookforum*. Greenberg's serial reports on Occupy Wall Street were published in the *New York Review of Books*, to which he is a frequent contributor.

The "occupy" in Occupy Wall Street has become a catchword, a #hashtag, a worldwide symbol that represents, among other things, a new uncorrupted form of grassroots activism. The American Dialect Society has named it "The Word of the Year" for 2011. It narrowly defeated the acronym FOMO ("fear of missing out"), which describes the obsessive need to stay abreast of news on Facebook, Twitter, and other social networking sites.

In a way, the two words are antonyms, one presenting itself as a cure for the other. Occupation can't be virtual; it has to occur face-to-face, because what it offers is an antidote to the empty gaze of the screen. One of the chief appeals of Zuccotti Park and the other encampments was their gritty communalism, their primal physicality, the spontaneous, live-action experience they offered. People didn't come to pay homage to a celebrity as they would at a music festival, or to hear a speaker as they would at a political rally or church. They didn't come to witness a performance, they came to *be* the performance, and what they were enacting was a kind of unscripted political theater in which argument, polemics, complaint, proposals, and insights were experimentally exchanged.

"Revolution without poetry is dead," one activist told me. "We don't do politics, we do political theater." This placing of the imagination over doctrine, of Dadaist gestures over disciplined marches, this belief that "theater is the political art form par excellent" (as another organizer put it to me, paraphrasing Hannah Arendt), is partly why OWS is so attractive to professional performers and artists. Protesters turned the public square into a political spectacle, presenting their occupations as a kind of social experiment, and they did so not on rural communes or in lofts or abandoned buildings but in the visible, inhospitable financial districts of America's major cities.

What most captivated visitors was the sense of equality in the encampments; the timid as well as the stentorian felt listened to and heard. No matter who they were, visitors were recorded, photographed, archived, YouTubed, and live-fed on a plethora of global Web channels, imbuing them with a sense of personal historical importance. The meek, it seemed, had inherited the earth, or at least a small part of it. Spontaneous gatherings in the encampments would begin with the exhortation to defer to the "traditionally marginalized": the shy, the unpolished, the less educated, the nonwhite. Patience was required; a rare, almost writerly attentiveness was encouraged and prized. People would formulate ideas, express rage, deliver opinions, outline grand political solutions, and then be treated to the thrill of having their words shouted back at them by the "people's mic."

The practice of giving everyone an equal chance to be heard was an article of faith in the occupation zones. One eloquent activist told me of his "nausea" at finding himself dominating a working group. "People were looking at me, listening to me, deferring to me. As an anarchist, I felt ashamed. I was stifling conversation, the free exchange of ideas. I was repressing collective creativity. I stepped back, and others came forward with better ideas, different perspectives. Spontaneity was able to flow again."

Occupation marked a major innovation in modern American political activism, a return to what is basic about assembly and democracy and simple human contact—a return, some of the protesters liked to point out, to a constitutional right enshrined in the First Amendment, even if it had been sparked by the actions of people living in Egypt under a totalitarian regime. Just as important, it marked a rejection of the stratagems and calculations of party politics and traditional organizational methods. Therein lay much of Occupy's threat. It functioned outside the arena of traditional political prizes: power, influence, access, the right to make laws.

Celebrities who visited Zuccotti Park were treated more as a nuisance than as objects of starstruck awe. Organizers regarded them with caution. The public square wasn't a place for the famous to preen. Occupy, after all, was anticonsumerist, antihierarchical—and who was higher on the totem pole of capitalist social status than the megafamous? It became an emblem of the movement's integrity not to succumb to the cult of celebrity, which, in any event, was an aspect of American culture they wished to overturn. They were more deferential to artists and intellectuals, such as Bill McKibben, Joseph Stiglitz, and Slavoj Žižek, to name just a few who came around to conduct teach-ins and offer practical support.

The rapper Jay-Z visited Zuccotti Park, then proceeded to market through his website an Occupy Wall Street T-shirt designed by his company, Rocawear. Representatives of OWS demanded that he stop selling the T-shirts. A man named Grim, speaking for OWS to the entertainment news website

TMZ, said, "Jay-Z, as talented as he is, has the political sensibility of a hood rat and is a scrotum. To attempt to profit off of the first important social movement of fifty years with an overpriced piece of cotton is an insult to the fight for economic civil rights."

Several popular entertainers have offered to participate in fund-raising concerts for OWS—for a time the movement was the new measure of cool. Wisely, organizers have been reluctant to accept the help, worried that performers would be unable to step back and defer to the nonhierarchichal message. Though they need the money, commercial purity is the movement's greatest asset, and the will of core organizers to protect it is one of Occupy's most admirable traits.

As a counterculture, OWS must remain inviolate—untainted by the mainstream culture it wishes to replace. The public encampments provided a chance to remove the scales from people's eyes and help them see how much of their "consciousness," as protesters would unabashedly say, had been colonized by the reigning economic system. It was the act of occupying that provoked these personal epiphanies, the unpredictable free-for-all of the twenty-four-hour public space. What mattered, a full-time organizer explained to me, was "the living, breathing vibrant quality of waking up in that space among others, of going to bed there, of knowing it is always there as a kind of ongoing generating station, an electrical sustaining force for those off-site."

Yet it was almost by accident that occupation became the central philosophical principle of the movement. Protesters first decided to lay down their sleeping bags in Zuccotti Park without much expectation that their stay would last or even be noticed beyond a small circle of activists and police. The movement's extraordinary popular resonance burst upon them like a storm. The extent of what they had lost didn't become entirely clear until after they were expelled, two months later, from the political Eden of Zuccotti Park and the other encampments around the country.

Afterward, protesters began speaking of themselves as having been forced into "the diaspora." They had become part of a floating citizenry of displaced persons, political nomads who had been driven from their land. Their confiscated tents became a symbol of their bond with those who had lost their homes in the foreclosure crisis and, beyond that, with the world's dispossessed. (Some protesters began covertly pitching tents in parks and bank lobbies, filling them with cement as symbols of their tenacity, their permanence, their intention to press on.) Romantic and rhetorical as it was, the analogy carried a certain moral force. Many had paid a price at the hands of the police, having been beaten and pepper-sprayed and jailed.

Almost immediately, organizers began staging "flash occupations," actions that took over public space for a day or a few hours and then quickly dispersed. The concept of occupation always had a metaphorical component—"occupy minds," "occupy faith," "occupy imagination"—but in order for the metaphor to have meaning, a permanent physical occupied space, a camp and headquarters, was required. And it had to be in the center of urban commercial life, visible and outdoors. Los Angeles mayor Antonio Villaraigosa, a former president of the American Civil Liberties Union with sympathy for OWS's message, offered protesters a vacant bookstore in a shopping mall that the city owned to replace their encampment. The offer was refused. "People don't join Occupy to be in an office," an organizer told me.

Still, the temporary flash occupations could be thrilling in a theatrical way. On December 1, for instance, several hundred protesters gathered at the steps to Lincoln Center Plaza in Manhattan to await the end of the final performance of Philip

Glass's opera *Satyagraha*, about the life of Gandhi. The idea was to dramatize their affinity with Gandhi's method of non-violent resistance. The large public plaza was barricaded as if to prevent a terrorist attack. Inside the barricades a couple of dozen police yawningly stood guard, stamping their feet in the cold. Another phalanx of police guarded the curb on Columbus Avenue, forcing demonstrators to cram together on the narrow sidewalk, hemmed in and easily controlled—the police tactic known as "kettling." Protesters who climbed over the barricades were thrown back onto the sidewalk like bundled sacks or arrested and carried away by police. It was the opposite picture of the heyday of Zuccotti Park, when protesters swarmed the square and police looked in from the outside.

Nevertheless, the mood was festive. Some protesters wore high-peaked papier-mâché hats, and a large green Lady Liberty puppet, a frequent attendee at occupations, was held aloft. As a gesture of reverence, many removed their shoes, despite the cold weather.

As operagoers left the theater, protesters called out to them to join the gathering, amiably pointing out that they were the contemporary embodiment of the Gandhian way that the audience had just witnessed onstage. A few cheered, a handful joined the demonstration, most hurried away into cabs or waiting cars. Then, in a show of solidarity with the movement, Philip Glass appeared, reciting Gandhi's poem about "Thrusting back evil/And setting virtue on her seat again," the demonstrators repeating every word in a firm, cadenced voice that was reminiscent of Glass's music.

For a few hours, high culture, public space, and political action had movingly converged. But by midnight it was over; all went their separate ways. With no encampment to return to, the demonstration seemed to have occurred in a vacuum, leaving few traces, its evanescence offering little to build on.

Occupation presented politics not as a set of issues but as a way of being. It offered a release from subjectivity. In the open public forum, people became emboldened, exactly as the Constitution had conceived them to be. Private indignation about the state of the country multiplied in the public square, taking on another form. Crucially, it gave the movement a way to recruit and expand. The outdoor, free-flowing nerve center promoted critical thought. "People get together," as one organizer put it to me, "they talk, they argue, they assess the way things are and the way they could be. They make sense of the world, together." She added, "Occupation says to our representatives, to our government, that they do not represent us. That's why we've made this space our own, a space that does represent us."

People readily spoke of occupation in spiritual terms. It was "a soul movement," "a transformational movement." A protester at Zuccotti Park quoted to me a passage from John in the New Testament: "He became Man and lived among us." He pointed out that the literal translation of the word for "lived" in the text is closer to "dwelt" or "tented." "He tented among us," said the protester, gesturing at the tents in the park. An Episcopal priest who was active in the movement told me, "I wear my collar now, which I never did before. With Occupy Wall Street, the collar is deconstructed, the clerical symbol becomes something else. You no longer represent this institution that stands apart on its spiritual hill. You are joining in."

Reverend Michael Ellick of Judson Memorial Church in New York compared open occupied spaces to public spaces in the first century of Christianity, when "all kinds of people could come together. It didn't matter who you had been before you arrived, a prostitute, a merchant, a beggar, a tradesman. All were equalized in the name of the spirit. It was about faith and real-life issues, not just faith alone as a disembodied entity."

The task of every generation was to redefine what justice is. It was part of the process of discovering who you were. Ellick added, "Maybe we are always living in the Roman Empire in one form or another and these movements that revitalize what is right are essential to civilization."

Occupation is primarily a cultural movement, one that transcends politics; or that is how it wishes to be seen. Political impact and cultural impact are not the same thing; one is concerned with policy, the other with the way we think about our lives. Occupation seeks to address our spiritual yearnings, our domestic ideals, our economic needs. Its ultimate ambition, laughable to some, magnificent to others, is to become a society unto itself.

Unions Build the Middle Class

David Madland, Karla Walter, and Nick Bunker

The authors are with the Center for American Progress Action Fund. David Madland, director of its American Worker Project, has written articles, books, op-eds, and commentaries on public opinion and on economic issues including retirement and jobs. Karla Walter, a senior policy analyst, focuses primarily on improving the economic security of American workers through higher wages and benefits and by promoting their rights. Nick Bunker, a special assistant with the economic policy team, works on issues related to economic security and employment conditions.

Why should anyone—especially those who are not union members—care that union membership is at record lows and likely to fall even further? The simplest answer is that if you care about the middle class, you need to care about unions—and the American middle class is struggling.

The middle class receives close to the smallest share of the nation's income it ever has since the U.S. Census Bureau started collecting data, in 1967. In 2010, the middle 60 percent of all Americans garnered only 46 percent of the nation's income, down from highs of around 53 percent in 1968. The middle class has weakened over the past several decades because the rich secured the lion's share of the economy's gains. The share of pretax income earned by the richest 1 percent of Americans more than doubled between 1974 and 2007, climbing to 23.5 percent from 9 percent, according to Thomas Piketty and

Emmanuel Saez. In contrast, incomes for most Americans were nearly flat over this same period, and median income after accounting for inflation actually fell in working-age households between 2001 and 2007, a period generally regarded as prosperous. As a result, the share of income going to the middle class has declined over the past forty years.

There are many reasons for the dramatic weakening of the middle class, including technology, trade, and increasing pay for college graduates. But a key explanation—though one that's too often overlooked—is the decline in the percentage of the workforce that is unionized.

The chart below shows that the percentage of unionized workers tracks very closely with the share of the nation's income going to the middle class—those in the middle three-fifths of income earners. As the percentage of workers in unions has declined, so have the fortunes of the middle class.

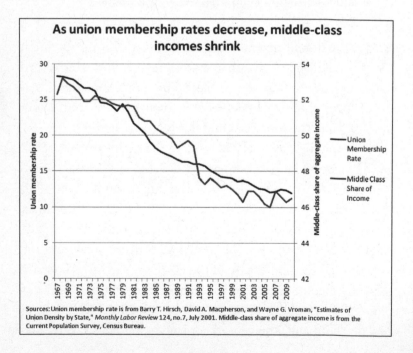

As union membership rates decrease, middle-class incomes shrink

Sources: Union membership rate is from Barry T. Hirsch, David A. Macpherson, and Wayne G. Vroman, "Estimates of Union Density by State," *Monthly Labor Review* 124, no. 7, July 2001. Middle-class share of aggregate income is from the Current Population Survey, Census Bureau.

Less than 7 percent of workers in the private sector are members of unions today, down from around 30 percent in the late 1960s. Public-sector unionization remained stable for decades—at 37 percent in 1979 and in 2012—but is under significant threat from conservative political opposition and could start declining as well. All told, less than 12 percent of the total workforce is unionized, and this percentage is likely to continue falling.

Even though unions have weakened, they are still critically important to the middle class: the states with the lowest percentage of workers in unions—North Carolina, Georgia, Arkansas, Louisiana, Mississippi, South Carolina, Tennessee, Virginia, Oklahoma, and Texas—all have relatively weak middle classes. In each of these states, the share of income going to the middle class (the middle 60 percent of the population by income) is below the national average, according to Census Bureau figures. In fact, academic studies indicate that the decline in union density explains as much of today's record level of inequality as does the increasing economic return of a college education.

Unions make the middle class safe by ensuring that workers have a strong voice in both the market and in our democracy. When unions are strong they are able to guarantee that workers are paid fair wages, receive the training they need to advance to the middle class, and are considered in corporate decision-making processes. Unions also promote political participation among all Americans and help workers secure government policies that support the middle class, such as Social Security, family leave, and the minimum wage.

As unions have become weaker over the past four decades, they have gradually lost their ability to perform these functions—and the middle class has withered. In order to rebuild America's middle class, we need to rebuild the labor movement.

Occupy Wall Street: The First Quarter and Beyond

George Gresham

George Gresham is president of 1199 Service Employees Internal Union, the largest health care workers' union in the United States, with over 350,000 members in New York, New Jersey, Massachusetts, Maryland, Florida, and Washington, D.C. He is the fifth president in the union's seventy-six-year history and has also served as vice president of its executive board. The grandson of a Virginia sharecropper, he spent his early childhood in the state's segregated schools. His father was a Teamster.

In the world Wall Street has made, quarterly results are the measure of all things. At the three-month anniversary of Occupy Wall Street, the results were impressive; only the most jaded cynic could deny it.

Political leaders obsessed with the debt and deficits have been forced to focus on jobs and inequality. Tax breaks for the wealthy that were untouchable before September 17, 2011, are suddenly in the crosshairs of Congress. Giant corporations that pay no taxes are finally being called to account, and more progressive taxes are being promoted in Albany, New York, and elsewhere.

Still, the cynics can say that the tents are gone from Zuccotti Park and that the encampments across the country are disappearing one by one. In their eyes, Occupy Wall Street is just another sinking stock, one more bubble ready to burst.

Of course, this is why we need a longer time frame to appreciate the remarkable achievements and lasting promise of the Occupy movement. Like all of America's great reform movements, Occupy Wall Street is attacking problems that seemed insoluble and uniting people who never realized they had interests in common. Students drowning in debt, workers without health care, retirees denied pensions, the unemployed of all stripes and party affiliations—they're all united now in a way they weren't before September 17.

To those of us in the labor movement, it's clear that Occupy Wall Street is doing what only the most tenacious organizers can: forging a way forward when progress seems impossible. Whether we formed our unions in the coal mines of Appalachia, the assembly lines of Detroit, or the hospitals of New York, we recognize when the political and economic systems are stacked against the working class, and we recognize the enormous effort required to even the scales.

For decades, labor, the left, and progressives of every kind have warned about the scourge of inequality in America. It was Occupy Wall Street that finally jump-started a real conversation about how and why the richest four hundred Americans have more wealth than the bottom 150 million combined.

Occupy Wall Street has reshaped the national debate as quickly and dramatically as any social movement in American history. Before fall 2011, America had no common language to explain the crash of 2008 and its causes. Now we can see and describe the chasm separating the 99 percent and the 1 percent. The Occupy movement might be mocked as naïve for lacking a specific set of demands, but it has brilliantly identified the one fundamental problem of our time.

Because Occupy Wall Street has drawn attention by marching across bridges and sitting down in streets, some critics call it a lawless mob. But Occupy's peaceful protesters are firmly in the tradition of the civil rights movement. Having grown up in the segregated South, I understood that civil rights activists sat down at lunch counters not to break the law but to fix it. That's what America's real freedom movements have always done. Abolitionists, suffragists, gay rights activists— they've all pushed to reform the laws that betray America's values.

We in labor know all about laws that need fixing. In our union, 1199 SEIU United Healthcare Workers East, another movement born on the streets of New York, our hospital workers had to push beyond the bounds of existing law when they joined together a little more than fifty years ago. A loophole then in the nation's labor law denied virtually all hospital workers the right to form unions. But the workers, many of them living in poverty, felt a union was their only way forward, so they struck for fair wages and demanded recognition from their hospitals.

Hospital officials quickly condemned the strikers for their "revolution against law and order"—words that must sound familiar to Occupy protesters. During the strike, the hospitals conceded very little, and after forty-six days the impoverished caregivers had to settle. Like the Occupiers forced from their encampments, the workers had to retreat from the streets and call survival a victory. Yet, after an intense advocacy campaign, hospital workers won union rights in 1963, when Governor Nelson Rockefeller signed a bill granting collective-bargaining rights to New York City's hospital workers. After decades of organizing, the once-impoverished caregivers have become the bedrock of our city's working class. We know that movements with humble beginnings can do great things.

Nevertheless, despite all the progress our members have made—expanding far beyond the five boroughs to unite with over 350,000 caregivers up and down the East Coast—none of us are insulated from the chill wind blowing through today's economy. America's middle class is living on a knife edge, and all of us need the Occupy movement to keep focusing Washington's attention on that fact. Occupy has done it when no one else could. It's reminding us of the hard-fought achievements of our past while giving us hope for the future.

Yes, the movement is fragile. No billionaire brothers are funding it. But the millions of Americans it's inspired promise to make Occupy Wall Street as powerful, resilient, and long-lasting as any of the other great American reform movements.

Where Is the Demand for Redistribution?

Ilyana Kuziemko and Michael I. Norton

Ilyana Kuziemko is an assistant professor of economics and public affairs at Princeton University. Michael I. Norton is an associate professor at the Harvard Business School.

R esearch shows that Americans are united in believing that wealth inequality in the United States is at much too high a level. The top 20 percent own some 85 percent of the wealth, but Americans want them to own just 32 percent; similarly, while the bottom 40 percent own essentially none of the wealth—in part because so many are in debt—the desire is for that group to own some 25 percent. These patterns hold true across the population, even among people of different income levels and political affiliations. While every group of Americans surveyed desires *some* inequality, no group—from the poorest liberals to the wealthiest conservatives—desires an America remotely as unequal as the country is.

Does that sentiment automatically translate into support for policies that would decrease inequality? Americans often fail to connect their distaste for inequality with support for policies that would tend to decrease it—from higher taxes on the rich to greater social spending on the poor. In surveys from the early 2000s, for example, few Americans reported believing that the Bush tax cuts would help the middle class, yet the majority still expressed strong support for them. Moreover, large groups of low-income voters—those most aided by progressive tax and transfer policies—regularly support politicians who oppose redistribution. No Democratic candidate for president has won the votes of the majority of the white working class in over thirty years; in the 2010 midterm elections, these voters supported Republicans by a margin of two to one.

In short, there's a disconnect between Americans' support for greater equality of income and wealth distribution and their support for policies designed to achieve that equality. Under what circumstances might we expect these two attitudes to converge? One commonsense possibility is that in times of economic crisis, when poorer Americans become more aware of the disparities in wealth in the United States—through the loss of their jobs, insurance, and homes—the demand for redistribution may rise.

Surprisingly, however, support for redistribution has fallen since the recession began in 2008: between April and October of 2008, the share of Gallup survey respondents saying they felt that income should be spread more evenly among Americans fell from 68 percent to 58 percent, and if anything it has decreased slightly since then. That is, during a period in which the unemployment rate increased by nearly 40 percent while the largest banks were bailed out by taxpayers, Americans substantially decreased their support for redistribution. Other surveys—including the General Social Survey—have documented similar trends, again even among those Americans who identify themselves as earning low incomes.

Why do low-income voters—more often than not the victims of rising inequality—so often oppose redistribution? Even more puzzlingly, why would their opposition to redistribution increase during the recession?

Our research suggests that, far from being surprised that many working-class people oppose redistribution, we might actually expect their opposition to rise during times of turmoil—despite the fact that redistribution appears to be in their economic interest. We suggest that people exhibit a fundamental loathing for being near or in last place, or what we call last-place aversion. This fear can lead people near the bottom of the income distribution to oppose redistribution because it might allow people below them to catch up with them or, even worse, leapfrog past them. Economic recession likely makes the fear of falling closer to last place even more real for people already toward the bottom of the distribution, meaning that their support for redistribution might also decrease.

We have documented last-place aversion in a variety of set-

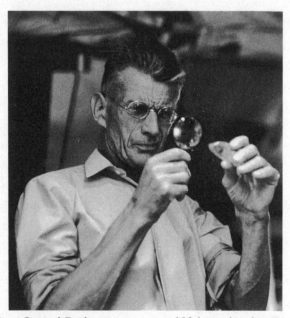

Perception: Samuel Beckett peers at a goldfish used in his *Film* (1965), starring Buster Keaton and based on Bishop Berkeley's principle *"esse est percipi"* (to be is to be perceived). Why do people vote against their own interests? Kuziemko and Norton argue that how we see ourselves may ultimately determine what we do in the polling booth. *(Corbis)*

tings. In one laboratory experiment, individuals are randomly given different amounts of money and are then shown their place in the resulting income distribution. Next they are asked to choose between two options. In one, they receive a very small amount of money, which is less than the difference between them and the person directly above. The other option is to place a win-lose bet, in which they will either win enough money to jump over the person above them, or lose money and fall even further behind. The last- and second-to-last-place players are by far the most likely to opt for the gamble, even though they actually have the least money to lose; players higher up in the income distribution, on the other hand, are perfectly happy to play it safe and not gamble. These results suggest that people in last place are willing to risk losing money for the chance to jump over the players just above them, and second-to-last-place players feel they need to defend against this possibility. Indeed, when asked to explain their decisions, many of our participants openly stated that they were driven at least in part by the simple desire to get out of—or stay out of— last place.

In another experiment, people are again randomly given various amounts of money and shown their place in the distribution, with each rank separated by one dollar. Each person is then given an extra two dollars that must in turn be given either to the person directly above or directly below. Because each rank is separated by one dollar, giving two dollars to the player below means that this person leapfrogs ahead of the giver. Nonetheless, the large majority of players choose to give the two dollars to the player below; giving money to someone who already has more than you is presumably not a very attractive option. However, nearly half the players in second-to-last place choose to give the extra money to the person above rather than below. Why? Apparently, giving money to someone who already has more than you can be less painful than giving the money to the person below you—but only when that behavior causes you to fall into last place yourself.

We also documented last-place aversion outside the laboratory by surveying a sample of Americans about their attitudes toward an increase in the minimum wage. The minimum wage obviously affects low-income workers disproportionately, and thus it is reasonable to expect that most low-wage workers would support an increase. Indeed, we generally do observe this pattern, with one major, and telling, exception: those making just above the minimum wage, $7.25 per hour, are far more likely to oppose an increase than those making $7.25 or below or those making more than $9.00. That is, people making $7.50 per hour would rather forgo a small raise than take the chance that an increase in the minimum wage will cause them to earn the "last-place" wage themselves—and to be tied with workers previously below them.

Of course, the results of our experiments and surveys must be used cautiously to develop predictions about when and why voters will support or oppose redistributive policies. However, one lesson is clear: our experiments generally made people focus on those close to them in the distribution. In one, they were allowed to gamble for a chance to jump over the person directly above them; in the other, they had to decide whether to give money to the person directly above or below them. In essence, the experiments made those low in the distribution focus on each other instead of on those far above them. The behavior of these "low-income" individuals suggests that they were laser-focused on getting away from the bottom, even if it meant behaving badly toward their fellow poor *and* even if it meant giving money to someone better off than themselves (the rich).

Enter the Occupy movement—in all of its incarnations,

from Occupy Wall Street to Occupy Tuscaloosa. Occupy seems to anticipate the power of last-place aversion in shaping people's political attitudes, and offers a competing and compelling narrative aimed at shifting people's focus from keeping those below them down to paying attention to those far above them. Simply put, Occupy Wall Street divides the world into just two groups: the top 1 percent and the bottom 99 percent. Stating the issue this way focuses the attention of people at the bottom of the distribution to those at the top   rather than on each other—and implicitly suggests that anyone not in the top 1 percent ("them") is one of "us." Will the rhetoric work? Alternate formulations have already arisen, such as "We are the 53 percent," which divides Americans into those who pay federal income taxes and those who do not. In other words, the us-versus-them mentality is powerful but also malleable. To the extent that these different narratives prove enduring, they have the potential to shape debates on wealth redistribution and economic policy in the coming years. While it is too soon to tell if Occupy Wall Street has staying power, its rhetoric has the potential to continue to alter the discussion about redistribution and inequality.

U.S. Cultural Decline:
The Overlooked Intangibles

Brandon Adams

Brandon Adams taught undergraduate economics courses
at Harvard University for eight years.

The tone of our national debate is typically formal and self-
righteous. We focus on cold, big-picture variables: budget
deficits, unemployment numbers, stock prices. Few commentators bother to tackle the large, messy questions about culture.
Still, it seems reasonable to ask the question: is it possible that,
culturally, we're a bit too messed up to mind the store? Three
cultural trends relevant to our past and future economic paths
would seem to indicate that we might be: first, a shortened
attention span, when the complexity of our economy is increasing at a rapid clip; second, a decline in savings rates (broadly
construed); and, third, a decline in societal trust levels.

As author James Gleick says, entertainment and communication get "faster" every year by most measures—beats per
minute, frames per second. What implications does this faster
world have for our long-run economic capacity? A faster world,
characterized by more general "noise" per unit of time, can
diminish overall productive capacity in two main respects.
First, it can crowd out mental energy that could be used in productive ways. Second, it can lessen our tolerance for what moves
slower. It's astonishing how far the process can go—one may
feel that voice communication is too slow, for instance, and
prefer texting. Some of us could never have envisioned such a
change. Still, from the perspective of individuals, the decline in

attention span that has come with a faster world may have both positive and negative effects: our newly limited ability to concentrate may act like a governor on the "happiness treadmill," with adjustments assuring that none of us has too good or too bad a time. Yet from the perspective of the nation as a whole, our ever-shortening attention span negatively affects our long-run economic capability. It's likely it also affects our plasticity—the ability of the economy to respond to negative/adverse shocks.

While in theory the impressive improvements in digital communication and social media of the past decade should lead to substantial improvements in our ability to coordinate complex productive activity, in fact they seem to lead to a fractalization of concern with the self. We're documenting and sharing our own lives at a faster pace; we live in an age of cultural hyperinflation. What you get, at the end of the day, is a frenetic but listless population. We're wrecking our attention spans at a time when we need them, more than ever before, to tackle the relentless complexity of the modern economy.

Let's relate the decline in the American savings ethic to an unusual phenomenon: the national increase in the popularity of tattoos. While time-series data in this realm leave much to be desired, crude measurements indicate that the trend is real. A 1936 study found that 6 percent of people were tattooed; the number has risen to around 15 percent in the past decade. The number of women with tattoos quadrupled between 1960 and 1980. While no one listed in *People* magazine's 1980 "Who is the most beautiful woman?" survey had a tattoo, seven of the ten women listed by the international men's monthly *FHM* as "sexiest women in the world" in 2008 did.

Are tattoos—ironically, in spite of their permanence—a credible signal that one lives for today? In many social contexts, it's valuable to send the message that you are the kind of person who lives for the moment. A tattoo serves as a signaling device. It is sufficiently costly that it creates a separating equilibrium — it allows those who live for the day to credibly convey that fact. Is it a stretch to relate the number of tattoos to the declining U.S. savings rate? I will throw the rise in obesity into the mix as well. Among American adults between twenty-four and seventy, the percentage of those who are overweight jumped from 44.8 percent in 1960 to 66 percent in 2004, with those being obese increasing from 13.3 percent to 32.1 percent during the same period. By 2012, 35.7 percent of U.S. adults and 16.9 percent of children qualified as obese. Excluding the percentage of those whose obesity has a medical provenance, the increase may be said to point to something like the same shortsightedness: obesity is a consequence of a lifestyle while tattoos are an advertisement of it, but the phenomenon at heart is the same.

For economists of the Austrian school, gross domestic product statistics are fairly meaningless as a measure of economic progress. The important thing is not level of economic output but rather the proportion of output devoted to investment as compared with the portion that is consumed. Investment increases long-run economic capacity; consumption represents a drawdown of economic assets and therefore represents a depletion of long-run capacity. Needless to say, economists of the Austrian school are not pleased with recent U.S. economic trends. Their thinking can also be applied to the world of human capital. A week in the library represents an investment in human capital; a week drinking beer at the beach represents consumption, or a decrease in human capital. The United States is not depleting its human capital in a massively irresponsible way, but I'd suggest that to the extent that human capital accumulation is a competition, we have been losing ground, and perhaps at a increasing rate.

The problem within the United States is not only an under-accumulation of human capital but also a misdirection in the investment of human capital. As Pacific Investment Management cofounder Bill Gross says, "Something is wrong when there's a shortage of computer engineers and an oversupply of financial engineers." Financial bubbles push too much talent in one direction, as was true with technology and Internet-related businesses during the dot-com bubble. In economic terms, the United States suffers from a subjective discount rate that is too high, in both real capital accumulation and human capital accumulation. To a greater extent than is good, we value current consumption over future consumption. This is very likely a matter of preference—Americans are expressing a preference for current consumption, and any move to a higher savings regime might well lower overall utility, which includes today's utility plus the discounted value of all future utility. So, as in previous examples, the United States might be behaving rationally from the standpoint of economics, yet in a way that is detrimental to its long-term economic health.

Francis Fukuyama argues, in *Trust: The Social Virtues and the Creation of Prosperity* (1995), that the level of trust is a forgotten variable in macroeconomics and has substantial power in explaining the structure, evolution, and performance of particular economies. The U.S. economy, in Fukuyama's view, ranked very high in trust. In the United States, people trust not only their extended family but also, sometimes, those they have just met; this general amicability, which might lead to two people who meet in a bar one night starting a business together the following week, has been a source of dynamism and strength for the United States in the world economy.

The long downturn that started in 2008 will result in substantial declines in the overall level of trust in U.S. society. It is simply a matter of how far trust levels will fall. High levels of unemployment and generally tenuous employment situations will be a leading factor in the fall in trust. The grossly unequal distribution of wealth and income in the United States is less of a problem when most people's incomes are growing and people feel that the economy is strong and fluid. In such an environment, upward mobility is a palliative for otherwise unacceptable levels of inequality. During a sharp and prolonged recession, mobility is stunted and inequality becomes sharply apparent because the wealthy, although they may have suffered huge losses, still have a cushion to support them through hard times. The poor and the middle class feel, justifiably, that the brunt of the downturn is borne by them. Our service economy seems particularly vulnerable to a decline in the legitimacy of wealth; when the difference between the guy driving a luxury car and his valet comes to be seen as simply a matter of luck, connections, and perhaps guile, and class mobility comes to be seen as stifled, people can't be expected to get along.

We've lived through a time where rent-seeking in the economy reached unheard-of levels (the financial sector peaked at 42 percent of total U.S. corporate profits in 2006); the benefits of this rent-seeking accrued to those who ensconced themselves in power in financial firms. So much of these firms' capital bases had been paid to employees that, for the financial sector as a whole, equity was possibly negative in fall 2008, just two and a half years after the beginning of the (predictable) fall in housing prices.

The U.S. government led a banking-sector recapitalization of unprecedented proportions. The details of the bailout began coming to light in the year or two after it occurred. Nothing we've learned so far has encouraged the view that talent and hard work, rather than connections and guile, are the engine of wealth creation. The political commentator Kevin Phillips once said that finance is the "most subsidized, petted, and socialized industry in the United States." Surely even Phillips was amazed by the aggressiveness of the bailouts and subsidies. Given that credit creation and asset ownership from 1990 to 2010 have been among the most subsidized activities in history, what kind of sense does it make to redistribute based on future income, when those subsidies are likely to decrease dramatically going forward?

Government policymakers' language lately has been the language of bailouts and emergency measures. This language acts insidiously to destroy trust levels. Very often, we heard policymakers remark that this or that bailout had to happen because, whatever the long-term cost of the bailout, it was outweighed by the risk of catastrophe in the near term. What this language does, with respect to trust levels, is to shorten everyone's time horizons; if government officials are implying that tomorrow doesn't matter as much because we might not get there, then sooner or later, this short-term frame of mind is going to seep into everyday individual interactions.

Consider the opening of Robert Axelrod's *The Evolution of Cooperation:* "Under what conditions will cooperation emerge in a world of egoists without central authority?"Axelrod suggests that the crucial requirement is repeated interaction. In short-term interactions, people tend to defect toward their own short-term interest. In a *Mad Max*–type world, where human interactions are random and short-lived, we can expect harsh interaction. Unwittingly, government officials, in their policy justifications and in their manner of speech, are creating a shorter-horizon mode of decision making that will tend to cause dissolution of trust in some measure.

In making the case for his proposed health care program to the public on July 22, 2009, President Obama emphasized that the status quo was unacceptable and implied that without a major, centrally directed change, medical costs would soar uncontrollably over time, severely straining individuals and breaking Medicare and Medicaid. In framing his case in these terms, he created anxiety and fear about the future. Arguably, the effect of these emotions is to shorten people's overall decision-making horizon, creating a lower-trust society.

Robert Putnam's *Bowling Alone*, an extensive documentation of antisocial behavior and the decline of civic organizations, created a sense of nostalgia for the communitarian ethic of the past but little real longing to re-create community in the modern era. The psychologist Mihaly Csikszentmihalyi notes that people enjoy time with family, but they tend to enjoy time with friends more, and they enjoy times of "flow" most of all — times when they are fully immersed in activities, often solitary, that they are extremely passionate about. The modern human being in wealthy societies is constantly in search of these high-intensity "flow" experiences, and the drop-off in (essentially more boring) community activity is a consequence.

The observed behavior of modern, rich societies suggests that this fracturing of community, in favor of a society where individuals are more free to pursue their own conception of optimal experiences, can go a very long way. The wealthier a society, it seems, the fewer the counterweights against individualism. Communitarian restrictions provided by history, religion, and family ties are more often than not simply cast aside.

Although some of the consequences of individualism are regrettable, it might well be the case that our current fractured, individualistic, short-horizon society is optimal in terms of cumulative overall happiness. In the absence of a comprehensive framework/philosophy that suggests how life should be lived, for better or worse, in early twenty-first-century Western nations, we have adopted the moral philosophy of the economist: the best course of action is that which maximizes the sum of happiness of individuals.

In the long term, the United States is following the playbook of a failed empire. This playbook consists of a weak political will abroad, an unsustainable trade balance, increasing public debt (to the point where default or very high inflation is inevitable), a declining culture (at least in terms of fundamental cultural variables associated with economic performance), the financialization of the economy and its influence on rent-seeking activity, and—finally—an inability as a nation to make difficult, long-term political choices. What's the appropriate strategy when you're going through a financial crisis in the midst of a broader, long-run decline? We haven't figured that out yet.

Where does this leave us? Complexity in the system will likely have to decrease; we're no longer capable, culturally, of holding things together in the current form. It's an uphill battle, fought against natural resource constraints, unfavorable demographics, and treacherous government finances, and we're just not up for it. What's likely is that a communitarian ethic will assert itself in the United States and other rich nations out of necessity; widespread failings at the macro level will force people to pay increased attention to their immediate environment.

Civil Society at Ground Zero

Rebecca Solnit

Rebecca Solnit lives in San Francisco and is an activist and the author of thirteen books, including *Storming the Gates of Paradise: Landscapes for Politics* (2007) and *Infinite City: A San Francisco Atlas* (2010).

On Tuesday, November 15, 2011, I awoke in lower Manhattan to the whirring of helicopters overhead, a war-zone sound that persisted all day and then started up again on that Thursday morning, the two-month anniversary of Occupy Wall Street and a big day of demonstrations in New York City. It was one of the dozens of ways you could tell that the authorities took Occupy Wall Street seriously, even if they profoundly mistook what kind of danger it posed. If you ever doubted whether you were powerful or you mattered, you had only to look at the reaction to people like you camped out in parks from Oakland to Portland, Tucson to Manhattan.

Of course, "camped out" doesn't quite catch the spirit of the moment, because those campsites were the way people had come together to bear witness to their hopes and fears, to begin to gather their power and discuss what was possible in our disturbingly unhinged world, to make clear how wrong our economic system is, how corrupt the powers that support it are, and to begin the search for a better way. Consider it an irony that the campsites are partly for sleeping, but also symbols of the way we have awoken.

When civil society sleeps, we're just a bunch of individuals absorbed in our private lives. When we awaken, on campgrounds or elsewhere, when we come together in public and find our power, the authorities are terrified. They often reveal their ugly side, their penchant for violence and for hypocrisy. Consider the liberal mayor of Oakland, who spoke with outrage of people camping without a permit but had nothing to say about the police she dispatched to tear-gas a woman in a wheelchair, shoot a young Iraq war veteran in the head, and assault people while they slept. Consider the billionaire mayor of New York who dispatched the NYPD on a similar middle-of-the-night raid on November 15. Recall this item included in a bald list of events that night: "tear-gassing the kitchen tent." Ask yourself, When did kitchens really need to be attacked with chemical weapons?

Does an eighty-four-year-old woman need to be tear-gassed in Seattle? Does a three-tours-of-duty veteran need to be beaten until his spleen ruptures in Oakland? Does our former poet laureate need to be bashed in the ribs after his poet wife is thrown to the ground at the University of California's Berkeley campus? Admittedly, this is a system that regards people as disposable, but not usually so literally.

In September 2011, the latest protests against that system began. The response only confirms our vision of how it all works. They fought fire with gasoline. Perhaps being frightened made them foolish. After all, once civil society rouses itself from slumber, it can be all but unstoppable. (If they were smart they'd have tried to soothe it back to sleep.) "Arrest one of us; two more appear. You can't arrest an idea!" said the sign held by a man in a Guy Fawkes mask in reoccupied Zuccotti Park on November 17.

The day before, in San Francisco, one hundred activists occupied a Bank of America, even erecting a symbolic tent inside it in which a dozen activists immediately took refuge. At UC-Berkeley, setting up tents on any grounds was forbidden, so the brilliant young Occupiers used clusters of helium balloons to float tents overhead, a smart image of defiance and sky-high ambition. And the valiant UC-Davis students, after several of them were pepper-sprayed in the face while sitting peacefully on the ground, evicted the police, chanting, "You can go! You can go!" The police went.

Occupy Oakland was busted up three times and still thrived. To say nothing of the other 1,400 occupations in the movement.

Alexander Dubček, the government official turned hero of the Prague Spring uprising of 1968, once said, "You can crush the flowers, but you can't stop the spring." The busting of Zuccotti Park and the effervescent, ingenious demonstrations elsewhere are a reminder that, despite the literal occupations on which this protean movement has been built, it can soar as high as those Berkeley balloons and take many unexpected forms. Another OWS sign, "The beginning is near," caught the mood of the moment. Flowers seem like the right image for this uprising led by the young, those who have been most crushed by the new economic order, and who bloom by rebelling and rebel by blooming.

Now world-famous Zuccotti Park is just a small concrete and brown marble–paved scrap of land surrounded by tall buildings. Despite the "Occupy Wall Street" label, it's actually two blocks north of that iconic place. It's rarely noted that the park is within sight of, and kitty-corner to, Ground Zero, where the World Trade Center towers crumbled.

What was born and what died that day a decade ago has everything to do with what's going on in and around the park, the country, and now the world. For this, al-Qaeda is remarkably irrelevant, except as the outfit that long ago triggered an incident that instantly released both the best and the worst in our society. The best was civil society. As I wandered in the Zuccotti Park area during the week of November 14, 2011, I was struck again by how much of what really happened on the morning of September 11 has been willfully misremembered. It can be found nowhere in the plaques and monuments. We need memorials to the coworkers who carried their paraplegic accountant colleague down sixty-nine flights of stairs while in peril themselves; to Ada Rosario Dolch, the principal who got everyone in the High School for Leadership and Public Service building, a block away, safely evacuated, while knowing her sister had probably been killed in one of those towers; to the female executives who walked the blind newspaper seller to safety in Greenwich Village; to the unarmed passengers of United Flight 93. We need monuments to ourselves, to civil society. The only monument civil society ever gets is itself, and the satisfaction of continuing to do the work that matters, the work that has no bosses and no paychecks, the work of connecting, caring, understanding, exploring, and transforming.

One of the complicating factors in the Occupy movement was that so many of the thrown-away people of our society—the homeless, the marginal, the mentally ill, the addicted—came to Occupy encampments for safe sleeping space, food, and medical care. These economic refugees were generously taken in by the new civil society, having been thrown out by the old uncivil one. Complicating everything further was the fact that the politicians and the mainstream media were more than happy to blame the Occupiers for taking in what society as a whole created, and for the further complications that ensued.

Civil society contains all kinds of people, and all kinds showed up at the Occupy encampments. The inclusiveness of such places was one of the great achievements of this movement. (Occupy Memphis, for instance, reached out to Tea Party members.) Veterans, students, their grandparents, hitherto apolitical people, the employed and unemployed, the housed and the homeless, and people of all ages and colors, were drawn in along with the unions. And, yes, there are also a lot of young white activists, who can be thanked for taking on the hard work and heat. We can only hope that this broad coalition will hang together awhile longer.

Just as civil society is all of us, so some of us crossed over to become that force known as the state, and even there, the response was more varied than might be imagined. New York City councilman Ydanis Rodriguez got scraped up and arrested by the NYPD when he tried to walk past a barricade two blocks from Wall Street while the camp was being cleared. Retired New York Supreme Court judge Karen Smith got shoved around and was threatened with arrest while acting as a legal observer. A councilwoman in Tucson, Regina Romero, became a dedicated advocate for the Occupy encampment there, and when the San Francisco police massed on the night of November 3, five supervisors, the public defender, and a state senator all came to stand with us.

I got home at 2:00 a.m. and wrote, "Their vows to us felt like true representative democracy for the first time ever, brought to us by the power of direct democracy: the Occupy movement. I thought of the *Oath of the Horatii*, David's great painting in the spirit of the French Revolution. The spirit in the plaza was gallant, joyous, and ready for anything. A little exalted and full of tenderness for one another. Helicopters hovered overhead, and people sent back reports of buses and massed police in other parts of town. But they never arrived."

Former Philadelphia Police captain Ray Lewis actually came to Wall Street to get arrested. "They complained about the park being dirty," he said. "Here they are worrying about dirty parks when people are starving to death, where people are freezing, where people are sleeping in subways, and they're concerned about a dirty park. That's obnoxious, it's arrogant, it's ignorant, it's disgusting."

The army, or some of its most honorable veterans, were with the Occupiers, too. In the Bay Area, members of Iraq Veterans Against the War were regular participants, and Occupy Wall Street had its larger-than-life ex-marine, Shamar Thomas, clad in worn fatigues and medals. He famously told off the NYPD early on: "This is not a war zone. These are unarmed people. It doesn't make you tough to hurt these people. *It doesn't.* Stop hurting these people!"

To my delight, one day I ran into him, almost literally. He was still wearing his fatigues and medals and carrying a sign that said, on one side, "There's no honor in police brutality," and on the other, "NO WAR."

The grounds of my hope have always been that history is wilder than our imagination and that the unexpected shows up far more regularly than we ever dream. In 2010, no one imagined an Arab Spring, and no one imagined, in 2011, an American Fall—even the people who began planning for it the summer before. We don't know what's coming next, and that's the good news. My advice is just of the most general sort: Dream big. Occupy your hopes. Talk to strangers. Live in public. Don't stop now.

I'm sure of one thing: there are a lot more flowers coming.

The Making of the American 99 Percent and the Collapse of the Middle Class

Barbara Ehrenreich and John Ehrenreich

Barbara Ehrenreich is the author of *Nickel and Dimed: On (Not) Getting By in America*, now in a tenth-anniversary edition with a new afterword. John Ehrenreich is professor of psychology at the State University of New York, College at Old Westbury. He is the author of *The Humanitarian Companion: A Guide for International Aid, Development, and Human Rights Workers*.

> *Class happens when some men, as a result of common experiences (inherited or shared), feel and articulate the identity of their interests as between themselves, and as against other men whose interests are different from (and usually opposed to) theirs.*
>
> —E. P. Thompson, *The Making of the English Working Class* (1963)

The "other men" (and of course women) in the American class alignment are those in the top 1 percent of the wealth distribution—among them the bankers, hedge fund managers, and CEOs targeted by the Occupy Wall Street movement. They have been around for a long time in one form or another, but they only began to emerge as a distinct and visible group, informally called the superrich, in recent years.

Extravagant levels of consumption helped draw attention to them: private jets, multiple fifty-thousand-square-foot mansions, twenty-five-thousand-dollar chocolate desserts embellished with gold dust. But as long as the middle class could still muster the credit for college tuition and occasional home improvements, it seemed churlish to complain. Then came the financial crash of 2007–2008, followed by the Great Recession, and the 1 percent to whom we had entrusted our pensions, our economy, and our political system stood revealed as a band of feckless, greedy narcissists, and possibly sociopaths.

Still, until a few months ago, the 99 percent was hardly a group capable of (as Thompson says) articulating "the identity of their interests." It contained, and still contains, most "ordinary" rich people, along with middle-class professionals, factory workers, truck drivers, and miners, as well as the much poorer people who clean the houses, manicure the fingernails, and maintain the lawns of the affluent.

It was divided not only by these class differences but most visibly by race and ethnicity—a division that has actually deepened since 2008. African Americans and Latinos of all income levels disproportionately lost their homes to foreclosure in 2007 and 2008, and then disproportionately lost their jobs in the wave of layoffs that followed. On the eve of the Occupy movement, the black middle class had been devastated. In fact, the only political movements to have come out of the 99 percent before Occupy emerged were the Tea Party movement and, on the other side of the political spectrum, the resistance to restrictions on collective bargaining in Wisconsin.

Occupy could not have happened if large swaths of the 99 percent had not begun to discover some common interests, or at least to put aside some of the divisions among themselves. For decades, the most stridently promoted division within the 99 percent was the one between what the right calls the liberal elite—composed of academics, journalists, media figures, etc.—and pretty much everyone else.

As *Harper's* magazine columnist Thomas Frank has

brilliantly explained, the right earned its spurious claim to populism by targeting that "liberal elite," which supposedly favored reckless government spending requiring oppressive levels of taxes, supported "redistributive" social policies and programs that reduced opportunity for the white middle class, created ever more regulations (to, for instance, protect the environment) that translated to fewer jobs for the working class, and promoted kinky countercultural innovations like gay marriage. The liberal elite, insisted conservative intellectuals, looked down on "ordinary" middle- and working-class Americans, finding them tasteless and politically incorrect. The "elite" was the enemy, while the superrich were just like everyone else, only more "focused" and perhaps a bit better connected.

Of course, the "liberal elite" never made any sociological sense. Not all academics or media figures are liberal (Newt Gingrich, George Will, Rupert Murdoch). Many well-educated middle managers and highly trained engineers may favor latte over Red Bull, but they were never targets of the right. And how could trial lawyers be members of the nefarious elite, while their spouses in corporate law firms were not?

"Liberal elite" was always a political category masquerading as a sociological one. What gave the idea of a liberal elite some traction, though, at least for a while, was that the great majority of us had, as far as we knew, never knowingly encountered a member of the actual elite, the 1 percent who are, for the most part, sealed off in their own bubble of private planes, gated communities, and walled estates.

The authority figures most people are likely to encounter in their daily lives are teachers, doctors, social workers, and professors. These groups (along with middle managers and other white-collar corporate employees) occupy, for the most part, a much lower position in the class hierarchy. They made up what we described in a 1976 essay as the "professional managerial class." As we wrote at the time, on the basis of our experience of the radical movements of the 1960s and 1970s, there have been real, long-standing resentments between the working class and middle-class professionals. These resentments, which the populist right cleverly deflected toward "liberals," contributed significantly to that previous era of rebellion's failure to build a lasting progressive movement.

As it happened, the idea of the liberal elite could not survive the depredations of the 1 percent in the late 2000s. For one thing, it was summarily eclipsed by the discovery of the Wall Street–based elite and their crimes. Compared to them, professionals and managers, no matter how annoying, were pikers. The doctor or school principal might be overbearing, the professor and the social worker might be condescending, but only the 1 percent took your house away.

There was, as well, another inescapable problem embedded in the right-wing populist strategy: Even by 2000, and certainly by 2010, the class of people who might qualify as part of the liberal elite was in increasingly bad repair. Public-sector budget cuts and corporate-inspired reorganizations were decimating the ranks of decently paid academics, who were being replaced by adjunct professors working on subsistence incomes. Media outlets were shrinking their newsrooms and editorial budgets. Law firms had started outsourcing their more routine tasks to India. Hospitals beamed X-rays to cheap foreign radiologists. Funding had dried up for nonprofit ventures in the arts and public service. Hence the iconic figure of the Occupy movement: the college graduate with tens of thousands of dollars in student loan debts and a job paying about ten dollars an hour, or no job at all.

These trends were in place even before the financial crash hit, but it took the crash and its grim economic aftermath to awaken the 99 percent to a widespread awareness of shared danger. In 2008, the stated intention of "Joe the Plumber" to earn a quarter-million dollars a year still had some faint sense of plausibility. A couple of years into the recession, however, sudden downward mobility had become the mainstream American experience, and even some of the most reliably neoliberal media pundits were beginning to announce that something had gone awry with the American Dream.

Once-affluent people lost their nest eggs as housing prices dropped off cliffs. Laid-off middle-aged managers and professionals were stunned to find that their age made them poison to potential employers. Medical debts plunged middle-class households into bankruptcy. The old conservative dictum—that it was unwise to criticize (or tax) the rich because you might yourself be one of them someday—gave way to a new realization that the class you were most likely to migrate into wasn't the rich, but the poor.

Here was another thing many in the middle class were discovering: The downward plunge into poverty could occur with dizzying speed. One reason the concept of an economic 99 percent first took root in America rather than, say, Ireland or Spain is that Americans are particularly vulnerable to economic dislocation. We have little in the way of a welfare state to stop a family or an individual in free fall. Unemployment benefits do not last more than six months or a year, though in a recession they are sometimes extended by Congress. At present, even with such an extension, they reach only about half the jobless. Welfare was all but abolished in the late 1990s, and health insurance has traditionally been linked to employment.

In fact, once an American starts to slip downward, a variety of forces kicks in to help accelerate the slide. An estimated 60 percent of American firms now check applicants' credit ratings, and discrimination against the unemployed is widespread enough to have begun to warrant congressional concern. Even bankruptcy is a prohibitively expensive, often crushingly difficult status to achieve. Failure to pay government-imposed fines or fees can even lead, through a concatenation of unlucky breaks, to an arrest warrant or a criminal record. Where other once-wealthy nations have a safety net, America offers a greased chute, leading down to destitution with alarming speed.

The occupation encampments that enlivened approximately 1,400 cities in fall 2011 provided a vivid template for the 99 percent's growing sense of unity. Here were thousands of people— we may never know the exact numbers—from all walks of life, living outdoors in the streets and parks, very much as the poorest of the poor have always lived: without electricity, heat, water, or toilets. In the process, they managed to create self-governing communities.

General Assembly meetings brought together an unprecedented mix of recent college graduates, young professionals, elderly people, laid-off blue-collar workers, and plenty of the chronically homeless for what were, for the most part, constructive and civil exchanges. What started as a diffuse protest against economic injustice became a vast experiment in class building. The 99 percent, which might have seemed to be a purely aspirational category early in the fall of 2011, began to will itself into existence.

Can the unity cultivated in the encampments survive as the Occupy movement evolves into a less centralized phase? All sorts of class, racial, and cultural divisions persist within that 99 percent, including distrust between members of the former liberal elite and those less privileged. It would be surprising if they didn't. The life experience of a young lawyer or a social worker is very different from that of a blue-collar worker whose job may rarely allow for biological necessities like meal or bathroom breaks. Drum circles, consensus decision making, and masks remain exotic to at least the 90 percent. "Middle-class" prejudice against the homeless, fanned by decades of right-wing demonization of the poor, retains much of its grip.

Sometimes these differences led to conflict in Occupy encampments—for example, over the role of the chronically homeless in Portland, Oregon, or the use of marijuana in Los Angeles—but amazingly, despite all the official warnings about health and safety threats, there was no "Altamont moment": no major fires and hardly any violence. In fact, the encampments engendered almost unthinkable convergences: people from comfortable backgrounds learning about street survival from the homeless, a distinguished professor of political science discussing horizontal versus vertical decision making with a postal worker, military men in dress uniforms showing up to defend the Occupiers from the police.

Class happens, as Thompson said, but it happens most decisively when people are prepared to nourish and build it. If the "99 percent" is to become more than a stylish meme, if it's to become a force to change the world, eventually we will have to confront some of the class and racial divisions that lie within it. We need to do so patiently, respectfully, and always with an eye to the next big action—the next march, or building occupation, or foreclosure fight, as the situation demands.

PART III

SOLUTIONS

Occupy K Street

Paul Volcker

Paul Volcker was chairman of the Federal Reserve
from 1979 to 1987 and chairman of the Economic
Recovery Advisory Board under President Barack
Obama from 2009 to 2011. The so-called Volcker rule,
a section of the 2010 Dodd-Frank Wall Street Reform
and Consumer Protection Act that restricts proprietary trading, is named for him.

I don't know just where the Washington, D.C., area ranks in
income distribution among American cities. I do know just
by looking that it must be high. Here we are in the midst of the
Great Recession, and the place is booming. Big, bulky office
buildings, prestigious new apartments, McMansions in the
suburbs, four-star hotels all over, fancy restaurants, thriving
cultural centers, a convention center, on and on. We also know
the main industry. It's manned by lawyers, lobbyists, trade
associations, lots of ex-congressmen—and it concentrates on
one product: influence.

Money isn't exactly new in politics, but it sure is growing
exponentially. It shows up not just in elections but day by day,
month by month, in a growing flood of finance and talent, to
influence laws and regulations and officeholders. And in this
process, the end result is ever more complexity and loss of
clarity.

Citizen representation before all levels of governmental
authority is a part—an absolutely necessary part—of American democracy. It's hard to think of a legislative or regulatory

process without consultation. But when "representation" is so imbued with money, one is entitled to wonder: are there no limits?

Can it really be true that our government is for sale?

I hope not.

But the threat makes it worth occupying K Street.

Interview with Emmanuel Saez

Kathleen Maclay

Emmanuel Saez is one of the economists whose research gave Occupy Wall Street the slogan "We are the 99 percent." In a series of papers published between 2003 and 2010, Saez and French economist Thomas Piketty showed that the top 1 percent of American households accounted for about two-thirds of all income gains in the period 2002–2007. The top 1 percent saw their incomes increase more than 10 percent a year when adjusted for inflation, while the rest of the households—the 99 percent—had income increases of 1.3 percent a year. From 2007 to 2008, the average real income for the top percentile fell 19.7 percent (resulting in a drop in the top percentile income share from 23.5 percent to 20.9 percent), and average real income for the bottom 99 percent also fell sharply, by 6.9 percent. The decline for the 99 percent was the greatest year-to-year decline since the Great Depression.

Kathleen Maclay works in the University of California-Berkeley Media Relations office.

KATHLEEN MACLAY: What do you make of the Occupy Wall Street protesters' claims that they "are the 99 percent"? Do you feel they are connecting—deliberately or not—with the bottom 99 percent that you have studied and written about?

EMMANUEL SAEZ: One of the most striking developments of the U.S. economy is how the top 1 percent has pulled away from the bottom 99 percent. Because the top 1 percent has captured about half of income growth since the 1970s, income growth for the bottom 99 percent has been only about half of the macroeconomic growth we always hear about in the press.

How is it possible that in a democracy the bottom 99 percent gets only half of economic growth? In a well-functioning democracy, the bottom 99 percent should be able to call for policies that will make the economy work better for the vast majority they are.

KM: Why do you think the Occupy Wall Street protests are happening now?

ES: The 2008 economic crisis was largely the consequence of deregulated finance running amok. Even before the crisis, economic gains for the bottom 99 percent had not been that great. Although it was necessary to bail out Wall Street to prevent greater economic damage, the public got the impression that the government stepped in to help Wall Street without asking any significant sacrifice from Wall Street in return. As the Democratic Party has been in power since 2009, this triggered first a right-wing backlash against government. Although the Occupy Wall Street protest, along with many sister movements in Europe, also starts from a disillusion about government action, it comes with the constructive feeling that there must be a way the government can make things better.

KM: What are the key causes for the substantial income gaps in the United States today? What role does the size of the federal deficit play, if any?

ES: New technologies and globalization cannot explain the dramatic increase in the U.S. income gaps because countries in continental Europe—such as France or

Germany—and Japan are going through the same technological and globalization forces yet are not experiencing such a dramatic increase in income gaps.

This implies that institutions, government policies and regulations, and social norms play a central role in shaping income gaps. To put things simply, the U.S. income gaps shrank significantly after the Great Depression with the New Deal policies of stringent regulations and progressive taxation and widened significantly after the Reagan revolution that undid those regulations and progressive taxation.

KM: You have written that "we need to decide as a society whether this increase in income inequality is efficient and acceptable and, if not, what mix of institutional reforms should be developed to counter it." Do you find the situation efficient and acceptable? Why or why not?

ES: The extraordinary increase in income concentration in the United States from 2002 to 2007 was driven in large part by surging profits in the real estate and financial sectors made possible by deregulation. As we know, the financial–real estate bubble is what triggered the 2008 Great Recession that we are still struggling with.

Therefore, it seems clear today that this increase in inequality was inefficient and hence unacceptable.

In my view, the administration in Washington, D.C., should have been much more aggressive both in reregulating finance and increasing progressive taxation. This would have been beneficial both to prevent such excesses from happening again and to fund the Wall Street bailouts and the stimulus packages necessary to fight the recession. Back in 2009, those policies could have been easily explained to the public and could have gathered both popular and congressional support.

KM: If the situation is unacceptable, what reforms in terms of economic and tax policy might offer the best counterbalances?

ES: History and empirical evidence is again the best guide here. [Thomas] Philippon and [Ariell] Reshef have shown a striking correlation between financial deregulation and relative wages in the financial industry in the Unites States over the twentieth century.

Similarly, there is a strong negative correlation between pretax income concentration and the progressivity of the tax system in the United States. Naturally, economists should and do argue about whether regulation and progressive taxation can stifle growth. Contrary to free market dogma, the historical experience of most Western countries in the post–World War II decades shows that high regulation and highly progressive taxation can be associated with rapid and sustained economic growth.

KM: You direct the Center for Equitable Growth at UC-Berkeley. Can you define equitable growth?

ES: Equitable growth is economic growth that is widely and fairly distributed so that it benefits all: a tide that lifts all boats. Virtually all Western countries experienced strong and yet equitable growth in the decades following World War II. This shows that growth and equity can go hand in hand.

Since the 1970s, growth has slowed down in most Western countries and has become much less equitable, especially in English-speaking countries such as the United States. Hence the interest among economists in understanding what policies could usher in a new era of equitable growth.

KM: How and why did you become so interested in and engaged in the subject of income inequality?

ES: Market economies have obviously been very successful at producing growth, but this growth often comes with large economic disparities. Those disparities matter, because people live in society and care about how they do relative to others. Historically, inequality has always been one of the very top criticisms of market economies. Hence, inequality is not only a technical subject for economic researchers but an issue that can stir passion among the broader public, which makes it worthy of study.

Although I started studying mathematics at the École Normale Supérieure in Paris, I quickly realized that economics was the field where analytical tools could be used to cast light on deep issues in society—such as income inequality and what the government could or should do about it.

KM: Do you support the protests? Why or why not?

ES: I definitely support the protests, as I think it is high time for the U.S. government to acknowledge and tackle head-on the issue of increasing income concentration. With political will and public support, there is no doubt in my mind that the government can have a major impact on inequality.

Protests are extremely important to make the public and the press aware of issues. In that sense, peaceful protests should play an important role in all societies, including our perfectible democracies. We know from history and from recent events that protests sometimes can change governments and have a decisive influence on policymaking.

KM: Do you think the protests are having or may have significant impact, or are they more just an expression of frustration by those outside the circles of Washington and financial industry decision makers?

ES: The attention-grabbing success of the protests is already a sign of a significant impact. Whether they will have real policy consequences remains to be seen. The current disillusion among the public with the ability of government to accomplish anything positive is unfortunately not the best environment.

I wish those protests had started exactly three years ago, when hope in a better government was running high. Let us hope that a constructive alternative can arise from disillusion.

Taxing High Earnings

Peter Diamond and Emmanuel Saez

Peter Diamond is professor emeritus of economics at the Massachusetts Institute of Technology. In 2010 he was awarded the Nobel Memorial Prize in Economic Sciences. Emmanuel Saez is professor of economics at the University of California-Berkeley. In 2009 he was awarded the John Bates Clark Medal, and in 2010 he was named a MacArthur Fellow.

Congressional Republicans are opposed to any increase in the 35 percent tax rate on the highest earnings, the rate that has been in place since 2003. The Obama administration would like to see a lapse in the Bush tax cut for the top earners and go back to the 39.6 percent top tax rate in force from 1993 to 2000, during the Clinton administration. We think that the marginal tax rate on the top 1 percent (roughly, earnings above $400,000) should be much higher. We favor a top tax rate near or in the range of 50 percent to 70 percent: 50 percent being the top tax rate in force from 1982 to 1986, during the Reagan administration, and 70 percent being the top tax rate in force from 1965 to 1981, under Presidents Johnson, Nixon, Ford, and Carter. We reach this conclusion by combining widely accepted notions of fairness in taxation with empirical analysis of the tax revenue loss (and so efficiency cost) as a consequence of how top earners are likely to change their behavior in response to higher taxes. We do not pin down a single number, because a good number depends on fairness factors, about which judgments differ, and on behavioral effects, about which estimates vary; but, allowing for these uncertainties, the gain from a much larger increase than is discussed by politicians is pretty clear.

The U.S. government collects most of its revenue from taxes on earnings. How much of these taxes should be collected from the highest earners and how much from the rest of workers? Whatever the overall level of revenue being raised by the government, the choice of tax rates on different earnings levels remains important. Taxing earnings takes money from people and alters their economic behavior, both because they have less money and because they get to keep only the after-tax fraction of any additional earnings. People vary in their ability to bear the cost of paying taxes, so that fairness concerns call for those with higher earnings to pay a larger share of earnings to support government expenditures. However, as the marginal tax rate on earnings gets higher, it lowers the incentive to earn. When people work less because of taxes on additional earnings, their choice of how much to earn ignores their contribution to government revenue—a contribution that supports government spending and government transfer programs, which help others. Since their decisions do not reflect their impact on everyone, their choices will not be efficient from the perspective of the entire economy. While it is common to hear opposition to a particular tax increase because it affects earnings or jobs, by itself such analysis is not a basis for analyzing taxes, since every tax on earnings affects earnings or jobs. The key question is to make a choice of tax rates based on the trade-off between greater fairness from larger tax burdens on those better able to bear the burden and more efficiency losses as tax rates get higher. This is the classic issue in the design of an income tax, referred to as the equity-efficiency trade-off, which is at the core of analyses of what is called the optimal income tax problem.

To approach this equity-efficiency trade-off, we need to think about the outcome of taxation in two dimensions: (1) the fairness of collecting taxes in different proportions of earnings for those with different earnings levels and (2) how much the levels of tax rates affect economic behavior of different people. For the first question we need to ask how much we care about taking a further dollar of revenues away from some group—for example, those earning above $400,000—compared with taking that dollar from, say, the median family, with an income of $52,700: given the level of expenditures to be financed, choosing to take less revenue from the highest earners requires taking more revenue from people with lower earnings (or using revenue from some other tax). People will naturally differ in their evaluation of the fairness associated with differences in taxation of high earners and average earners. We proceed from the principle that it is much better to take a dollar from the group of people earning over $400,000 than from those with much lower earnings. Economists refer to the relative weighting of dollars remaining in the hands of different earners as a normative question—one that calls for an ethical judgment, not a scientific economic evaluation.

Consistent with a wide variety of approaches to this normative issue is the conclusion that there should be greater willingness to take tax dollars from the highest earners when the income distribution has more inequality, as we have experienced over recent decades. The share of total income going to the top 1 percent of income earners has increased dramatically, from 9 percent in 1970 to 23.5 percent in 2007, the highest level on record since 1928 and much higher than in European countries or Japan today. Meanwhile, the top tax rate has fallen by half, from 70 percent to 35 percent.

In contrast with the normative concern about the taxation of those with different earnings levels, the impact of taxes on efficiency is a "positive question"—a question for which there is an empirical answer, although one that it is not easy to measure accurately; and we have only a range of plausible answers. As a first approximation, the efficiency loss is related to the extent to which tax revenue is lower because of the behavioral response to higher marginal tax rates through reduced reported earnings. That is, to what extent do higher marginal tax rates cause tax revenue to go down because earners simply report less income? Lower reported income comes from a combination of doing less work and so earning less, arranging to be paid in a form that is taxed less heavily (tax avoidance), and not reporting income actually earned (tax evasion). To collect more revenue from higher earners, there is a need to tax them at a higher rate, but higher rates tend to increase the overall efficiency loss. Hence the equity-efficiency trade-off.

A starting place for thinking about a suitable tax rate to set on the highest earners is to estimate the tax rate that maximizes the revenue from this group. Any higher rate would lose revenue while also lowering the financial position of these high earners. We do not favor rates so high that we harm the finances of the highest earners and lose tax revenue in the process. Any lower rate gives up revenue to leave the highest earners better off. How much lower one thinks the rate should be depends on the level of one's concern about the income of the highest earners relative to the level of one's concern about taxpayers with lower earnings.

Consider an increase in the tax rate on earnings above the level of $400,000. If there were no behavioral response, then the revenue would go up by the size of the tax rate increase times the total amount of earnings above $400,000. The average income for this group is roughly $1.2 million, so there is $800,000 of taxable income per person for an increase in the tax rate on earnings above \$400,000. This ratio of income above the cutoff of \$400,000 (\$1.2 million) to the cutoff (\$400,000) is pretty much constant as we move further up the income distribution—for example, an average of \$1.5 million above a cutoff of \$500,000. In technical terms, the constancy of this ratio implies that the top earnings distribution is a Pareto distribution. This ratio for a Pareto distribution can be described in terms of a parameter a that will be used in the tax formula below, with the value of a roughly 1.5.

For the formula, we also need to consider the behavioral response to raising the tax rate. Economists have long studied how much on average people change their hours of work, and thus their earnings level, when they get a pay increase. Workers respond to their wages net of the additional taxes from additional earnings—the net-of-tax wage, or the wage multiplied by one minus the tax rate. The same empirical calculation of the response of earnings to wage changes provides a way to estimate how much earnings change when the tax rate changes. It is convenient to measure this in percentage terms—the percentage change in earnings for a 1 percent change in the after-tax wage. This is the key remaining empirical ingredient to evaluate the impact, on revenue, of a tax increase on top earners, and it is referred to as the elasticity e of top incomes with respect to the net-of-tax rate.

The formula for the tax rate that maximizes revenue from the top earners, τ^*, is simple—in terms of the parameters defined above, it is given by the equation

$$\tau^* = 1/(1 + a\,e)$$

This formula does not refer just to the income tax rate but to the combination of all taxes that together determine how much consumption spending can come from additional earnings.

Thus it combines the federal income tax, the Medicare tax, and state and local income and sales taxes. The top U.S. marginal tax rate, combining all taxes, is 42.5 percent, while the top federal income tax rate is 35 percent. We have a good estimate of a of 1.5, but only a range of estimates of e. The connection between the estimate of e and the top total tax rate and federal income tax rate is shown in the table below.

Tax Rates to Maximize Revenues from Top Earners

Elasticity of taxable income	Total tax rate	Federal income tax rate
0.1	87%	84%
0.25	73%	68%
0.5	57%	51%
0.75	47%	41%
1	40%	32%

For the top tax rate of 42.5 percent to be the revenue-maximizing value, the elasticity would need to be 0.9, close to one—solving from $0.425 = 1/(1 + 1.5 \times e)$. But this value for the elasticity is well above the majority of the best estimates.

There is a large body of literature using tax reforms to estimate the elasticity e relevant for this revenue-maximizing tax formula. The literature has focused primarily on the response of reported income, either adjusted gross income or taxable income, to net-of-tax rates. Adjusted gross income measures earnings, while taxable income measures earnings minus deductions. Deductions are also influenced by tax rates. Some deductions, like mortgage interest payments, reflect changes in house purchases and so represent a distortion related to taxation. In contrast, the deduction for charitable giving represents a change that benefits others and should not be considered a distortion in the same way.

Part of the behavioral elasticity is due to real economic responses such as labor supply and business creation, but part is due to tax avoidance and evasion responses. A number of studies have shown substantial responses of reported incomes that happen quickly and come from the tax avoidance margin at the top of the distribution; but no compelling study to date has shown substantial responses along the real economic responses margin among top earners. In other words, top earners can move taxable income between years to subject them to lower tax rates, for example by changing the timing of charitable donations and other deductions. But existing studies do not show much change in actual work being done. Jonathan Gruber and Saez are often cited for their substantial taxable income elasticity estimate ($e = 0.57$) at the top of the distribution. However, they also found a small elasticity ($e = 0.17$) for income before any deductions, even at the top of the distribution. Both numbers help inform a suitable choice, since some of the increase in deductions, such as charitable giving, should not be viewed as a full efficiency loss.

As a start, we follow the link from elasticity to tax rate as given in the formula above. For the Pareto parameter $a = 1.5$, if $e = 0.25$, a midrange estimate from the empirical literature, then the tax rate to maximize revenue, $\tau^* = 1/(1 + 1.5 \times 0.25) = 73$ percent, is substantially higher than the 42.5 percent top U.S. marginal tax rate in 2011 (combining all taxes). Before exploring further steps, we review the issue of tax avoidance.

When a tax system offers tax avoidance or evasion opportunities, the tax base in any given year is quite sensitive to tax rates, so that the elasticity e is large, and the revenue-maximizing top tax rate is correspondingly low. Two important qualifications must be made. First, many of the tax avoidance channels, such as retiming or income shifting, produce increases in tax revenue in other years or other tax bases, and hence do not decrease the revenue-maximizing tax rate as much as would appear if one were looking only at income tax revenues in a single year. That is, moving taxable income between years, or from earned income to capital gains, does not eliminate all of the tax revenue that would be collected without the change: there is a drop in revenue from the tax base being reduced and a rise in tax revenue from the tax base to which the income has been moved. For the impact on total tax revenue, both of these must be considered, and ignoring the additional effect gives too low an estimate of the revenue-maximizing rate.

Second, and more important, the tax avoidance or evasion component of the elasticity e is not an immutable parameter, but can be reduced through base broadening and tax enforcement. Thus, while base broadening and decreased tax rates overall go together to produce a given level of revenue, base broadening and increased tax rates on high earners (and so further decreases in tax rates on lower earners) can go together insofar as high earners make more use of tax avoidance strategies than lower earners. For example, if the Internal Revenue Service pursues tax cheats more vigorously, this not only raises revenue (beyond the cost of more stringent enforcement) but also changes the relationship between tax rates and tax revenues, and so the tax rates that bring in more revenue.

As an illustration using the different elasticity estimates of Gruber and Saez for high-income earners, the top tax rate to maximize revenue (including all taxes) using the 2011 taxable income base (and ignoring tax externalities—both increases in revenue in other years and the value of changes in charitable donations) would be $\tau^* = 1/(1 + 1.5 \times 0.57) = 54$ percent, while the revenue-maximizing top tax rate if we legislated a broader income base with no deductions would be $\tau^* = 1/(1 + 1.5 \times 0.17) = 80$ percent. Taking state and payroll tax rates as fixed, such rates correspond to top federal income tax rates equal to 48 percent and 76 percent, respectively. These calculations give us a range of values, with the appropriate one, including the factors that are not included in these two calculations, lying somewhere in between. Although considerable uncertainty remains in the estimation of the long-run behavioral responses to top tax rates, the elasticity $e = 0.57$ is a conservative upper-bound estimate of the elasticity and so a conservative lower-bound estimate of the implied revenue-maximizing top tax rate. Therefore, the case that considerably higher rates at the top than at present would still raise more revenue appears robust in the context of the standard model of income taxation.

Starting with a value for the tax rate that maximizes revenue, we can ask how much lower the tax rate should be to recognize a positive value for higher incomes for top earners. That is, consideration of the fairness dimension, which can be captured by the extent to which we value higher incomes for top earners as opposed to higher incomes for lower earners, lowers the tax rate from the rate that maximizes revenue, which shows no concern for a larger financial outcome for top earners. People will differ in the extent of their concern for top earners compared with lower earners. We now alter the formula above for the revenue-maximizing tax rate to a rate that also reflects a normative weight given to top earners, which we denote τ^{**}. This now involves three key parameters. In addition to the parameter a of the earnings distribution and the parameter e for the response of earnings to tax rates, we introduce a parameter g to represent the normative weight to put on high earners. The parameter g measures the concern for the income of the top earners relative to a weight on the revenue needed by government (reflecting the normative weight on lower earners, who must provide revenue not coming from the top earners).

$$\tau^{**} = (1 - g)/(1 - g + a\, e)$$

If we set g close to zero, this is saying that additional income for those averaging $1.2 million is of very little importance relative to the incomes of lower earners, who have to pay higher taxes if the highest earners pay less (and also reflecting the elasticity that is plausibly lower on lower earners). For example, with $a = 1.5$ and $e = 0.25$, the total top tax rate with g equal to zero is 73 percent. Increasing g to 0.1 or 0.2 lowers the tax rate in the formula to 71 percent and 68 percent. Those rates would be obtained with top federal income tax rates of 67 percent and 63 percent, respectively. Because the government should be concerned about income distribution, the weight g for top-bracket tax filers is small relative to that of the average person in the economy, so that g is small for plausible normative concerns and the optimal rate is close to the rate that maximizes revenue. A commonly calculated example has g proportional to the inverse of the level of income. In this case, the last dollar of income of someone with twice as much income gets half as much weight as does the last dollar of income of the lower earner. For example, weight g at the $1,364,000 average income of the top 1 percent in 2007 is only 3.9 percent of the weight g of the median family, with an income of $52,700. When the weight g for the top earners is very small, the tax rate that balances fairness considerations with revenue needs is close to the rate that maximizes revenue. Formally this can be seen by doing some calculations using the formula above.

To some readers, marginal income tax rates on the top percentile of earners within a range of 48 percent to 76 percent may seem implausibly high. One way to judge how seriously to take such numbers is to consider whether elements left out of the analysis push for a significantly different answer. Two such elements are capital income and lifetime or long-term career considerations.

As long as capital income (dividends, capital gains) is taxed less heavily than labor income, the ability to convert some labor income into capital income is a reason for limiting the difference between tax rates on the two types of income—that is, an argument for a somewhat lower labor income tax to limit the extent of such conversions. It is also an argument for limiting the extent to which dividends and capital gains are taxed less heavily than earnings.

Perhaps most critically, does a calculation based on estimates of how earnings in a typical year depend on taxes that year still apply when recognizing that people earn and pay income taxes year after year? First, earlier decisions made by the taxpayer, such as what level of education and which career to pursue, affect later earnings opportunities. It is conceivable that a more progressive tax system could reduce incentives to accumulate human capital—advanced degrees, for instance— in the first place. The logic of the equity-efficiency trade-off would still carry through, but the elasticity e should reflect not only short-run labor supply responses but also long-run responses through education and career choices. While there is a sizable multiperiod optimal tax literature using life-cycle models and generating insights, we unfortunately have little compelling empirical evidence to assess whether taxes affect earnings significantly through those long-run channels.

Second, there is significant uncertainty about future earnings. Thus a thirty-year-old recognizes that earnings at age fifty might or might not be much higher than earnings at thirty. Net-of-tax earnings will not be as uncertain with a tax system that has lower tax rates on lower earnings, because revenues are also coming from higher tax rates on higher earnings. In other words, we should think of the rise in tax rates with earnings as a form of insurance about future earnings levels. In addition to providing insurance directly, this tax rate structure makes investing in human capital less risky.

A third consideration is the heightened concern about taxing the earnings of those with limited ability to borrow. That is, people can save and borrow to have consumption levels that need not exactly match earnings levels. It is consumption, not income, that is at the heart of distributional concerns. But many people, particularly young people, have limited ability to borrow against future earnings. This affects not only the efficiency of the timing of their consumption but also, as has become clearer since the onset of the financial crisis, the ability of people to start new businesses. This is both an argument for taxing capital income (and so taxing earnings less heavily while raising a given level of total revenue) and for tax rates that rise with earnings level, given that on average there is a higher level of wealth (available to support start-ups) among the highest earners, compared with those with lower earnings.

Fourth, the results described above apply in a situation in which individual earnings are equal to the productivity of the worker. There are strong reasons to suspect that pay and productivity diverge for some workers, especially at the top of the income distribution. It is particularly difficult to measure the actual economic contribution of managers working in complex organizations. Therefore, top earners might be able to partly set their own pay by bargaining harder or working at influencing compensation committees. Naturally, the incentives for top earners to make such efforts for higher pay for the same amount of work are much stronger when top tax rates are low. In this scenario, in the long run, cuts in top tax rates can still increase reported incomes at the top, but the increases in top 1 percent incomes now come at the expense of the remaining 99 percent—insofar as top-rate cuts stimulate harder bargaining for higher pay at the top but not overall economic output. In a model including such considerations, if top earners are overpaid relative to their productivity, the optimal tax rate is naturally higher than in the standard model. Public perceptions of the extent to which top earners are paid for productivity or overpaid play a key role in the policy debate about top tax rates. Empirically, it is difficult to estimate divergences between pay and productivity, and to determine whether such divergences respond to top tax rates.

Although the average federal individual income tax rate of top-percentile tax filers was 22.4 percent in 2007, the top percentile paid 40.4 percent of total federal individual income taxes. Therefore, the taxation of very high earners is a central aspect of the tax policy debate not only for the equity-efficiency trade-off reasons we have analyzed but also for overall revenue raising. For example, setting aside behavioral responses, increasing the average tax rate on the top percentile from 22.4 percent (as of 2007) to 29.4 percent would raise revenue by 1 percentage point of gross domestic product. Indeed, even increasing the average tax rate of the top percentile to 43.5 percent, which would be sufficient to raise revenue by 3 percentage points of GDP, would still leave the after-tax income share of the top percentile more than twice as high as in 1970. Of course, increasing upper-income tax rates can discourage economic activity through behavioral responses, and hence potentially reduce tax collections, creating the standard equity-efficiency trade-off discussed above. Nevertheless, we conclude that a significant increase in the tax rate on the top earners to finance lower taxes on lower earners would be valuable. This conclusion should be part of any discussion of increases in tax revenues as part of addressing our unsustainable budget trajectory. Perhaps a marginal income tax rate of 49 percent, which has an attractive symbolic content, being less than half, and just below the rate set in the early Reagan years, would be a plausible number, far more likely to be too low than too high in light of both fairness and efficiency concerns.

Commentary

J. Bradford DeLong

J. Bradford DeLong, a former assistant secretary of the U.S. Treasury, is professor of economics at the University of California-Berkeley and a research associate at the National Bureau for Economic Research.

Peter Diamond and Emmanuel Saez argue in the previous essay, "Taxing High Earnings," that the right marginal tax rate for the United States to impose on our richest citizens is somewhere in the range of 50 percent to 70 percent.

It is an arresting assertion, given the tax-cut mania that has prevailed for the past thirty years, but Diamond and Saez's logic is clear. The superrich command and control so many resources that they are effectively satiated: increasing or decreasing how much wealth they have has little or no effect on their happiness. So no matter how large a weight we place on their happiness relative to the happiness of others—whether we regard them as praiseworthy captains of industry who merit their high positions or as parasitic thieves—we simply cannot do anything to affect it by raising or lowering their tax rates.

The unavoidable implication of this argument is that when we calculate what the tax rate for the superrich will be, we should not consider the effect on their happiness, for we know that it is zero. Rather, the key question must be the effect of changing their tax rate on the well-being of the rest of us.

From this simple chain of logic follows the conclusion that we have a moral obligation to tax our superrich at a rate close to the peak of the Laffer curve: to tax them so heavily that we raise close to the most possible money from them—the point beyond which their diversion of energy and enterprise into tax avoidance and sheltering would mean that any extra taxes would not raise but reduce revenue.

The utilitarian economic logic is clear. Yet more than half of us are likely to reject the conclusion reached by Diamond and Saez. We feel that there is something wrong with taxing our superrich until the pips squeak so much that further taxation reduces the number of pips. And we feel this for two reasons, both of them set out more than two centuries ago by Adam Smith—not in his most famous work, *The Wealth of Nations*, but in his far less often discussed book *The Theory of Moral Sentiments*.

The first reason applies to the idle rich. According to Smith:

> A stranger to human nature, who saw the indifference of men about the misery of their inferiors, and the regret and indignation which they feel for the misfortunes and sufferings of those above them, would be apt to imagine, that pain must be more agonizing, and the convulsions of death more terrible to persons of higher rank, than to those of meaner stations.

We feel this, Smith believes, because we naturally sympathize with others (if he were writing today, he would surely invoke mirror neurons). And the more pleasant our thoughts about individuals or groups are, the more we tend to sympathize with them. In Smith's words, the fact that the lifestyles of the rich and famous "[seem] to be almost the abstract idea of a perfect and happy state" leads us to "pity...that any thing should spoil and corrupt so agreeable a situation! We could even wish them immortal."

The second reason applies to the hardworking rich, the type of person who

> devotes himself forever to the pursuit of wealth and greatness....With the most unrelenting industry he labors night and day...serves those whom he hates, and is obsequious to those whom he despises....In the last dregs of life, his body wasted with toil and diseases, his mind galled and ruffled by the memory of a thousand injuries and disappointments...he begins at last to find that wealth and greatness are mere trinkets of frivolous utility....Power and riches...keep off the summer shower, not the winter storm, but leave him always as much, and sometimes more exposed than before, to anxiety, to fear, and to sorrow; to diseases, to danger, and to death.

In short, on the one hand, we don't wish to disrupt the perfect felicity of the lifestyles of the rich and famous; on the other hand, we don't wish to add to the burdens of those who have spent their most precious possession—their time and energy—pursuing baubles. These two arguments are not consistent, but that does not matter. They both have a purchase on our thinking.

Unlike today's public-finance economists, Smith understood that we are not rational utilitarian calculators. Indeed, that is why we have collectively done a very bad job so far in dealing with the enormous rise in inequality between the industrial middle class and the plutocratic superrich that we have witnessed in the last generation.

Boycott!

Michael Lewis
Interviews Himself

Michael Lewis is the bestselling author of *Liar's Poker*, *Moneyball*, *The Blind Side*, *The Big Short*, and *Boomerang*. He lives in Berkeley, California, with his wife and three children.

What was your first reaction to the Occupy movement?

Some blend of glee and relief. Glee because, by both temperament and occupation, I have a rooting interest in socially disruptive behavior. Relief because I had begun to think such protests might never happen. Given the provocation—intense and effective political pressure from Wall Street to codify two sets of economic rules, one for people who work at giant Wall Street firms, the other for people who don't—I was surprised it has taken as long as it has for people to hit the streets. The chief cause of the financial crisis was what the government didn't do (regulate) rather than what it did (subsidize homeownership), and so it seemed strange to me that, until now, the most potent political reaction to the financial crisis has been an anti-government backlash. It was as if, after some infectious disease killed a million people, the only political reaction was a popular uprising to prevent the manufacture of antibiotics.

Have your feelings about the movement changed?

Yes.

How?

I think it is a bigger deal than I did when it first started. It's true in many cities that the campsites are being broken up, and the protesters dispersed. But it's pretty clear that they hit a nerve. People didn't like them living on their streets, but they liked what they stood for.

What evidence do you have to support any sweeping statement about American public opinion?

Did you see Obama's Kansas speech? [On December 6, 2011, President Barack Obama gave a speech in Osawatomie, Kansas, the city in which, on August 31, 1910, Theodore Roosevelt gave his "New Nationalism" address.] Clearly the White House strategy people have decided to fight the next presidential election on the issues that preoccupy the Occupy movement: radical economic inequality and the grotesque distortions in our politics that it causes. Plus various polls all showed that the American people more or less supported the movement—to the extent that many of the 1 percenters simply assumed they were 99 percenters.

The big complaint about the movement is that it doesn't know what it wants. If someone put you in charge of the movement, what would you have it do?

I'm not certain that they're wrong to be as woolly-minded about their goals as they seem to be. By not being too explicit about what they want, they attract anyone who is upset about anything. But if I were in charge I would probably reorganize the movement around a single, achievable goal: a financial boycott of the six "too big to fail" Wall Street firms: Bank of America, Citigroup, JPMorgan Chase, Goldman Sachs, Morgan Stanley, Wells Fargo. We would encourage people who had deposits in these firms to withdraw them, and put them in smaller, not "too big to fail" banks. We would stigmatize anyone who invested, in any way, in any of these banks. I'd try to organize college students to protest on campuses. Their first goal would be to force the university endowments to divest themselves of shares in these banks.

Do you really think that could work?

Yes. I think we could create a run on a bank.

If you are so sure that the movement is both important and just, why did you not yourself join them?

The one tent I own is too big. It would have stood out.

Any other reason?

I have small children.

What does that have to do with anything?

It's the excuse I use to get out of doing anything I don't really want to do. People seem to accept it.

You are evading the real question. You have written not one but two books about the financial crisis, in which you point out the evils of the current financial system. Since the Occupy movement began, your only contribution has been to write two short satirical pieces in which you designed a strategy for the 1 percenters to keep their money and continue to recruit Ivy League students. Why do writers think it's okay to be all talk and no action?

Okay, I'll tell you what happened. Twice I wandered around Occupy camps—in Washington and in San Francisco. There was one giddy moment when I thought I should get up and give a rousing speech about the evils of credit default swaps. After that, I just felt absurd. I was of no use.

Reforming Western Capitalism
Martin Wolf

Martin Wolf, associate editor and chief economics commentator at the *Financial Times*, is the author of *Fixing Global Finance* (2008) and *Why Globalization Works* (2004).

The criticisms of today's capitalism are both old and modern. Capitalism, critics argue, serves greed, exploits vulnerability, imposes inequality, suborns democracy, and despoils the environment. Capitalist economies are both unstable and unjust. The system works by promoting endless dissatisfaction today, to be sated by ever more consumption tomorrow.

In times of economic distress and high unemployment, such criticisms come once again to the fore. They were rampant in the 1930s, when many believed in the viability of a socialist alternative. They have returned today, albeit in a weaker form, since few now believe in any alternative. This is partly because of the failures of socialism. It is also because the remedies propounded in the 1930s did what they were supposed to do when used this time. Aggressive fiscal and monetary intervention stopped an incipient depression.

The reaction of those who believe in the virtues of a market economy to such criticisms is to reject them out of hand or, if they do not, to blame everything that has gone wrong on governments. This is a mistake, as both politics and policy.

Yes, the market economy has proved itself over two centuries uniquely able to generate sustained rises in prosperity. It has produced previously inconceivable increases in standards of living. It has poured forth a cornucopia of what were, not so long ago, unimaginable goods and services. Even the Chinese authorities endorse the market economy, though they hope to contain the demands for freedom that normally follow rising prosperity.

Married to science and technology—another great open system of competitive yet ordered human endeavor—the market economy has transformed the world. It has already allowed hundreds of millions of human beings to enjoy long lives, fast travel, easy communication, and exciting entertainment. It allows the remaining billions to dream of a comparable existence. To our ancestors of several millennia ago, our lives would be more like those of gods than of human beings.

Competitive market economies work. But they are, like all human inventions, imperfect: they are unstable, do not always deliver high-quality public goods, and do not automatically create the institutions on which they depend. Not least, market economies change and develop. As the economy changes, so will the law that governs it, the society that contains it, and the politics that surround it.

Ours is not the world familiar to Adam Smith more than two centuries ago. Today, markets are global, not local. The dominant businesses are limited liability companies, not personal proprietorships or partnerships. Debtors are made bankrupt, not thrown into prison. The biggest source of instability is the economy, not the weather. People expect governments to manage business cycles rather than accept them as acts of providence. They know the structure of the economy is likely to change, not remain immutable.

Crises accelerate change. They always have. Thus, the Great Depression in the 1930s shaped many of today's institutions and mechanisms, from the welfare state to financial regulation. Today's "crisis of capitalism" is another such occasion.

The needs of today have to be seen in the context of early

twenty-first-century globalization. This is a world in which the biggest economic stories are the "great convergence" and the breakdown of the financial and monetary systems. It is a world in which the provision of public goods matters, not just at local and national but also at global levels. It is a world of manmade money and a vast trade in financial claims. It is a world in which the economy is ever more global, humanity ever more urban, and the impact of economic activity on the planet ever more pervasive.

The thesis underlying the recommendations advanced below is that today's economic crisis reflects the interaction of contemporary developments—above all, globalization, the rise of emerging economies, the emergence of huge global macro-economic imbalances, the liberalization of finance, and three decades of rising leverage—with longer-term features of capitalism. Among those features are the principal-agent problems of the limited liability corporation, the tendency of capitalist finance toward instability, and the need to balance national democratic politics against the supranational logic of market capitalism.

Some of what is happening cannot, or should not, be changed: the rise of China, for example, or globalization. In some cases, there are inescapable trade-offs: between the need for financial activity and the risks of instability, for example. The aim is to make reforms that would put the market economy in a better state, without expecting either permanent solutions or perfection. Neither is available.

I will consider seven challenges: macroeconomic instability, finance, inequality and unemployment, corporate governance, taxation, money in politics, and global governance. Some concern the capitalist system as it is today. Others concern the context in which it operates. The reach is broad. But so is that of our economy.

*   *   *

Macroeconomic instability. One of the big debates in economics is whether a modern capitalist economy is inherently stable. Before the crisis, the orthodox view was that it would be stable if the economy was competitive and the central bank anchored inflation expectations successfully. Events have disproved this hypothesis.

The late Hyman Minsky, in his 1986 masterpiece *Stabilizing an Unstable Economy*, has provided the best account of why this theory is wrong. In a modern economy, periods of stability and prosperity sow the seeds of their own downfall. They create conditions in which leverage comes to be seen as a route to wealth for mediocre businesspeople and greedy individuals. Those engaged in the financial system will both create and benefit from the creation of such leverage.

In a world in which perils are underestimated, as they always are in good times, the provision of leverage explodes. Finance progresses from what Minsky called "hedge," in which interest and principal are to be repaid out of expected cash flow, to "speculative," in which only interest is to be paid out of cash flow but debt needs to be rolled over, and finally to "Ponzi," in which both interest and principal are to be paid out of expected capital gains.

In the short to medium term, supply of credit generates its own demand, because it raises asset prices and so validates further borrowing. Only when asset prices finally fall from unrealistic heights does reality return. But by then the financial system and the economy will be in severe crisis.

Does this sound familiar? It should. Just look at the debt explosion before the recent crisis and the consequent rise in leverage in many Western economies, not least the United States.

What is the answer to instability? There are three elements, if one puts to one side, as I would, the ideas that we should return to the nineteenth-century gold standard or eliminate banking. People will not accept the boom and bust or passive governments of the gold standard. The elimination of banking would require a far bigger crisis than the present one.

The first element is to accept that, as critics of capitalism, Karl Marx foremost among them, have noted since the nineteenth century, financial crises are inherent in free-market capitalism and cannot be eliminated. This is partly because of the way capitalism behaves. It is also because everybody — actors in the economy, regulators, and even economists — thinks and acts procyclically. (See Daniel Gross's "Countering the Dangers of Procyclicality," pp. 438–45.)

Second, so-called macro-prudential policy matters hugely. Regulators need to watch the buildup of leverage in the economy like hawks, because that is beyond the purview of individual financial institutions. They need to ensure adequate levels of loss-absorbing capital in financial institutions and also among the ultimate borrowers: no more mortgages equal to more than the value of underlying assets, to take an obvious example.

Finally, we need to emphasize the role of the government and its agencies, including central banks. These acted as stabilizing forces during the crisis. Indeed, they needed to do even more than they did. But they also acted as destabilizing forces before the crisis: in particular, central banks were too aggressive in preventing moderate recessions, thereby exacerbating the willingness to take risks, and governments were too willing to encourage excessive leverage in the household sector, to promote the dream of universal homeownership. (See "Your House as an ATM: The Myth of Homeownership," by Bethany McLean, in part 1.)

*   *   *

Finance. A complex financial system is an inherent and essential part of any modern market economy. It is needed to allocate savings, discipline businesses, provide insurance against risk, and manage payments. It is also based on a complex and fragile network of trust. The lesson of the crisis is a well-known one: such a complex system is prone to collapse at times of panic.

The need is to protect finance from the economy and the economy from finance. This means shock absorbers. In the presence of adequate shock absorbers, normal market disciplines can apply. Mistakes will still be made, on a huge scale. Perverse incentives are not the only explanation for these, as orthodox economists too often believe. People make mistakes. In an environment of fundamental uncertainty, they are influenced by the fads and fashions of the moment. But with a more robust structure, the system should be better able to survive mistakes.

What, then, are the specific answers? The first and most important is far more equity capital. The core financial institutions should not have true leverage of more than ten to one. A second is long-term, loss-absorbing, unsecured debt. A third element is special resolution regimes that allow the authorities to handle institutions on the brink of losing funding effectively.

A fourth, as the UK's independent commission on banking has recommended, is that the core business of managing the payments system and providing credit to households and small and medium-sized businesses should be treated as separate activities from investment banking, partly in order to strip implicit and explicit subsidies from the latter activities. This is a modern version of the Glass-Steagall Act of 1933. A fifth answer is to reconsider remuneration in complex financial institutions, to ensure the alignment of interests between management and the suppliers of debt finance.

In the case of such institutions, the interests of shareholders align poorly with those of the ultimate risk bearer, which is society at large and usually, though not exclusively, the taxpayer. This makes reliance on incentives that supposedly align the interests of management with those of shareholders extremely dangerous. They are still more dangerous if, as is usual, such incentives—stock options, for example—ignore downside risks. They are worse still if, as again is usual, the profitability of a financial strategy can only be assessed over a full leverage cycle. Against this background, it is necessary for regulators to insist that managers be paid substantially in long-term debt instruments of their firms, which can also be cashed in only after lengthy holding periods.

In addition to making finance more robust, it is also clear that greater allowance needs to be made for asymmetries of information. Too often, consumers do not—indeed cannot—understand what they are buying. They need protection from the sort of predatory practices seen so egregiously in subprime lending in the United States before the crisis.

Inequality and unemployment. As the Organisation for Economic Co-operation and Development showed in a 2011 report, high-income countries have seen a marked rise in inequality over the past three decades. This is captured, of course, in the brilliant Occupy Wall Street slogan, "We are the 99 percent."

This rise in inequality is the result of complex, long-term forces: globalization; technological change, including "winner-take-all" markets; the birth of new and dynamic industries, particularly information technology; changes in social norms; the rise of finance, including the increase in the ability to extract rent from the economy in a host of hard-to-monitor ways; and regressive changes in taxation.

Many of these changes are irresistible. But both the level of and the increase in inequality of earnings vary across countries.

This suggests that economic structure and policy can alter outcomes, particularly after taxes and social benefits. The United States and the United Kingdom, for example, saw far faster rises in the real incomes of the top decile than of the bottom decile of the household income distribution. In France, this actually went the opposite way.

Many would argue that inequality is unimportant. There are two possible responses. The first is that it is important if it matters politically. Some people on the free market side of the argument fantasize about abolishing such a political debate. But that is impossible. The second is that inequality of outcome has a powerful impact on equality of opportunity. It is vastly harder for children who grow up in poverty to obtain a decent education, for example, than it is for those brought up in more affluent and supportive conditions. Poverty blights both aspiration and achievement. It is dishonest to pretend otherwise.

What are the answers to inequality and long-term unemployment? These are huge challenges, with solutions that will inevitably vary from one society to another. Among those answers are greater explicit redistribution from the winners to the losers, and particularly the children of the losers; subsidization of low-income jobs, alongside higher minimum wages; huge efforts to improve the quality of education and child care; and, no less, a determination to sustain domestic demand effectively in the midst of a severe downturn, such as the one experienced in 2011–12.

Corporate governance. The core institution of contemporary capitalism is the limited liability corporation. It is a remarkable social invention. But it has deep drawbacks, of which the most important is its lack of accountability, other than to the market for goods and services itself.

Ignore the myth of shareholder control. In fundamental

respects, these entities are not owned, because the multiplicity of owners creates a huge collective action problem that insiders can easily exploit in their own interests. Corporations are, as a result, vulnerable to looting by management. This is what economic theory would predict. It is also what we see.

Many of the rewards supposedly provided to align the interests of top employees with those of owners, such as share options, instead create an incentive to manipulate corporate earnings at the expense of the long-term health of the company, the shareholders, and the long-term and committed employees on which a successful business depends.

What, then, are the answers? Unfortunately, no simple remedy to these failings exists. The corporation is the best institution we know for running large and complex businesses. It is certainly important to ensure that there is a level playing field for other forms of ownership, including partnerships and mutuals. It is equally important to encourage the creation of independent and well-informed boards. The case for granting a say in the guidance of the company to long-term workers seems to be strong. It is also sensible to ask shareholders to vote directly on pay. But it is impossible to believe that a diffuse body of often short-term shareholders would have the incentive and the information needed to influence corporate behavior in any profound way.

Taxation. Inevitably, this discussion raises questions about the role and limits of taxation. The general thrust of political discussion, outstandingly so in the United States, is against higher taxation. Yet taxes play a huge role in determining how the market economy operates, for both good and ill. They also finance the provision of essential public goods and services, including education. Finally, they make a big difference to the final outcome on ex post income distribution.

So what are the answers on taxation? Perhaps the biggest necessity is to remove the incentives for leverage embedded in both personal and corporate taxation. On the latter, shifts toward treating equity and debt equally should significantly reduce the fragility created during cyclical upswings. A broader issue is the desirability of shifting the burden of taxation from income to land and, more broadly, to wealth. An annual tax on large amounts of wealth at, say, 1 percent would have substantial merits: it would encourage the active use of wealth and would allow lower taxes on incomes. On income distribution, two big issues are the extent to which many of the richest people pay next to no tax at all, because of legal loopholes, including the ability to turn income into capital gains, taxed at a far lower rate. The candidacy of Mitt Romney has, rightly, brought the latter loophole into view. Finally, it is essential to increase international cooperation on taxation.

Money in politics. No bigger challenge exists than the relationship of the market to democratic politics. To some on the free market side, the answer seems to be that the former has all the legitimacy and so should have the ability to purchase the latter. To some on the anti-market left, the answer is that the market should be absorbed by politics completely. The latter approach is now almost entirely abandoned. The former remains intellectually vigorous, particularly in the United States.

The correct view is in between. Politics and the market interact. But both have their own legitimate spheres of operation. The market is based on the individual's role as producer and consumer. Politics is based on the individual's role as citizen. To function well, each needs to be protected from the other.

In the absence of a properly functioning set of protections, the bazaar (the sphere of the market) consumes the forum (the sphere of politics). The outcome is rule by affluent vested interests or, quite simply, plutocracy. Vested interests create closed political and economic systems. Thus they seek to undermine the open access upon which not only democratic politics but, no less, a competitive market economy depends. Protecting democratic politics from plutocracy is perhaps the biggest challenge to contemporary liberal democracy.

What are the answers? Just as the protection of the market from politics must come from legal and constitutional protections of private property and market activities, so the protection of politics from markets must come from restrictions on the use of private money, transparency about political giving, and the provision of public resources that allow a wider range of people to participate in politics.

Global governance. Last but certainly not least, today's capitalism is global. This creates a host of profound but inescapable challenges.

One of these challenges is how to regulate businesses that operate on a vast global scale. In the European Union, this has turned out to be particularly difficult in finance. To some extent, there is a choice: either to align support with regulation at the national level, and so break up the integrated financial system, or to align support with regulation at a higher level, and so move toward a more integrated European or even global regulation. In practice, the answer is a mixture of the two.

More broadly, the disjunction between the level at which politics operates and the levels at which business and the economy increasingly operate is a deep concern. Among the issues is how to provide a host of global public goods by agreement among a wide range of very different states. Those public goods include open markets, global monetary and financial stability, and security and global environmental protection. In all these areas, there are huge cross-border spillovers. As the human economy grows and its impact on the earth becomes more powerful, these pressures will rise.

A particularly important immediate challenge is global macroeconomic rebalancing and the reform of the global monetary system. The dominant role of the U.S. dollar has caused substantial difficulties for the United States itself, as the demand for liquid foreign currency reserves brought a flood of cheap money into the United States, which then helped cause the explosion of credit in the 2000s. Thus reform of the international monetary system to reduce dependence on the dollar is in the U.S. interest, even if it were to reduce the role of the dollar as a reserve asset.

What are the answers? In the long run, the answer must be to strengthen global governance, however unpopular that notion may be. The level of government must match the level of both the economy and the public goods that need to be provided. This shift to stronger global governance will require enormous imagination and courage. But the alternative is to leave significant aspects of human interaction unregulated. That will ultimately prove damaging. Some would argue that it has already proved to be so.

A crisis, it has been said, "is a terrible thing to waste." Ignore the grammar. Appreciate the sentiments. Capitalism cannot be replaced. Indeed, it should not be replaced. It is a uniquely flexible, responsive, and innovative economic system. It has enormous achievements. But it also has great fragility. The current crisis has revealed important areas for change at national and global levels. In the past, policymakers have found ways to make the necessary legal and institutional reforms in the end. They must do so again. Capitalism has always changed, in order to survive and thrive. It needs to change again.

How Occupy Wall Street Can Restore the Clout of the 99 Percent

Scott Turow

Scott Turow is a writer and attorney. He is the author of *Presumed Innocent* and the sequel *Innocent* (2010) and a frequent contributor to op-ed pages. He is a partner at the law firm of SNR Denton, specializing in criminal defense, and has written about and litigated capital cases. He is president of the Authors Guild.

Now that the Occupy Wall Street protesters have been driven from many of their encampments, I have an unusual suggestion for how they should next deploy their considerable energies: work across the nation for a constitutional amendment requiring Congress to regulate the expenditure of private money on elections.

Let me connect the dots. The heart of the protests is a lament about widening income inequality in the United States, brought about, in part, by a government that seems to favor disproportionately wealthy interests. The Occupiers have focused their outrage on the bailout of banks that reaped huge profits on mortgage-backed securities and are now profitable again, while millions of homeowners have been foreclosed upon or lost their jobs.

The best antidote to this imbalance of income and influence would be to greatly reduce the role of private funding in our elections. Nothing is more empowering to the well-heeled—corporations, unions, lobbyists, political-action committees, trade associations, and bundlers—than our political leaders' need to come to them, hat in hand, for the money to get elected.

Although the event has largely faded from memory, in 1974, in the wake of the national shame over Watergate, Congress established meaningful limits not only on campaign donations but also on the expenditure of private funds in an election. A loose assortment of odd bedfellows, including the Conservative Party senator James Buckley of New York and the American Civil Liberties Union, protested the laws as a violation of the First Amendment right of free expression.

While equating spending money with speech might strike many as implausible at first blush, the argument prevailed in *Buckley v. Valeo* (which I have called the twentieth-century equivalent of the Dred Scott decision of 1857, which exempted people of African ancestry from the rights of U.S. citizens). Since *Buckley*, an increasingly conservative U.S. Supreme Court has repeatedly struck down on First Amendment grounds efforts to curb private spending on elections. In 2010, in the *Citizens United v. Federal Election Commission* decision, the Court ruled that despite a long-standing ban on contributions to political campaigns by corporations and unions—because, after all, such entities aren't voters—they could now contribute as much as they liked as long as the expenditures weren't made in coordination with a candidate. (See Joel Bakan's "Psychopaths, Inc.: On Corporate Personhood," pp. 353–61.)

In reaching this result, the Court overruled a number of its own decisions, including one as recent as 2004 that had upheld parts of the McCain-Feingold campaign-finance reform legislation. In 2011, the Court invalidated an Arizona law that sought to counterbalance funding inequities by giving public financing to candidates in proportion to the privately financed spending of their opponents. This too, the Court said, violated free speech.

Yet the Supreme Court has made no effort to address the inherent conflict of its approach to the First Amendment with other constitutional principles. The bedrock of our democracy is embodied in the most famous line of the Declaration of Independence, "All men are created equal." Our belief in the equal dignity and value of every human being has led to the fundamental precept of one person, one vote — a tangible recognition that each citizen deserves an equal say in who governs her or him.

By treating money as an analog for speech, the Court's post-*Buckley* jurisprudence has figuratively allowed the rich to speak through microphones while the poor can barely whisper, and tolerates a situation in which the voices of contributors are amplified to the point that they drown out the opinions of mere voters. I have never understood how permitting the wealthy so much greater influence over the political process can be squared with the vision of equality on which the country was founded.

As the limits on spending have eroded, campaigns have grown exponentially more expensive — President Barack Obama raised and spent $750 million in 2008 and the number may be closer to $1 billion in 2012. This creates an appetite for political money that naturally can be best fed by the rich. Only 0.5 percent of Americans contributed $200 or more during the last general election cycle. Their generosity made up 82 percent of itemized contributions.

Nor should it be surprising that private contributions have grown in lockstep with income inequality: Our politicians are increasingly dependent on those who have the most and are accordingly reluctant to bite the hand that feeds them. In 2011 . polling, for example, almost three-quarters of Americans favored raising taxes on millionaires. Yet any such proposal has been consistently blocked in Congress, despite the overwhelming popular support for the idea.

Unfortunately, nothing less than a constitutional amendment is likely to reverse the situation. For now, the Court's conservative majority is firmly entrenched. And even were the Court to become more moderate, with the replacement of one of the conservative justices, the principle of *stare decisis*, of respect for prior decisions, would mean that any effort to erase the damage done since *Buckley* would necessarily be incremental.

As for the Occupy Wall Street movement, it has been criticized by some for not having a realistic agenda, even though polling shows that millions of Americans, including me, are sympathetic to the basic message of the protests, if not the violent engagements with police that have occurred in Oakland, California, and elsewhere.

So here is my suggestion for how the Occupiers can rally around a single goal and reinvigorate their movement. The Constitution can be amended by a two-thirds vote of each house of Congress, followed by ratification by three-fourths of the states. The demonstrators should head for the public spaces in Washington where protests have long been tolerated and demand that Congress amend the Constitution to change our campaign-finance system.

Meanwhile, those in tents across the nation should start going door-to-door with petitions, visiting legislators, and building alliances with good-government groups, all in service to a proposed amendment that might read something like this: "The Congress and the States shall regulate the direct and indirect expenditure of private funds on the electoral process in order to ensure that no group, entity, or individual exercises unequal influence on an election by those means."

It would be an uphill fight, of course, because passage of the amendment would mean convincing incumbents across the country to turn their backs on the system that put them in office. On the other hand, the expenditure limits that became law in 1974 passed by a two-thirds majority of each house of Congress, after President Gerald Ford's veto. And even if the amendment movement gains slowly, it will allow the Occupy adherents to press together toward a single intelligible goal, one that exploits the widespread loathing of the toxic effects of our current campaign-funding system and the lethal mixture of money and politics.

Most important, it will demonstrate that there is a political alternative to chagrined acceptance of the Supreme Court's edicts and move the debate from courtrooms to the town halls and legislative chambers where the will of the people is supposed to be done.

Psychopaths, Inc.:
On Corporate Personhood
Joel Bakan

Joel Bakan was born in East Lansing, Michigan, and resides in Vancouver, where he is professor of law at the University of British Columbia. His book *The Corporation* (2004), published in more than twenty languages and an international bestseller, inspired the critically acclaimed hit documentary of the same name, which Bakan wrote and co-created. He is working on a new documentary film based on his book *Childhood Under Siege* (2011).

The bizarre notion that corporations are "persons" and thereby entitled to constitutional rights is under attack, thanks in part to Occupy Wall Street activism and the Supreme Court's controversial campaign finance decision in *Citizens United v. Federal Election Commission* (2010). New York and Los Angeles have passed resolutions condemning corporate personhood, joining a growing number of cities, and Senators Bernie Sanders (I-VT) and Mark Begich (D-AK) have proposed a constitutional amendment that would exclude for-profit corporations from the rights given to natural persons by the Constitution. Democracy is well served by these initiatives, but more is needed to curb significantly the power and malfeasance of corporations: we need to go beyond the *fact* that corporations are legally conceived as persons and address the *kind* of persons—psychopaths—that they are created by law to be.

Through a strange legal alchemy, courts decided in the late

nineteenth century that corporations deserved the same constitutional rights as human beings. Until then, corporate personhood had been understood as a mere legal fiction, a limited device for enabling companies to operate as economic actors. "A corporation is an artificial being, invisible, intangible, and existing only in contemplation of law," as Chief Justice John Marshall held in 1819. "Being the mere creature of law, it possesses only those properties which the charter of its creation confers upon it."

WE THE PEOPLE, NOT WE THE CORPORATIONS
— Sign at an Occupy protest

The artificial being magically came to life in 1886, when the Supreme Court decided that corporate persons — "[no longer] imaginary or fictitious, but real; not artificial but natural," in the words of a contemporary lawyer — should have constitutional rights. Over the next two decades courts considered 288

APPLYING "EQUAL PROTECTION"

Of the cases in this court in which the 14ᵗʰ Amendment was applied during the first fifty years after its adoption, less than one half of one percent invoked it in protection of the Negro race, and more than fifty percent asked that its benefits be extended to corporations.
— Justice Hugo Black

AFRICAN AMERICANS   CORPORATIONS

(M. Wuerker)

Fourteenth Amendment claims by corporations (compared to just nineteen by African Americans, whom the amendment was originally designed to protect). Well into the 1930s, the courts routinely nullified laws at the behest of corporations claiming constitutional rights violations. This era of pro-business judicial activism—called the Lochner era, after the 1905 case *Lochner v. New York*, which exemplified it—ended in 1937, when President Franklin D. Roosevelt threatened to add five judges to the Supreme Court to shield his reforms from judicial attack.

Citizens United heralds the Court's return to its Lochner-era ways. The case, which invoked the First Amendment to nullify restrictions on corporate political spending, "elevate[s] corporations to a level of deference which has not been seen at least since the [Lochner-era] days when substantive due process was regularly used to invalidate regulatory legislation thought to unfairly impinge upon established economic interests," according to Justice John Paul Stevens in his dissenting opinion (quoting, in turn, from Justice Byron R. White's dissenting opinion in *First National Bank of Boston v. Bellotti*, a political spending case decided in 1978). As such, *Citizens United* reflects a broader judicial trend. Sixty-one percent of the Roberts court's decisions have been pro-business, according to a study by Lee Epstein, William Landes, and Richard Posner, compared with 51 percent for the Rehnquist court (1986–2005), 47 percent for the Burger court (1969–86), and 29 percent for the Warren court (1953–69). "The Roberts Court is undeniably conservative," says Steven Shapiro, national legal director of the American Civil Liberties Union, "but it is a particular kind of conservatism. This is not a libertarian court. It is not a states' rights court. It is a pro-business court."

Amending the U.S. Constitution to bar corporations from having constitutional rights would help curb pro-business judicial decisions. But, importantly, there would be little impact beyond that. The United States would become more like other nations, where corporations have no, or very limited, constitutional rights; nonetheless, ill-gotten corporate gains would remain. The fact is that corporate power and malfeasance are not rooted in the Constitution, which is why excluding corporations from the benefits it confers can have only limited effects.

The *corporation's* constitution, on the other hand, its legally mandated character, is a major source of corporate-caused ills in the world today—and that is where the real work needs to be done. Law not only confers personhood on corporations; it imbues them with unique personalities as well. The "best interests of the corporation" principle, a pillar of corporate law, compels managers and directors to place corporate interests above others, to exploit anything in any way that might yield profits, and to ignore whatever ill effects befall others. Self-interest, in other words, is the overriding imperative for corporate action. That characteristic well equips corporations to create wealth for shareholders, and jobs and useful products for

September 17, 2011: Day 1, Occupy Wall Street. *(Photograph by Gina Herold. Copyright © Gina Herold. Used with permission.)*

society, but it also makes them extremely dangerous institutions. Unable to feel genuine concern for others, experience guilt or remorse when they act badly, or have any sense of obligation to obey laws and ethical norms, corporate persons are, in effect, psychopathic beings.

Despite corporations' dangerous character, governments, especially over the last thirty years, have been in retreat from regulating and overseeing their behavior. Beguiled by free market ideology, and naïvely trusting that corporations will do right, governments have rolled back regulatory restraints and promoted self-regulation as an alternative. The results have been disastrous and include two recent crises—the 2008 financial meltdown and the 2010 Gulf of Mexico oil rig explosion—that were consequences of government's failure to rein in reckless corporate behavior. In hindsight, it was no surprise that financial institutions, driven by promises of huge profits and with few regulatory constraints in place to stop them, would carelessly grant risky loans, repackage the resulting debt as securities, and build exotic derivatives schemes. Nor was it a surprise that British Petroleum, a company with a string of serious environmental and safety infractions dating back at least to the 1990s (though strategically hidden by its carefully cultivated green image), would, if it could, cut corners to save money when constructing and operating its deep-sea wells. The same harmful dynamic has played out across numerous other areas—workers' rights and safety, children's well-being, consumer protection, and democratic processes, to name a few—as governments continue their retreat from effective regulatory roles.

That retreat is fueled in part, I believe, by dangerous misconceptions about the corporation's true nature. The concept of corporate social responsibility has evolved to suggest that corporations can care about social and environmental interests, not only profits. This has, in turn, fostered a belief, widely held among activists, governments, and business groups, that corporations can be trusted to regulate themselves and refrain from causing harm. They can, the logic goes, therefore be freed from regulatory restraints—deregulated—without risking bad behavior. "There has been a transfer of authority from the government to the corporation," as Samir Gibara, former chair and CEO of Goodyear Tire, describes it, "and the corporation needs to assume that responsibility; needs to really behave as a corporate citizen of the world; needs to assume the self-discipline that in the past, governments required from it." The notion that corporations, psychopathic at their institutional core, *can* be responsible, self-disciplined, and citizens of the world is oxymoronic. Yet it powerfully serves today to sugarcoat, and hence justify, governments' continuing retreat from regulation—the "transfer of authority from the government to the corporation," as Gibara calls it.

Psychopaths are notorious for masking their dangerously self-obsessed personalities with charm, and corporate psychopaths have made an art of it with social responsibility. It is crucial not to confuse the charm (carefully constructed by marketers and public relations practitioners) and the reality. Corporate social responsibility is—can only be, in light of the corporation's legally mandated nature—a *strategy* for serving corporations' ends, whether by warding off regulators, deflecting criticism, or attracting customers. It can never be an end in itself. That would be illegal. As a result, assuming a mantle of corporate social responsibility is, in essence, "like putting a good-looking girl in front of an automobile to sell an automobile," as the late economist Milton Friedman once told me. "That's not in order to promote pulchritude. That's in order to sell cars."

That helps explain why flagrant social *irresponsibility* is so often the handiwork of social responsibility's loudest advocates.

Enron and AIG were paragons of corporate social responsibility before they collapsed, in 2001 and 2008, respectively, under the weight of reckless greed and criminality. Pfizer, a company intent on doing "more good for more people than any other company on the planet," as its former CEO Hank McKinnell once stated, was later revealed to be one of the world's worst corporate criminals. BP, a social responsibility leader—"Can business be about more than profits? We think so" ran a prominent ad campaign—blatantly and routinely ignored safety and environmental standards, most destructively in connection with the above-mentioned oil rig explosion. And on it goes.

Governments, and the citizens who elect them, must give up on the fantasy of corporate benevolence and treat corporations for what they really are—psychopathic institutions, incapable of genuine social responsibility and unable to regulate themselves. That means requiring, *by law*, that they be socially responsible, not trusting and hoping that they will be. Restoring the ability and will of governments to protect public interests through democratically created and effectively enforced regulatory laws is, I believe, the best way to push back against corporate rule and malfeasance. To that end, I offer the following general prescriptions:

Government regulation should be reconceived, and relegitimized, as the principal means for bringing corporations under democratic control and ensuring that they respect the interests of citizens, communities, and the environment.

Regulations should be made more effective by staffing enforcement agencies at realistic levels, setting fines sufficiently high to deter corporations from unlawful behavior, strengthening the liability of top directors and managers for their corporations' illegal behaviors, barring repeat offender corporations from government contracts, and suspending the charters of corporations that flagrantly and persistently violate the public interest.

Regulations designed to protect the environment and people's health and safety should be based on the precautionary principle, which prohibits corporations from acting in ways that are reasonably likely to cause serious harm, even if definitive proof that such harm will occur does not exist.

Regulatory systems should be reformed to improve accountability and avoid "agency capture" by industry, which currently serves to undermine their integrity, and the "revolving door" flow of personnel between government and business should be stopped. Though corporations have a place in representing their concerns to government and cooperating with government on policy initiatives, their current status as "partners" with government endangers the democratic process. At a minimum, their influence should be scaled back to a degree commensurate with that of other organizations, such as unions and environmental, consumer, and human rights groups.

Elections should be publicly financed, and corporate political expenditures phased out (in light of *Citizens United*, this would require a constitutional amendment, such as Senators Sanders and Begich propose, or a reversal by the Supreme Court in some future case). Additionally, electoral reforms that might bring new voices into the political system and encourage disillusioned citizens to return to it, such as a move to proportional representation, should be pursued.

Most important, we need to embrace a subversive truth—
that corporations are our creations. They have no lives,
no powers, and no capacities beyond what we, through
the governments we elect, give them. That is why it
is our fundamental right—indeed, our duty as citizens
in a democracy—to limit their actions in the name of
public interests.

Occupy Democracy

Robert B. Reich

Robert B. Reich is Chancellor's Professor of Public Policy at the Richard and Rhoda Goldman School of Public Policy at the University of California-Berkeley. He has served in three administrations, most recently as secretary of labor under President Bill Clinton. He has written twelve books, including *Aftershock* and *The Work of Nations*, which has been translated into twenty-two languages, and the bestseller *Supercapitalism*.

The surge of cynicism about government isn't about government's size. It comes from a growing perception that government isn't working for average people. It's for big business, Wall Street, and the very rich instead.

This is where the Occupy movement comes in. Its core message is that the increasing concentration of income and wealth poses a grave danger to our democracy. Our problem isn't government; it's who government is *for*. And if there's a core strategy for the movement in the years ahead, it's that we must reoccupy our democracy by organizing and mobilizing average Americans to get big money out of politics.

In a December 2011 Pew Center poll, 77 percent of respondents said too much power is in the hands of a few rich people and corporations. This view is understandable. Consider:

Wall Street got bailed out but homeowners caught in the fierce downdraft caused by the street's excesses have gotten almost nothing.

Big agribusiness continues to rake in hundreds of billions in price supports and ethanol subsidies. Big Pharma gets extended patent protection that drives up everyone's drug prices. Big oil gets its own federal subsidy. But small businesses on the Main Streets of America are barely making it.

American Airlines uses bankruptcy to ward off debtors and renegotiate labor contracts. Donald Trump's businesses go bankrupt without impinging on Trump's own personal fortune. But the law won't allow you to use personal bankruptcy to renegotiate your home mortgage.

If you run a giant bank that defrauds millions of small investors of their life savings, the bank might pay a small fine but you won't go to prison. Not a single top Wall Street executive has been prosecuted for Wall Street's megafraud. But if you sell an ounce of marijuana you could be put away for a long time.

Not a day goes by without Republicans decrying the budget deficit. But the biggest single reason for the yawning deficit is big money's corruption of Washington.

One of the deficit's biggest drivers—Medicare—would be significantly lower if Medicare could use its bargaining leverage to get drug companies to reduce their prices. Why hasn't it happened? Big Pharma won't allow it. It threatened to scuttle President Obama's health care law unless Medicare was barred from negotiating lower drug prices. Medicare's administrative costs are only 3 percent, far below the 10 percent average administrative costs of private insurers. So why not tame rising health care costs for all Americans by allowing any family to opt in? That was the idea behind the public option in the draft health care bill. Health insurers stopped it in its tracks.

The nation's health bill would also be lower if Medicare

and Medicaid could make payments to doctors and hospitals conditional on their moving from a "fee for service" system— in which they get more money the more tests and treatments they provide—to a "fee for healthy outcomes" system, where they'd get paid for keeping people healthy. Why hasn't this come about? Health insurers, big hospital chains, Big Pharma, and the American Medical Association are opposed.

The other biggest budgetary expense is national defense. America spends more on our military than do China, Russia, Britain, France, Japan, and Germany combined. The basic defense budget (the portion unrelated to the costs of fighting wars) keeps growing; in 2011 it was about 25 percent higher than it was a decade ago, adjusted for inflation. That's because defense contractors have cultivated sponsors on Capitol Hill and located their plants and facilities in politically important congressional districts. We keep spending billions on cold war weapons systems like nuclear attack submarines, aircraft carriers, and manned combat fighters that pump up the bottom lines of Bechtel, Martin Marietta, and their ilk but have nothing to do with twenty-first-century combat.

The widening deficit is also being driven by declining tax receipts. That's only partly due to the fact that most Americans have less income to tax these days. Yet the richest Americans are taking home a bigger share of total income than at any time since the 1920s. Their tax payments are down because the Bush tax cuts reduced their top rates to the lowest level in more than half a century and cut capital gains taxes to 15 percent. Congress hasn't even closed a loophole that allows mutual fund and private equity managers to treat their incomes as capital gains.

The four hundred richest Americans, whose total wealth exceeds the combined wealth of the bottom 150 million Americans put together, pay an average of 17 percent of their income in taxes. That's lower than the tax rates of most day laborers and child-care workers.

Social Security payroll taxes continue to climb as a share of total tax revenues. Yet the payroll tax is regressive, applying only to yearly income under $110,100 in 2012. And the share of revenues coming from corporations has been dropping. The biggest, like General Electric, often find ways to pay no federal taxes at all. Many shelter their income abroad, and every few years Congress grants them a tax amnesty to bring the money home.

Get it? "Big government" isn't the problem. The problem is the big money that's taking over government.

Government is doing fewer of the things most of us want it to do—providing good public schools and affordable access to college, improving our roads and bridges and water systems, and maintaining safety nets to catch average people who fall—and more of the things big corporations, Wall Street, and the wealthy want it to do.

Some conservatives argue that we wouldn't have to worry about big money taking over government if we had a smaller government to begin with. Here's what Congressman Paul Ryan told me when we were debating all this on ABC's *This Week*: "If the power and money are going to be here in Washington, that's where the influence is going to go...that's where the powerful are going to go to influence it."

Ryan has it upside down. A smaller government that's still dominated by money would continue to do the bidding of Wall Street, the pharmaceutical industry, oil companies, big agribusiness, big insurance, military contractors, and rich individuals. It just wouldn't do anything else.

If we want to get our democracy back, we've got to get big money out of politics. That won't be easy. It will take a movement—an Occupy movement—to do so, because it won't be done by the political system itself. That system is too dependent on big money.

Arguably the problem began in 1976, with *Buckley v. Valeo*. The Supreme Court upheld statutory limits on individual contributions, but it also found that spending money to influence elections is a form of free speech, protected by the First Amendment. Corporations invested more than $300 million in the 2008 presidential election, but the floodgates were not fully opened until 2010. In *Citizens United v. Federal Election Commission*, five Justices invalidated part of the McCain-Feingold 2002 campaign finance law that sought to limit corporate influence on elections. The Court found that corporations are people under the First Amendment.

Together, *Buckley* and *Citizens United* have given big corporations, Wall Street, and their lobbyists and trade associations, as well as very rich individuals, the ability to drown out the First Amendment rights of every other American. If money is speech, those who have the most money have the loudest and most powerful speech. If corporations are people, the biggest corporations are the most politically privileged people in the land. The voices of average Americans can't be heard because most of us don't have the dough to break through, and none of us are corporations.

These rulings would endanger democracy under any circumstance; but when income and wealth are as concentrated as they are today, the rulings give a small group of people—top corporate executives, rich Wall Street traders, billionaire hedge fund managers—the ability to effectively run the nation. Consider the Koch brothers (worth $25 billion each), who are bankrolling the Tea Party. Their petrochemical empire also finances candidates who will vote against environmental protection, lawsuits against environmental regulations already in place, and propaganda to convince Americans that climate change is unproven.

Reported lobbying expenditures have risen annually, to $3.5 billion in 2010. This sum understates the true extent of the problem because many influence peddlers don't register as lobbyists and many firms don't fully report their lobbying expenditures. Meanwhile, the revolving door between Washington and lobbying firms has turned into an open doorway. Half of the senators and 42 percent of House members who departed Congress between 1998 and 2004 became lobbyists. Although no reliable data exist past 2004, it seems likely that the percentages continue to climb because lobbyists' pay continues to soar.

We don't even know the extent of the political corruption because so much of it is secret. All we know is that the flow of money into politics has never been as large as it is now, no matter how you measure it—adjusted for inflation, as a percent of the total economy, relative to the number of elections, relative to the number of elected officials.

So-called Super PACs—typically run by former aides and associates of candidates running for office—are now vehicles for pumping unlimited amounts of money into political campaigns, without disclosure of the money's sources. Millionaires and billionaires aren't contributing their money out of sheer love of country. They have a more self-interested motive. Their political spending is analogous to their other investments. Mostly they want low tax rates and friendly regulations.

What can the Occupy movement do about this? Plenty.

For one, it can campaign for a constitutional amendment to strike down *Buckley* and *Citizens United*.

Second, it can mobilize to ensure that the president will nominate and the Senate confirm future Supreme Court candidates who will overrule these cases.

Third, it can push for legislation that, although consistent with *Buckley* and *Citizens United*, reduces the influence of money in politics. Examples of such legislation are campaign finance laws that match public dollars with dollars raised by individual campaigns; laws that require full disclosure of contributors to Super PACs and other so-called independent groups; laws that bar elected or appointed officials from lobbying government for a decade or more after they serve; and laws that require broadcasters to set aside free time for candidates who abide by campaign finance restrictions.

How should the Occupy movement proceed to accomplish this? When Occupiers have sought to make their voices heard by joining together in public spaces for weeks and months at a time—one of the few ways average people can still be heard— they've been told their First Amendment rights are limited, and they have been evicted. The New York State Court of Appeals, along with many mayors and other officials, says Occupiers can picket—but what they did instead was set up encampments. Yet it's the encampments themselves that have drawn media attention (along with the police efforts to remove them).

Our courts and public officials have stood the First Amendment on its head. Money is considered speech, and corporations are considered people—but when average people peacefully assemble to protest the consequences of these judgments, they're told the First Amendment gives them no right to assemble for weeks or months. They may only picket, during daylight hours. Yet a bunch of people carrying pickets isn't news. When it comes to making views known, picketing is no competition for big money. Ordinary people don't have much money, which is precisely the problem. The only way they can be heard in this age of big money with big voices is to make a ruckus.

What do I mean by making a ruckus? Not engaging in violence. If Occupiers and other citizens were to shift tactics from passive resistance and civil disobedience to violence, it would spell the end of the movement. The vast American middle class that now empathizes with the Occupiers would promptly desert them. There's another alternative. If Occupiers are expelled from specific geographic locations, the movement should shift to broad-based organizing, around the simple idea at the core of the movement: it's time to occupy our democracy.

Taxing the 1 Percent of the 1 Percent

David Cay Johnston

David Cay Johnston is the tax columnist for Reuters. He also teaches the property, tax, and regulatory law of the ancient world at Syracuse University's law and business schools. In 2001 he received a Pulitzer Prize for his coverage of taxes for the *New York Times*. His book *Perfectly Legal* won the 2004 book of the year award from Investigative Reporters and Editors and, like his 2008 book, *Free Lunch*, was a bestseller. He is also the author of *The Fine Print* (2012). The father of eight grown children, he lives in Rochester, New York, with his wife.

The rich—the really rich—are different from the 99 percent. They are also very different from most of the 1 percent.

Understanding that Congress taxes the really rich differently than everyone below them is central to understanding why America's economy is failing to deliver enough jobs, enough income, and enough wealth so the 99 percent can prosper. It's not just that the top 1 percent within the 1 percent have a lot more. Thanks to Congress, for tax purposes they can look like paupers even though they may own a dozen mansions, yachts big enough to include a helipad or even a submarine, and, to get between homes and ship, his-and-her jets. It's possible to have all that and pay no income taxes. It's all perfectly legal, a free lunch for the superrich thanks to the fine print that very few in the mainstream news media report on.

To understand this, let's start with the numbers (all in 2010 dollars) and some perspective on how it is the 1 percent within the 1 percent get the most favored treatment. Think about income as a ladder with 100 rungs. The poorest person is on the bottom rung, the person with the highest income is on the top rung, and someone stands right in the middle at the median point, where half make more and half less. Where would the median be? Go ahead, stop reading for a moment and take a thoughtful guess. Ask anyone else around you to take his or her best guess, too.

First, let's look at the source of most income for the 99 percent: paychecks. The median gross paycheck in 2010 was $26,364, or $507 a week, the lowest since 1999. Since that year, median weekly income has hovered in a narrow range between $507 and a peak, in 2007, of $521. To put that in perspective, of the 150.4 million people who earned a paycheck in 2010:

A third of them, 50.3 million, made less than $15,000.
Their average pay for the year was just $6,049.
Three out of four workers made less than $50,000.
The 1 percent jobs started at $200,000.
Half of the 1 percent were paid less than $300,000.
There were 93,725 people paid more than $1 million.
The 81 highest-paid workers averaged $79.6 million.

A worker at the threshold of the 1 percent made less than eight times the median wage, while the 81 highest-paid workers made almost four hundred times what those at the bottom of the 1 percent earned for their labor. Even those earning at the threshold of the top tenth of 1 percent, which was just under $500,000, are much closer to the median-wage worker than those at the very top.

We move on to a broader measure of income, one that includes not just paychecks but pensions and unemployment benefits, profits from small business, dividends and interest from stocks and bonds, and, especially for those at the top, capital gains from selling stocks for more than they cost. Our measure is adjusted gross income, the last number on the front page of your tax return. We will go by taxpayer, which is roughly equal to household. Married couples who file a joint return count as one taxpayer. In 2009, the latest year for which we have this data, the median income was $633 a week—a smidgen more than $32,900 per year. That is the lowest since 1996, when the median was $32,207. Median income peaked in 2001 at $35,125, or $2,225 a year more than in 2009. Median is a good measure, often used by economists to give us an idea of what is typical. Keep in mind, however, that there is no limit on top incomes: as they soar, the median should rise. When the top soars and the median stays flat, it means the bottom half are relatively worse off.

Now let's look at the 1 percent using national data. To get into the top 1 percent, you needed an adjusted gross income of just under $350,000 in 2009. That's more than ten times the median of about $32,900, a slightly larger gap than for wages alone. Nearly half of the top 1 percent made less than $500,000. That is a lot of money compared with the median, but still just fifteen times the median. The top half of the 1 percent— 729,000 taxpayers—enjoyed more income than the 70 million taxpayers in the bottom half of the entire income distribution. Go higher still, to the top hundredth of the 1 percent, a bit more than 15,000 taxpayers. They made a nickel out of every dollar going to all Americans in 2008, four times their share of income before President Reagan took office. That means the 99.99 percent used to get 98.72 percent of all income but now must get by on less than 95 percent, according to analysis of tax data by Emmanuel Saez and Thomas Piketty.

Let's go even higher, to the top 400 taxpayers, whose

incomes were treated as a state secret during the George W. Bush administration but made public again a few days after Barack Obama was inaugurated. Together they earned 1.3 cents out of every dollar of income, an average of $274 million each, or more than $750,000 every day of the year in 2008. That was double their income share in 1992. More significantly, 1.3 cents out of every dollar was the income share of the top 9,925 taxpayers the year Reagan was elected, and now just 400 taxpayers get that slice of the income pie.

The 400 are not even the top of the ladder, just the top of the ladder as measured by income that Congress requires be reported. Before we get to the top incomes, let's take a look at tax burdens within the 99 percent and within the 1 percent. The 2008 median wage was $26,000, in round numbers. That year the top 400 made nearly $274 million each, as noted. For both, we will count the full payroll tax. Half gets deducted from paychecks. The other half represents wages that workers never see that are taxed at 100 percent. We will add that extra half of the payroll tax to the worker's gross pay, raising it to almost $27,989 for the median-wage earner and adding almost $836,000 for the top 400. The Social Security tax is applied to all of the median-wage worker's income but to just the first $102,000 earned by the top 400. The Medicare tax is applied to all wages and made up about 8 percent of the income of those in the top 400.

The results:

Median-Wage Worker		Top 400
$ 29,989	2008 Income	$ 279,969,823
$ -2,156	Income Tax	$ -49,588,538
$ -3,978	Payroll Tax	$ -835,713
$ -6,134	Total Tax	$ -50,424,251
21.9%	Tax Rate	18.4%

The working stiff pays 3.5 cents more in taxes out of each dollar she earns working, even though each person in the top 400 makes more than nine thousand times as much money.

Among the top-400 group, 30 taxpayers paid less than 10 percent of their income taxes, and some may have paid nothing, Internal Revenue Service data show. Another 101 paid between 10 percent and 15 percent of their income, and another 112 paid up to 20 percent. So of the 400, at least 243 paid a lower tax rate than our worker earning the median wage.

One reason for those low rates is that the top 400 can take deductions denied to millions in the 99 percent. For example, fewer than half of homeowners get to deduct mortgage interest—because they make too little to be among the 33 percent of taxpayers with itemized deductions. Those in the top 400 also can deduct unlimited amounts of property tax. Billionaires John C. Malone, the cable television magnate, and Ted Turner, the founder of CNN, both own more land than the combined area of Rhode Island and Delaware. Think of the subsidy to all those $100 million mansions.

Contrast this with the almost four million taxpayers in the 99 percent who are not allowed to deduct their property taxes. The reason? That's a story in two parts about how Congress coddles the 1 percent at the expense of families in which both parents have jobs that pay well. In 1968 the Johnson administration revealed that 155 families making more than a million dollars in inflation-adjusted income paid no federal income tax. The next year Congress passed, and President Nixon signed into law, the minimum tax. It limited how many tax credits, oil depletion allowances, and other tax breaks rich investors could use to limit their income. Then came the 1986 Tax Reform Act. All of the 1969 provisions limiting investment tax breaks were repealed. In their place was a new levy, the alternative minimum tax, or AMT.

To this day most of the news media describe the AMT as a levy on the rich to make sure they pay some taxes. (Editors at the *New York Times* defend this as "shorthand.") In reality, the AMT takes away the standard deduction, personal exemptions for taxpayers and their dependents, deductions for state income tax and local property tax deductions, and deductions for miscellaneous items, including union dues. The law raises the income taxes of married couples and some single parents who own their own homes, have two or more children, and live in the high-tax states, which just also happen to be the ones with the better-paying jobs. I call it the anti-married tax.

Congress also put in a provision that raised by a third the amount people caught in the AMT have to pay in medical bills before they can deduct them—to 10 percent, instead of the 7.5 percent for most taxpayers. This means that if you or someone in your family gets cancer or needs expensive surgery not covered by insurance, Congress raises your income taxes.

Under the temporary income tax cuts championed by President George W. Bush in 2001, the AMT was designed to increase, and the official projection was that it would bring in close to $600 billion before the cuts expired, making up for a third of the projected revenue loss from the Bush cuts. The extra AMT funds were counted as offsets to the tax cuts, and if not for them, Bush would not have been able to get through the cuts for the top tenth of 1 percent, who got 12.5 percent of the tax savings.

It was assumed that about 25 million taxpayers would come under the AMT. However, each year since, Congress has passed a temporary fix, called the AMT Patch, that limits the AMT to no more than four million taxpayers, mostly two-income career couples who stand on income ladder rungs 75 to 99½. This patch meant that the revenue losses were much larger than what the public was told, not $1.3 trillion from 2001 to the end of 2010, but almost $2 trillion and with interest of almost $2.5 trillion.

Ponder that for a moment. Politicians who spout "family values" raise taxes on parents who both work and buy a home and on those with a grave illness or injury to help pay for tax cuts for the 1 percent.

The money the added tax on the sick raises is not much, perhaps $50 million annually, based on my analysis of reports by the nonpartisan and widely respected Tax Policy Center. That's a mere drop in the federal income tax bucket. However, the symbolism—taxing the sick and dying to give tax relief to the richest among us—is appalling. Since I first explained this in the *New York Times* in 1999, Congress has done nothing to fix it, an indication of how little regard our lawmakers have for the 99 percent.

Some people look at the taxes paid by the 1 percent and the top 400 and say they pay more than enough tax. Critics note that the top 1 percent make a fourth to a fifth of all reported income but pay close to 40 percent of all federal income taxes. True, but the incomes of those at the top have been growing much faster than their taxes, meaning their burden is easing. Further, the measure is not the number of dollars paid but the share of income paid. That is what tells you how much of a burden tax is.

Why should those who make more pay lower rates than those who make less?

The idea that those who make more pay a higher rate is nearly twenty-five hundred years old. Indeed, the development of that idea is so intertwined with the birth of democracy that it is one of its defining features. The ancient Athenians, after living through two centuries of tyranny in which the rich paid little tax, devised a moral principle. Without civilization—without the laws that define property, the courts to settle disputes, and the power to enforce the law—no one had any wealth, they reasoned, because in man's natural state, in the wilderness, no one's property was safe from marauders.

In Athens, with its civilizing rules, people could get rich and keep their property safe. The Athenians maintained that the rich had a moral duty to pay more in taxes to sustain the civilization that made their riches possible. They also concluded that being rich did not give you any greater voice in politics—one man, one vote, regardless of income. They even started out choosing people for government jobs by lot, except for the position of *strategos* (general). Those in government positions were held to standards of strict accountability, which ensured integrity.

Every worldly philosopher, from Plato and Aristotle to Adam Smith, Jeremy Bentham, David Ricardo, James Mill and his son John Stuart Mill, Karl Marx, Alfred Marshall, and John Maynard Keynes, wrote in favor of progressive taxation. Milton Friedman even invented the negative income tax, implemented by Congress as the earned income tax credit, a form of progressive income tax. Friedman also favored a progressive consumption tax. These economists all understood the idea of marginal utility. An extra dollar of weekly income can mean the difference between eating on the last day of the week or going hungry, a real issue in America today with burgeoning numbers of people needing food stamps and relying on free staples from food banks. On the other hand, if a top Wall Street trader made one dollar less, it would have no impact on his welfare.

Taxing high incomes at a higher rate is a way for society to reap some benefit from those who grew wealthy because they were educated by taxpayers, kept healthy by taxpayer-funded medical discoveries, drove to work on taxpayer-financed roads, and relied on the taxpayer-financed law enforcement and military to protect their fortunes.

While many people claim that the progressive income tax is a Marxist idea, the concept was more than two millennia old when Marx came along. Perpetuating this canard helps the 1 percent, and especially the richest of those in the 1 percent, sell the idea that what matters is how many dollars of tax they pay, not what share of their incomes. Rather than being communist or even liberal, progressive taxation is the most conservative practice in Western civilization, in the classic meaning of the word: time-tested and enduring. Those who favor flat taxes and oppose progressive taxation are not conservatives but radicals and reactionaries, and ahistorical at that.

The top-400 data go back only to 1992, but in 1961 the top 398 taxpayers, who each made on average $14.3 million in today's money, paid 42.4 percent of their income in federal income taxes, compared with 18.1 percent in 2008, when they averaged nineteen times as much income in real terms. During those same years, the bottom 90 percent saw their income tax rate fall by just 2.4 percentage points, while the top group's fell by 24.3 points. And the Reagan-era increases in Social Security taxes took back all of that and more from the bottom 90 percent.

What we have not discussed so far are the people who do not show up in the official data: people who are higher up the income ladder than even the top 400. These superhigh incomes are not the result of capital gains from selling businesses — which are taxed at just 15 percent (though there are easy ways to defer those taxes when selling a business). The biggest incomes go to those who are by far the highest-paid workers in history. Congress allows them to get paid now but delay for years or even decades reporting their compensation on their income tax returns. Who are these lucky workers? Hedge fund, private equity, and other managers of investment partnerships.

The typical hedge fund imposes two fees on investors. There is a 2 percent annual fee on the value of accounts. Then the manager gets 20 percent of any increase in value (and nothing if the fund loses money). John Paulson charges 44 percent, which is why in 2008 and 2009 he was able to make $9 billion; but Paulson was not required to report most of his income. The reason is that the 44 percent fee, the bulk of his compensation for his labors, is paid in the form of shares of the investment partnership. This is known as "carried interest," and Congress allows those whose compensation comes in this form to pay taxes on these shares only when, and if, they sell. Any income these managers get from those shares, however, is taxable.

A number of hedge fund managers have consistently been paid $1 million per day or more for years. Yet, unlike most workers, they do not have income taxes taken out before they get paid. This is how George W. Bush treated his 10 percent share of the Texas Rangers baseball team, reporting all of his $17 million as capital gains. In turn, all of that money and the profits his partners made came from taxpayers, not the market. That is because the Rangers got local, state, and federal tax subsidies of $202 million but sold the team for a profit of just $168 million.

The reality is that Congress taxes the richest of the richest much more lightly than it taxes a working stiff making $26,000 a year and even a two-income professional couple making $500,000. And the really rich who don't work can live tax-free. All they have to do is borrow against their assets, which they can do for less than 2 percent annual interest. To understand this, imagine you have $5 billion and want to spend $20 million a year. You borrow the $20 million, and at year's end you owe less than $400,000 in interest. Your fortune should have grown by more than that. If it grew 5 percent, you are ahead by almost $30 million. Now you roll over the old loan and take out a new one, and your fortune keeps growing, while your tax bill is zero if you own tax-free bonds and stocks that pay no dividends.

Frank and Jamie McCourt, who owned the Los Angeles

Dodgers, paid no income taxes after 2003, while spending more than $100 million through 2008, records in their divorce case show. Warren Buffett's main holding, Berkshire Hathaway, pays no dividends. He revealed that his 2010 income was $62.8 million, not nearly enough to make the top 400 list. He paid $6.9 million in federal income tax, an effective rate of 11 percent. Viewed as a share of his wealth, however, Buffett's income tax came to less than two-tenths of 1 percent. Buffett believes that his tax rate should be higher, and that for the superwealthy the estate tax rate should be set so high that it ensures we have a society of economic merit, not inherited wealth.

As Buffett told me in 2001, repealing the estate tax is the economic equivalent of "choosing the 2020 Olympic team by picking the eldest sons of the gold-medal winners in the 2000 Olympics.... We would regard that as absolute folly in terms of athletic competition...we have come closer to a true meritocracy than anywhere else around the world.... You have mobility so people with talents can be put to the best use. Without the estate tax, you in effect will have an aristocracy of wealth, which means you pass down the ability to command the resources of the nation based on heredity rather than merit."

Yet we have lowered the top estate tax rate from 55 percent to 35 percent, and we have rules that allow perpetual or dynasty trusts that favor whom you have as parents over your hard work in determining whether you prosper. Our laws help explain why America today has less income mobility than Western Europe, as numerous studies have documented in the past decade.

How did we get to this state of affairs—flat to falling wages for most, tens of millions with no work or less work than they want, heavier taxes for the median-wage worker than the top 400, and laws enabling tax-free living for the richest of the rich?

In a word: Congress.

For years in lectures I have urged people to test just how well Congress listens to the thousands of lobbyists representing rich people and the big corporations with all the campaign donations, speaking fees, and post–Capitol Hill jobs to hand out. Corporations occupy Congress. Doubt that? Dial the Capitol switchboard at 202-224-3121, ask for your representative's office, and request a five-minute appointment, in private, at the lawmaker's convenience back in the home district. In more than a decade of recommending this, I have yet to have a single person tell me he or she scored a private meeting. Some have told me they were asked if they were campaign donors (asking that question is potentially a crime), and others have said they were lectured on what they should think about the issues they raised with the staff.

Want change? Want the progressive tax system that defines democracy? Want an end to rules that favor the already rich over the strivers and that tax the gravely ill to help the 1 percent? You can have it. Just do the work to elect a different Congress, one that represents the people, not the moneyed people — a Congress that will write different laws not just on taxes but on every aspect of society to fulfill the six noble purposes laid out in the preamble to our Constitution.

It will not be easy. It will take time. But, then, the whole idea of democracy and its civil twin, progressive taxation, is that we rule ourselves. Just as outsourcing jobs has not been good for incomes, neither has outsourcing politics to someone else because too many of us were too busy and preferred another rerun of *Law & Order* to the duties of citizenship.

The Short Sell: An Interview with Matt Taibbi

Tom Verlaine

Matt Taibbi writes about finance and politics for *Rolling Stone* magazine and is the author of *Griftopia: Bubble Machines, Vampire Squids, and the Long Con That Is Breaking America* (2010) and several other books. Tom Verlaine is a songwriter in New York City.

TOM VERLAINE: Do you think any president will create a mandate on income inequality?

MATT TAIBBI: No, I don't think so. I think Barack Obama will make income inequality an issue in the 2012 campaign, but that's a very different thing than saying something might ever be done about the problem.

TV: Regarding OWS, Ben Bernanke has said he's sympathetic to the protesters. Vikram Pandit said he'd like to meet them. I don't think that crew is interested in changing anything, do you?

MT: Vikram Pandit would like to meet them—and push them into a giant threshing machine. One thing that's striking about this whole phenomenon is the complete tone-deafness with which the movement has been met by the likes of Dimon, Mike Bloomberg, and Mitt Romney. When they talk about OWS, they literally sneer, or else they roll their eyes as if to say, "That's so quaint—protests." Every last one of them is outraged at the mere suggestion that they did anything wrong and really believes the whole movement is driven by jealousy.

Rolling Stone journalist Matt Taibbi (left) and songwriter Tom Verlaine. *(Photograph of Matt Taibbi by Sacha Lecca for RollingStone.com. Photograph of Tom Verlaine by Jimmy Rip.)*

TV: Do you see OWS growing? Perhaps spinning off some smaller groups, maybe with their energies more focused on one particular complaint?

MT: I think OWS in some form or another has to keep growing and will. Ultimately the movement has exactly the message that's needed and will attract followers— we represent the disenfranchised many against the super-connected few. OWS occupies the same space in society that a true labor-friendly political party would: it serves as a counterbalance to money, connections, and bureaucratic mechanism by representing sheer numbers. (At least that's the idea.) The problem is that most Americans are not really part of an organized labor workforce anymore, so it's pretty hard to organize them as workers. But as consumers and citizens, large numbers of people are starting to share the same complaints. We've all seen housing prices plummet, we've paid for bailouts, we've watched as people who stole from us are not prosecuted. These are things the 99 percent have in common. Once they realize their collective power as depositors and customers, and organize around that idea, they will have a real movement.

TV: "End the Fed" is one OWS "battle cry." The Federal Reserve has always been so mystifying. Do you think it needs to exist?

MT: The Fed needs to be reformed seriously. It's been used as an unofficial bailout mechanism for Wall Street for too long. Here's the irony of the Fed: most of the bankers who depend on its cheap cash for survival are rabid ideologues who believe there should be no "handouts" or "government interference" in our lives. They have utter contempt for single moms on welfare. And yet they're perfectly willing to take billions in zero-interest cash from the Fed and lend it to us at 5 percent or 20 percent (as credit cards) or even back to the state at 3 percent, a scheme that's essentially a government license to print money.

The Fed has become like a Santa Claus who doesn't give coal in stockings anymore. Everyone gets presents no matter how much they suck.

TV: Outside of the corrupt officials here and there, I still think unions are good. How do you feel about them? Helpful? Necessary? Past their prime?

MT: I think unions are very necessary and we need to expand them and also to alter their form somehow. Clearly right now the problem with unions is that they lack true international heft. If autoworkers in Detroit strike, they have no influence on autoworkers in China or Mexico. A union's power is limited when there's an absence of true solidarity. They need to get to a point where workers in China are in sync with workers in Europe and America. Much easier said than done, of course.

The other thing we need are true consumer unions. We need people who are, say, customers of/depositors with JPMorgan Chase to organize. We need to be able to come to banks and say, "You will lose 9 percent of your deposits tomorrow if you don't put a halt to X practice." Right now, customers who are ripped off by their banks or by other major companies have almost no recourse beyond the class-action suit, which is a clumsy method of response in addition to being expensive and overly dependent upon the whims of judges.

TV: Have you read the CFED 2012 "Scorecard" showing that half of Americans are one crisis away from poverty? How do you interpret this?

MT: Most Americans are stretched extremely thin; that's no secret. The health care system is the biggest culprit here—one funkily costly illness puts your average person on his back within a few months. Fixing that would go a long way toward curbing that problem.

TV: Many folks seem to think that OWS needs a spokesman or a point man to really get across, while others think the kind of informal, "scatter" method currently used is actually something new and beneficial. What do you think?

MT: I think eventually OWS will be well served by one voice and one leader or set of leaders. But that might be a long way away. Right now it just needs to grow and absorb all the anger and discontent, and being vague helps it rather than hurting it. But eventually, you'd want a Dr. King type to come forward and be the voice and the coordinator.

TV: No one in OWS addresses the Social Security tax, yet everyone I talk to agrees that it is actually a crime. After all, the $1,000 in Social Security tax someone paid in 1970 represented, say, a year's rent. Now it's maybe a half month's rent. One economist proposed the Social Security amount-due be paid to a special personal savings account, thus accruing interest, and that it be attached to a will should something happen to the payee. Sounds good to me! Then create some sort of tax, perhaps only a state tax, much higher for higher-income folks, to fund aid to the poor and elderly. No one, it seems, has ever proposed a payback of all Social Security tax collected to the payees not receiving Social Security benefits. Of course, it's not so simple—but is it so absurd an idea?

MT: Not sure if I have an opinion on this. The thing is, Social Security tax paid by the wealthy still ends up being used most of the time—by politicians improperly raiding the Social Security fund.

TV: The recent SOPA showdown-slowdown was interesting—seeing part of the 99 percent acting as de facto lobbyists. Do you think there will be more of this type of action? Or could there be more involving other areas of legislation?

MT: Absolutely, and I think this is an appropriate use of OWS as a political entity. Some people seem reluctant to deign to get into the process, but I think it's useful and can really help.

TV: When TARP's first draft got rammed through the Senate in '08, overnight constituent phone calls to Congress got the kibosh put on an absurd, maybe criminal, giveaway to the banks. Of course, they redrafted and got their "needs" taken care of, but it was another instance of the vox populi preventing the 1 percent from getting exactly what they want. I'm kind of skeptical of any power growing from grassroots advocacy, but I'd really like to be more positive. Do you think Occupy can really change anything?

MT: I think Occupy already has changed something. For instance, the foreclosure settlement I believe would have been far worse for consumers had the Obama administration not feared the reaction of an OWS-influenced public. It still has to keep growing and be a vague threat to public order, but if it does that, it will have a huge influence in ways both tangible and intangible.

TV: Do you have any news about the Sergey Aleynikov case?

MT: He got sentenced to seven years in jail, last I heard. [On February 16, 2012, a couple of weeks after this interview, Aleynikov's conviction was reversed. He was acquitted and, on February 17, released from prison, having served a one-year sentence.]

TV: High-frequency trading: do you see an end to that?

MT: Not anytime soon. There are a few members of Congress with bees in their bonnet over HFT, but they don't have many allies. I think it'll take a "flash crash" on a larger scale to bring about a ban.

TV: Everyone I know thinks the repeal of the Glass-Steagall Act was a mistake. Do you?

MT: Absolutely. Investment banks are inherently risky in their behaviors. Commercial banks, on the other hand, should be completely conservative in their outlook. Merging the two is madness. How can you take a massive depository institution like Chase or Wells Fargo and allow it to build up huge swaps portfolios—essentially, huge betting positions? The only reason you would do this is to blur lines between professions, increase the dumb power of banks, make insider dealing easier, and so on. There's no legitimate reason to allow these mergers.

TV: Has the day-to-day trading on Wall Street made a casino out of the equities market?

MT: It's worse than a casino. In a casino you actually have to post money before you make a bet. In the derivatives markets anyway, banks and hedge funds can build up huge positions without putting a dime down. These mountains of unregulated swaps create the potential for huge sucking whirlpools of losses. In a real casino, all the losses average out—it's a zero-sum game. Not so in the modern Wall Street.

TV: A friend of mine who worked on Wall Street said it is without question all insider trading, all "tips" and lobbyists behind the scenes suggesting ideas for legislation that would lead to all sorts of "lucrative" business. She suggests everyone who has stocks dump them if the loss isn't too great. She said it's mostly only the wallet boys—the 1 percent—who make money in the stock market, and they've rendered Wall Street itself useless for the 99 percent. Do you think so?

MT: Clearly the people who make real money in the equities markets (and other markets) are the ones that use insider-trading schemes, be it HFT (which is just computerized insider trading) or a word or two about interest rate changes or a new bailout plan or unemployment stats that get leaked out ahead of time. I think insider dealing is epidemic, much worse than people imagine. The rest of us who are "invested" in mutual funds or whatever are not playing the same game.

TV: Other than the five points you laid out in a piece for *Rolling Stone* in October 2011, do you see any specific actions OWS can take this year?

MT: I think OWS needs to target a specific problem or institution and then apply all its resources toward achieving that one goal. I'm involved with an OWS group engaged in just that sort of activity, can't elaborate. But OWS needs a show of force.

TV: It's curious—OWS had a certain irony from the start in that the overwhelming bulk of stock market activity no longer occurs on Wall Street—to the extent that Goldman Sachs is the last of the big firms still on Wall Street. What do you think?

MT: "Wall Street" is much more a state of mind than a place. There's more "Wall Street" in the Hamptons, Davos, and St. Croix than there is on Wall Street and Maiden Lane, probably. It's truly an international archipelago.

TV: Would you ever advise someone to buy stocks unless you had a "can't go wrong" tip?

MT: Sure. I still think the stock market can work for people. It's an enormously efficient way of raising money, and some great ideas get turned into global institutions overnight on the NYSE. It just needs a little better policing.

TV: You have far more access to the mechanics of the markets these days than most professors and economists. If you had some bucks to put back, where would you put them?

MT: I can tell you all my extra cash goes to home principal. I'm as clueless about personal finance as I am about fashion. If I ever had a lot of money, I'd probably buy a safe house on some random Francophone island somewhere, maybe some goats.

TV: After your vampire squid story broke, are you persona non grata on Wall Street or do they in fact trust you more and give you greater access?

MT: A little bit of both. Some won't talk to me. I've been disinvited to speaking functions because of angry

Goldman folk, but I also get calls from people in and around Wall Street trying to teach me things/point me in directions. I'd say I get more of the latter call.

TV: Regarding the European situation, do you see the ECB pulling out a form of TARP for the PIIGs?

MT: Some sort of bailout is inevitable.

TV: While China is the largest holder of U.S. Treasury bonds, it's suspected that the Chinese are also the biggest traders on Wall Street in U.S. equities. Have you seen any indication of that?

MT: I don't know about that, but I do know there are theories that foreign powers are engaged in coordinated, terroristic assaults on our financial markets. I don't think that's outside the realm of possibility. If I had a hundred billion dollars and hated America, I sure would get a kick out of inflating speculative bubbles here and so on. Why not?

TV: It seems to many that the SEC [Securities and Exchange Commission] are either lazy or disinterested. Do you think they've done their job?

MT: They absolutely have not done their job. They've actually gone out of their way to not do their job. The recent *New York Times* piece about the SEC granting waivers to companies accused of fraud, allowing them to raise money without the restrictions that usually come with such accusations, is a classic example. Can you imagine a single black mom caught cheating on her TANF [Temporary Assistance for Needy Families] welfare benefits being allowed to continue receiving welfare? Never in a million years would that happen. But the SEC essentially did that for banks over three hundred times in the last decade. The senior SEC staff are all refugees from the very firms they should be targeting. Hence the soft touch. And how about no major MBS [mortgage-backed securities] cases? Pathetic.

TV: What do you think the case of Fabrice Tourre says about Goldman Sachs or about banking generally?

MT: That it doesn't cost much to hire a big investment bank to commit highway robbery. Goldman in that case allowed hedge fund creep John Paulson to use Goldman's name in putting a portfolio of crappy mortgage derivatives together—Goldman called this "renting the platform"—for just fifteen million bucks. The scheme cost two European banks a billion dollars. A billion in damages for fifteen million in fees that Fabulous Fab and friends barely saw even a tiny percentage of. That tells me they're not only crooks, they *enjoy* being crooks.

TV: If you were put in charge of Occupy what would you do?

MT: Organize mass depositors' strikes and other actions with the concrete aim of breaking up the "too big to fail" banks, which are a threat to national security. They are vulnerable, and this is the quickest way to show America that OWS means business and must be dealt with.

TV: Is there one gigantic action you'd recommend that you think would actually change or begin to change the system?

MT: I think OWS needs to function like a giant short-selling fund, only without the profit motive—it has to have the power to identify corrupt companies and put them out of business, whether through consumer strikes or other political actions. I think it's possible to develop this capability.

TV: A certain kind of economist tends to stay awake at night worrying about how to solve the crisis. Do you think there are any people in finance like that?

MT: The question is, who's thinking about how to solve the crisis for his own benefit, and who's thinking about it in the sense of, let's solve it for the greater good? We saw in the Goldman/Abacus/Timberwolf case that Goldman, when it saw trouble coming, acted not to sound a general alarm but to secretly trade on the knowledge, often against their own clients. There are probably more people of that ilk on Wall Street than any other.

Smart Loans
Eliot Spitzer

Eliot Spitzer served as attorney general (1999–2006) and governor (2007–2008) of the state of New York. He attended Princeton University and Harvard Law School, where he was an editor of the *Harvard Law Review*. He is the author of *Government's Place in the Market* (2011).

If chapter one of Occupy Wall Street can be seen as a visceral cry of protest against the twin trends of rising inequality and declining opportunity that are gripping our nation, then chapter two must be a clarion call for real reform in areas that alter these troubling trajectories. The current policy debates are uniformly lacking in creativity and scope. They are minimalist in the context of the magnitude of the challenges we face.

Let's agree on a couple of easy starting points: the competitiveness of the United States over the long term depends upon our ability to be more innovative, creative, and nimble with intellectual capital. We can no longer—nor should we want to—win based upon having lower wages. We ceded pure wage competition long ago to the labor-rich nations of Asia, Latin America, and increasingly Africa. We no longer have a monopoly on capital, which is as mobile as an email; and access to resources and mass markets favors the newly arrived forces of China and India.

If we are going to improve American intellectual capital so we can generate the patents, products, and ideas of the future, we need to fix how Americans pay for higher education. We are struggling now with student debt that is in order of magnitude not too dissimilar to the tsunami of housing debt that crashed down on us in 2008. This crisis results from a simple fact: for too long we have asked students entering college and graduate school to choose one of two unappetizing options: pay astronomical tuition bills up front or amass enormous debt that demands fixed, sky-high monthly payments the moment they graduate and enter the workforce. These options serve as barriers to educational opportunity, since many cannot afford upfront tuition payments or qualify for the needed loans. They also distort career choices, since for most the obligation to repay loans immediately has reduced the ability to choose socially desirable jobs such as teaching, forcing the pursuit of the highest-paying job regardless of personal or social utility.

Yet there may be a third way that eliminates the educational financing problem. Milton Friedman, perhaps the most important conservative economist of the past fifty years, first proposed the idea, and James Tobin, a Keynesian from the more liberal wing of economic studies, then refined and tried to effectuate it. If two Nobel laureates of decidedly differing worldviews agree, it must be worth at least a quick look. Robert Reich, in his masterful book *Aftershock*, embraces the concept as well. It is, moreover, successful and commonplace in Europe and Australia.

Marketed under the uniquely unappealing name of "income-contingent loans"—I would suggest we call them "smart loans" instead—the concept is simple: instead of paying up front or taking loans with repayment schedules unrelated to income, students would accept an obligation to pay a fixed percentage of their income for a specified period of time, regardless of the income level achieved.

The beauty of this is that the single greatest barrier to education is eliminated. Everybody can go: no cash is needed up front. And the magnitude of your repayment is calibrated to what you earn, permitting greater freedom with respect to choice of jobs. Does this require those who earn more to pay more? Yes, but that is a fair transaction. Repayment is calibrated to the payback you get from the education. The numbers can be arranged such that the government—which is the lender—is made entirely whole, and educational opportunities are increased exponentially. We would eliminate the problem of student debt that now crushes opportunity.

Suppose a university charged $40,000 a year in annual tuition. A standard twenty-year loan in the amount of $160,000 ($40,000 times four) would produce an immediate postgraduate debt obligation of $1,228.50 per month, or $14,742 per year, not sustainable at a salary of $25,000 or anything close to it. Under a smart loan program, the student could pay about 11 percent of his income, with an initial debt of $243 per month, or $2,916 per year, which is more feasible at a job paying $25,000. If, after five years, the student's salary jumped to $100,000, payments would jump accordingly and move up over time as income increased. After twenty years, assuming ordinary income increase, the loan would be paid off.

Yes, this model raises all sorts of complex subsidy issues: Do we let lower-income earners stop repaying after twenty years even if they haven't repaid in full? Should higher-income earners subsidize lower earners by paying for the full twenty years even if they have repaid their individual debts in full? Should we set a minimum-income threshold, below which no repayment is required? Should we set an annual cap on repayments for exceptionally high earners? Should we make the percentage paid progressive, so as income increases a slightly higher percentage is paid each year? These questions are not easy, but they can be resolved.

For those who question the administrative complexities of smart loans, the answer is easy: the IRS can serve as the collection agency, making enforcement almost universal and driving costs down to a negligible level. It works in other nations.

Why should we be especially interested in this idea now? Despite all the money we spend on K–12 education, we are woefully underfunding higher and postgraduate education, and few areas are more important to retooling our economy. Things are only getting worse: college endowments have fallen, making aid harder to fund. Family savings have taken a huge hit, limiting the capacity to pay up front and obtain loans. Investments in higher education have fallen because of state budget crises.

Conservatives support the "income-contingent" model, as Friedman did, because they acknowledge that education is a social good that receives inadequate investment. Because it is hard to collateralize an education, unlike a piece of machinery, the market has a hard time funneling as much capital to education as it should. Education is a classic "public good"— undervalued by the market when positive social externalities are considered—and this financing structure helps to overcome the market's failure at minimal public expense. For liberals, the allure of the model is that it removes a significant barrier to education for the nonwealthy, and it frees employment decisions from the yoke of pure income maximization.

The success of income-contingent loans overseas has prompted sufficient study to provide blueprints for what the domestic models could look like. The foreign experience also prompted Yale to put in place a small pilot program, which it terminated in 1978. Though unsuccessful for administrative and collection-related reasons, the Yale program did benefit Yale law student Bill Clinton. If Occupy Wall Street wants a next chapter, this is a model worth embracing.

Enough with Occupying Wall Street: It's Time to Start *Pre*occupying Wall Street

Lawrence Weschler

Lawrence Weschler, a longtime contributor to *The New Yorker* (where he covered popular upsurges in Poland, South Africa, Latin America, and Belgrade, among other places), is the director of the New York Institute for the Humanities at NYU. He is the author of *Uncanny Valley; The Passion of Poland; A Miracle, A Universe: Settling Accounts with Torturers;* and *Calamities of Exile.*

Tyrannies all over the world—and here I include the tyranny of the market that the proponents of unfettered capitalism (which is to say, by and large, the system's increasingly concentrated winners, and all those handsomely paid-off apologists and retainers they regularly choose to hide behind)—exist in the ironclad certainty that people are nothing more than meat on sticks. Anything that their subordinates, their inferiors, their underlings are or have beyond that exists at the sheerest whim of the regime. Indeed, the notion that human beings have absolute rights simply by virtue of their humanity—the right, for instance, not to be tortured, on the one hand; or to secure lodging, a decent livelihood, adequate health care, and so forth, on the other—arises initially as a wild, untethered assertion in the face of eons of stark evidence to the contrary. But it is a magical assertion.

"We hold these truths to be self-evident, that all men are created equal, that they are endowed by their Creator with certain unalienable Rights, that among these are Life, Liberty and the pursuit of Happiness." The truly revolutionary advance in that declaration is contained not so much in such words as "truths," "self-evident," "unalienable," or "created equal" as in the calm self-certainty of that opening phrase: "We hold." The text does not launch out with "It is manifestly self-evident that" or some similar construction, as strict logic might seem to dictate. I mean, either it is or it isn't self-evident, right? Except that in this instance, the self-evidence of the assertion does in fact remain hidden, fugitive, immanent at best, until people rise up to embrace it, to hold fast to its insistence (mutually pledging their lives, their fortunes, and their sacred honor in the process). It is holding such truths to be self-evident that first makes them so—and, more specifically, doing so in concert, alongside others.

I first began to think along these lines several decades back, when I had the privilege of reporting from Poland during the early eighties and thereby got to witness the astonishing Solidarity upsurge firsthand. As it happens, one of the principal architects of that seismic convulsion, Adam Michnik, was in New York City in November 2011 and paid a visit to the Occupy Wall Street encampment at Zuccotti Park when it was in full bloom. We were talking a few hours afterward, and he told me he'd recognized a kindred spirit. "Sort of like Poland a few years before the actual Solidarity uprising in 1980," he explained. "The prologue to that moment, say Poland in 1976, when Polish workers began to rise up and say NO. They weren't yet sure what it was they wanted, what they wanted to say YES to, but they had become absolutely convinced of what they did not want, what they could no longer abide—and that is the beginning of the end for the regime."

His comments put me back into those days, in the early 1980s, when Solidarity was going full throttle: a movement that would, within less than a decade and notwithstanding temporary setbacks here and there, go on to rout one of history's vastest totalitarian regimes—a regime so entrenched and so stolid that hardly anyone beforehand had so much as granted himself permission to imagine its full eradication. Back in those days, the nascent mass movement's theorists—people like Michnik—used to speak of Solidarity as an expression of "the subjectivity of the Polish nation," by which they meant the Polish people's sudden insistence that they no longer be treated as the objects of other people's histories but instead start behaving as the subjects of their own. What began as almost a grammatical transformation—as basic as the leap from "Please, please stop doing that to us" to "Damn it all, we simply won't take this anymore"—ultimately had profound, world-upending implications.

As indeed might—one almost shudders to think it—the new movement under way here at the very heart of the capitalist market. (There's that joke of a few years back, to the effect that in 1989 capitalism defeated communism and in 2008 it defeated democracy, though that was never exactly right: in 1989 it was a mass people's uprising that overthrew communism, albeit one that was overwhelmed by the very rampaging neoliberal capitalism that went on to overwhelm Western democracy as well in 2008, a seemingly totalizing triumph that, on the other hand, may yet now be proving short-lived.)

And after having so brilliantly rallied oppositional energies in the fall of 2011, one way of phrasing the question now facing the Wall Street Occupiers and their as-yet homebound supporters all around the country, as the movement enters its next phase, might well be framed as, "How do we get from that inchoate *no* to a more focused *yes?*"

That the movement is entering a new phase can hardly be doubted: Merely occupying public squares in towns and hamlets all around the country was never in and of itself supposed to have been the point (though for a few weeks there it seemed to be becoming so); for that matter, as has been noted, the encampments themselves were becoming increasingly problematic, attracting all sorts of homeless, often mentally unstable elements whose care in a less savagely cost-cutting era would have been the wider society's obvious responsibility; having to divert substantial energies to sanitation and other similar day-to-day requirements; gradually wearing out their welcome with neighboring residents and businesses (those non-stop drum circles); etc. Given such problems, as well as the relentless onset of the coming winter, it could be and indeed has been argued that the various municipal authorities did the movement an unintended favor by shutting down the encampments themselves (and especially doing so in such a repeatedly ham-fisted way).

Nor need the remarkable upwelling of a radically participatory form of democracy within the camps, no matter how bracing and potentially valuable in the long run, in itself be fetishized as the point of the exercise. The fact is that at some point the Occupiers are going to need to sharpen their demands, or at least widen their tactical and strategic vision. They are going to need to find a way of reaching out to constituencies well beyond their original cohort, including millions of fellow citizens who, while they may not have the time or the life situation or the disposition to be able to join the diehards in encampments, would nevertheless love to be offered some concrete way into the movement, a practical means of expressing their anger and frustration, to say nothing of sheer human solidarity with one another. It is becoming the responsibility of Occupy Wall Street (just as it was the responsibility of the original antiwar mobilizers back in the Vietnam days) to find some way of building bridges to those people.

Phrased differently, if the greatest single contribution of the Occupy Wall Street movement to the progressive cause was the way it quickened a vital sense of narrative drive that had gone all but moribund over the past thirty years (through such captivating innovations as the 99 percent meme), that sense of vitality had begun to flag noticeably once again, and it was becoming imperative that the movement find a way of ratcheting the narrative up another several notches.

In doing so, the movement ought to build on another of Occupy Wall Street's greatest conceptual breakthroughs, the insight that it's become pointless to address our concerns to the politicians—a political system virtually completely paralyzed, evenly divided between bullies and weenies, with a president for all intents and purposes veritably palsied with compunction and misgiving. You don't occupy Capitol Hill: you occupy Wall Street. And the formulation needs to remain the same: it's time to stop addressing our concerns to the hired help; from now on we deal directly with the masters.

So, where are we today?

While the big corporations sit on piles of cash, small businesses are failing to thrive because people are not spending; and people are not spending because they either have already lost their jobs or live in justifiable fear that they may lose them soon. Fully a quarter of current mortgage holders are underwater, meaning they owe more to the banks than their houses are worth, with foreclosure only a family financial hiccup away. The possibility of moving anywhere else (where there might be a job) is likewise closed to them if they don't want to lose everything they've put into their houses, since housing markets generally have seized up as a result of the crisis.

Meanwhile, recent college grads groan under the weight of unprecedented amounts of debt—loans of the sort students in most other countries were never required to take on to fund what most everywhere else is seen as a self-evident public good; having an educated populace is, after all, to everyone's advantage. These loans were taken out with the assurance that the resultant degrees would lead to jobs that would allow the loans to be repaid: jobs that no longer exist.

With the general exception of the notorious 1 percent (who've been making out like bandits all through this period, just as they did throughout the previous three decades), the vast majority of Americans have pulled back on their spending; hence businesses lay off more workers. Then tax revenues decline and local governments in turn lay off more teachers, police, and firefighters, who therefore no longer spend, and so forth.

And what does government seem capable of doing in the face of all this? Not much. If anything, the wheels of governance seem more bollixed and mired than those of the economy. One party is being held hostage by a Tea Party pretty much entirely untethered from any understanding of its own actual economic interests, a faux populist insurgency lashed into existence by one group of billionaires (the Koch brothers and their ilk) and prodded along via the Pavlovian rantings of opinion-shapers employed by another (Murdoch and his), the rage of its members cleverly channeled toward the governments and civil servants that have (granted) proved so hapless in trying to deal with the crisis rather than toward the financial behemoths that created the crisis. The other party, alas, ever since the days when the Clinton-Rubin regime engineered its grand surrender (for purposes of all that excellent fundraising), has been captive to that same finance industry, a sinister embrace that their new leader, President Obama, for whatever the reason (personal psychological issues, heartfelt political conviction, meritocratic identification, Stockholm syndrome, a despairing realpolitik sense of what can be achieved—who knows and who cares?), has proven singularly incapable of sundering.

Bailouts—at full value, dollar for dollar—get lavished upon the banks and finance industry whose recklessness got us into the mess, without the slightest requirement that those institutions turn around and help the economy at large. While everyone else suffers, the executives take unconscionable bonuses, and meanwhile sluice good portions of the rest of their bailout funds into paying lobbyists and their designated candidates to gut even the mildest of regulations intended to forestall any further such criminal recklessness in the future. Is it any wonder that people are furious, alienated, and thrashing about for a response with any hope of opening up any sort of future prospect?

It is against that backdrop that I offer the following proposal. I should say first of all that I am by no means the first to be thinking along these lines (other such proposals have been bubbling up all over); nor is this sort of proposal the only one that need be pursued. It would constitute one activist foray among many. But it does strike me as the sort of direct action that the evicted Occupiers and their sympathizers around the country ought to be considering.

It grows out of the marvelously suggestive insight embodied in that classic old Yiddish story, the one in which, as you remember:

> Schlomo is up again all night, tossing and turning, and by three in the morning Rivka, his long-suffering and increasingly exasperated wife, has had it. "Enough already with the tossing and turning, Schlomo!" she exclaims. "What's keeping you up like this night after night, and me too while we're at it?" "It's Moishe across

the lane," explains Schlomo, trembling. "I owe him ten rubles, due tomorrow, and I don't have it." To which Rivka, climbing out of bed and heading over to the window, retorts, "Is that all? Geesh, no problem." She opens the shutter, leans out, and yells, "Moishe!" A few moments pass till Moishe across the way angrily flings his window open: "For God's sake, Rivka, what could you possibly want at this hour?" "It's Schlomo," she explains. "He owes you ten rubles in the morning, and he doesn't have it!" Whereupon she latches her shutter back up and returns to bed. "There," she tells her husband, "now *you* go to sleep and let *Moishe* stay up all night worrying."

What would it be like if activists were to spend the next several months developing, articulating, and organizing toward a major national mortgage and student loan strike? A loan strike could be slated to begin—provided enough people signed on in advance (and I'm talking hundreds of thousands, millions), and unless a concrete set of intervening demands was squarely met in the meantime—on some specific preannounced date in the intermediate future. Why not, say, on November 1, 2012, right at the climax of the presidential campaign?

Such a set of demands is hardly as radically over the top as it may first appear. No less a figure than Martin Feldstein, the former chairman of Ronald Reagan's own Council of Economic Advisers, argued in a *New York Times* op-ed piece, on October 12, 2011, that the country will never get out of its economic rut until the problem of underwater mortgages is squarely addressed. "House prices are falling because millions of homeowners are defaulting on their mortgages," he wrote, "and the sale of their foreclosed properties is driving down the prices of all homes. Nearly 15 million homeowners owe more than their homes are worth; in this group, about half the mortgages exceed the home value by more than 30 percent." Noting the strangulating effect of this situation on the economy as a whole, he went on to propose that, in order "to halt the fall in house prices," the government would be best advised to reduce mortgage principal that exceeded 110 percent of the value of the home. He noted that approximately eleven million of fifteen million "underwater" homes fell into this category. He said, further, that if all those eligible were to take part, "the one-time cost would be under $350 billion"—a cost he proposed could be divvied up evenly between the banks (which is to say, their shareholders) and the government.

A similar calculus could be applied to student loans. The real scandal here, apart from the sheer scale of individual indebtedness, is that the rates of the loans in question (I have friends who are locked into Citibank to the tune of coming on 10 percent), while they might have made sense in the day when prime was 4 or 5 percent, become utterly usurious at a time when the Fed has been busy shoveling money at those same banks at well-nigh zero percent, supposedly in order to help rev up the economy. Maybe those loans should be reset at just a few points above current prime—or the overhanging principal reduced according to some fairer systemic formula (no total loans to exceed $25,000, with less onerous schedules for repayment, or some such plan). For that matter, there may be other ways of parsing the resetting of underwater mortgages (for example, allowing for the temporary recasting of the mortgage payment into a non–interest-paying rental, without loss of accrued stake in the property in the interim).

The Occupy movement would need to enlist the advice of sympathetic economists and loan experts to craft the precise terms of the respective demands. In addition to the alleviation of tremendous amounts of individual and family anxiety and suffering, the more generalized goal of the reset—and incidentally, why is it that up till now in this crisis only the improvident banks and investment houses have been allowed to reset the terms of their deals, without any penalty, whereas none of the rest of us have been accorded similarly revivifying largesse?—would be to free up all sorts of spending money at the lower reaches of the economy, where it might actually do some good.

The naïvely self-deluding flaw in Feldstein's proposal, alas, is that he aimed it at the government. It's past the time for pundits like him to start getting real: this government, paralyzed and trammeled as it is these days, is never even going to consider, let alone act upon, anything of the sort. But our strategy circumvents that dead end entirely.

Again: once the precise terms of the demand have been framed, a national campaign could kick into gear in which underwater mortgage holders and overstrained postgraduate students would be invited to sign a statement to the effect that if by some specific date, some equally specific number of fellow debtors had likewise signed on to the plan, and if their grievances had not been satisfactorily addressed in the meantime, then all of them would simply stop paying the banks. *It would become the banks' problem*—and a problem from hell at that, for as lavishly as the banks' executives have been paying themselves, the underlying institutions are still in pretty delicate shape. Let *them* stay up all night worrying about it. Let them figure out how to get their lobbyists to get their government retainers to respond in a fashion that would avert such a terrifying looming eventuality.

I can already hear the baying screeches welling up from the coddled opinionati—almost a whole other charm of the proposal. Not fair! Against the rules! (Wait a second, isn't it the lender's responsibility to ascertain the viability of the loan in question, and isn't the prospect of default the supposed reason they've been allowed to rake in all that intervening interest? Is it our fault if they weren't able to calculate the eventual consequences of all these decades' worth of their compounding insouciant arrogance?) Moral hazard! (*Now* they start worrying about moral hazard?) What about those who played by the rules? (You mean an earlier generation that never had to rack up these sorts of student debts because college was much cheaper? You mean homebuyers who happened to secure their loans before the bubble and back when regulations still prevented the sorts of predatory practices to which their neighbors succumbed? Beyond which, this crisis affects all of us equally, with the exception again of that impervious 1 percent. If neighborhoods don't recover as a whole, no one in them is going to have a secure horizon.) And finally, that last-ditch all-purpose room-clearer: Class warfare! (Yeah: right.)

A further charm of the proposal is that many of those it seeks to engage would be distinctly easy to organize: in many neighborhoods, house after house is underwater, and it would just be a question of going door to door. A similar pattern pertains to recently graduated students, who tend to congregate, unemployed, in the same watering holes and in any case can be reached via their alumni organizations. (Indeed, one could deploy one group to organize the other.) Once reached, such reengaged individuals could form the basis for a significant widening of the innovative mass-participatory democratic impulse so brimmingly in evidence at the various occupations. Something old and ailing, the economy, might receive a vivifying jolt; and in the process something new and dynamic and gleamingly hopeful might quicken into being.

However, it's important to neither underplay what is being asked of signers nor leave them to their own devices once they do sign. People are being asked to put their livelihoods on the line (all the money they have tied up in their houses, often their entire retirement savings; the prospect of a complete collapse in their credit ratings; a mountain of potential legal fees, etc.). While organizing the signers, the movement would also need to develop support systems: legal-aid cooperatives, alternative credit societies, and the like (cooperatives whose seed funding could be provided by supporters not directly called upon to sign the growing commitment petitions, and which could in themselves grow into vital alternative institutions).

A final virtue of this proposal would be the way it so vividly lends itself to narrative elaboration. From the start, reporters would be tracing the upward arc of the organizing dynamic: they wouldn't be able to help themselves—this is storytelling catnip. A few hundred signatures the first week, a few thousand the week after, suddenly several tens of thousands more. Were sufficient signatures to be gathered before the deadline, the odds are the signers would never even be called upon to make good their threat, so spooked would the financial powers that be have become at the prospect.

On top of all that, such a plan would constitute a recovery of the great American tradition of direct action, running as it does from the true Founding Fathers (with their actual tea party and then a Declaration of Independence in which they chose to address the world at large rather than addressing the king, let alone his mere representatives) through Shays's Rebellion (Shays in that sense having been another of the Founding Fathers), the Jacksonian movements, and the Populist movements of the Gilded 1880s–90s (which began with farmers creating granges and other work-arounds to undercut the railroad monopolies, and industrial workers uniting to wrest back some measure of control from the robber barons), and then to the FDR era (Hoovervilles, etc.) and the activism of the civil rights and Vietnam eras.

As was the case with FDR, the point would not be to over-throw capitalism so much as to save it from itself, to usher in a more humane capitalism, and specifically to address the yawn-ing wealth gap that has so dramatically come to deform our current period. Much as the strategy of Republican *éminence grise* Grover Norquist has been to starve the beast (to under-mine tax revenues so relentlessly that government has no choice but to contract), ours ought to be to create a situation the only way out of which would be a vast realignment of wealth and resources. (There would likely be no way the banks could meet the sudden shortfalls occasioned by meeting all those loan demands, short of government rescue, and no way the govern-ment in turn could provide such relief without substantial wealth taxes.)

Thinking more long-term: the U.S. political system is completely rigged against the formation of third parties, but eventually (though only long-term, not right now), the strategy could be for the resultant movement to take over the dead husk of one of the superannuated political parties (much as the pop-ulists ended up doing with the Democratic party under Wil-liam Jennings Bryan).

But in order to be successful, such an effort would finally have to overcome the specter of race politics that has so bedev-iled American history to date. One of the main reasons the populists ultimately failed with Bryan is that the rich were able to pit poor whites against disenfranchised blacks: had those poor whites made common cause with their black counter-parts—demanding, among other things, their immediate reenfranchisement—the resultant votes could well have put Bryan over the top. Similarly, the only way FDR was able to push through his New Deal legislation was with an alliance of congressional northern liberals and southern racist commit-tee chairmen, one premised on agreement that any serious addressing of the scandal of Jim Crow segregation in the south would be put off for yet another generation. And surely, as has often been noted, a good part of the impetus behind the current Tea Party has been white panic at the sight of a black president. But another one of the nice things about the loan strike strategy is precisely the fact that there are as many underwater loans and dependent children groaning under the weight of egregious student debt among the Tea Party folk as anybody else. A loan strike movement could have the collateral benefit of peeling off substantial portions of the Tea Party (helping some of its members at long last to see the way they've been lashed into acting against their own financial interests), such that we might be verging on a moment when the curse of race politics in America could finally be superseded.

The point, in sum, is for all of us, holding fast to self-evident truths, to move beyond merely occupying Wall Street and to start *pre*occupying Wall Street, to unsettle the nights of its denizens and to wend our way into *their* dreams. And the time to be doing so is now.

Reframing the Debate

Tyler Cowen and Veronique de Rugy

Tyler Cowen is Holbert C. Harris Professor of Economics at George Mason University and general director of the Mercatus Center. His latest book is *An Economist Gets Lunch* (2012). Veronique de Rugy, a senior research fellow at the Mercatus Center, writes a column for *Reason* magazine, is a contributor to the *Washington Examiner*, and blogs at "The Corner" at *National Review Online*.

From the start, the Occupy Wall Street movement framed its argument around the claim that protesters spoke for the 99 percent, or the vast majority of Americans whose interests have been sacrificed to the fortunes of the ultrarich 1 percent. Within that framework, protesters expressed unhappiness about income inequality, the shrinking of the middle class, and the influence of the wealthy and well connected in politics. Perhaps most of all, they are unhappy that those they consider responsible for the financial crisis have paid no price for the damage they inflicted.

Each of these complaints has some validity, but there are other and perhaps more fruitful ways in which to frame the debate. Let's examine the representative claims made by the Occupiers to see how they may be misconstruing the problems and why some of their proposed solutions may make things worse rather than better. And what might an OWS agenda actually look like?

*   *   *

*Claim 1: **Wall Street is the main force holding back poor Americans.*** Wall Street has contributed to some very real problems, but the core issues for poor Americans are often health care, education, and the cost of renting an apartment or buying a house. The best way to improve living standards and increase options for future success is to move toward greater competition and accountability in each of those areas, areas that usually have little to do with the financial sector per se.

Contrary to common belief, the U.S. health care system is hardly market-based. Instead it gives us the worst features of both private and public systems, but the public-sector component plays a very large role. For instance, nearly half of all health care spending comes from tax dollars. Public spending on health per capita is greater than in all other Organisation for Economic Co-operation and Development countries, except Norway and the Netherlands. U.S. health care also is dominated by public-sector rules, regulations, and severe barriers to entry. Previous government policies have locked in an employer-based system, and consequently, most consumers don't know or even necessarily care what their health insurance costs. They have no way to reduce those costs, and little incentive to do so, even if they could. This lack of price transparency has numerous perverse effects, such as poor service and unresponsive doctors and insurance companies. For poorer Americans, subsidies to private health insurance mean it can be hard to find good doctors who accept Medicaid. Also, most states have structured their markets in such a way that few individuals are able to make meaningful choices among providers in a given area. The predictable result is spiraling costs that price many people out of the market for health care and health insurance. Navigating the health care sector ought to feel more like going to Walmart and McDonald's—quick service, low prices.

Monopoly is even more pronounced in K–12 education—
and further removed from any possible connection to Wall
Street "banksters." Over 90 percent of students in elementary
and secondary education attend traditional public schools,
which have produced a mediocre record of improvement over
the past forty years. According to the National Assessment of
Educational Progress, which has tracked reading, math, and
science scores since the early 1970s, graduating high school
seniors have made no gains in basic academic knowledge over
that time period. Yet per-pupil funding has more than doubled,
and the number of teachers per student has reached an all-time
high. Americans are now paying more than twice as much as
they did forty years ago for roughly the same product. It is no
surprise that public schools produce significantly lower rates of
parental satisfaction than both private schools and public
schools in which students voluntarily enroll.

The typical high school graduate faces a dilemma: the contemporary economy increasingly rewards students and workers
who can perform higher analytic tasks. Harvard economists
Claudia Goldin and Lawrence F. Katz have documented the
strong relationship between education and income growth.
Briefly, technological changes increase the demand for higher-
skilled and better-educated workers, but our educational system
isn't supplying them. That's a bigger problem than anything
stemming from finance, and it is why we see high unemployment
at the same time that we see lots of help-wanted ads for engineers
and computer support workers. OWS protesters who have called
for more access to affordable higher education ignore a more
basic problem, namely that K–12 systems are not preparing students for colleges, even lower-tier community colleges.

Increasingly, families elect to pay high prices to live in
highly ranked school districts. Cornell economist Robert
Frank measures what he calls the toil index: the number of

hours that median earners must work each month to be able to rent a house in a school district of at least average quality. He finds that the number grew by 62.4 percent between 1970 and 2000—from 41.5 to 67.4 hours per month.

Housing prices are inflated by a host of government policies, ranging from zoning rules that reduce the supply and variety of housing to mortgage-interest deductions that drive up housing costs. Indeed, across the board, poor Americans suffer from fewer choices and options in the areas that most directly affect their futures. Yet when it comes to basics such as health insurance, education, and housing, Wall Street is hardly the culprit.

We'd like to see the OWS movement focus its attention on the on-the-ground battles to lower the cost of living and improve public services for poor Americans. Those ends are usually achieved through greater competition and accountability. For instance, more districts should experiment with greater choice for K–12 schools, and that means the dollars could follow individual students as schools compete based on curricula, specialization, reputation, and parental satisfaction. School districts from Oakland, California, to New York City are already experimenting with such funding mechanisms, and research by Caroline Hoxby of Stanford University shows that increasing competition among schools generally increases both student achievement and satisfaction rates. A stronger commitment to firing the bad teachers and paying more to the good ones would help as well.

Claim 2: The top 1 percent is where the true class warfare is.

A lot of the ongoing wealth drain is from young to old through government redistribution, not just from working Americans to Wall Street. There is a systematic transfer of wealth from the relatively young and poor to the relatively old and wealthy. To put it slightly differently: the Occupiers should not be occupying Wall Street, they should be occupying AARP.

Roughly 40 percent of the federal budget goes to Americans over the age of sixty-five, mainly through Medicare and Social Security (this number includes the 28 percent of Medicaid spending that goes to older people). Assuming no significant changes in benefit levels, by 2030 these payments will consume 54 percent of the budget, and they will likely squeeze out just about everything else. Medicare, in particular, is the program behind the explosion of federal spending going forward.

Yet older Americans are in decent financial shape by historical standards. Their average net worth has increased almost 80 percent over the past twenty years. While official poverty numbers suggest that 15.9 percent of the elderly live in poverty, these numbers do not reflect how the elderly have fared over the last ten years or how their circumstances compare with those of other groups. Looking at consumption and income data to assess changes in living standards, University of Chicago's Bruce Meyer and James Sullivan of the University of Notre Dame show that those sixty-five and older have much lower poverty rates than most other demographic groups and that these rates have fallen sharply over time. Few other groups have enjoyed as much improvement in living standards over the past three decades. In fact, younger Americans are the ones getting poorer, especially relative to the elderly. Unfortunately, this progress is not reflected in U.S. Census poverty estimates.

A recent report by the Pew Research Center notes the divide: "In 2009, the typical household headed by an adult 65 or older had $170,494 in net worth, compared with just $3,662 for the typical household headed by an adult younger than 35.... The current gap is by far the largest since the Census Bureau began collecting these data in 1984. Back then, the age-based wealth gap was 10:1. By 2009, it had ballooned to 47:1."

What's more, a 2011 paper by University of Massachusetts-Amherst's Jeffrey Thompson and Timothy Smeeding of the

University of Wisconsin-Madison shows some dramatic and indeed depressing results. While the poverty rate for all households remains below levels reached during the economic downturns of the early 1980s and early 1990s, poverty has climbed substantially and reached a thirty-year high for households whose head is under thirty-four and for childless households with heads under fifty-five.

The point is not to start a class war against elderly Americans. Rather, we should consider the means-testing of both Social Security and Medicare, as well as a greater emphasis on fixing K–12 education. As a nation, the ratio of what we spend on the old compared with what we spend on the young is much higher than in the social democracies of Europe. American politics is largely to blame for the discrepancy. The elderly vote at high rates and the young do not. The elderly are also more likely to change their vote in response to a politician's position on benefits to...the elderly. This helps to explain why our system is broken and biased against the interests of the young.

Claim 3: *The top 1 percent are basically fraudsters and financial tricksters.* What of the impression that the typical 1 percenter is a Wall Street villain straight out of an Oliver Stone movie—an investment banker, a hedge fund operator, or a corporate raider who made his or her profits by firing long-term employees? The reality is different. To qualify for membership in the 1 percent in 2009, you needed to be part of a "tax unit" that pulled in $343,927 or more. That's a healthy income, to be sure, but only a third of the way to being a millionaire. Also, incomes grow much faster at the top end of the income distribution than in the middle or at the bottom end. That is, the disparity in income among that top 1 percent is very large.

The occupational spread of the 1 percent ranges far afield of Wall Street. A 2010 study by Jon Bakija of Williams College,

Adam Cole of the Treasury Department, and Bradley T. Heim of Indiana University finds that, along with financial-sector workers, the top 1 percent also comprises realtors, lawyers, doctors and other medical personnel, and executives and managers. In fact, excluding capital gains, in 2005 13.9 percent of taxpayers in the top 1 percent worked in finance. Focusing on the 0.1 percent of income earners, the study also finds that those in all the occupations in the group experienced rapid increases in income between 1993 and 2005, with higher gains in percentage terms going to real estate professionals than those in the financial sector. The latter had the third-fastest real income growth of all professions in the top 0.1 percent.

Perhaps more to the point, the 1 percent are often important creators, like J. K. Rowling and the late Steve Jobs rather than, say, Bernie Madoff. Fundamentally, Rowling and Jobs became wealthy by creating products that other people wanted, not by running scams. Their fortunes, however, were multiplied by the growth in globalization and technology. For instance, Rowling was able to tap into a market far beyond her native England, and she also leveraged her characters' popularity through movies and toys and other brand extensions. Similarly, Jobs and Apple benefited from free-trade agreements that allow for cheaper production costs and broader sales opportunities.

Consider two Swedish discount firms: the furniture maker IKEA and the clothing store H&M. Their ability to move beyond the relatively small domestic market in Sweden means that they gain access to a world of opportunity, but it also means they're paying top price for managerial expertise in global markets. The top managers earn more and the shareholders earn more, and perhaps some local retailers go out of business, but this tale of inequality is hardly a story of villains. Contrary to the beliefs of the Occupiers, a lot of the spread of incomes between top and bottom is happening for understandable reasons and through causes that are difficult to remedy.

Finally, fraud, rip-offs, and so forth are by no means the exclusive province of the top 1 percent. Plenty of bad behavior and bad practices are demonstrated by TV repairmen, used-car salesmen, small-business owners, and indeed many other professionals, including college professors and journalists. This gets back to the point that the 1 percent versus the 99 percent is not the fundamental distinction. The fundamental divide is between makers and takers—namely, those who produce something of value and those who gain at the expense of others, usually through a mix of political connections and fraud. We find both makers and takers, in great numbers, in the 1 percent but also in the 99 percent.

Claim 4: More broadly shared prosperity can be achieved through redistribution of income. General economic growth lifts everyone's income, even if the incomes of those at the top increase a lot more. However, taxes on the 1 percent can't be increased excessively without consequences for the average American.

Making the U.S. tax system more progressive, while it sounds like a tempting remedy, won't solve a lot of the major problems. In fact, the United States already has a more progressive tax system than do the social democracies worldwide. According to Organisation for Economic Co-operation and Development data, the top 10 percent of households in the United States pays 45.1 percent of all income taxes (both personal income and payroll taxes combined) in the country. In part, this finding probably reflects the greater role played in the tax system by refundable tax credits, such as the earned income tax credit and the child tax credit, and it also reflects the higher earnings at the top in the United States. Meanwhile, the average tax burden for the top 10 percent of households in OECD countries is 31.6 percent of the revenue intake, well below the American percentage.

What of the argument that high marginal rates of taxation will cause the wealthy to work less and create less? A paper by Peter Diamond and Emmanuel Saez suggests an increase in marginal rates of taxation on the wealthy to 70 percent. (See "Taxing High Earnings," pp. 317–29.) The opposite view is expressed by Michael P. Keane, in a recent survey article in the *Journal of Economic Literature*: "In a model that includes human capital, I show how even modest elasticities—as conventionally measured—can be consistent with large efficiency costs of taxation." In other words, even if higher taxes don't discourage the efforts of those who are wealthy, they decrease the incentive for individuals to become wealthy in the future. The point is not that current tax rates are necessarily the correct ones, only that we should not overestimate the gains from trying to tax the rich more heavily. It's a core economic lesson that trade-offs are everywhere.

Higher tax rates on the very wealthy also frequently lead to deal renegotiations that cause the wealthy to keep their previous share of the surplus. If J. K. Rowling had to pay higher taxes, for instance, she likely could demand a better deal from her publishers for her next book. The appearance of higher published tax rates on the wealthy doesn't necessarily mean the wealthy are bearing the actual burden.

Putting taxes aside, America's spending is less progressive than that of most European nations. According to the OECD data, while Sweden, Denmark, and Finland spend almost a third of their GDP on social transfers and Germany and France devote about a quarter, America redistributes 14 percent of its national income to social transfers. In other words, rather than make the tax system much more progressive, we should redistribute government spending in a more progressive way. That is the remedy suggested by the data on societies with lesser inequality.

Another recommendation of many commentators is that capital be taxed at a higher rate. The United States, however, already imposes a relatively heavy tax rate on capital, unlike most other OECD countries. First, according to OECD data, our federal capital gains tax rate of 15 percent is quite average. In fact, about a dozen advanced economies—for example, those of the Netherlands and New Zealand—have long-term capital gains tax rates of zero. Second, before being taxed at the individual level by taxes on dividends and capital gains, corporate profits in the United States are taxed at the business level—at the second-highest "on paper" rate of all OECD countries— and then again at the individual level by taxes on dividends and capital gains. Providing a lower rate for dividends and capital gains at the individual level is one way to partly alleviate the distortion from the other tax rates. And while some companies can avoid the heavy corporate rate by keeping their profits abroad, many don't have that luxury. Furthermore, stashing profits abroad may hurt the American economy, including domestic wages.

If shared prosperity is the goal, there is strong evidence that the differences in lifestyle and well-being between the very rich and the rest of us have narrowed dramatically in the last few decades. The vast majority of Americans have broad access to new pharmaceuticals, air travel, nutritious and cheap food, the Internet, and virtually all the technical innovations that the superrich have access to. Also, the data show that home and car ownership, access to higher education, and more have increased at all levels of income over the past thirty to forty years. On the whole, if one compares the quality of life of the very rich and the rest of us, one finds that it has become more alike than people routinely assume. Furthermore, less-well-educated groups have gained more leisure time than better-educated groups over the past forty-five years.

Such trends extend beyond material goods. Inequality in personal happiness, as measured by surveys and other questionnaires, is not growing in the United States. The relative measures of happiness and satisfaction in the United States are comparable with those in Sweden and Denmark, two countries that most progressives and, one assumes, many OWS protesters look at with envy.

We understand that Occupy Wall Street has some valid complaints. But a reframing of the problem is more likely to lead to sustainable remedies than the original viewpoint. By focusing on a narrowly defined division—the 1 percent versus the 99 percent—the movement misses the larger political dynamics of old versus young, makers versus takers, and the broader prevalence of fraud in American life. More important, decentralization of power and an increase in choice and competition in fiscal, educational, health care, and other policy areas would lead to more satisfying and equitable outcomes.

Voluntary Financial Transactions Tax
Brandon Adams

Brandon Adams taught undergraduate economics courses at Harvard for eight years.

A core tenet of Occupy Wall Street is that our economic system is rigged because of the overwhelming influence of money on the U.S. political process. Protesters tend to believe that capital has been protected at every turn for thirty years while labor has been trodden upon. The predictable result is that capital has all the power and economic inequality is at an all-time high.

I have a policy I'd like to suggest for anyone who supports Occupy Wall Street: a Voluntary Financial Transactions Tax (VFTT).

In *Confidence Men* (2011), Ron Suskind writes that, early in his administration, President Obama asked budget director Peter Orszag directly about immediate steps that might be taken to raise revenue. Orszag's number one suggestion: a financial transactions tax. Suskind reports, "Obama said, in one meeting, 'We are going to do this!' Summers disagreed; it never materialized."

Many years before Lawrence Summers received $5.2 million in a year for one day per week of work, or gave $135,000 speeches at Goldman Sachs, he wrote an academic paper titled "When Financial Markets Work Too Well: A Cautious Case for a Securities Transactions Tax." The case that Summers laid out in that paper was, in fact, not too cautious; he clearly supported a financial transactions tax. However good the logic was behind a financial transactions tax in 1989, when Summers wrote the article, the logic behind such a tax now seems dead perfect.

First, our deficit for fiscal year 2011 was $1.3 trillion. It's time to start thinking about intelligent ways to raise money.

Second, inequality in the United States has never been higher. In 2010, the top 1 percent accounted for almost 24 percent of all income and nearly 36 percent of the nation's wealth. A financial transactions tax hits where any new tax should— the upper echelons of income and wealth.

Third, a financial transactions tax would decrease the level of extremely short-term trading in the market, which would likely act to reduce volatility and improve the long-run market ecology. High-frequency trading firms have been recording record profits while providing dubious social value. In 1989, Summers concluded that "there are strong economic efficiency arguments to be made in support of some kind of Securities Transaction Excise Tax that throws 'sand into the gears,' to use James Tobin's (1982) phrase, of our excessively well-functioning financial markets."

The cumulative volume of financial transactions today is so monstrous that even minuscule rates of tax on financial transactions would yield huge revenues. A 0.2 percent tax on a wide range of financial transactions would likely yield in the neighborhood of $200 billion per year.

Here is my vision of the Voluntary Financial Transaction Tax: if you commit to support the VFTT, you're committing to donate, in 2012 and beyond, 0.2 percent of your financial transactions to a charity of your choice. This voluntary tax requires minimal calculation; every end-of-year brokerage statement lists the dollar amount of cumulative purchases and sales for the year.

A VFTT truly has a grassroots flavor in that once many

people have endorsed it, there will be increased pressure for financial firms to voluntarily adopt it. Indeed, supporters of the VFTT should not support businesses that choose not to pay the tax. Social shame will likely be an effective transmission mechanism for broad adoption of the VFTT among the wealthy.

Widespread adoption of a VFTT makes it more likely that Congress will consider a bill to sign a financial transactions tax into law. This should be viewed as the long-term goal.

Medicare for All

Jeff Madrick

Jeff Madrick is a regular contributor to the *New York Review of Books* and a former economics columnist for the *New York Times*. He is editor of *Challenge* magazine, visiting professor of humanities at Cooper Union, and senior fellow at the Roosevelt Institute and the Schwartz Center for Economic Policy Analysis at the New School for Social Research. He is the author of the book *The Case for Big Government* (2009), which was named one of two PEN Galbraith Non-Fiction Award Finalists, and *Age of Greed* (2011).

There is no voice when no one is listening.

Democracy is the term used to describe America today. Yes, Americans can vote. Yes, there is a free press. Yes, Americans can answer ill-put survey questions, whose results are read. It is hard to imagine, though, that Americans have any sense that their frustrations are being seriously listened to. The major media reflect centrist conventional wisdom, which in turn shapes American opinion in a feedback loop through conventional terminology. Survey results reflect the way American frustration is channeled into acceptable positions—positions of the moment. Thus, for example, Americans seemed to believe that their economic frustrations in 2011–12, which grew out of a combined unemployment and underemployment rate of nearly 20 percent, were the result of federal deficits or government spending in general. According to the surveys, they were most disturbed by government spending before the 2010 elections.

Because Washington framed the debate, and the Obama administration before the 2008 election emphasized budget balancing in light of political surveys conducted by Democratic pollster Stan Greenberg, among others, the jobs crisis that had been developing almost without pause since early 2008 was neglected by the mainstream media. Both Democrats and Republicans in Washington were mostly worried about long-term budget deficits, which they believed had to be dealt with sooner rather than later. There was little room for further discussion in the media. Only after the 2008 election did the Obama White House demand payroll tax cuts to stimulate growth, as it became clear that the economy was weakening. The administration seemed to fear making the move before the election. Only a couple of months later, the White House pivoted again to focus on deficits. "Winning the Future" again focused on cutting the deficit, not creating jobs. In his 2011 State of the Union address, the president proposed a five-year freeze on some spending programs. His budget for 2012 was composed two-thirds of spending cuts and only one-third of tax increases. The next pivot—a full-fledged jobs program—was not advanced by the president until September 2011.

Did all the talk of spending cuts truly address the confusion and frustration of Americans who had lost jobs and were unable to find new ones? Surely it was also clear that many Americans opposed the bailout of the banks. Did anyone truly represent this view in Washington? For the most part, the Republicans would not, just as they were mostly absent on jobs. The Republican view remains all about cutting government to spur growth.

Under a Democratic president, we did not hear very often— yes, there were occasions the president got angry—that the banks still had their share to pay. In the meantime, the Wall

Street elite affected to take every modest scold from the president as deeply wounding, an attack on the American Dream.

Obama did not do much to amend the rescue. He asked Congress to adopt the Volcker rule, mostly opposed, as far as we can tell, by his economic team, and the subject of much criticism from Wall Street. The rule sensibly limited risky proprietary trading—that is, securities trading with a bank's own funds. Treasury Secretary Timothy Geithner went on a cheerleading tour. He kept talking about how successful the $700 billion Troubled Asset Relief Program and the enormous Federal Reserve package were in getting America back on track.

The financial-markets panic was stopped by these policies, but America did not get back on track. The simple fact is that the Treasury Department—that is, the taxpayers—took the financial risk and Wall Street reaped the rewards. It should not have been that way. He who takes the risks should reap the lion's share of the rewards. Those who don't take the risks deserve, at best, modest compensation. Wall Street made a fortune and paid its bankers enormous bonuses.

Neither Republicans nor Democrats are listening to such complaints. Everyone in Washington seems, at least, to be on the same side. So why speak up? Why get involved? Indeed, measures of civil engagement such as voting, interest in public affairs, and attendance at political meetings are down in America. Does this suggest people are happy?

The Tea Party developed out of some of these frustrations and organized itself politically around antigovernment themes. Republicans in Washington have heard its united voice, which they partly interpret as meaning no taxes on the rich. Are they really reading the Tea Party members right? Is the Tea Party leadership truly representing those frustrations? It may yet lose force.

The Occupy Wall Street movement has succeeded in

giving voice to the many others by focusing on two rhetorical and related enemies: "Wall Street" and "the 1 percent." Wall Street greed, not simply outsized misjudgments by otherwise well-meaning bankers, brought financial markets and the economy down. Washington's part was to ignore what was going on.

OWS touched a live nerve. The American people knew it was Wall Street that sparked the crisis and that huge money at the top was unfair. A fine 2010 paper by Jon Bakija, Adam Cole, and Bradley Heim shows how much of the income of nonfinancial and financial executives alike in the top 0.1 percent was tied to Wall Street gains. According to Bakija, Cole, and Heim,

> [I]n 2005, non–financial executives, managers, and supervisors make up 42.5 percent of the top 0.1 percent of the income distribution, and financial executives make up 18.0 percent, so together the two groups account for slightly more than 60 percent of the top 0.1 percent.... The pay of executives, managers, and financial professionals tracks the movement of the stock market. This makes sense for obvious reasons in finance.... it also makes sense for executives and managers because much of their pay comes in the form of stock options.... The connection between the pay of executives, managers, and financial professionals and movements in the stock market could be illustrated by showing the share of national income going to executives, managers, and supervisors, and to financial professionals, who are in the top 0.1 percent of the income distribution over time.... A graph of this would show distinct peaks during the Internet bubble and the housing bubble.

Focusing on the 1 percent was key to OWS activists' success. But the other component of their success was that their

Percentage of primary taxpayers in top 0.1 percent of the distribution of income (excluding capital gains) that are in each occupation

	1979	1993	1997	1999	2001	2002	2003	2004	2005
Executives, managers, supervisors (non-finance)	48.1	45.7	48.4	47.1	42.6	40.6	40.5	40.9	42.5
Financial professions, including management	11.0	14.1	14.7	16.4	19.1	19.0	17.8	18.7	18.0
Lawyers	7.3	6.5	6.3	5.9	7.1	8.2	8.8	8.0	7.3
Medical	7.9	13.3	6.8	4.4	5.2	6.8	7.6	6.3	5.9
Not working or deceased	5.4	2.5	3.5	3.8	4.0	3.7	3.7	3.8	3.8
Real estate	1.8	1.3	1.8	2.1	2.5	2.9	3.0	3.3	3.7
Entrepreneur not elsewhere classified	3.9	3.0	2.8	2.7	2.8	2.9	3.2	3.0	3.0
Arts, media, sports	2.2	3.3	3.5	3.5	3.3	3.6	3.4	3.3	3.0
Business operations (nonfinance)	1.5	1.7	2.3	2.2	2.7	2.7	2.2	2.7	2.9
Computer, math, engineering, technical (nonfinance)	2.3	2.3	3.1	4.7	4.0	3.0	3.1	3.0	2.9
Other known occupation	2.9	2.1	2.2	2.6	2.5	2.5	2.4	2.5	2.7
Skilled sales (except finance or real estate)	2.2	2.9	2.9	2.6	2.4	2.3	2.3	2.3	2.3
Professors and scientists	0.8	0.8	0.7	0.8	0.9	0.9	0.9	0.9	0.9
Farmers & ranchers	1.4	0.2	0.5	0.5	0.5	0.5	0.5	0.5	0.6
Unknown	1.4	0.5	0.5	0.9	0.7	0.6	0.8	0.7	0.5

Addendum: detail on executives, managers, and supervisors

	1979	1993	1997	1999	2001	2002	2003	2004	2005
Executive, non-finance, salaried	32.0	21.8	19.4	18.0	15.4	13.9	14.3	14.5	14.0
Executive, non-finance, closely held business	5.3	12.8	15.7	15.2	13.7	14.2	13.7	14.3	15.6
Manager, non-finance, salaried	4.9	4.1	5.5	6.2	5.4	4.5	4.7	4.1	4.0
Manager, non-finance, closely held business	2.5	3.5	4.8	4.8	5.1	4.9	5.0	5.0	5.8
Supervisor, non-finance, salaried	1.6	1.4	1.0	1.2	1.2	1.1	0.9	1.1	1.0
Supervisor, non-finance, closely held business	1.8	2.0	1.9	1.8	1.8	1.9	1.9	2.0	2.2
Addendum: executives, managers, supervisors, finance	59.0	59.7	63.1	63.5	61.6	59.6	58.4	59.6	60.5

Source: authors' tabulations of Statistics of Income individual income tax return data.

From "Jobs and Income Growth of Top Earners and the Causes of Changing Income Inequality: Evidence from U.S. Tax Return Data," by Jon Bakija, Adam Cole, and Bradley T. Heim, November 2010, updated January 2012.

Used with permission.

cause was not precisely economics. They were about injustice. That was the source of their strength. Put simply, they were asking: Why is poverty so high in America? Why have wages been stagnant in America for so long? Why do so many have no health care? Why aren't the banks and Washington providing mortgage relief or business loans? Why are Wall Streeters again making so much money, while the economy remains in the doldrums? Why should we trust national leadership that does not respond to these issues in a concerted fashion?

Of economists and policymakers they were implicitly asking: Why did you let Wall Street do this to us, and why are they still getting away with it? Was this good economic theory? If not, why didn't you stand up and shout out that something was not right?

New York City mayor Mike Bloomberg said Congress led Wall Street to make bad subprime loans. It is nonsense. Most mainstream economists scoffed at the idea. He said that the Obama stimulus failed. It is again nonsense. Yet he lectured OWS participants as he evicted them from Zuccotti Park: they should live by the power of their ideas, he said—implying, of course, that they had none. The power of Bloomberg's ideas was the $250 million or more of his own money he spent on three mayoral campaigns. How can the OWS movement and its sympathizers take his comments seriously when his ideas are devoid of any real sense of justice and disregard the true contours of power and free speech in America?

When people ask why OWS and its offshoots don't have a political agenda, the movement's answer is basically a question: What are your solutions, and why hasn't our democracy implemented them? If you are so smart, why are we in this mess?

OWS activists wanted to give anger and frustration a voice, and they could only do that through public demonstration and assembly—and, occasionally, resistance. They succeeded. Voice only exists if someone is listening. By demonstrating publicly, banging on drums, marching through the streets, and occupying Zuccotti Park and other public places throughout the nation, actions for which so many within the establishment and within the Washington policymaking tribe had scorn, they forced those who opposed them to listen. Those who took part in OWS had a voice, and that voice talked about injustice.

Where do they go from here? The groups are splintering. Some are pursuing policy objectives. Others are sitting in where they perceive there are problems: at foreclosures and in front of the Capitol, for example. They are shining a light on injustice. They did not lose momentum even as they were evicted, sometimes violently, across the nation. The United Nations rapporteur for free expression demanded an explanation from the United States for its having suppressed the right to free speech.

Of all the ironies, the greatest is that OWS has become an American brand, even an icon. It assures the movement's permanent influence. It is dangerous to be a brand. It suggests a longer life than the OWS critics had anticipated. OWS protesters need not occupy Zuccotti Park anymore. But they need visibility, a reminder that their brand exists.

I am still wedded to the older school of political reform. I think the protesters can constructively pursue some specific policies. If they choose do to so, I'd recommend focusing on only two.

The first is Medicare for All. Rising health care costs and unjust distribution of health care services are America's biggest domestic problems. Education and infrastructure do indeed demand attention; but rising health care costs can either bankrupt the nation over time or result in such a mean-spirited level of unjust triage that political stability will be endangered. To cut federal programs such as Medicare will mean requiring the

Medicare is signed into law on July 30, 1965: President Lyndon B. Johnson flips the pages of the bill as former president Harry S. Truman waves the handful of pens used during the signing ceremony. Standing behind them are Lady Bird Johnson, Vice President Hubert Humphrey, and Bess Truman. *(LBJ Library, photograph by Yoichi Okamoto)*

elderly either to use private health care insurance, which will be more expensive, or to do without health care benefits they need. For example, raising the Medicare eligibility age to sixty-seven from sixty-five will reduce federal spending but increase private spending significantly, according to the Kaiser Family Foundation. Many will simply drop out and not be covered. How long will Americans put up with this? The Tea Party and the OWS movement are relatively peaceful outgrowths of deepening anger and frustration, but without government response, anger may grow.

Almost everyone on Medicare likes it. It is simple, efficient, and relatively cheap. The costs per beneficiary rise significantly more slowly than do costs in the private health care sector. It is not an outrageously generous plan. It has high co-pays, for example. Some have calculated that the typical private plan, on

WHY MEDICARE FOR ALL?

The principal cause of soaring federal spending after 2025 is the inefficiency of the nation's health care system. While the issue has been widely discussed, few, if any, of the budget balancing plans proposed in 2011 offered serious health care reforms. The basic facts are well known. About 17 percent of U.S. national income is spent on health care; the figure includes both public and private spending. France, next closest among major nations in health care spending, devotes about 11 percent of its GDP to it. On a per capita basis, America spends 50 percent more than nations such as Norway, Switzerland, and Canada.

Rising costs will drive up government expenditures on Medicare and Medicaid in the late 2020s and 2030s far more rapidly than will the effects of an aging population. The Congressional Budget Office has estimated that health care costs will rise to roughly 25 percent of GDP by 2025 and 37 percent in 2050.

Higher Medicare and Medicaid spending will be, by far, the most important driver of federal deficits in the future. Social Security increases are minor by comparison.

"Obamacare," or the Patient Protection and Affordable Care Act (2010), will place some downward pressure on the growth of health care spending by reducing provider payments and other measures. It will also test ways to reduce expenditures by emphasizing quality of care over quantity of care such as through single comprehensive payments for treatment rather than payment by procedure.

Medicare for All would be a far more effective way of reforming the health care system. It is, however, politically impractical, if not impossible, given the lobbying efforts of health care companies and providers. Americans also seem to retain an ideological fear of government-run health care. The phrase "socialized medicine" has rung alarms in America since the 1930s, when Franklin Delano Roosevelt tried but failed to establish a national health care system.

That does not mean that Medicare for All should be abandoned as an idea, especially by the idealists of OWS. It can cover all Americans adequately while probably reducing costs by eliminating enormous marketing and overhead costs of insurance companies. It would operate similarly to Medicare today, covering almost all necessary procedures based on a contribution by both employees and employers. Just as it now covers almost all of the elderly, it could cover almost all of America. Special provisions would have to be made for those who are independent contractors and those who do not work full time. Such a single-payer system would also enable government to negotiate drug prices, control reimbursements for providers, and develop incentives for preventive care and reduced use of heroic medical procedures.

Savings from a single-payer plan versus the current mix of for-profit health insurance companies would come partly from reduced marketing and administrative costs, which alone are estimated to amount to $200 billion to $300 billion a year. Congressman John

Conyers Jr. (D-MI) has introduced a Medicare for All bill: H.R. 676, "The United States National Health Care Act," or "Expanded & Improved Medicare for All" (2009). It has won some support in Congress and from physicians, including the seventeen-thousand-member Physicians for a National Health Program (PNHP), approximately 2.5 percent of all doctors in the United States. Conyers's proposal is, in fact, more generous than Medicare, eliminating the 20 percent co-pays and most deductibles. Given the savings from reduced administrative and marketing costs, and also from more widespread reimbursement controls, Conyers and his allies believe the out-of-pocket costs to most Americans would be significantly reduced from current levels of pay for employer-supported plans. Nevertheless, some new taxes would be levied to finance it. A less generous plan, which retained 20 percent co-pays, for example, except for the poor, would in turn require few taxes to finance it.

The best evidence that such plans can work is that successful versions of them are in place in many countries, and they largely result in superior health outcomes compared with the American system. Beyond the fact that those who are covered under similar plans pay far less for health care than U.S. citizens, a 2010 Commonwealth Fund study of seven countries (the United States, Australia, Canada, Germany, the Netherlands, New Zealand, and the United Kingdom) ranked America last overall and last or next to last in the following measures: quality of, access to, and efficiency of care; equity of care between high- and low-income individuals; and the chance of living a long, healthy, and productive life.

Medicare for All remains implausible politically, but so was the success of OWS. Is another miracle possible?

average, is better. However, Medicare is *universal*. It would also give government the authority to negotiate drug prices and establish better preventive medicine through wiser incentives— a serious chance to reduce overall health care costs as a share of gross domestic product.

My second reform would be the public financing of all national elections. Dollar amounts devoted to lobbying are obscenely high today. The financial establishment has watered down the Dodd-Frank financial reregulation legislation (the Dodd-Frank Wall Street Reform and Consumer Protection Act, H.R. 4173). Health care companies defeat good reform. The defense industry makes sure Congress spends ever more. Energy companies maintain their tax breaks and prevent reforms to fossil fuel usage.

The source of the power? It is all a function of the huge cost of elections, which gives these rich companies and their executives their sway. It also gives the rich the power to prevent higher taxes on their incomes and to change or lighten regulations. Public financing of elections would eliminate much of this influence.

Energy directed by the young and newly roused could make progress in these two areas. These two reforms could in themselves transform America.

But I am not urging the OWS protesters to turn their

attention to these two policies. They must go with their own instincts. Remarkably, they refuse to appoint leaders, though there are many who have become leading organizers. They still respect everyone's opinions. As of this writing, specific change is not yet for them—at least not for many of them. For now, they are content to shine the light on the many injustices they find. For me, so far, that is more than enough.

Countering the Dangers of Procyclicality

Daniel Gross

Daniel Gross, economics editor at Yahoo! Finance, is the author of *Dumb Money: How Our Greatest Financial Minds Bankrupted the Nation* (2009) and *Better, Stronger, Faster: The Myth of American Economic Decline* (2012).

In seeking to recover from the massive self-inflicted wounds of the Great Panic of 2008 and the Great Recession of 2008–9, analysts frequently repair to the disciplines of economics and history. As they should. The U.S. response to the Crash of 1929 and the Great Depression offers a useful playbook. As a former PhD student of American history turned financial journalist, I find it shocking how much the American system has forgotten about the experience of the New Deal — or, worse, how little it knew about it in the first place.

But as we consider how we might avert future catastrophes, I'd argue it's worth looking to two other disciplines: physics and engineering.

Even with the reforms and vows never to repeat the mistakes of reckless leverage, the U.S. economy still struggles with design specifications that don't account for a powerful natural force: procyclicality. Procyclicality is the dangerous, predictable tendency of our financial, political, regulatory, media, and cultural systems to amplify and boost existing trends and wavelengths as they gain strength.

The laws of physics, it turns out, pertain to economics. Trends and objects moving in a particular direction tend to keep doing so. As they increase in size, they gain momentum and speed, which helps them gain still more size and still more velocity. Think of a snowball that starts at the top of a mountain as a few tightly packed snowflakes and winds up at the bottom as a twenty-foot-diameter boulder capable of crushing anything in its path.

We've seen this happen time and again in the financial markets and in the economy at large. The United States is a highly procyclical country. This is how our commercial culture rolls. When one person hits on a good idea, whether it's a social networking company, a railroad, or a yogurt shop, five or ten other people quickly mimic it. Rather than discouraging people from attacking entrenched incumbents, the success of first-movers simply encourages a host of second-movers to rush in. When ten mail-order clothing retailers have received funding, it's that much easier for the eleventh and twelfth. The completion of one $10 billion leveraged buyout simply sets the stage for five more. Financial procyclicality melds with media procyclicality. As booming companies grow in size, they emerge as marketing, advertising, and lobbying forces—and there's nothing the media love more than blowing up a hot new trend into the next big thing.

Procyclicality has its virtues. Booms and boomlets whip up capital and enthusiasm, and spread new ideas, concepts, and business models at warp speed. The dynamism builds large industries and economic force overnight: six transcontinental railroads instead of one in the late nineteenth century; four online booksellers instead of one in the late 1990s; in 2011, hundreds of daily deal sites (Groupon, LivingSocial, and so forth) instead of three or four.

Procyclicality also leads to greater volatility and ever-larger crashes. Think of a boat on which all the passengers rush to the port deck railing at the same time to catch a glorious view, causing the vessel to keel over sharply. Then they all rush at once to the starboard deck in an effort to right it. Instead of stabilizing, the ship capsizes.

In the past decade, we've seen several troubling examples of procyclicality.

Housing finance. As housing prices boomed in the years after 2001, homeownership turned from a way of guaranteeing stable shelter to an investment scheme. As prices rose and froth developed, procyclicality embedded into the system inflated the bubble further. As housing grew more expensive and leveraged, the industry—with regulators and politicians nodding their assent—pushed housing to become even more expensive and leveraged. Fannie Mae and Freddie Mac, the government-sponsored enterprises, continually raised the limits for the size of loans they'd make. Rather than react to higher prices by raising mortgage standards, the vast lending industry lowered them—developing so-called affordability loans that didn't require down payments, or that offered teaser interest rates, or that didn't even require borrowers to make the full interest payment each month. And they've been procyclical on the down side. Post-bust lenders have tightened standards and made it harder to get a loan, which only exacerbates the decline.

Banks. The worst of the excesses in mortgage lending arose in the shadow-banking sector—largely unregulated lenders like Countrywide Financial that got their funding from Wall Street investment banks. The same procyclical tendency was evident in the regulated banks. Bankers follow a simple formula: size × leverage = greater profits. As banks agglomerated more and more capital, they realized they could bolster returns by layering debt upon existing debt, or stowing it in off-balance-sheet vehicles, which is how Citigroup wound up with a trillion-dollar balance sheet backed by only a skinny layer of capital. The larger the bank, the easier it was (and the more sense it made) for it to take larger risks.

Financial markets. When the stock market began to melt down in 2008, a third form of procyclicality came to the fore. Information technology and competition among exchanges have combined to lower the cost of executing a trade to just a few cents. This encouraged and abetted the growth of high-frequency trading operations, funds and investors that use computer programs to make hundreds of thousands or even millions of trades a day in an effort to capture tiny price movements. With so much trading put on autopilot, and with a series of trip wires triggering investors to sell when prices are falling, or to buy when prices are rising, the procyclicality of high-frequency trading is obvious. The flash crash of May 6, 2010, when the market apparently fell more than six hundred points in five minutes—*for no particular reason!*—was the most vivid example of this tendency. Intra-day swings of several hundred points have become commonplace.

Fiscal policy. Fiscal policy is highly procyclical, especially at the state and local levels. When states receive a gusher of revenues from capital gains taxes, or cities grow fat on real estate transfer taxes, budgeteers don't stash the money away. Rather, they establish the high-water mark as a new, highly elevated baseline. Of course, as we've seen, revenues can fall rapidly when markets crash—federal revenues fell 16.5 percent in fiscal 2009. That leaves gaping budget deficits, and it pushes policymakers to engage in austerity programs at precisely the wrong time in the economic cycle.

Clearly, the U.S. economy and its financial system and

markets need a greater level of countercyclicality—standards, forces, devices, and instruments that arise as countervailing forces to balance the immense procyclical forces of financial trends.

Countercyclicality is already built into many of our systems. On hot summer days, when use of air-conditioning is already at a high level, customers crank it up even more, placing stress on the system. Many utilities have established countercyclical incentives and programs whereby certain large users— universities, office buildings—commit in advance to dial down their usage automatically when everyone else is ramping it up. Paying users to turn down their lights a few days a year is much cheaper than building an extra power plant and keeping it on standby for hundred-degree days. When it comes to fiscal policy, countercyclicality helped stop the Great Recession of 2008–9 from turning into a repeat of the Great Depression. But we—regulators, the Federal Reserve, the political system, policymakers, even the media—need to do much more.

Housing finance could be—and should be—much more countercyclical. As prices rise, for example, entities like Fannie Mae and Freddie Mac, which dominate the mortgage market, should tighten standards rather than loosen them. After all, they (and the taxpayers who stand behind them) have much more to lose when the typical mortgage is $500,000 compared with $250,000. In years during which prices rise, they should demand higher credit scores, greater or equivalent down payments, or the purchase of mortgage insurance. By contrast, after prices have fallen precipitously, as they have in recent years, mortgage lenders should act in a countercyclical manner. They could loosen standards on credit scores, or increase the acceptable loan-to-value ratio, or simply be a little more aggressive on extending credit. Doing so would help provide some vital ballast to the market. In addition, when the typical home sells for $160,000 instead of $230,000, lenders are assuming less risk on any given deal.

Even with the passage of the Dodd-Frank bill and a more vigilant set of regulators on the job, the doctrine of "too big to fail" has not been consigned to history. When large, systematically important institutions run into trouble, there will always be intense pressure to bail them out, regardless of what the law says. In fact, the U.S. banking industry is more concentrated today than it was in 2007. The large banks will always want to be larger. That means we have to get much more serious about putting countercyclical incentives in place that make it less profitable for banks to be larger, or to make them think twice.

The higher capital standards imposed by the 2010 Dodd-Frank Wall Street Reform and Consumer Protection Act, and envisaged by the emerging Basel III global standards, are a good start. But they don't go far enough. It would be useful to have a steeply progressive set of capital requirements, so that as banks surpass milestones—$1 trillion in assets, $1.5 trillion in assets, $2 trillion in assets—they are required to hold proportionally more capital in safe assets. Banks could still pile their balance sheets to the sky; it just wouldn't be quite as profitable to do so. By the same token, deposit insurance should be steeply progressive.

When a two-story structure in the middle of an open field falls down, the collateral damage it imposes is minimal. When a fifty-story skyscraper in the middle of a city falls over, it can take down other buildings and vital infrastructure. Banks are the same way. Small banks can get into only so much trouble, and their failure won't make much of a dent in the Federal Deposit Insurance Corporation insurance fund. As we saw in 2008 and 2009, the failure of massive banks can swamp the FDIC fund. The FDIC already charges differential insurance premium rates for small and large banks. But the lion's share of the differential in the rates stems from the FDIC's assessment of risk. As we've seen, however, banks that appear to be low-risk institutions can quickly become high-risk ones. It would make better sense—and be much more countercyclical—to focus on size rather than perceived risk. Again, banks could grow as large as they wanted. But the system would make it less profitable, rather than more profitable, for them to do so.

The nation's financial markets have plenty of countercyclical measures built into them. Trading limits kick in on days of significant volatility. The commodity exchanges have made a practice of raising margin requirements for traders in products whose prices have risen rapidly, such as gold or silver. They respond to the rising use of leverage by, in effect, requiring participants to put up more capital to maintain positions. These standards can have the effect of tamping down speculation in already frothy markets.

High-frequency trading is the real procyclical danger in the markets. Here we have another obvious countercyclical tool at our disposal: a financial transactions tax. Rather than ban a particular practice, regulators can simply make it less economically appealing. As economists like to say: if you want less of something, tax it. Imagine the United States were to impose a so-called Tobin tax, a levy of a few cents on every trade of a financial instrument—bonds, stocks, derivatives, commodity futures. It would raise a lot of money without imposing much of a cost on buy-and-hold investors. But it would really discourage the legions of procyclical high-frequency traders who trade millions of shares in an effort to gain a penny, or a fraction of a penny, in profits—and who really provide no economic benefit. (See Brandon Adams's Voluntary Financial Transactions Tax proposal, pp. 422–24.)

To a significant degree, federal fiscal policy is countercyclical. In 2008 and 2009, at a time when private sector demand was falling, the public sector did its part to boost demand, through automatic stabilizers like food stamps and unemployment insurance. The Federal Reserve cut interest rates and engaged in quantitative easing, and the federal government passed a large, $787 billion stimulus program. There's much more that can be done, especially at the state level, where budget officials are required to balance their budgets each year. Many states have reserves or rainy-day funds. In 2011, North Dakota, which is experiencing a boom thanks to renewed oil and gas exploration and oil production, set up a legacy fund that channels a chunk of oil-related taxes into a pool that can't be raided for several years. More states should mimic North Dakota. They could set up spending caps that limit increases in appropriations to a fixed amount—4 or 5 percent—and dictate that revenues rising above that level be shunted aside into reserves.

It's hard to be countercyclical. When industries grow larger, they are better able to influence policy and protect existing practices. Aside from embedding countercyclicality into standards, policies, and the structure of markets, we have to train ourselves to push back against prevailing trends. That's difficult. It's not much fun being countercyclical. It takes guts to stand up at a party and tell everybody to stop drinking, or to shut down the all-you-can-eat chocolate fountain, or turn off the cheap supply of credit. Still, performing the difficult tasks would help us avoid having to make much harder and more painful choices down the road. Nobody likes a buzzkill. But if we had empowered the countercyclical buzzkills in 2006 and 2007, we wouldn't be suffering from this long and pronounced procyclical hangover.

Principal Reduction: How to Reduce the Mortgage Burden

Felix Salmon

Felix Salmon is the finance blogger for Reuters and has been blogging since 1999. He arrived at Reuters from Condé Nast's Portfolio.com, where he originated the Market Movers financial blog. He also wrote daily commentary on Latin American markets for news service Bridge News; worked and freelanced for a variety of publications, including *Euromoney* magazine; helped set up the New York bureau of financial website InterMoney.com; and created the Economonitor blog for Roubini Global Economics. He is a graduate of the University of Glasgow and has worked in the United States since 1997.

There's a lot of blame to go around when it comes to the causes of the financial crisis, but at heart, it was about debt—or, as the financial markets like to call it, leverage. Investment banks created highly leveraged mortgage-backed securities that blew up; commercial banks backed up their holdings of super-senior debt instruments with little or no capital; homeowners bought houses with no money down, paying for them by borrowing amounts they could never afford to repay.

In many ways, the debt-fueled housing bubble was the financialization of America carried to its logical conclusion. From the early 1980s onward, economic growth was increasingly a function of leverage: small improvements magnified by being turbocharged with debt. A little debt can do wonders for growth—but like a drug addict, the economy eventually needs that much debt just to stand still, and ends up having to take on more and more leverage to sustain the growth it's used to.

With leverage, of course, comes danger—what finance types call "systemic risk." If the debt stops getting rolled over, as happened in 2007, then the entire economy can come to a screeching halt, with the loss of trillions of dollars in wealth, not to mention millions of jobs across the country. When the party stops, as happened in 2008, a new word enters the lexicon: deleveraging. It's a central paradox of finance: while the economy needs credit in order to grow and to create jobs, it also needs to reduce the total amount of debt outstanding, in order to reduce not only individual and corporate debt burdens but also the risk of another massive crunch.

Deleveraging is always a painful process. When done on a nationwide scale, it often takes the form of inflation, which tends to hurt the poorest members of society in a particularly invidious way. When done on a case-by-case basis, it involves the loss of a lot of wealth: your liability is my asset. (The money in your checking account, for instance, is counted toward your bank's total liabilities. If your bank repudiated your claim to that money, then it would be richer, but you would be poorer.) Nevertheless, deleveraging is necessary. And every so often, it's possible to find a positive-sum way of making it happen: a plan that makes *everybody* better off.

How can writing down debts ever benefit a creditor, the person to whom those debts are owed? The answer lies in the fact that if a debt is not going to get paid off in full anyway, the creditor's best interest lies in simply maximizing the value of what he does end up receiving. Let's say you owe me $1,000— but then you come and tell me that you can't afford to pay me back. You're faced with a choice. Either you empty out your checking account and I take everything in it, which is $250, or you can find some money elsewhere and give me $450 in settlement of the debt. If I'm sensible, I'll take the $450—and I'll leave you with a working checking account.

Compared to the $1,000 I had in the first place, I'm worse off, but that's a sunk cost at this point, and there's no point crying over spilled milk. I have to face the situation as I find it today, and make the best of it.

You'd think that banks, in particular, would be alive to the sunk-cost fallacy—partly because denial is a pretty bad business strategy at the best of times and partly because they all worship at the altar of something called "mark to market." That is, they check to see what their loans are worth every day (or at least every quarter) and then value the loans at what they're worth in the real world rather than how much was borrowed in the first place. Yet banks—and this probably comes as little surprise, at this point—can and do behave in surprisingly irrational and childish ways. A lot of the time, especially when it comes to dealing with homeowners, they seem more interested in inflicting misery than in maximizing their own financial returns.

All of this comes into starkest focus with respect to mortgages. America has millions of underwater homeowners, many of whom are behind on their payments and all of whom are significantly less likely to pay off their mortgage in full than they would be if they actually had equity in their houses.

It's simple logic, used by every company and commercial real estate operation in the land. If you owe more than your property is worth, and you can walk away from that property and discharge your debt in full, then you should absolutely do so: indeed, the Mortgage Bankers Association did exactly that in 2010. It had a $75 million mortgage on its Washington, D.C., headquarters but sold the building for $41 million, moved out, and is renting elsewhere, relieved of the burden of $75 million in debt.

Banks hate it when people walk away from their homes. (The act is often called "jingle mail," because you're essentially mailing in your keys to the bank.) At the same time, they're often enormously reluctant to do the one thing that is completely effective at preventing people from doing that, which is to reduce the principal due on the mortgage so that the amount of the mortgage is lower than the value of the home. The U.S. government, too, has been reluctant to push this as a solution: its attempts to encourage banks to refinance mortgages have all been centered on reducing monthly mortgage payments rather than the total amount owed. In fact, many government-backed mortgage modifications actually *increase* the total principal amount because of various fees tacked on during the modification process.

Even if your mortgage payments go down, it can still make all the financial sense in the world to stop paying them, especially if you run into trouble. If you can rent a nice place for less than your mortgage payments, and if you have no real prospect of owning any positive equity in your home for the foreseeable future, it makes sense to free up a lot of cash flow by just stopping payments on your house. This is especially true when banks can take well over a year even to start foreclosure proceedings.

The result is a huge "shadow inventory" of homes overhanging the market. These homes aren't yet for sale but will at some point get foreclosed on, depressing values across the neighborhood. As a result, in 2011, no one wanted to buy—and house prices continued to fall, despite record low mortgage rates of less than 4 percent.

So what *should* happen when people get into trouble making their mortgage payments on a house that is underwater? After 2008, banks tended to do one of two things. They waited for an interminable amount of time, then initiated foreclosure proceedings and kicked the family out of their home.

Alternatively, they worked out a mortgage modification that didn't reduce the amount owed by a single dollar, thereby maximizing the probability of a redefault and of the homeowner having to go through the same painful process all over again.

There are multiple ways of doing this better. The simplest is just for the banks to unilaterally reduce the principal amount owed on a mortgage. It's much more effective, always, for a bank to reduce principal and keep the interest rate constant than it is to do what they tended to do after 2008, which was to keep the principal constant and reduce the interest rate. Why don't they reduce principal? They don't because doing so involves writing down the value of the mortgage on their books—something they're bound to do sooner or later, but which they'd much rather do later than sooner.

As the depressed stock prices of every bank in America in 2011 attested, however, no one really believed the values that the banks put on their mortgages—they weren't kidding anyone. Coming clean on the true value of their mortgage portfolio might hurt banks' quarterly earnings, but it wouldn't necessarily hurt their share price. Once the mortgages are marked down to a reasonable level, banks can be much more sensible about how they're going to deal with homeowners in difficulty.

There are circumstances in which banks have shown themselves willing to take losses on the mortgages they own. One is when they sell a big portfolio of mortgages to some third-party investor: such portfolios are often sold at just 10 percent or 20 percent of the face value of the mortgages if a lot of those mortgages are in default. Another scenario, and it happens pretty frequently, is the short sale, in which a homeowner sells a house and hands over all the proceeds to the bank, and in turn the bank writes off the mortgage, even though it isn't fully paid off. Then, of course, there's the worst scenario of all: you fall behind on your mortgage, and the bank forecloses on your property, taking over the deed to the house. At that point, the bank will turn around and sell the property, almost certainly for less money than it was owed on the mortgage, and take a loss.

All of these mechanisms open up possibilities for keeping homeowners in their homes, even after they've fallen behind on their mortgage payments: you just need a little imagination. For instance, let's say you're a bank that has foreclosed on a home. Standard operating procedure in such a situation is normally to kick the occupants out, put the house up for auction, and take whatever you can get for it. But there's no rule saying you have to do that; indeed, there's no rule saying that you have to evict the home's occupants at all. Instead, why not rent the house back to them at the market rate? The market rent will almost certainly be lower than what they used to have to pay in mortgage payments, and at the same time you get to avoid kicking the family out of their home. Everybody wins in this case. The family gets to stay where they are, the neighborhood isn't blighted by a boarded-up home being sold at auction by an owner who doesn't care about it, and the bank gets a healthy income stream rather than a modest sale price.

And if the bank prefers to get cash rather than be a landlord? No problem: it can simply sell the property to someone happy to rent it out to the current occupants. Many such organizations and individuals exist: in days of record low interest rates, people with money often jump at the opportunity to make a decent rental yield on their investment, especially if they're helping out a family in straitened circumstances at the same time. Often, such a rental contract will include a clause allowing the former owners to buy the house back at a pre-set price: the new owner might ask for a 10 percent profit after one year, a 15 percent profit after two years, and so on. If the family members manage to qualify for a mortgage to buy their house back, then the new owner will sell it to them—for less than the occupants originally paid but more than the new owner/landlord paid. Again, everybody wins.

Similarly, if a bank sells a defaulted mortgage for a fraction of its face value, then there are lots of ways in which the new owner can keep the former homeowners in their house and still make money. The principal amount can be reduced, of course, as can interest payments—and you probably wouldn't be surprised to learn how much simple and sympathetic human contact can help.

Most of the time, homeowners have no ability to get through to a sensible human being at their mortgage company who can understand what they're saying and help them make empowered decisions with regard to any possible mortgage modification. Instead, they get the standard runaround: they're constantly being asked to fax in documents that always seem to then go missing. By contrast, if you buy a mortgage and approach the homeowner with good will and a genuine desire to find a reasonable solution, it's amazing how often something mutually beneficial can be worked out. Indeed, a company called American Homeowner Preservation (AHP) is doing just that: it has set up a hedge fund devoted to buying pools of defaulted mortgages and keeping the homeowners in their homes, and it is making good money doing so. All it takes, really, is a little bit of compassion and an ability to be inventive—rather than following exactly the same script every time.

AHP started with a simpler, nonprofit model: it would act as a broker, putting together willing buyers with underwater homeowners. The homeowners would do a short sale to the buyers at the home's market value, and the buyers would lease the house back with an option to repurchase. That model didn't work, because the banks refused to cooperate. While they were okay with short sales in general, they were emphatically not okay with any short sale that involved sellers remaining in their home. Tired of fighting and losing endless battles with the banks, AHP decided it would be a lot easier to buy the mortgages themselves. That way, AHP didn't have to deal with impenetrable and illogical bureaucracies all day.

The banks have a reason for making it hard for people to sell their homes and stay in them regardless: they're worried that lots of other homeowners will attempt the same stunt. However, it only makes sense to sell your house if you're significantly underwater on your mortgage. And if you're significantly underwater on your mortgage, then it probably makes sense to sell your house whether you get to stay in it or not.

Indeed, one of the more evil tricks of America's banks is that the very people who need the most help with their mortgages—people who are far underwater—are also the people least likely to be able to get it. If you bought your home at the top of the market and it's now worth a lot less than you borrowed to buy it, you'll probably be rejected for the kind of mortgage refinancing that everybody else can get with no difficulty. As a result, if you're current on your underwater mortgage, banks and investors reckon that mortgage is worth not less than par (because it's underwater) but, rather, *more* than par—about 106 cents on the dollar, on average. On a $200,000 mortgage, investors will pay a $12,000 premium just to be able to collect your high-interest mortgage payments, which you can't reduce because you're not allowed to refinance.

It's a little bit crazy: if these homeowners were rational, especially if they live in a nonrecourse state like California, they would just mail their keys in to their bank and be done. That's certainly what the *bank* would do, in the same situation. (In 2009, for instance, Morgan Stanley mailed back the keys to five San Francisco office buildings worth $1.5 billion rather than pay the mortgage on those buildings out of its record profits that year.)

Instead of reacting with gratitude to the fact that these underwater homeowners are paying their mortgages in full, though, banks punish those homeowners by forcing them to continue paying the high interest rates they locked in when they bought at the top of the market. Mortgage rates had never been lower than they were in 2011, which meant that mortgages that couldn't be refinanced to a lower rate were particularly valuable to banks.

If you're current on your mortgage, the banks won't let you refinance, and if you're behind on your mortgage, they won't let you stay in your home, even if you have a willing buyer waiting with the cash to buy the house and let you do just that. There's only one exception to this rule, and it's a fascinating one. If a bank bought its mortgages below par rather than lending the money out itself, then it's quite likely to be open to the idea of principal reductions. For instance, when Wells Fargo bought Wachovia and when JPMorgan Chase bought Washington Mutual, they bought those banks' mortgage portfolios at a large discount to par. It turns out that those mortgages—the ones bought from Wachovia and WaMu—have been getting modified with principal reductions.

The behavioral psychology here is very easy to understand. No bank wants to admit that it wrote idiotic loans by writing down its own assets from par. Meanwhile, it's much easier to write *up* an acquired asset, which is what Wells and Chase did, by putting some smart principal-reduction plans in place. (Some principal reductions, indeed, have even been done for homeowners who are current on their mortgages.) Economically speaking, of course, what the banks are doing here makes no sense at all. Either writing down option-ARM (adjustable-rate mortgage) loans makes sense, from a profit-and-loss perspective, or it doesn't. If it does—and, yes, of course it does—then the banks should do so on *all* their toxic loans, not just the ones they bought at a discount.

The solution, then, is clear. We need to encourage banks—and servicers—to mark their mortgages to market, and to do whatever makes sense if they're being realistic about how much those mortgages are worth. And while it's okay to assume that homeowners will develop an emotional attachment to their homes and pay more than necessary to stay in them, it's not okay to take advantage of that fact to extract thousands of dollars a year in extra mortgage payments from those homeowners.

More generally, principal reduction in mortgage modifications has to become the rule rather than the exception. The reason the government's efforts to fix the mortgage market have failed so miserably is that those efforts have centered on interest payments, not the total amount owed. A sluggish housing market will act as an economic drag for as long as millions of homeowners owe vastly more than their house is worth.

If done right, these policies can be implemented in a positive-sum way, leaving everybody—including the banks doing the write-downs—better off. For instance, the government could impose higher capital standards on banks that insist on marking underwater defaulted mortgages at par, and give the banks an incentive to write down principal that way, while making the whole banking system safer at the same time.

Not all deleveraging can be done this efficiently or painlessly, but that's a great reason to grab this low-hanging fruit while we can. If we don't want the United States to continue to suffocate under the weight of far too much debt, we have to start making serious efforts to bring our debt burden down. This one's a no-brainer. Let's do it.

How Bankruptcy Contributed to the Mortgage Crisis and How It Could Help the Economy Recover

Michelle J. White and Wenli Li

Michelle J. White is a professor of economics at the University of California-San Diego, visiting professor at the Cheung Kong Graduate School of Business, Beijing, and research associate at the National Bureau of Economic Research. Wenli Li is a senior economic adviser and economist with the Federal Reserve Bank of Philadelphia.

Occupy Wall Street protesters held an Occupy Our Homes campaign on December 6, 2011, in several U.S. cities to disrupt foreclosures and evictions. In line with the focus on preventing foreclosures, this essay offers some modest proposals to change bankruptcy law in ways that would help to reduce foreclosures.

A bit of background is useful. First, the mortgage crisis that led to the 2008 financial crisis, the recession, and our economic malaise is far from over. Several million foreclosures have occurred, and most predictions are that foreclosures will double or triple by the time housing markets recover. Among mortgages that originated during the housing bubble, 6.4 percent have ended in foreclosure, and an additional 8.3 percent are in serious default and likely to go into foreclosure, according to November 2011 figures from the Center for Responsible Lending. The large number of foreclosures increases the supply of homes for sale, pushing down home prices—which are

Occupy Our Homes, January 6, 2012: In Oakland, California, activists stand on the steps of a foreclosed home that they reoccupied, on a day that brought such actions nationwide. *(Justin Sullivan, Getty Images)*

still falling in fifteen of twenty metropolitan areas for which data are available. The falling prices will put even more mortgages underwater in the future, resulting in a continuing drag on the economy.

Second, economists agree that when homeowners default on their mortgages, lenders have an inefficiently strong incentive to sell homes in foreclosure rather than allow homeowners to keep their homes by renegotiating the terms of the mortgages. When lenders foreclose on a house and sell it for less than the amount owed on the mortgage, they lose the difference between the amount owed on the mortgage and the proceeds of selling the house, and in addition they must pay foreclosure costs. However, lenders do not bear the unquantifiable social costs of foreclosure, stemming from and including the health problems former homeowners experience due to stress; the sagging performance of their children, who are forced to move and transfer to new schools; the decline in value of nearby houses; neighborhood blight as houses are vacated and not maintained; and cuts in public service by local governments due to plummeting property tax revenues. Even the start rate of new businesses drops, since traditionally homeowners tap their home equity for the capital to open a business. Because mortgage lenders do not bear any of these costs, they have an incentive to foreclose too often.

Third, the various government programs to stop foreclosures, including HAMP (Home Affordable Modification Program), the Federal Housing Administration's FHASecure program, HOPE for Homeowners (a joint project of the FHA and HUD, or Housing and Urban Development), the Home Affordable Refinance Program (a program of the Treasury and Department of Housing and Urban Development), and Fannie Mae's HomeSaver Loan program, have helped very few homeowners. This is because these programs generally require that lenders consent to mortgage modifications, and lenders rarely do so.

How could bankruptcy law help in reducing foreclosures? In the past, homeowners in financial distress often filed for bankruptcy in order to save their houses. Bankruptcy helps them in several ways. The automatic stay on legal actions against debtors stops foreclosure at least temporarily and gives financially distressed homeowners breathing space to sort out their finances. It also ends garnishment of debtors' wages. Unsecured debts such as credit card loans, installment loans, and medical debts are discharged in bankruptcy, although the terms of homeowners' mortgage contracts cannot be changed. Along with ending wage garnishment, the discharge of unsecured debt in bankruptcy increases debtors' ability to pay. In the past, homeowners in bankruptcy often used the extra money to repay their mortgage arrears and keep their homes. Also, homeowners in bankruptcy could file a plan to spread the cost of repaying their mortgage arrears over three to five years.

If they made all the repayments required under the plan, then the original mortgage contract was reinstated.

Bankruptcy law was reformed in 2005 to make it less debtor-friendly. Some types of debt that previously could be discharged in bankruptcy became nondischargeable. Homeowners with income above the median level in their state were required to use some of their future income to repay unsecured debt. The most important change, however, was that filing became much more costly and difficult. Lawyers' fees and filing fees rose from less than $1,000 before the reform to around $2,000 afterward (for debtors who do not file repayment plans) and $3,500 (for debtors who file repayment plans). Other hurdles were also put in place by the reform, including requirements that bankruptcy filers undergo credit counseling before filing, take a financial management course before receiving a debt discharge, and file copies of their pay stubs and income tax returns with the bankruptcy court even if they had never filed tax returns in the past. These and other requirements fall heavily on the most financially distressed debtors, who often can no longer afford to file for bankruptcy.

By making bankruptcy more difficult and costly, the reform caused the number of filings to plummet, from around 1.5 million per year in 2004 to only 600,000 in 2006. In 2011 research, I argued that an unintended effect of bankruptcy reform was to sharply increase the number of mortgage defaults, since homeowners who could no longer have their unsecured debts discharged in bankruptcy were more likely to default on their mortgages. I estimated that even before the mortgage crisis began, bankruptcy reform caused the default rate to rise by 23 percent on prime mortgages and 14 percent on subprime mortgages. The number of additional mortgage defaults was 225,000 per year.

How could bankruptcy law be changed to help solve the foreclosure crisis?

My first proposal is to reduce debtors' costs of filing for bankruptcy, thus making it easier for financially distressed homeowners to use bankruptcy to save their homes. This could be done by eliminating some of the hurdles to filing that were adopted as part of the 2005 bankruptcy reform.

My second proposal is to allow bankruptcy judges to change the terms of homeowners' mortgage contracts in bankruptcy. A version of this change was part of proposed legislation to deal with the mortgage crisis: the Helping Families Save Their Homes in Bankruptcy Act of 2009. Although the act was adopted, the bankruptcy provision was dropped. Under the proposal, bankruptcy judges would have the power to reduce the principal amount of homeowners' mortgages to the current market value of the home if the mortgage was underwater and to reduce the interest rate on mortgages to the current market level. Unlike HAMP and HOPE or the other government programs designed to aid homeowners, this legislation would allow bankruptcy judges to change the terms of mortgage contracts without lenders' consent.

The main criticism that has been made of this proposal is that it would reduce the availability of mortgage loans and cause interest rates on mortgages to rise. Yet bankruptcy judges have the power, under existing legislation, to change the terms of mortgage loans on investor-owned and vacation properties. (They do not have this power for owner-occupied primary residences.) Research has shown that there is little difference between the availability and terms of mortgage loans for (a) vacation homes or investor properties (with mortgages that can be modified in bankruptcy) and (b) owner-occupied primary residences (with mortgages that cannot be modified). Both types of mortgages are offered on the same terms because lenders' losses are in fact smaller when mortgages in default are modified in bankruptcy—their losses when mortgages are modified are approximately 20–25 percent of the mortgage principal, compared to 50 percent or more when foreclosure occurs. These results suggest that allowing mortgage modification on owner-occupied primary homes would not change the supply of mortgage credit.

Another criticism of the proposal is that many homeowners would use bankruptcy to modify the terms of their mortgages even if they have the ability to pay according to the original mortgage terms. However, homeowners who wished to use bankruptcy to change their mortgages would have to file a repayment plan in bankruptcy, live on a bankruptcy trustee–supervised budget for five years, and have the bankruptcy filing on their credit records for up to ten years. These costs dissuade homeowners from using bankruptcy except when they would otherwise default on their mortgages and lose their homes.

Occupy Global Capitalism
Jeffrey D. Sachs

Jeffrey D. Sachs is an economist and the director of the Earth Institute at Columbia University. He is the author of, among other books, *The Price of Civilization* (2011).

O ccupy Wall Street erupted in September 2011, eight months after a youth upheaval brought down the government of Tunisia and spread to Cairo, Madrid, Tel Aviv, Santiago, Athens, and dozens of other cities around the world. From Wall Street, the movement quickly spread to hundreds more cities across the United States and the globe, including to Moscow at the end of 2011, in the wake of rigged elections. Nor did the global upheavals end there. Youth protesters took to the streets of Nigeria early in 2012, while massive demonstrations continued in Moscow and broke out in several central European countries, including Romania and Slovakia. These protests show no sign of ending any time soon.

Of course, this kind of cross-border contagion is nothing new. Revolutions, protests, and anticolonial upheavals have often traveled across national boundaries. The year 1848 saw a wave of antimonarchical upheavals across Europe. Russia's October Revolution in 1917 spurred several failed attempts at revolution in Europe. Anticolonial movements leaped from India and Indonesia in the late 1940s across Asia and Africa in the 1950s and 1960s. Nineteen sixty-eight was a year of global youth protest, and in 1989, anticommunist revolutions spread like wildfire across central and Eastern Europe. The 2003 U.S.

war on Iraq spurred coordinated antiwar protests around the world, showing how a global protest movement could be quickly organized with online support.

Yet the Occupy movement is distinctive. It is a wave of social protest that spans rich and poor countries alike. While each country swept up in protest has its distinctive political and economic grievances, there are important commonalities in the aims of the protests in countries as disparate as Tunisia, Egypt, Israel, Spain, Chile, and the United States. The protests can reasonably be labeled Occupy Global Capitalism. They mark a popular revulsion against a global economic system that has caused vast inequalities in income, claimed new victims of poverty and mass unemployment, and that lacks a moral and political framework oriented to the needs of the millions of people being left behind by global economic change.

Global capitalism has arisen during the past thirty years as a system of deep contradictions. On the positive side, global corporations have created a deeply interconnected network of production and finance that is fueling worldwide technological advance at an unprecedented rate. The mobile phone revolution is Exhibit A; never before in history has a technology spread so far and so fast across the globe. From a mere eleven million mobile subscribers in 1990, almost entirely in rich countries, there are more than six billion mobile subscribers today, covering almost all the world. Private companies chasing market profits have brought hundreds of millions of the world's poorest people into mobile telephony, mobile banking, and the interconnected digital age.

Yet global capitalism has also created massive new hardships and has sapped the political will and perhaps even the ability of national governments to respond to the needs of those hurt or left behind by economic change. Many of today's multinational corporations are more powerful than the host governments. By virtue of their immense financial wealth and their credible threat to move jobs across borders, the corporate giants push local politicians to ease regulations, lower corporate tax rates, and weaken or abolish environmental and labor standards. The "race to the bottom" is evident in every sphere of government: business relations, financial regulation, accounting practices, tax policy, labor standards, environmental regulation, and the compliance of boards and managers with fiduciary responsibilities.

If corporate threats to decamp are not enough, corporate enticements to politicians (a.k.a. kickbacks and campaign contributions) are even more potent. Business lobbies pay the ever-rising campaign bills of the politicians, offer lucrative jobs to friends and family, pay direct bribes, and increasingly make national politics a game of corporate power. Conglomerates, such as Rupert Murdoch's News Corporation, that own the mass media increasingly make or break political careers.

Top CEOs, unleashed by deregulation and unhindered by weakened trade unions, are the ultimate winners, especially in the United States, where corporate governance is weak. Many CEOs act with impunity, taking home unconscionable incomes that they award themselves in a rigged compensation process. They game the political system through their financing of political parties and politicians and play off one government against the next in order to advance their agenda of dismantling government oversight.

Market forces are also playing a direct role in rising inequality. On the positive side, we need to remember that global markets are succeeding in advancing new products and technologies at falling prices. Computers, mobile phones, tablets, digital cameras, televisions, and other consumer goods of the digital age are now within the reach of billions of people, poor as well as rich. Vast numbers of people are being pulled out of poverty by global economic growth, especially in former low-income countries such as China and India—today's middle-income emerging markets, or EMs. (For further discussion of EMs, see Nouriel Roubini's "Economic Insecurity and Inequality Breed Political Instability," pp. 150–63.) China is certainly the world leader in transformation and the country with the largest effects in reshaping the world economy, but Brazil, India, Indonesia, and dozens of other countries are also experiencing market-led dynamism and reshaping the global economy and balance of power.

Yet the distribution of economic gains has been startlingly uneven. Workers with low skills and low levels of educational attainment typically see little advancement, and those stuck in rural villages of poor countries and inner cities of rich ones are falling behind. The income "prize" is being won by those with the education and training to take up information and communication technologies (ICTs): notably those with high school degrees or higher in the emerging economies and college graduates and specialized technicians in the rich countries. In the past, a young American man could enter the middle class with a high school diploma and a job at the local factory. No more. Those factory jobs are gone, lost either to robotics and other automation or to outsourcing to lower-cost emerging economies. As a result, a generation of young people without a college degree is trapped, and the gap between the education haves and have-nots has soared. College-educated parents in the United States raise college-educated kids, while poor families without an education raise kids who are also most likely destined for economic hardship. Americans like to see their country as the land of social mobility and opportunity for all, but studies show that the United States now has perhaps the least social mobility within the entire Organisation for Economic

Co-operation and Development, as indicated by the highest correlation of educational attainment between parents and children.

Here, then, is the picture of today's global capitalism: a ferociously productive juggernaut that brings new high-tech products to the marketplace but ruthlessly divides societies according to power, education level, and income. The rich are getting richer and more politically powerful; the poor are being left behind, without decent jobs, income security, an income safety net, or a political voice. This scenario, with suitable amendments for national conditions, is being replicated across the world as global capitalism brings one country after another into its production systems and web of political influence.

And what has become of the supposed ability of representative democracies to tame and regulate the excesses of the capitalist system? The basic premise of the "mixed economy" is that market dynamism can be combined with democratic equality. Capitalism can promote innovation and growth, while government ensures that all citizens can secure their basic need for health care, education, suitable shelter, and household income sufficient to preserve dignity and raise healthy and educated children.

In Scandinavia, the mixed economy is known as social democracy; in Germany, as the social market; in the United Kingdom, as the third way; and in the United States, as the social-welfare state. Yet the premise of the mixed economy — that a strong state should tame the marketplace while leaving it dynamic — is under extreme duress except in northern Europe (Scandinavia, Germany, Finland, and Netherlands), where the model remains intact. In the United States, the United Kingdom, southern Europe, Israel, and almost all of the world's middle-income countries, the overriding political and financial power of corporate capitalism has nearly obliterated the functioning of the mixed economy, with the state in retreat or mainly serving corporate interests.

The poor, unskilled, and unemployed are increasingly left to fend for themselves. Corporate-backed politicians lack the will, and the governments lack the tax revenues, to fund the social safety nets and regulations needed to keep corporate greed in check. The social welfare state is dying—being replaced, in essence, by a corporatocracy: government organized by and for the interests of powerful multinational corporations. In these circumstances, it's understandable that nearly one in two Americans lives in a low-income household.

In most of the world, young people have grown up in an age of political cynicism and corruption, if not brutal repression. America's "millennials," typically defined as the generation born during 1980–95, so roughly seventeen to thirty-two years old in 2012, grew up witnessing an era of unprecedented inequality of income, a catastrophic financial bubble, and a contagion of corporate fraud led by Wall Street. They have reached the age of majority and have tried to find jobs in the worst financial crisis since the Great Depression. They have never experienced firsthand a government that champions the principles of a mixed economy, regulation of corporate abuse, and fair redistribution of income.

The economic circumstances of Tunisia and Egypt, while seemingly very different from those of the United States and Europe, are decidedly part of the same global market economy. Both the Tunisian and Egyptian economies are sites of major foreign investments by European and American companies. Both have been pulled by the same forces of global trade, production, and investment. Both countries experienced major increases in inequality in recent decades, resulting from a combination of market dynamics and corruption. Both the Zine al-Abidine Ben Ali and the Hosni Mubarak regimes were long backed by Europe and the United States, and in return the regimes offered ample opportunities for European and U.S. investors. When the Arab Spring began, the first impulse of the major Western powers was to back the existing decrepit regimes rather than to support the protesters. Only when the tide turned in favor of the street protesters did the Western powers come around to declare support for the Arab Spring.

Across high-income and middle-income countries, today's youth are confronting the realities of global capitalism. Good middle-class jobs are scarce, squeezed out by technological change and low-wage competition from Asia. Tuition for higher education, the ticket out of poverty and economic insecurity, is soaring and already out of reach of most of this generation. More than 70 percent of American young people ages twenty-five to twenty-nine do not have a bachelor's degree. Many more than one third enroll in higher education, but large numbers are forced to drop out because they simply cannot afford to stay in school. Other young people drop out much earlier because they attend woefully underprovisioned public schools in low-income neighborhoods. For Hispanic men aged twenty-five to twenty-nine, the proportion enrolled in higher education is a dismal 11 percent, and for African American young men, the proportion is 16 percent. Far more African American young males have spent time in prison than have completed a college degree.

As factory jobs have disappeared, the ranks of unemployed youth have soared in the United States, Europe, and the Middle East. Up to 2007, before the financial bubble imploded, the construction sector was providing at least some employment alternative for many high school graduates. During the period from 2001 to 2007, the U.S. Federal Reserve Board and the European Central Bank kept interest rates very low and credit easily available in order to stoke a construction boom that soaked up millions of workers. Yet the bursting of the bubble during 2007–8 ended this source of jobs. Since the construction bubble will not soon reappear, neither will its millions of jobs. Youth unemployment rates are generally between 20 and 40 percent across North Africa and southern Europe, and a lower but still crushing rate of around 15 percent in the United States.

Another recent global factor adds to the explosive brew. Since 2005, the world-market prices of primary commodities—including staple grains (wheat, maize, rice), minerals such as copper, and fossil fuels (oil, gas, and coal)—have soared. China's rapid economic expansion has created a surging demand for primary commodities, causing food and energy prices to soar and real incomes of urban households (especially poor households) to fall. Falling incomes have fueled the global unrest.

It is notable where the protest movements have erupted and where they have not. Northern Europe, with its social democracy, has largely been bypassed. In the social democracies, unemployment rates (including among youth) are generally moderate, and unemployed workers are helped with active labor market policies, including job matching and job training. Young families receive transfer payments and guarantees of maternal and paternal leave time and child care. Public revenues largely or fully cover the tuition costs at universities and technical schools. The entire support effort is made possible by high levels of taxation (typically between 40 and 50 percent of gross domestic product) to fund these publicly provided investments. However, even in these countries we should be careful not to idealize the situation. Right-wing nationalist parties have arisen to stoke public discontent with immigrant populations at a time of economic hardship.

Most of the protests have taken place in countries characterized by high levels of economic inequality, widespread discontent with political corruption, and frayed or nonexistent social-support programs. These conditions obviously characterized the regimes of Ben Ali and Mubarak, but they also apply in the surprising cases of Chile and Israel. By macroeconomic standards, both Chile and Israel are unquestioned success stories. Economic growth is high, corruption is lower than in surrounding countries, and unemployment, too, is fairly low. Yet both Chile and Israel have extremely high levels of income inequality, with among the highest Gini coefficients—used to measure inequality—of the members of the Organisation for Economic Co-operation and Development. (See, in part 2, Ariel Dorfman's "In the Footsteps of Salvador Allende"; Nora Lustig, Alejandra Mizala, and G. Eduardo Silva's "¡BastaYA! Chilean Students Say 'Enough'"; and Neri Zilber's "Occupying the Israeli Street.") The rich are very rich and very powerful. Quality education is out of reach of many poorer families. The social safety net is tattered. And financial scandals have brought down a shocking number of Israel's top politicians.

The Occupy movement and related protests worldwide have erupted, then, against a backdrop of four grim economic realities of global capitalism: (1) chronically high unemployment rates for young people; (2) high tuition costs that put the quality education and training needed for today's labor market out of reach for most young people; (3) corrupt governments uninterested in addressing the needs of the losers and laggards of globalization; and (4) the abrupt collapse of a decadelong financial bubble that was fed by a mix of lax monetary policies, financial deregulation, and flagrant corruption within leading financial companies, and that temporarily boosted employment in the construction industry.

The Occupy movement is therefore a protest against both the prevailing politics and prevailing economics. The Arab Spring was often described as only a political upheaval, but the economic causes of the upheaval are just as real and urgent (see Chris Stanton's "From Tahrir to Zuccotti: Justice but No Peace in Egypt," pp. 239–44). The new governments across North Africa will have to address the needs of their dispossessed populations, including the mass of unemployed youth, or these governments will find themselves the targets of continuing protests and unrest, as we see in Egypt.

In the United States and Europe, the situation is comparable if less extreme. In 2012, the Occupy protests may be temporarily eclipsed by the U.S. elections, or perhaps by a modest drop in the unemployment rate, but the underlying crisis of income inequality, high joblessness, and lack of access to quality education and skills is chronic and not cyclical. America's Occupy movement, or a successor, will be long-lived, even as specific protests and tactics wax and wane.

The core issue for the future, in my view, is whether the Occupy movement marks a true turning point—the start of a new era of progressive governance—or whether corporate power will maintain its chokehold on national politics. Those of us in the progressive movement should have few illusions of any kind of quick win against decades of increasing corporate power. Deeply entrenched corporate interests are certainly not willing to cede the field without a struggle. Wall Street has shown its political staying power even after infuriating the public by requiring trillions of dollars of bailout funds. The 2012 political campaigns will be the ideal opportunity for large corporate donors to reassert their political primacy through an ample flow of campaign financing.

Yet despite the long odds against political change, and despite the ability of big corporate money to buy access to power and policy, a new progressive era is possible. We had a swing from corporate power to progressive politics twice before in American history: at the end of the Gilded Age of the late nineteenth century and during the Great Depression of the 1930s. In both of those historic circumstances, U.S. income inequality and corporate corruption had soared, leading to a catastrophic financial crisis. In both cases, widespread public protests and dramatic electoral change ushered in an era of progressivism in which the federal government reasserted its political authority over big business and mobilized the instruments of federal power to regulate large private firms and redistribute income to ensure a social safety net. These were the services of the unparalleled Roosevelt family: Republican Theodore Roosevelt of the Progressive Era and nephew-by-marriage and distant cousin Franklin Roosevelt of the New Deal. The first Progressive Era lasted a quarter century (from around 1896 to 1917), and the New Deal era lasted for a bit over thirty years (from around 1933 to 1968).

The progressive challenge today may be tougher, however. It is by no means sure that our national governments are really up to the challenge, even if public pressures finally force politicians to reassert authority over corporate capital. In the earlier progressive eras, economies were national rather than globalized. The United States' giant corporations were truly "American" and could be forced to play by national rules. With globalization, the national governments still have some sway, but far less than before. Companies can and already do take advantage of dozens of international tax havens or low-tax production sites. Corporate regulation and taxation—such as a financial transactions tax—will only function and will best function with ample international cooperation and coordination of such policies. Creating a single national policy is hard enough; coordinating such a policy throughout the G20, for example, is an extremely heavy lift. But it must be done.

For these reasons, the next progressive era will need to be a global one, with a global awakening to the necessity of regaining regulatory control over corporate power, to tax high incomes, to close down tax havens, and to coordinate the development of new industries (such as renewable energy and improved education and health systems) that will gainfully employ millions of properly trained young people. The agenda is large. The Occupy Global Capitalism movement, if it comes to see itself as such, is the starting point of a generation of change.

What is to be done? The Occupy movement has been repeatedly accused of being a protest without a cause. This is flagrantly false. Its cause is the reform of the political economy of global capitalism. It looks equally to progressive political change and progressive economic change. While there is no single platform to arise from the global movement, the main demands are clear enough:

> Politics in the hands of the 99 percent, not of the 1 percent that control the large corporations
>
> Rebuilding a mixed economy with a proper balance of markets and government
>
> Ending reckless wars and downsizing the military
>
> Shifting public funds into training and education so that young people can develop the skills needed for gainful employment
>
> Taxing the rich and the financial sector, including with a financial transactions tax
>
> Building or rebuilding a social safety net and active labor-market policies more along the lines of northern Europe
>
> Reinventing key services, such as health and education, to bring them within reach of everybody, rich and poor
>
> Global cooperation to put this agenda into effect

One intriguing detail can be a touchstone for the way forward. Today's youth already changed politics in 2011, even though the new progressive era is yet to truly arrive. Authoritarian rulers were toppled, and long-standing social crises were brought dramatically and vividly to the public's view. Part of this success can be attributed to the participants' mastery of ICTs and to the power of social networking. Today's millennials are the networked generation, and those networks have gone global just as multinational capital went global thirty years ago. Civil society is gaining strength by inventing new methods of social cooperation. Global civil society will increasingly be positioned to challenge, and to help reform, the global economy. We are entering an era of networked politics, education, health care, energy systems, and other key parts of our global economy. An era of transformation and reform is at hand.

Debt Jubilee

Michael Hudson

Michael Hudson is research professor of economics at University of Missouri-Kansas City, and a research associate at the Levy Economics Institute of Bard College. He is a former Wall Street analyst and consultant, president of the Institute for the Study of Long-Term Economic Trends, and a founding member of the International Scholars Conference on Ancient Near Eastern Economies.

On November 3, 2011, Alan Minsky, programming director of Southern California's KPFK-FM, interviewed economist Michael Hudson. The policy recommendations below consolidate the ideas Hudson expressed on the show.

Setting up a more fair banking and financial system requires changing tax favoritism as well. There are a number of good proposals for reform. One of the easiest and least radical is to set up a public option for banking. Instead of relying on Bank of America or Citibank for credit cards, the government would set up a bank and offer credit cards, check clearing, and bank transfers at cost. The idea throughout the nineteenth century was to create this kind of public option. There was a post office bank, and that could still be created to provide banking services at cost or at a subsidized price. In Russia and Japan the post office banks are the largest of all.

Providing a public option would limit the ability of banks to charge monopoly prices for credit cards and loans. It also would eliminate the kind of gambling that has made today's financial system so unstable and put depositors' money at risk. Ideally, I would like to see banks act more like the old savings banks and savings and loan institutions. In fact, the most radical regulatory proposal I would like to see is the Chicago Plan, promoted in the 1930s by the free marketer Herbert Simon. You make banks do what textbooks say they are supposed to do: take deposits and lend them out in a productive way. If there are not enough deposits in the economy, the Treasury can create money and supply it to the banks to lend out. However, you would rewrite the banking laws so that normal banks are not able to gamble or play speculative games.

The obvious way to do this is to reinstate the Glass-Steagall Act (1933) so that banks can't gamble with insured deposits. This way, speculators would bear the burden if they lost, not be in a position to demand "taxpayer liability" by threatening to collapse the normal vanilla banking system. The idea is to shape markets so as to steer the banks to lend for actual capital formation and to finance homeownership without credit inflation that simply bids up prices for houses as well as for other real estate, stocks, and bonds.

Financial reform requires tax reform, because much of the financial problem stems from the tax shift off real estate and finance onto labor and industry. The most obvious fiscal task that most people understand—and support—is to restore the progressive tax system that existed before 1980, and especially before the Bill Clinton and George W. Bush tax cuts. However, the key isn't just income tax rates as such. It's the kind of taxes that should be levied—or how to shift them back off labor onto property, where they were before the 1980s. You need to restore the land taxes to collect the "free lunch" that is not really "free" if it is pledged to pay the banks in the form of mortgage interest.

Over the past few decades the tax system has been warped

more and more by bank lobbyists to promote debt financing. Debt is their "product," after all. As matters stand, much higher taxes must be paid on earnings and dividends on equity financing than on cash flow financed with debt. This distortion needs to be reversed. In a nutshell, the tax shifts since World War II have left more and more of the land's site value to be capitalized into interest payments on bank loans. The banks have ended up with what used to be taken by landowners. There is no inherent need for this. It doesn't help the economy; it merely inflates a real estate bubble. Economic growth and employment would be much stronger if income tax rates were lowered for most people. Property owners and speculators would pay. There would be fewer free lunches and more "earned" income.

Speculators have borrowed largely to make capital gains. In 1913, capital gains originally were taxed as normal income. The logic was that capital gains build up a person's savings, just as earning an income does. The financial and real estate interests fought back, and today there is only a tiny tax on capital gains—a tax that sellers don't have to pay if they plow their money into another property or investment to make yet more gains. When Wall Street firms, hedge funds, and other speculators avoid paying normal taxes by saying that they don't "earn" money but simply make capital gains, this is where a large part of today's economic inequality lies. I would tax these asset-price gains (mainly land prices) either at the full income tax rate or even higher.

I would close down tax avoidance in offshore banking centers by treating offshore deposits by Americans as "earned but hoarded" income and tax it at 90 percent. You restore the rates of the Eisenhower administration. You reinstate criminal penalties for financial fraud and tax evasion by misrepresentation.

To restore the kind of normalcy that made America rich, debts need to be written down—and the politically easiest way to cut through the tangle is to write them off altogether. A debt write-down sounds radical and unworkable, but it's been done since World War II with great success. It is the program the Allies carried out within the German economy during that country's 1947 currency reform. This was the policy that created Germany's economic miracle. America could experience a similar miracle.

Keeping bad debts on the books will handcuff the economy and cause debt deflation by diverting income to pay debt service rather than to spending on goods and services. We are going into a new economic depression — not just a Great Recession — because most spending is on finance, insurance, and real estate, not on goods and basic services. Markets are shrinking, and unemployment is rising.

Debt cancelation can be done across the board or more selectively, by applying what's been New York State law since

The Athenian statesman, lawmaker, and poet Solon (638–558 BC) instituted a set of laws called *seisachtheia*, which not only canceled all current debt but wiped old slates clean, ending debt peonage. *(Sarnese Collection, Museo Archeologico Nazionale, Naples)*

before the Revolution, going back to when New York was still a colony. I'm referring to the law of fraudulent conveyance. This law says that if a creditor lends to a borrower without having any idea how the debtor can pay in the normal course of business, without losing property, the loan is deemed to be fraudulent and declared null and void. Applying this law to defaulting homeowners would free the homes that are in negative equity throughout the country. It would undo the fraudulent loans that banks have made, the trick loans with exploding interest rates, balloon mortgages, and so forth. As part of the rules to define what constitutes "fraudulent" or irresponsible lending, mortgage debt service should be reduced to the rate that former Federal Deposit Insurance Corporation chair Sheila Bair recommended: 32 percent.

I would support government employment projects to guarantee full employment. My first caveat is to warn against these projects turning into a military giveaway. My second caveat is to prevent this full-employment program from creating a later privatization giveaway to Wall Street—that is, infrastructure that the government will sell off to the ruling party's major campaign contributors for pennies on the dollar. Privatizers add on interest and financial fees and high executive salaries and bonuses, and they charge monopolistic access fees. The financial sector first creates a problem by loading the economy down with debt, and then "solves" it by demanding privatization sell-offs under distress conditions. To promote full employment, the aim should be to invest public money such that the Republicans and Democrats cannot later turn around and privatize the capital investment at a giveaway price. The privatizers and their banks would like to install tollbooths on new bridges and get a free ride to turn America into a tollbooth economy—but that's really another story.

Another Way to Resist Wall Street: Copies, Smuggling, and "Globalization from Below"

Gordon Mathews

Gordon Mathews is professor of anthropology at the Chinese University of Hong Kong. The narrative below is adapted from *Ghetto at the Center of the World: Chungking Mansions, Hong Kong* (Chicago: University of Chicago Press, 2011).

Mathews, an American, embedded himself for four years in the Hong Kong shopping mall that director Kar Wai Wong immortalized as a den of iniquity in *Chungking Express* (1994). There, far from the spoils of the 1 percent but not as far as one might think, another, grittier side of globalization may be found.

I wait in the decrepit customs area of Kolkata airport with my friend, a man I'll call Saabir. A handsome Muslim in his twenties, from the Kolkata neighborhood of Kidderpore, Saabir is an illegal temporary worker in Chungking Mansions, a ramshackle seventeen-story building in the heart of Hong Kong's tourist district. He moonlights as a merchant, taking China-made clothing back to India to pay for his flights. Saabir is mercilessly abused by customs officials in Kolkata, something he dreads and fears as he gets off the plane and collects his luggage. He knows he has no choice but to endure it; he supports his parents and his pregnant wife in Kidderpore with his earnings. Although he pays off customs officials when that's possible, more often he simply puts up with their abuse, doing all he can to avoid paying extra duties or losing extra days as his merchandise waits for customs' arbitrary processing. I ask one customs official, a portly middle-aged man in street clothes—most officials don't bother wearing uniforms—why there is so much trouble with these goods, and he screams at me, "Why should we let this man in? He is bringing in Chinese clothing, but we can make these clothes in India!" Saabir doesn't have the nerve or the power to reply, "But my goods are what Indian people want to buy."

Clothing and other goods that Saabir and his fellow traders bring back from Hong Kong fill markets in India and Africa. This is globalization as experienced by most of the world: the 80 percent of people across the globe who have never seen a real iPhone and certainly don't own a credit card but who buy smuggled or copy merchandise from distant countries offered in their local street markets.

The Occupy Wall Street protesters directly confronted the financiers of Wall Street, as did protesters in cities throughout the developed world. At Chungking Mansions, a 1961 former luxury high-rise–turned–bazaar, there's another kind of activity challenging Wall Streets the world over—not protesters but informal traders, merchants who deal in cheap copy goods, and street peddlers. When we think of globalization, we usually think of multinational corporations with their multibillion-dollar budgets and batteries of lawyers. Challenging this "globalization from above" is "globalization from below": traders buying merchandise under the radar of the law and transporting these goods by container or in their luggage across continents and past borders, to be sold by street vendors at minimal prices with no questions asked. This is business without lawyers and copyrights, run through skeins of personal connections and wads of cash.

Located in a largely upscale neighborhood called Tsim Sha Tsui, Chungking Mansions is home not just to traders, merchants, and temporary workers but also to asylum seekers from

Africa and South Asia who are in flight from the political tyranny and economic deprivation of their home countries, and to low-budget travelers and tourists from around the world. With its frenetic comings and goings and its warren of insider shops, the complex has been viewed variously as a developing-world heart of darkness in Hong Kong's epicenter and as (according to *Time* magazine) Asia's "best example of globalization in action." Those who brave the throngs are surprised to find themselves in something that looks rather more like the markets of Kolkata, Kathmandu, or Kampala. Africans in bright robes or hip-hop gear sell clothing, Pakistani men in skullcaps entice passersby into restaurants, Nepalese whisper "hashish?" to the white people who are their typical customers, and slinky Indonesian women mingle with European hippies and Indian touts who direct tourists to overnight quarters on the building's upper stories. Such accommodations range in price and accoutrement from cell-like windowless single rooms to flatscreen-TV-equipped suites. Chungking Mansions is the only building in Hong Kong with free South Asian TV—Indian, Pakistani, and Nepali channels are broadcast.

Chungking Mansions is little more than a hundred yards from the Peninsula, one of Hong Kong's fanciest hotels, and K11 and iSQUARE, two of its newest shopping malls. Sex workers engage in business in the building, although generally not the Chinese, Thai, and Eastern Europeans found in some of Hong Kong's more upscale hotels, but Indians and Africans. One Kenyan sex worker I met calculated carefully how many customers she needed to service and how much money she needed to make each week to be able to eventually start a store in Nairobi and support her young daughter. A cautionary and perhaps apocryphal tale makes the rounds concerning an African trader who was relieved of fifty thousand dollars by a Chinese sex worker while he took a shower.

Redefining globalization: Entrance to Chungking Mansions, the seventeen-story Hong Kong shopping mall, and a Pakistani restaurant within. *(Both photographs courtesy Gordon Mathews)*

In the 1990s, when the building was still undergoing its transition from high-end tenancy to eyesore to international bazaar, Pakistani gangs were said to roam the corridors, intimidating the then largely South Asian merchants. In 2011, with its tidy signs and watchful CCTV cameras, Chungking Mansions has a more peaceable, even bourgeois, aura. The building no longer has any problem with criminal gangs, except for the drug dealers who sometimes lurk around the building's corners. As one Pakistani phone stall proprietor told me, "Why should anyone extort money? We can make money much more easily by selling mobile phones!"

Pakistani and Indian merchants are in Chungking Mansions because they were able to obtain the right to live in Hong Kong at some point in the decades before its return to China in 1997. They may feel a degree of alienation from Chinese Hong Kong, choosing to settle in the one place within the region that doesn't seem Chinese. As the proprietor of a jewelry stall told me, "Hong Kong is Chinese; I feel like an outsider in Hong Kong. But when I enter this building, I don't feel like an outsider. I feel like I'm home." Indeed, Chungking Mansions' corridors echo with the music and videos and news reports of South Asia; Hong Kong Chinese stand out whenever they enter the building, as they do in the evenings when they frequent the half-dozen fashionable curry restaurants on the upper floors of the complex.

Many of the South Asian managers of phone stalls and other businesses in Chungking Mansions rely on temporary workers such as Saabir for their labor. The majority of the Indian workers come from Kidderpore. Connections with family and friends have enabled them to work in Hong Kong. Upon arrival they are given fourteen-day tourist entry permits, twice renewable. They can stay 180 days a year in all. They work twelve-hour days for four hundred dollars a month, far higher than most wages in Kolkata.

South Asians run restaurants, guesthouses, and money-exchange offices, but the most typical businesses are the mobile phone stalls, of which there are over a hundred; my best estimate, judging from conversations with clerks about sales totals and my own statistical calculations, is that 20 percent of phones now used in sub-Saharan Africa have passed through Chungking Mansions. The phone business is both potentially very lucrative and also very risky.

One key to the trade is to find cheap China-made phones that consistently work well (no easy task). Another is to find sources for so-called fourteen-day phones—Nokia and other top brands returned by their original European owners within two weeks after purchase, then warehoused and sent to Hong Kong for sale at half or less of their original price—or for good-quality copy phones made in factories in south China and smuggled across the China–Hong Kong border. As a Pakistani smuggler told me, "I just look confident, and Hong Kong customs never bothers me." He is lucky never to have had his goods confiscated, but the odds are on his side: the Lo Wu and Lok Ma Chau border crossings between Hong Kong and China are among the busiest in the world, and most goods make it past the border checkpoints without being noticed.

A second key to these merchants' trade is to find regular customers. A steady supply of ten customers a week, most typically African but also South and Southeast Asian, buying eight hundred phones each, is more than enough for a stall to make a tidy profit, especially since this trade is off the books. Merchants could sell via the Internet, but since most traders don't have credit cards or other reliable currency instruments, this would be quite dangerous: the word from merchants and traders alike is that only face-to-face trade can be trusted. Some merchants crow over the traders they can fool, and vice versa. A trader from Mali told me he would never cheat his customers, though he himself has often been cheated. "I'm a Muslim," he says, "and Allah is watching me." A Pakistani merchant exulted, "I sold that African guy two hundred fourteen-day phones as if they were new, and he believed me! How stupid he was! I made eight thousand dollars just like that!" Another Pakistani merchant ruefully related, "I gave a customer credit for forty thousand dollars because I'd known him for five years, and he seemed trustworthy. But then he never came back. I called him over and over back in Tanzania, but first they said that he's gone, and next they said that they'd never heard of him." It's a common story, but most merchants talk neither of cheating nor of being cheated, but only of their ongoing efforts to make a living in a business whose parameters, due to ever-changing exchange rates, an ever-changing flow of customers, and an ever-changing array of phones for sale, are always difficult.

Mahmood, a Pakistani friend, sells phones primarily to African traders. None of his phones on offer has a price sticker. Instead, traders approach and ask the wholesale price of a particular model. Mahmood asks the trader about a comparable model. If the trader knows nothing about it, Mahmood raises his initial price 10 percent, based on the customer's ignorance of the game. If the customer recognizes the model Mahmood has mentioned, Mahmood knows to keep his price low: he has a worthy adversary. From there, the haggling takes days, with offers and counteroffers made until the last possible moment, while the trader's van waits outside.

Such a deal might be for a thousand or more phones, typically weighed to the final ounce of the thirty-two-kilogram baggage limit imposed by airlines such as Ethiopian or Emirates. Within two days, the phones will be sold in the street markets of Nairobi, Dar es Salaam, or Lagos. Mahmood sells an array of phones: branded Chinese models, unbranded knockoffs, used phones, copies of well-known brands (intellectual property rights, it probably goes without saying, are mostly honored in the breach in Chungking Mansions), and of course fourteen-day phones. He never bothers with new Nokias, Samsungs, Sony Ericssons, or iPhones—who in the developing world could afford such extravagant products?

The African traders in Chungking Mansions—overwhelmingly male, as is the largely Muslim Chungking Mansions as a whole—come from virtually every sub-Saharan country. Most deals are carried out in U.S. dollars (African banks' letters of credit may not go far)—I've seen a single trader pull as much as thirty thousand dollars out of his pocket. It's a highly competitive system, with nothing less than the pooled fortune of one's family at stake. Only half of first-time traders ever return, I'm told. Those who do, who avoid being cheated and learn to navigate customs, may come back to Chungking Mansions month after month, year after year, buying goods in Hong Kong or in south China at factories across the border and carrying them home.

Hong Kong is safer than mainland China to do business in, but with less potential for truly making a killing in the market. "The big fish go to China," a Tanzanian trader told me. "We little fish stay in Hong Kong." Guangzhou and other cities in mainland China are viewed by traders as places where, in the words of one, "You can get rich quickly, and lose everything quickly." In this man's view, fortunes can be made, but the chance of being cheated is also relatively higher than in Chungking Mansions. There are several reasons: English isn't spoken nearly as much as in Hong Kong, and the lack of a lingua franca is said to make it all the more likely that one will be cheated. In addition, it's said, laws aren't followed. As one Chungking Mansions merchant, a man who has lived for years in China, explained to me, "The problem with the mainland Chinese is that they will agree to anything until they get your deposit. But once they have your money, they will deliver whatever they want. You have a contract, but for them it has no meaning at all. It's like a piece of toilet tissue."

Another risk is borders: if the trader is carrying copy goods, as many are, theoretically these can always be confiscated, although they rarely are. The biggest danger for most African traders I've spoken with is the border of their own country. As a Ghanaian trader in electrical items told me, "Sometimes, I can make as much as fifty percent profit, other times no.... Sometimes you get bogged down in the airport or the harbor, waiting—your goods may lose value. Some people want to cheat the customs. If you want to cheat them and are caught, that's a problem. But if you go the legal way, the charges on the goods are higher. If I have my way, I would rather cheat them."

A Nigerian trader in computers told me, "Customs is the hardest part of my business. Some customs guys will take fifty dollars, others two hundred, others a thousand. Some need a suit, others shoes to get the job done.... Yes, it's corruption, but they don't call it corruption—it's like you're returning a favor." In Nigeria, importing many types of goods, such as clothing, is strictly illegal, despite the fact that Nigeria doesn't make these goods. Payment of bribes is inevitable. Despite their illegality, Chinese-made goods are ubiquitous in Nigeria; traders are fulfilling the needs of a market desperate for their wares.

The schemes are often ingenious. A Congolese trader explained to me how to send three used cars by container around the Cape of Good Hope to Matadi, where they would be driven overland to Kinshasa—then asked me to invest in the venture, saying, "I can guarantee you three hundred percent profit." The gas tanks of the cars could also be loaded with mobile phones, he added, which would never be seen by customs agents. A Kenyan trader buys an item of clothing she likes in Hong Kong and then orders ten thousand copies from a factory in China, which she ships back home under her own label. Another East African trader buys knock-off Jacuzzis, made by a south China company and sent back home to be sold to cabinet ministers and business magnates who want televisions, CD players, and computers in their baths.

For Saabir, despite the abuse he suffers at Kolkata airport, back in Kidderpore the rewards of his life become clear. His family's main breadwinner, he is accorded respect and has paid for his two sisters' weddings. On one trip, he proudly showed me videos of the many hundreds of wedding guests his Hong Kong salary had paid for, and when he wheeled his shiny new white motorcycle around the streets of Kidderpore, he was followed by an array of starry-eyed youth.

I've traveled repeatedly to India and Africa with temporary workers and traders, sometimes alone with goods, on runs for friends. In East Africa, I saw how a new trader can make a mistake, costing him his savings. The man had bought five thousand dollars' worth of Chinese-made copy phones and had asked me to deliver them to a friend of his to sell; having registered in Hong Kong as an asylum seeker, he could not leave. He hadn't realized that among his sophisticated friends, such phones would be viewed as garbage; he lost most of his money.

I spent several days with a West African trader in Dubai. His dream was to find the source of the copy goods he bought, thereby cutting out the middleman. He knew that the factory was in south China, but our Internet searches showed only the original European company, not the maker of the copies. I kept telling him that no maker of copies would advertise that fact on a website, but he didn't believe me. Our efforts, of course, were fruitless.

An African legislator I interviewed damned the traders who went back and forth between his country and China: "They are always trying to beat the system by avoiding customs.... When they reach the market, they play on the ignorance of clients by not telling them that these are counterfeit goods or used goods; they try to sell them for the price of the original." His view is contested by most traders. Some acknowledge cheating their customers — "I get good mobile phones for my family and friends in the city, but cheap copies for villagers. They don't know any better," a trader from Gabon told me. Yet most insist that competition with other traders keeps them honest: they cannot afford to cheat customers, or their business will be lost, they say. Beyond this, some traders tell me, is that with all the difficulties of manufacturing in Africa, from government corruption to high infrastructure costs, the only way that African consumers can get goods is through the work of traders like themselves. While the buyers back home sometimes pay high prices for shoddy goods, more important is the fact that they can get these goods at all. A Ghanaian trader, packing exactly eight hundred phones, which put him just at the thirty-two-kilogram limit, said to me as he was preparing to leave Chungking Mansions for his long return flight, "Of course we're helping our country in our trading. Before, only a very tiny number of Ghanaians had mobile phones, but now almost everyone does. That's because we bring them the phones." A Kenyan trader said to me, "Nobody in my country can buy an original brand of suit, or an original phone by a famous company. It's too expensive. But these copies can show them good things. Traders are bringing the world to Africa. They are bringing home goodness!"

It may not last: African traders are in increasing danger of being pushed aside by Chinese companies moving into Africa, looking to eliminate the African-trader middlemen. African traders and asylum seekers in Hong Kong wonder whether China is better or worse for Africa than the West was: the dominant view I hear is that China of course seeks to exploit Africa, but at least without the self-righteous rhetoric of Western powers, which is seen to cloak exploitation in hypocrisy.

The morality of the China-Africa trade is thus quite complicated. And what of the morality of Chungking Mansions itself? The building is remarkably peaceful: fights do occasionally break out between different ethnic groups, but not nearly as much as might be expected. In many businesses, Indians and Pakistanis work side by side. They say that they get along with each other in Chungking Mansions in a way that they sometimes don't back home because of their common desire to make money and their unwillingness to let national enmity get in the way of that desire. In its relative peacefulness, Chungking Mansions may be seen as a neoliberal success story; at the same time, as with neoliberalism everywhere, its trade is based on exploitation, not least of the people eventually buying its goods.

What's clear is that Chungking Mansions' denizens, from the richest property owner to the poorest temporary laborer or asylum seeker, are among the developing world's elite, by virtue of the fact that they were able to hop on a plane and fly thousands of miles to come to Hong Kong. This is an exclusive club that comprises third-world success stories. It's a place where people can potentially get rich.

The merchants and traders who do business in Chungking Mansions don't think much about Wall Street. They may frantically worry about currency fluctuations that may destroy their profits in a blink; the 2008 economic crisis has had a huge effect on many of the merchants and traders I know. As a Kenyan said to me, "Many people in my country depend on the remittances of their relatives working overseas. When those relatives lose their jobs, people in my country can't buy things, like the phones I bring back." These traders are dependent on the global economic order led by Wall Streets around the world, but they don't seek to destroy Wall Street and its ilk. They don't seek to confront the 1 percent of the truly wealthy but to become part of that 1 percent themselves. At this they will almost certainly fail: as compared with the financiers in their skyscrapers in the financial exchange across Hong Kong harbor, these traders are mice nibbling at the crumbs left beneath the tables of kings; but in their activities, evading copyrights and border controls, they are nonetheless gnawing at the foundations of those kings' tables.

Some in the Hong Kong government would prefer that this trade not exist, but the police can't easily stop it. As soon as even undercover police enter Chungking Mansions, lookouts alert their coworkers; an illegal worker need only step out from behind a counter to blend in with the crowd of customers, and nothing in his or her passport indicates anything less than full legality. Copy goods can be distinguished easily enough from originals by the trained eye, but undercover agents—typically white or Chinese—are largely blind to the subtleties of fakes, and get nowhere. "If a white or a Chinese guy in a suit and tie asks me for six hundred copy Nokia phones," a Pakistani merchant told me, "of course he's an undercover cop or a Nokia agent. Who else could he be?"

The police do act quickly when violence or overt robbery takes place, appearing within two to three minutes of such incidents. Trading is another matter. "As long as these cases don't affect Hong Kong people, then we don't care very much," one police officer told me. In following Hong Kong's neoliberal mantra of "let business proceed unimpeded," Chungking Mansions hums right along.

Multinational corporations, as well as global institutions such as the World Bank, despise this form of globalization and seek to make it legal, taxable, and subject to regulatory over-sight; but this is impossible. The anthropologist Carolyn Nord-strom estimates that less than 5 percent of goods passing through the world's ports are ever inspected. If strict enforce-ment of customs and border controls were ever to take place, globalization would vanish in much of the developing world. It won't happen: these players are far more nimble than the agents from above who seek to police them. Controlling the flow of copy, smuggled, or otherwise illicit goods across the globe is a chimera—an outcome that might be likened, perhaps, to nar-cotics agents stanching the flow of drugs worldwide. How on earth would they ever be able to? They cannot—they will always be outwitted.

The merchants and traders in Chungking Mansions are no saints of anticapitalism, and globalization from below is in its way almost as exploitative as globalization from above. If the traders and merchants of Chungking Mansions ever Occupy Wall Street, it will be to grab a share of its wealth rather than to protest its inequities. Nonetheless, they have an essential role to play in combating Wall Street, a role that may ultimately be more important than that of the Occupy Wall Street protest-ers. As Wall Street and the Euro-American capitalist order slowly crumble, globalization from below may outlast global-ization from above as the primary engine of the world's econ-omy. Chungking Mansions is an old building, and it will eventually be torn down. But the trade that goes on in Chung-king Mansions may be not the world's past but its future.

Coda: "The Last Capitalist on Wall Street"
Brandon Adams

Apart from editing the finance journal *Grant's Interest Rate Observer*, which he founded, James Grant, the subject of the profile below, is the author of, among other books, *Mr. Speaker: The Life and Times of Thomas B. Reed, the Man Who Broke the Filibuster* (2011), *Mr. Market Miscalculates* (2008), and *Money of the Mind* (1992).

Brandon Adams taught undergraduate economics courses at Harvard University for eight years. He interviewed Grant during the third month of the 2011 Occupy protests.

James Grant's most striking quality is his intellectual confidence. He does not hedge his answers; he does not cater to the persuasion of the interviewer; he does not strive to be popular or politically correct; he's not afraid to offend even his customers: he notes that hedge funds are for "friends, fools, and family." His office is at 2 Wall Street, just across from the New York Stock Exchange, and it houses Grant and four studious, highly intelligent-looking young men. Grant notes that he is "the last capitalist on Wall Street."

He presented me with a highly unusual view of the crisis, but one that I ultimately found fairly persuasive. He believes that "the root cause of so many of our problems is statism." Echoing Friedrich Hayek (1899–1992), he believes that the confrontation with "more and more legalisms and interventions" drains people and leads toward lethargy and withdrawal—as he puts it, "an endless low-level flu."

Grant has developed a reputation as something of a perma-bear ("I've made that bed myself," he says), but to me his pessimism comes across not as fear that the world will end but rather a realization that we will putter along in a listless state, unable to reach anything close to potential. He looks back fondly toward America's immediate postwar years, but he does not see any great moral separation between people of today and those of earlier generations. He suggests that Wall Street has never been a bastion of societal responsibility: "I'm not sure when the era of moral purity on Wall Street occurred."

He believes that in a previous generation, Wall Street greed largely translated into improved life on Main Street, through improved capital allocation and capital availability, but he suggests that that transmission mechanism has been largely broken. The primary causes were federal intervention in markets, a legalistic culture ("Dodd-Frank [the 2010 Wall Street Reform and Consumer Protection Act] is twenty-two hundred pages"), and the passing of the partnership form of organization on Wall Street.

The partnership form of organization was associated, in Grant's view, with measured risk taking and a much more long-term orientation. "Partners were forced to keep most of their money in the partnership, and, at retirement, they were taken out at book value," Grant says, referring to the accumulated equity of the partners. This system led to greater stewardship and to a more harmonious relationship with social worlds outside Wall Street; in the 1950s, 1960s, and 1970s, "there was nothing outsized about the wealth Wall Street partners accumulated or the way they lived."

Grant thinks that the "magic credit card" that the United States enjoys as a result of being the world's reserve currency is ultimately "a sweet poison" that has contributed to the United States' lack of global competitiveness. He refers to our ongoing trade relationship with the Chinese as a "symbiotic relationship of looming bankruptcy." Regarding Japan's long stagnation, Grant suggests that there's considerable danger that we've over-learned supposed economic lessons from Japan's management of the crisis and underlearned cultural ones; he senses in the United States, as in Japan, "a reluctance to confront failure." The United States has, like Japan, "prolonged the workout." He believes that the United States made a serious policy mistake in subsidizing housing and mortgages to a tremendous extent, and he suggests that much of our political activity since then has been focused on "postponing the repricing and recognition of this great mistake."

Whether or not one agrees with Grant's views, there should be a general concession that he is one of the best advocates of free market capitalism in the land. There were times when I found myself in fairly strong disagreement with him — for example, he favors a flat tax over a progressive tax system — but in no way did it seem that he had come upon any of his opinions easily. His view of human nature seems to be that it is subject to great vicissitudes; he believes that people are capable of extraordinary feats but also of remarkable laziness and greed if placed in the wrong institutional setting. He is a strong believer in personal charity, but he is against pretty much every form of government-mandated wealth redistribution, and he thinks that "everyone should have the experience of being taxed."

He holds no soft place in his heart for the Geithner-Bernanke-Paulson complex that managed economic life during the crisis. He believes that economic improvement requires "an election," and he notes that "in another life" Lawrence Summers wrote a paper, with Kim Clark, called "Unemployment Insurance and Labor Force Transitions," about, in Grant's words, "the effect of prolonged unemployment benefits on the propensity to look for work." Grant is of the view that when people are given the opportunity to take advantage of the government, they usually will. He's equally pessimistic about the laboring and capital classes; he cites a 2011 speech called "Control Rights (and Wrongs)," by Andrew Haldane of the Bank of England, which argues, essentially, that bankers are adept at estimating the extent of the freeroll that governments are offering them, and they make their bets accordingly.

I got the sense that Grant believes that any economic policy or product that is not readily comprehensible to him and his group of geniuses at 2 Wall Street must in fact be a sort of financial con game bound to have unfortunate consequences. In his book *Mr. Market Miscalculates: The Bubble Years and Beyond* (2008), he notes that he left the task of deciphering late-stage CDO offering memoranda to the brightest of his underlings, and when this young genius came back with no understanding whatsoever, he knew the world was in trouble. He jokingly suggests that "our monetary system seems to require a level of complexity for people too smart to work at NASA" and hands me a fully indecipherable Federal Reserve–sponsored research paper on the role of money in the macroeconomy.

We chatted a bit about David Einhorn's November 8, 2011, speech in Dallas on the deleterious effects of Bernanke's policy of committing to keep long-term interest rates near zero for the foreseeable future (those are my words, as Grant claims to have never uttered the phrase "foreseeable future"). Einhorn noted that once interest rates are low enough, substantive long-term investments in real projects become less sensitive to further reductions in interest rates—if projects make sense at 2 percent, they'll probably also make sense at 3 percent or 4 percent. He noted further that the real effects of very low long-term rates have been to: encourage speculation in commodities and real assets and thus exacerbate the gap between rich and poor; destroy incentives to save while also increasing the wealth one might need to reasonably retire—Einhorn believes the underlying motive to this policy is to force people into equities and other risk assets; and create an overall environment of extreme uncertainty that makes planning difficult for both households and firms. Though a seemingly strange pairing, Grant notes that "it is unlikely that David and I will disagree on any of these things."

Grant noted that artificially low interest rates "have always been good for the speculative classes." He and I briefly discussed the policy merits of a financial transactions tax; he said, predictably, that he was "against it"—"I'm against most intrusions into the free market." Grant suggested that our recent financial crisis was caused by the free market working around unnatural government interventions; the primary culprit, in his view, was the Chinese policy of recycling export earnings into U.S. dollar assets in an attempt to maintain the renminbi at an artificially low level. "This is not what is known as classical finance," he said. The policy proved to be world-destabilizing when coupled with the U.S. backing of Fannie Mae and Freddie Mac and other U.S. measures aimed at expanding the availability of mortgage loans.

Grant's views are not too difficult to summarize—he's a staunch believer in the resiliency of free markets, he's not a fan of progressive taxation or wealth redistribution, and he's against unwarranted complexity. He favors, in his words, a policy of "tough fairness." He believes that Obama, in creating an economic landscape that is governed by rules and regulations, is "creating a store that is too difficult to manage." Grant stated his views on Occupy Wall Street, as usual, without qualification: "I'm against it. They're for government-mandated wealth redistribution and I'm not." On November 17, 2011, the day that Occupy Wall Street literally occupied Wall Street, Grant, at six foot five, in a suit and bow tie, was given a hard time by some of the protesters near his building. He jokingly remarked to a nearby police officer, "It's not easy being in the one percent," to which the officer replied, "At the rate I'm racking up overtime, I'll be there soon."

Acknowledgments

I don't know that I have ever encountered a more unimpeachable group of writers than the contributors to this book. Their conviction trumped personal convenience and demands on their time.

Someone always has to say yes first. Michael Lewis signed on at the less-is-more stage of creation and made a virtue of my uncertainty. Jim Mairs and Starling Lawrence brought the idea into focus. Bob Buckley suggested the names of at least a quarter of the contributors and deconstructed economics for me. Albert Mobilio suggested the names of another quarter of the contributors and offered the shrewd and sympathetic advice of an editor who has done this kind of thing or something very much like it many times before. Brandon Adams contributed the book's first policy recommendation and conducted interviews. There was no question, conceptual or procedural, that I hesitated to ask him.

Jamie Pilkington urged me in the direction of accessibility and Deborah Karl in the direction of history and analysis; Deborah also served as de facto agent. Robin Wells, an economist and the book's guest editor, broke logjams so much more efficiently than I could have on my own that I wondered how the book could have proceeded without her. Andrew Wylie offered advice, and he and Jamie Pilkington are indirectly responsible for the book's having made its way first to Michael Pietsch and then to Geoff Shandler at Little, Brown. Geoff, my editor, did more to create the book's structure and orientation than anyone; his ideas are on every page. He and Liese Mayer applied the editorial equivalent of a combination of macro- and microeconomics, each paying attention to both big-picture and practical matters.

Mary Tondorf-Dick, Peggy Freudenthal, Karen Landry, Betsy Uhrig, Jayne Yaffe Kemp, Deborah Jacobs, Holly Hartman, and Ben Allen handled the work of sixty-seven contributors and interview subjects, working through their prose, equations, and charts and making improvements in presentation, content, and word choice. Others at Little, Brown who were welcoming, knowledgeable, and enthusiastic include Andrea Shallcross, Terry Adams, Nicole Dewey, Carolyn O'Keefe, Amanda Brown, and Theresa Giacopasi.

Jon Bakija, Adam Cole, and Bradley Heim's "Jobs and Income Growth of Top Earners and the Causes of Changing Income Inequality: Evidence from U.S. Tax Return Data" is cited in these pages fewer times only than Thomas Piketty and Emmanuel Saez's work. Jon answered a range of questions and allowed me to use one of the tables from the paper.

My siblings (a natural family communism prohibits me from singling out any one of them) and my mother, Celesta T. Byrne, encouraged me from the day the idea took hold; it happened to be my mother's eighty-ninth birthday. My husband, Ivan Solotaroff, delivered homemade Thai soup and bangers and mash to my desk. Through conversation and in other ways, Brian Stanton, Matt Wuerker, Jane Kornbluh, Alicia Whitaker, Linda Whitaker, Lisa Ross, Nancy K. Palmquist, Bob and Trish Linkenheimer, Candace Zee, Kristen Ward, Adrienne DiGiovine, MaryBeth Dillione, Diane LeBas, Mike Molloy, Rebecca Bancroft, Kati and Ray Sowiak, Laura and Brad

Zinker, Jim McIntyre, and Bill Thomas helped the project along. I am also grateful to Chris Buckley, Tom Buckley, Bobby Timmons, Resa Cornutt, and Steve Haeckel.

Occupy Wall Street provided the occasion for *The Occupy Handbook* and brought to the larger public the issues debated in its pages.

Notes

Janet Byrne / *Introduction: A Tale of Two Taxes*

xv Nobody lies groaning: Raoul Vaneigem, *The Revolution of Everyday Life*, tr. Donald Nicholson-Smith, 2nd ed. (London: Rebel Press and Left Bank Books, 1993), 124.

xvi According to the Spectrem Group: Robert Frank, "Millionaires Support Warren Buffett's Tax on the Rich," *Wall Street Journal*, October 27, 2011, http://blogs.wsj.com/wealth/2011/10/27/most-millionaires -support-warren-buffetts-tax-on-the-rich/; Alexander Abad-Santos, "The 68%: Polls Are Finding Support for a Millionaires Tax," *Atlantic Wire*, October 27, 2011, http://www.theatlanticwire.com/ business/2011/10/68-polls-are-finding-support-millionaires -tax/44212/; for the Spectrem Group, see http://www.spectrem.com/ about-spectrem-group.

xvi a Reuters headline: Reuters, "Paul Volcker Says Volcker Rule Too Complicated," November 9, 2011, http://www.reuters.com/article/ 2011/11/09/us-regulation-volcker-idUSTRE7A83KN20111109.

xvii median household income: All figures are from the U.S. Census Bureau, http://quickfacts.census.gov/qfd/index.html.

xvii A swing state, Pennsylvania is twenty-eighth: See http://www.tax foundation.org/research/show/22685.html; Binyamin Appelbaum and Robert Gebeloff, "Even Critics of Safety Net Increasingly Depend on It," February 11, 2012, http://www.nytimes.com/ 2012/02/12/us/even-critics-of-safety-net-increasingly-depend -on-it.html?_r=1&pagewanted=all; Jon Perr, "This Week in the War on the Safety Net," *Crooks and Liars*, February 14, 2012, http:// crooksandliars.com/jon-perr/this-week-in-the-war-on-the -safety-net.

xviii As the sociologists Kathryn Edin and Maria Kefalas: See Kathryn Edin and Maria Kefalas, *Promises I Can Keep: Why Poor Women Put Motherhood before Marriage* (Berkeley: University of California Press, 2005); Chris Hedges, "City of Ruins," *The Nation*, November 4, 2010, and see also Hedges's forthcoming *Days of Destruction, Days of Revolt,* with illustrations by Joe Sacco (New York: Nation Books, 2012).

xix As *Bloomberg Businessweek* pointed out: Drake Bennett, "David Graeber, the Anti-Leader of Occupy Wall Street," *Bloomberg Businessweek,* October 26, 2011, http://www.businessweek.com/magazine/david -graeber-the-antileader-of-occupy-wall-street-10262011.html.

xxi The *Washington Post's* Ezra Klein summarizes: Ezra Klein, "Wonkbook: Romney's Problem Isn't His Gaffes. It's His Policies," *Washington Post,* February 2, 2012, http://www.washingtonpost.com/ blogs/ezra-klein/post/wonkbook-romneys-problem-isnt-his-gaffes -its-his-policies/2012/02/02/gIQA0WeBkQ_blog.html.

xxi according to the *New York Times's* David Leonhardt, *reduce* taxes: David Leonhardt, "Generational Divide Colors Debate Over Medicare's Future," *New York Times,* April 5, 2011, http://www.nytimes .com/2011/04/06/business/06leonhardt.html.

xxii taxes for the poorest 90 percent: See http://ctj.org/pdf/ryan plan2010.pdf.

xxii For much of the 1970s, the highest marginal tax rate was 70 percent: For tax rates in relatively recent history, see Joel B. Slemrod, *Does Atlas Shrug? The Economic Consequences of Taxing the Rich* (Cambridge, MA: Harvard University Press, 2000).

Part I
HOW WE GOT HERE

Paul Krugman and Robin Wells / The Widening Gyre: Inequality, Polarization, and the Crisis

8 the "central problem of depression-prevention": Robert E. Lucas Jr., "Macroeconomic Priorities," *American Economic Review* 93, no. 1 (March 2003): 1–14.

9 Our understanding of American political economy has been strongly influenced: Nolan McCarty, Keith T. Poole, and Howard Rosenthal, *Polarized America: The Dance of Ideology and Unequal Riches* (Cambridge, MA: MIT Press, 2006).

13 an organized campaign that successfully induced many universities to drop it: David Colander and Harry Landreth, "Political Influence on the Textbook Keynesian Revolution: God, Man, and Laurie [*sic*] Tarshis at Yale," in *Keynesianism and the Keynesian Revolution in America: A Memorial Volume in Honour of Lorie Tarshis,* edited by Omar F. Hamouda and Betsey B. Price (Cheltenham, UK: Edward Elgar, 1998), 59–72.

14 There is also the motive suggested by Keynes's contemporary Michał Kalecki: Michał Kalecki, "Political Aspects of Full Employment," *Political Quarterly* 14 (October–December 1943): 322–31.

15 "The growing tension between the Obama administration and business": Mort Zuckerman, "Obama Needs to Stop Baiting Business," *Financial Times*, July 26, 2010.

Philip Dray / Take a Stand: Sit In

19 "We're with you. We're in the same boat": Robert V. Bruce, *1877: Year of Violence* (Indianapolis: Bobbs-Merrill Company, 1959), 125.

21 "The Republic had celebrated": David T. Burbank, *Reign of the Rabble: The St. Louis General Strike of 1877* (New York: Augustus M. Kelley, 1966), 12.

22 "The *laissez-faire* policy has been knocked out": Bruce, *1877*, 314–15.

24 "Why there? The food's supposed to be terrible": Seth Cagin and Philip Dray, *We Are Not Afraid: The Story of Goodman, Schwerner, and Chaney and the Civil Rights Campaign for Mississippi* (New York: Macmillan, 1988), 60.

25 "Ella, this is the thing!": Ibid., 66.

26 "If you went into Mississippi": Clayborne Carson, *In Struggle: SNCC and the Black Awakening of the 1960s* (Cambridge, MA: Harvard University Press, 1981), 50.

27 "I didn't recognize Bob at first": Jack Newfield, *A Prophetic Minority* (New York: New American Library, 1966), 76.

27 "The law down here": *McComb (MS) Enterprise-Journal*, August 30, 1961.

Michael Hiltzik / The 5 Percent

30 "It is no small": Richard L. Neuberger and Kelley Loe, *An Army of the Aged* (Caldwell, ID: Caxton Printers, 1936), 12.

30 As for public: Statistics are from the old-age security staff report to the Committee on Economic Security, January 1935.

31 "no place to go": See "letter to President Roosevelt Regarding Old-Age Pensions," at http://www.ssa.gov/history/lettertoFDR.html (accessed January 15, 2012).

31 As set forth: The letter is reprinted in Francis Everett Townsend, *New Horizons* (Chicago: J. L. Stewart Publishing, 1943), 138.

32 "The neighbors are going": Hearings, Economic Security Act, Senate Finance Committee (February 16, 1935), 1024.

32 "On Capitol Hill": Richard L. Neuberger and Kelley Loe, "The Old People's Crusade," *Harper's Monthly*, March 1936.

33 Anacostia Flats: For a definitive description of the Anacostia Flats assault, see Paul Dickson and Thomas B. Allen, *The Bonus Army: An American Epic* (New York: Walker & Company, 2004), 170ff.

33 "Well, Felix...this elects me": Richard Norton Smith, *An Uncommon Man: The Triumph of Herbert Hoover* (New York: Simon & Schuster, 1984), 140.

34 range of 43 to 46 percent: Thomas Piketty and Emmanuel Saez, "Income Inequality in the United States, 1913–1998," *Quarterly Journal of Economics* 118, no. 1 (2003): 1–39, updated to 2007 in August 2009.

35 "hillbilly paradise": Arthur M. Schlesinger Jr., *The Politics of Upheaval, 1935–1936* (Boston: Houghton Mifflin, 1960), 63.

36 He was not devoid: See Edwin Amenta, *When Movements Matter: The Townsend Plan and the Rise of Social Security* (Princeton, NJ: Princeton University Press, 2006), 223.

37 "everybody wastes": Hearings, Economic Security Act, House Committee on Ways and Means (January 29, 1935), 573.

37 "I knew the scheme": Walter Lippmann, "Dr. Townsend's Trillions," *Los Angeles Times*, January 10, 1935.

37 "Never explain": Benjamin Stolberg, "Dr. Huey and Mr. Long," *The Nation*, September 25, 1935.

37 "an economic impossibility": Neuberger and Loe, *An Army of the Aged*, 12.

38 "frankly for educational purposes": Frances Perkins, *The Roosevelt I Knew* (New York: Viking, 1946), 278.

39 "I do not know": Roosevelt, Address to the Advisory Council of the Committee on Economic Security, November 14, 1934.

39 "the kiss of death": Arthur Krock, "In Washington," *New York Times*, November 20, 1934.

40 total annual income: Hearings, Economic Security Act, House Committee on Ways and Means (January 21, 1935), 111.

40 "it is not within the picture": Ibid., 110.

41 "because it became a popular": Ibid., January 23, 1935, 200.

41 "Nobody has been fool enough": Ibid., February 4, 1935, 754.

43 "an astonishingly inept": William E. Leuchtenburg, *Franklin D. Roosevelt and the New Deal* (New York: Harper & Row, 1963), 132.

Raghuram Rajan / Inequality and Intemperate Policy

83 a Georgetown University report titled "Help Wanted": Anthony P. Carnevale, Nicole Smith, and Jeff Strohl, "Help Wanted: Projections of Jobs and Education Requirements Through 2018," Georgetown University Center on Education and the Workforce, June 2010, Washington, D.C., http://www9.georgetown.edu/grad/gppi/hpi/cew/pdfs/FullReport.pdf.

Daron Acemoglu and James A. Robinson / Against Political Capture: Occupiers, Muckrakers, Progressives

100 This piece draws heavily from many parts of our book, Daron Acemoglu and James A. Robinson, *Why Nations Fail: The Origins of Power, Prosperity, and Poverty* (New York: Crown, 2012), which introduces the concepts of inclusive and extractive institutions. See chapter 1 of *Why Nations Fail* and David W. Galenson, "The Settlement

and Growth of the Colonies: Population, Labor and Economic Development," in *The Cambridge Economic History of the United States,* Volume I: *The Colonial Era,* edited by Stanley L. Engerman and Robert E. Gallman (New York: Cambridge University Press, 1996), on the development of U.S. institutions. The Charter of Maryland, the Fundamental Constitutions of Carolina, and other colonial constitutions have been put on the Internet by Yale University's Avalon Project, at http://avalon.law.yale.edu/subject_menus/17th.asp. Alexander Keyssar, *The Right to Vote: The Contested History of Democracy in the United States,* rev. ed. (New York: Basic Books, 2009), is a seminal introduction to the evolution of political rights in the United States. Vanderbilt is quoted in Matthew Josephson, *The Robber Barons* (Orlando: Harcourt, 1934), 15. "The Great American Bubble Machine," Matt Taibbi's piece on Goldman Sachs, appeared in *Rolling Stone* magazine on July 9, 2009. Elizabeth Sanders, *Roots of Reform: Farmers, Workers, and the American State, 1877–1917* (Chicago: University of Chicago Press, 1999), stresses the agrarian roots of populism. The text of the Populists' Omaha Platform can be found at http://historymatters.gmu.edu/d/5361/. Roosevelt's quotes come from his speech, which is at http://www.theodore-roosevelt .com/sotu1.html. J. Bradford DeLong presents the historical data on the number of billionaires at http://www.j-bradford-delong.net/ econ_articles/carnegie/delong_moscow_paper2.html. Chapter 6 of *Why Nations Fail* discusses the case of Venice. Thomas Piketty and Emmanuel Saez, "Income Inequality in the "United States, 1913– 1998," *Quarterly Journal of Economics* 118 (2003): 1–39, with updates by the authors, is the basic source for the data on the increasing income share of the richest 1 percent of the population. Jacob S. Hacker and Paul Pierson, *Winner-Take-All Politics: How Washington Made the Rich Richer—and Turned Its Back on the Middle Class* (New York: Simon & Schuster, 2010), present conjectures as to why money has become more powerful in U.S. politics, and Larry M. Bartels, *Unequal Democracy: The Political Economy of the New Gilded Age* (Princeton, NJ: Princeton University Press, 2010), documents how the policy preferences of politicians match those of the rich. Quotes from the OWS webpage are from http://occupywallst.org/. Sidney Tarrow, "Social Protest and Policy Reform: May 1968 and the Loi d'Orientation in France," *Comparative Political Studies* 25 (1993): 579–607, discusses why French students in 1968 failed to achieve their goals.

Carmen M. Reinhart and Kenneth S. Rogoff / Causes of Financial Crises Past and Present: The Role of the This-Time-Is-Different Syndrome

118 Never mind the glaring imbalances: Maurice Obstfeld and Kenneth S. Rogoff, "Perspectives on OECD Capital Market Integration:

Implications for U.S. Current Account Adjustment," *Global Economic Integration: Opportunities and Challenges* (Kansas City, MO: Federal Reserve Bank of Kansas, 2001), for example, pointed out that massive sustained current account deficits (trade deficits) such as the United States was experiencing often end in collapses.

119 This is a "nutshell" version: Carmen M. Reinhart and Kenneth S. Rogoff, *This Time Is Different: Eight Centuries of Financial Folly* (Princeton, NJ: Princeton University Press, 2009).

120 On the left scale, we graph the index of capital mobility: Maurice Obstfeld and Alan M. Taylor, *Global Capital Markets: Integration, Crisis, and Growth* (Cambridge: Cambridge University Press, 2004).

122 For the post-1970 period, Graciela L. Kaminsky and Reinhart's: Graciela L. Kaminsky and Carmen M. Reinhart, "The Twin Crises: The Causes of Banking and Balance-of-Payments Problems," *American Economic Review* 89, no. 3 (1999): 473–500.

123 In table 1, we focus on a few quantitative parallels: Ibid.; these and other economic and financial indicators are analyzed in detail.

123 As Carmen M. Reinhart and Vincent R. Reinhart document: Carmen M. Reinhart and Vincent R. Reinhart, "Capital Flow Bonanzas: An Encompassing View of the Past and Present," *NBER International Seminar on Macroeconomics* 2008, edited by Jeffrey Frankel and Francesco Giavazzi (Chicago: Chicago University Press for the NBER, 2009), 1–54.

124 Capital inflows (see table 2) are, of course, the mirror image: Obstfeld and Rogoff, "Perspectives on OECD Capital Market Integration"; Obstfeld and Rogoff, "Global Current Account Imbalances and Exchange Rate Adjustment," *Brookings Papers on Economic Activity* 1 (2005): 67–146; and Nouriel Roubini and Brad Setser, "The United States as a Debtor Nation: The Sustainability of the U.S. External Imbalances," draft, New York University, New York, November 2004.

125 We have described the "inverted V" pattern: Reinhart and Rogoff, *This Time Is Different.*

127 Countless case studies of banking crises: Ibid.

127 Gerald Caprio Jr. and Daniela Klingebiel's evidence: Gerald Caprio Jr. and Daniela Klingebiel, "Bank Insolvency: Bad Luck, Bad Policy, or Bad Banking?," *Annual World Bank Conference on Development Economics*, edited by Boris Pleskovic and Joseph Stiglitz (Washington, D.C.: World Bank, 1996), 79–104.

128 The procyclicality of credit ratings: See Carmen M. Reinhart, "Default, Currency, Crises, and Sovereign Credit Ratings," *World Bank Economic Review* 16, no. 2 (2002): 151–70.

129 Investigating what came first, banking or currency crises: Kaminsky and Reinhart, "The Twin Crises."

129 Asli Demirgüç-Kunt and Enrica Detragiache, who employed a different approach: Asli Demirgüç-Kunt and Enrica Detragiache, "The Determinants of Banking Crises in Developing and Developed Countries," *IMF Staff Papers* 45 (1998): 81–109.

129 In 2002 Reinhart examined: Reinhart, "Default, Currency, Crises, and Sovereign Credit Ratings."

129 As Carlos Diaz-Alejandro recounts: Carlos Diaz-Alejandro, "Goodbye Financial Repression, Hello Financial Crash," *Journal of Development Economics* 19, nos. 1–2 (1985): 1–24.

131 This episode is not yet over: In Carmen M. Reinhart and Kenneth S. Rogoff, "From Financial Crash to Debt Crisis," *American Economic Review* 101, no. 5 (August 2011): 1676–1706, we show that, indeed, sovereign defaults often follow within a few years of a wave of banking crises.

Part II
WHERE WE ARE NOW

Nouriel Roubini / Economic Insecurity and Inequality Breed Political Instability

155 A study by Alan S. Blinder: Alan S. Blinder, "How Many U.S. Jobs Might Be Offshorable?," Princeton University Center for Economic Policy Studies Working Paper No. 142, March 2007.

156 a study by Nobel Prize winner Michael Spence: Michael Spence, "The Downside of Integrating Markets," *Foreign Affairs*, July/August 2011, https://www.foreignaffairs.com/articles/67874/michael-spence/globalization-and-unemployment.

163 a 2011 International Monetary Fund study: Andrew G. Berg and Jonathan D. Ostry, "Inequality and Unsustainable Growth: Two Sides of the Same Coin?," April 8, 2011, International Monetary Fund Research Department.

James Miller / Is Democracy Still in the Streets?

173 On the afternoon of August 2: A version of this work was delivered as part of a panel, The Fate of Participatory Democracy, at a conference on The Port Huron Statement at 50, University of California–Santa Barbara, February 2–3, 2012.

174 Graeber proposed implementing one of the most radical forms: For the instituting of participatory democracy within OWS, see David Graeber, "Enacting the Impossible: On Consensus Decision Making," *The Occupied Wall Street Journal*, October 23, 2011; Drake Bennett, "David Graeber, the Anti-Leader of Occupy Wall Street," *Bloomberg Businessweek*, October 26, 2011; and Jeff Sharlet, "Inside Occupy Wall Street," *Rolling Stone*, November 10, 2011.

174 "participatory and democratic to the core": Yotam Marom, "Occupy Wall Street Is Winning, So What's Next," *Metro Focus,* October 13, 2011, posted at http://www.thirteen.org/metrofocus/news/2011/10/were-winning---so-what-do-we-want/, accessed on January 4, 2012.

175 "the incompatibility of rule-by-consensus": James Miller, *"Democracy Is in the Streets": From Port Huron to the Siege of Chicago* (New York: Simon & Schuster, 1987), 326; reiterating an argument made by others, notably Jane J. Mansbridge in *Beyond Adversary Democracy* (New York: Basic Books, 1980).

175 "for anyone who joined in the search for a democracy of individual participation": Miller, *"Democracy Is in the Streets,"* 328.

175 An offshoot of a Quaker direct-action group: Andrew Cornell, "Anarchism and the Movement for a New Society: Direct Action and Prefigurative Community in the 1970s and 80s," *Perspectives,* 2009, posted at Institute for Anarchist Studies website http://anarchiststudies.org/node/292, accessed on December 28, 2011.

176 "While an organization is new and vital": George Lakey, from an interview in 2008, quoted in Cornell, "Anarchism and the Movement for a New Society."

176 the General Assemblies that have become a hallmark of the Occupy movement: See David Graeber, *Direct Action: An Ethnography* (Oakland, CA: AK Press, 2009), 234.

177 "Every person is free to do as they wish": "Quick guide on group dynamics in people's assemblies," recommended at http://www.nycga.net/about/, the official website of the New York City General Assembly, posted at http://takethesquare.net/wp-content/uploads/2011/07/Quickguidetodynamicsofpeoplesassemblies_13_6_2011.pdf, accessed on December 28, 2011.

177 "Prejudice and ideology must be left at home": Ibid. For the goal of a "new subjectivity," see Marina Sitrin, "Horizontalism," posted at http://marinasitrin.com/?page_id=108, accessed on January 1, 2012.

178 "If you want to see what real democracy, run horizontally, with full participation, looks like": GE, "News from the Front," posted at the 16beaver website, http://www.16beavergroup.org/journalisms09.23.11.htm, accessed on December 27, 2011.

178 "There is an energy and an amazing consensus process": DG, "Some Impressions from Saturday and Monday," posted at the 16beaver website, http://www.16beavergroup.org/journalisms09.23.11.htm, accessed on December 27, 2011.

179 "a much slower, painstaking struggle of creating alternative institutions": David Graeber, "Revolution in Reverse," in *Revolutions in Reverse: Essays on Politics, Violence, Art, and Imagination* (London: Minor Compositions/Autonomedia, 2011), 64.

179–80 the creation of an *indirect* democracy, much more intricate and extensive than the Spokes Council: Perhaps the most interesting effort to imagine such a national form of participatory democracy remains that of G. D. H. Cole, whose vision of Guild Socialism was informed by the experience of anarchosyndicalism as well as the theories of Rousseau.

180 "the most important negative liberties we have enjoyed since the end of the ancient world": Hannah Arendt, *On Revolution* (New York: Viking, 1963), 284.

181 Instead of single-mindedly pursuing a new form of "collective thinking": See John Gray, *Two Faces of Liberalism* (New York: New Press, 2000), who has come to a similar conclusion. Similar arguments appear in the work of William Galston, Bernard Williams, and Judith Shklar. My own views have been even more deeply shaped by the example of Montaigne, which I briefly describe in *Examined Lives* (New York: Farrar, Straus and Giroux, 2011).

181 "It is a way to create one, fleeting moment": Graeber, *Direct Action*, 407.

182 "the law of group polarization": Cass R. Sunstein, "The Law of Group Polarization," John M. Olin Law & Economics Working Paper No. 91, available at http://www.law.uchicago.edu/lawecon/workingpapers.

Robert M. Buckley / The Arc of Communism: Lessons for Occupy Wall Street?

185 erupted in often violent protests: Jonathan Sperber, *The European Revolutions, 1848–1851* (Cambridge: Cambridge University Press, 2005), 1.

185 "the springtime of the peoples": John Merriman, *A History of Modern Europe: From the French Revolution to the Present* (New York: W. W. Norton, 1996), 715.

186 some crushed by tanks: Grazina Miniotaite, *Nonviolent Resistance in Lithuania: A Story of Peaceful Liberation* (Boston: Albert Einstein Institution, 2002).

187 the plight of the poor: Daron Acemoglu and James A. Robinson, "Why Did the West Extend the Franchise? Democracy, Inequality and Growth in Historical Perspective," *Quarterly Journal of Economics* 115 (November 2000): 1167–99.

187 "which would eviscerate old Paris neighborhoods": Colin Jones, *Paris: The Biography of a City* (New York: Viking, 2005), 318 n. 1.

187 more died in the 1871 event: Donny Gluckstein, *The Paris Commune: A Revolution in Democracy* (Chicago: Haymarket Books, 2011), 162.

188 "The obligation to share in public": Edmund Wilson, *To the Finland Station* (New York: NYRB Classics, 2003), 278.

188 while the moment may have passed: Acemoglu and Robinson, "Why Did the West Extend the Franchise?," *Quarterly Journal of Economics* 115 (November 2000): 1167–99.

188 The result of this enfranchisement: In England, which has the best data on income distribution for the nineteenth century, the Gini coefficient increased from about 0.40 in the 1820s to a level of 0.62 in 1871.

188 measure of inequality...in the United States today: Gini figures are from the World Bank and/or the U.S. Census Bureau, and unless otherwise noted are for the most recent dates.

189 "What succumbed in these defeats": Francis Wheen, *Karl Marx: A Life* (New York: W. W. Norton, 2000), 156–57.

189 not a bad deal: Angus Maddison, *The World Economy: A Millennial Perspective* (Paris: OECD, 2001), chapter 1.

189 one of the most influential books ever published: Wheen, *Karl Marx*, 113.

190 U.S. after-tax income distribution is significantly more regressive: Sidney Weintraub, "U.S. Tolerance of Income Inequality," Center for Strategic and International Studies Working Paper, no. 121, January 2010.

190 becoming Gordon Gekko: Tyler Cowen, *Marginal Revolution Blog*, December 17, 2011; and Tyler Cowen, "Why Is Income Inequality in America So Pronounced? Consider Education," *New York Times*, May 17, 2007.

190 What Is to Be Done: The title (with a question mark at the end) of a 1902 political pamphlet Lenin wrote about what a new communist state should do; it was drawn from a novel of the same name by the Russian revolutionary Nikolai Chernyshevsky (1828–1889).

191 increase regulatory oversight: Deniz Igan and Prachi Mishra, "Making Friends," *Finance & Development* 48, no. 2 (June 2011): 27–29, discuss how regulations are "purchased," while Miret Padovani and Rajna Gibson Brandon, "The Determinants of Banks' Lobbying Activities," *Swiss Finance Institute Research Papers*, no. 11-56, November 2011, discuss the size and trends in bank lobby expenditures.

191 the United States has had one of the largest increases in corruption: Transparency International computes measures of corruption and ranks countries by these measures. The United States fell from a ranking of sixteenth least corrupt country in 2001 to twenty-fourth least corrupt in 2011. Greece and Italy had large declines over this period. Spain and Iceland experienced declines similar to the United States, with the latter declining to thirteenth and the former to thirty-first.

193 a Gini coefficient 25 percent lower than that of the United States: World Bank Development Indicators.

194 in keeping with a culture's sense of fairness: Brazil's Gini coefficient fell from 0.61 in 1998 to 0.54 in 2009, a very large drop in inequality.

194–95 almost four times that of Japan's: On South Africa, see Alan Cowell, "In Britain, Minding the Income Gap," *New York Times*, November 25, 2011. On the differences between the United States and Japan, see Thomas Piketty and Emmanuel Saez, "The Evolution of Top Incomes: A Historical and International Perspective," *American Economic Review: Papers and Proceedings* 96, no. 2 (May 2006): 200–5.

Salvador Martí Puig / "15M": The Indignados

211 "the most interesting political development since the death of Franco": Diego Beas, "How Spain's 15-M Movement Is Redefining Politics," *Guardian*, October 15, 2011.

211 the "when" can explain to a large extent the "why" and the "how": See Sidney Tarrow, *El Poder en Movimiento: Los Movimientos Sociales, la Acción Colectiva y la Política* (Madrid: Alianza Editorial, 1997).

212 the protesters called themselves the *indignados: Indignados* has been translated into English as "the outraged." The term was borrowed from the title of a pamphlet written by Stéphane Hessel, published a few months earlier in France and, against all forecasts (and to the author's surprise), a bestseller. See, in these pages, Robert Zaretsky's "From Resistance to Revolution à la française," 245–55.

212–13 Carlos Taibo…cites three main issues: Carlos Taibo, *Nada Será Como Antes: Sobre el Movimiento 15-M* (Madrid: Ediciones de la Catarata, 2011).

213 principal motives of the protesters: Kerman Calvo, Teresa Gómez-Pastrana, and Luis Mena, "Movimiento 15M: ¿Quiénes Son y qué Reivindican?," *Zoom Político* 2011/4, Laboratorio de Alternativas, Madrid.

213 "There's not enough bread for all this chorizo": In colloquial Spanish, the term *chorizo* means "thieves" — hence the play on words.

213 "Focused on robbing you": This slogan is another play on words, based on the PP's campaign slogan, *Centrados en ti* (Focused on You).

213 "Yes We Campo": This is a playful adaptation of Obama's "Yes We Can," with "campo" referring to the camps set up by the *indignados* in public squares and on avenues throughout Spain.

214 some of the reasons for the movement's longevity and reach: Calvo, Gómez-Pastrana, and Mena, "Movimiento 15M: ¿Quiénes Son y qué Reivindican?"

215 economist Albert O. Hirschman: See Albert O. Hirschman, *Retóricas de la Intransigencia* (México City, México: Fondo de Cultura Económica, 1992). Hirschman's theory contradicts, for example, that of the economist and social scientist Mancur Olson (1932–1998). See Olson's *The Logic of Collective Action: Public Goods and the Theory of*

Groups (Cambridge, MA: Harvard University Press, 1965), *The Rise and Decline of Nations* (New Haven, CT: Yale University Press, 1982), and *Power and Prosperity* (New York: Basic Books, 2000).

215 in the larger municipalities…the protest vote was even greater: Manuel Jiménez Sánchez, "¿Influyó el 15M en las Elecciones Municipales?," *Zoom Político* 2011/4, Laboratorio de Alternativas, Madrid.

Robert Zaretsky / From Resistance to Revolution à la française

245 motto of his paper: *Camus at Combat: Writing 1944–1947*, ed. Jacqueline Lévi-Valensi (Princeton, NJ: Princeton University Press, 2006), 12.

245–46 "a true democracy, freed from the reign of money": John Sweets, *The Politics of Resistance in France, 1940–1944* (DeKalb, IL: Northern Illinois University Press, 1976), 218.

246–47 "They make a favor": *Simone Weil: An Anthology*, ed. Siân Miles (New York: Weidenfeld & Nicolson, 1986), 11.

247 The Charter called for: For the text in full, see http://blogs.mediapart.fr/mot-cle/conseil-national-de-la-resistance.

248 attainment of such *droits acquis:* A comprehensive discussion can be found in Maurice Larkin, *France Since the Popular Front* (New York: Oxford University Press, 1988), 128–32.

248 the Gestapo soon captured and tortured Hessel: Stéphane Hessel, *Danse avec le siècle* (Paris: Seuil, 2007).

250 "anger at injustice still intact": See http://blogs.mediapart.fr/mot-cle/conseil-national-de-la-resistance.

250 "at the final stage where the end is not far": Stéphane Hessel, *Indignez-vous!* (Montpellier: Editions Indigène, 2010), 1.

252 "those who made me dream of another destiny": See http://sites.univ-provence.fr/veronis/Discours2007/transcript.php?n=Sarkozy&p=2007-01-14.

253 "militant act, a communal gesture": *Libération*, December 10, 2010.

253 "It is, instead, small books that cost 30 sous which are to be feared": Ian Davidson, *Voltaire: A Life* (New York: Pegasus, 2010).

254 an administrative Trojan horse: *Manifeste d'économistes atterrés* (Paris: Les Liens qui libèrent, 2010), 42–43.

254 a "swindle" and "disaster": Arnaud Montebourg, *Votez pour la démondialisation* (Paris: Flammarion, 2011), 29.

David Madland, Karla Walter, and Nick Bunker / Unions Build the Middle Class

273 The share of pretax income earned by the richest 1 percent: Thomas Piketty and Emmanuel Saez, "Income Inequality in the United States, 1913–1998," *Quarterly Journal of Economics* 118, no. 1 (2003): 1–39, updated to 2008 in July 2010.

Ilyana Kuziemko and Michael I. Norton / Where Is the Demand for Redistribution?

280 Research shows that Americans are united: M. I. Norton and D. Ariely, "Building a Better America—One Wealth Quintile at a Time," *Perspectives on Psychological Science* 6 (2011): 9–12.

280 few Americans reported believing that the Bush tax cuts would help: L. M. Bartels, "Homer Gets a Tax Cut: Inequality and Public Policy in the American Mind," *Perspectives on Politics* 3 (2005): 15–31.

281 far from being surprised: I. Kuziemko, R. W. Buell, T. Reich, and M. I. Norton, "Last Place Aversion: Evidence and Redistributive Implications," working paper, Princeton University, 2012.

Brandon Adams / U.S. Cultural Decline: The Overlooked Intangibles

286 entertainment and communication get "faster" every year: James Gleick, *Faster: The Acceleration of Just About Everything* (New York: Pantheon Books, 1999).

287 15 percent in the past decade: Anna Swan, "Tattoo Statistics," Associated Content (accessed August 14, 2009), http://www.associated content.com/article/31975/tattoo_statistics.html?cat=7.

287 The number of women with tattoos quadrupled between 1960 and 1980: "Infinite Tattoos Blog" (accessed August 14, 2009), http://infinitetattoos.wordpress.com/2008/07/.

287 seven of the ten women listed by the international men's monthly *FHM*: "100 Sexiest Women in the World 2008," *FHM*, July 2008.

288 from 44.8 percent in 1960 to 66 percent in 2004: "Statistics Related to Overweight and Obesity," U.S. Department of Health and Human Services (accessed August 14, 2009), http://www.win.niddk.nih.gov/publications/PDFs/stat904z.pdf.

288 By 2012, 35.7 percent of U.S. adults and 16.9 percent of children: Tara Parker-Pope, "Obesity Rates Stall in U.S. but Stay Stubbornly High," *New York Times*, January 18, 2012.

289 Francis Fukuyama argues: Francis Fukuyama, *Trust: The Social Virtues and the Creation of Prosperity* (New York: Free Press, 1995).

290 rent-seeking in the economy reached unheard-of levels: "Greed and Fear," *The Economist*, January 22, 2009.

291 In short-term interactions, people tend to defect: Robert Axelrod, *The Evolution of Cooperation* (New York: Basic Books, 1985).

292 Robert Putnam's *Bowling Alone*: Robert Putnam, *Bowling Alone: The Collapse and Revival of American Community* (New York: Simon & Schuster, 2001).

292 The psychologist Mihaly Csikszentmihalyi notes that: Mihaly Csikszentmihalyi, *Flow: The Psychology of Optimal Experience* (New York: HarperCollins, 2008).

Part III
SOLUTIONS

Kathleen Maclay / Interview with Emmanuel Saez

311 "What do you make of the Occupy Wall Street protesters' claims": Grateful acknowledgment is made to Kathleen Maclay for permission to use an abridged version of her October 7, 2011, interview with Emmanuel Saez, http://newscenter.berkeley.edu/2011/10/07/wall-street-protests-echo-researchers-findings-on-growing-income-gap/.

Peter Diamond and Emmanuel Saez / Taxing High Earnings

317 Congressional Republicans are opposed: This essay draws on our analysis in Peter Diamond and Emmanuel Saez, "The Case for a Progressive Tax: From Basic Research to Policy Recommendations," *Journal of Economic Perspectives* 25, no. 4 (2011): 165–90, DOI: 10.1257/jep.25.4.165, which contains discussion of this approach and relevant references. The authors are grateful to Henry Aaron and Janet Byrne for valuable comments on earlier drafts.

318 The U.S. government collects most of its revenue: The taxation of capital income is discussed in James Banks and Peter Diamond, "The Base for Direct Taxation," in *Dimensions of Tax Design: The Mirrlees Review*, edited by the Institute for Fiscal Studies (Oxford: Oxford University Press for the Institute for Fiscal Studies, 2010), chapter 6, 548–648; and Diamond and Saez, "The Case for a Progressive Tax."

319 the median family, with an income of $52,700: U.S. Census Bureau, "Median Household Income for States: 2007 and 2008," American Community Surveys, September 2009.

319 The share of total income going to the top 1 percent: Thomas Piketty and Emmanuel Saez, "Income Inequality in the United States, 1913–1998," *Quarterly Journal of Economics* 118, no. 1 (2003): 1–39, series updated to 2007 in August 2009; and Anthony Atkinson, Thomas Piketty, and Emmanuel Saez, "Top Incomes in the Long Run of History" (forthcoming, *Journal of Economic Literature*).

321 This ratio for a Pareto distribution: The top tail of the income distribution is closely approximated by a Pareto distribution characterized by a power law density of the form C/z^{1+a} where $a > 1$ is the Pareto parameter. Such distributions have the key property that the ratio of average income for those above a high cutoff to the cutoff is the same for all cutoffs in the top tail and equal to $a/(a - 1)$. For the U.S. economy, the cutoff for the top percentile of tax filers is approximately $400,000, and the average income for this group is approximately $1.2 million, so that the ratio equals 3 and hence $a = 1.5$.

321 This is the key remaining empirical ingredient: Formally, this elasticity is an income-weighted average of the individual elasticities across top-bracket tax filers. It is also a mix of income and substitution effects, as the reform creates both income and substitution effects in the top bracket. Emmanuel Saez ("Using Elasticities to Derive Optimal Income Tax Rates," *Review of Economic Studies* 68 [2001]: 205–29) provides an exact decomposition.

322 Thus it combines the federal income tax: Since these earners are above the maximum earnings subject to the Social Security payroll tax, that rate does not matter for this calculation.

322 The top U.S. marginal tax rate: The top tax rate is 42.5 percent for ordinary labor income when combining the top federal individual tax rate of 35 percent, uncapped Medicare taxes of 2.9 percent, and an average combined state top income tax rate of 5.86 percent and average sales tax rate of 2.32 percent. The average across states is computed using state weights equal to the fraction of filers with adjusted gross income above $200,000 who reside in the state as of 2007 (Internal Revenue Service, *Statistics of Income: Individual Income Tax Returns for Year 2007*, Publication No. 1304 [Washington, D.C.: Government Printing Press, 2009]). The 2.32 percent average sales tax rate is estimated as 40 percent of the average nominal sales tax rate across states (as the average sales tax base is about 40 percent of total personal consumption). As the 1.45 percent employer Medicare tax is deductible for both federal and state incomes taxes, and state income taxes are deductible for federal income taxes, we have $((1 - .35) \times (1 - .0586) - .0145)/(1.0145 \times 1.0232) = .575$ and hence $\tau = 42.5$ percent.

322 The literature has focused: Emmanuel Saez, Joel Slemrod, and Seth Giertz, "The Elasticity of Taxable Income with Respect to Marginal Tax Rates: A Critical Review" (forthcoming, *Journal of Economic Literature*), offers a recent survey, while Slemrod, ed., *Does Atlas Shrug? The Economic Consequences of Taxing the Rich* (Cambridge: Harvard University Press, 2002), looks at studies focusing on the rich.

323 Jonathan Gruber and Saez are often cited: Jonathan Gruber and Emmanuel Saez, "The Elasticity of Taxable Income: Evidence and Implications," *Journal of Public Economics* 84 (2002): 1–32.

323 However, they also found a small elasticity: Ibid., table 9, p. 24.

324 As an illustration using the different elasticity estimates: Gruber and Saez, "The Elasticity of Taxable Income."

326 For example, weight *g* at the $1,364,000 average income: Thomas Piketty and Emmanuel Saez, "Income Inequality in the United States, 1913–1998," *Quarterly Journal of Economics* 118, no. 1 (2003): 1–39, updated to 2008 in July 2010.

328 In a model including such considerations: Thomas Piketty, Emmanuel Saez, and Stefanie Stantcheva, "Optimal Taxation of Top Labor Incomes: A Tale of Three Elasticities," NBER Working Paper No. 17616, 2011.

329 the top percentile paid 40.4 percent: Internal Revenue Service, *Statistics of Income: Individual Income Tax Returns for Year 2007.*

329 increasing the average tax rate on the top percentile from 22.4 percent: In 2007, the top percentile of income earners paid $450 billion in federal individual taxes (Internal Revenue Service, 2009, *Statistics of Income: Individual Income Tax Returns for Year 2007*), or 3.2 percent of the $14,078 billion in GDP for 2007. Hence, increasing the average tax rate on the top percentile from 22.4 to 29.4 percent would raise $141 billion, or 1 percent of GDP.

329 increasing the average tax rate of the top percentile to 43.5 percent: The average federal individual tax rate paid by the top percentile was 25.7 percent in 1970 (Thomas Piketty and Emmanuel Saez, "How Progressive Is the U.S. Federal Tax System? A Historical and International Perspective," *Journal of Economic Perspectives* 21, no. 1 [2007]: 3–24) and 22.4 percent in 2007 (Internal Revenue Service, *Statistics of Income: Individual Income Tax Returns for Year 2007*). The overall average federal individual tax rate was 12.5 percent in 1970 and 12.7 percent in 2007. The pretax income share for the top percentile of tax filers was 9 percent in 1970 and 23.5 percent in 2007. Hence, the top 1 percent after-tax income share was 7.6% = 9%*(1 – 0.257)/(1 – 0.125) in 1970 and 20.9% = 23.5% x (1 – 0.224)/(1 – 0.127) in 2007, and would have been 16.1% = 23.5% x (1 – 0.435)/(1 – 0.177) with a tax rate of 43.5 percent on the top percentile (which would increase the average tax rate to 17.7 percent).

J. Bradford DeLong / Commentary

330 Peter Diamond and Emmanuel Saez argue in the previous essay: Grateful acknowledgment is made to J. Bradford DeLong for permission to use a slightly modified version of his December 1, 2011, blog post, "The 70% Solution: Taxing the Rich Department," http://delong.typepad.com/sdj/2011/12/the-70-solution-taxing -the-rich-department.html.

Martin Wolf / Reforming Western Capitalism

336 "Reforming Western Capitalism": An earlier version of this piece appeared as "Seven Ways to Fix the System's Flaws," *Financial Times,* January 22, 2012, http://blogs.ft.com/martin-wolf-exchange/ category/us/.

341 A fourth, as the UK's independent commission on banking has recommended: Independent Commission on Banking, Final Report,

September 2011, http://www.ecgi.org/documents/icb_final_report _12sep2011.pdf.

342 high-income countries have seen a marked rise in inequality over the past three decades: "Growing Unequal? Income Distribution and Poverty in OECD Countries," 2011, http://www.oecd.org/docu ment/4/0,3343,en_2649_33933_41460917_1_1_1_1,00.html.

Joel Bakan / Psychopaths, Inc.: On Corporate Personhood

353 The bizarre notion that corporations are "persons": Most ideas and some key passages in this essay are based on passages in my book *The Corporation: The Pathological Pursuit of Profit and Power* (New York: Free Press, 2004); one or two passages draw on my *Childhood Under Siege: How Big Business Targets Children* (New York: Free Press, 2011).

353 Senators Bernie Sanders (I-VT) and Mark Begich (D-AK): Senate Joint Resolution 33; see http://thehill.com/images/stories/blogs/ flooraction/Jan2011/sjres33.pdf.

355 Sixty-one percent of the Roberts court's decisions: Lee Epstein, William M. Landes, and Richard A. Posner, "Is the Roberts Court Pro-Business?," December 17, 2010, http://epstein.usc.edu/research/ RobertsBusiness.pdf; see also Adam Liptak, "Justices Offer Receptive Ear to Business Interests," *New York Times*, December 18, 2010.

355 "The Roberts Court is undeniably conservative": ACLU, "Supreme Court Ends Pro-Business Term with Important First Amendment Rulings," www.aclu.org/organization-news-and-highlights/supreme -court-ends-pro-business-term-important-first-amendment.

359 one of the world's worst corporate criminals: Pfizer received the largest criminal fine in history, $1.3 billion. *Collins v. Pfizer Inc.*, 04-11780, U.S. District Court, District of Massachusetts. See, for instance, Cary O'Reilly, "Pfizer Pays Record $1.3 Billion Penalty for Drug Misbranding," Bloomberg, October 17, 2009.

Robert B. Reich / Occupy Democracy

362 In a December 2011 Pew Center poll: See http://www.people-press .org/2011/12/15/section-2-occupy-wall-street-and-inequality/.

Tom Verlaine / The Short Sell: An Interview with Matt Taibbi

382 Ben Bernanke has said he's sympathetic: For Federal Reserve chairman Ben Bernanke's comments, see his October 4, 2011, testimony before the Joint Economic Committee; full text at http://www .federalreserve.gov/newsevents/testimony/bernanke20111004a .htm?loc=interstitialskip. In an interview with *Fortune* magazine managing editor Andy Serwer on October 12, 2011, Citigroup CEO Vikram Pandit was asked about the protesters and replied, "I'd be

happy to talk to them anytime they want" (http://finance.fortune
.cnn.com/2011/10/12/me-and-vikram-down-by-zuccotti-park/).

385 CFED 2012 "Scorecard": For the Corporation for Economic Development, see http://assetsandopportunity.org/scorecard/.

387 Sergey Aleynikov case: See Peter Lattman, "Appeals Court Overturns Conviction of Ex-Goldman Programmer," *New York Times*, February 18, 2012," http://dealbook.nytimes.com/2012/02/17/ justice-dealt-setback-in-case-against-ex-goldman-programmer/; Azam Ahmed, "Former Goldman Programmer Gets 8-Year Jail Term for Code Theft," *New York Times*, March 18, 2011; and Matt Taibbi, *Griftopia: Bubble Machines, Vampire Squids, and the Long Con That Is Breaking America* (New York: Spiegel & Grau, 2010), 229.

390 After your vampire squid story broke: Matt Taibbi, "The Great American Bubble Machine," *Rolling Stone*, July 9, 2009.

391 *New York Times* piece about the SEC: Edward Wyatt, "SEC Is Avoiding Tough Sanctions for Large Banks," *New York Times*, February 3, 2012.

391 the case of Fabrice Tourre: See Taibbi, *Griftopia*, 235–36; Grant McCool, "Goldman's Tourre Seeks Appeal in SEC Fraud Case," Reuters, September 22, 2011.

392 Goldman/Abacus/Timberwolf: See, for example, Louise Story and Gretchen Morgenson, "SEC Case Stands Out Because It Stands Alone," *New York Times*, May 31, 2001; Narayanan Somasundaram, "Goldman Sued for $1.07 Billion Over Timberwolf CDO," Reuters, October 28, 2011.

Lawrence Weschler / Enough with Occupying Wall Street: It's Time to Start Preoccupying Wall Street

398 It is holding such truths to be self-evident: This piece was originally published on Robert Scheer's *Truthdig* website on December 9, 2011, expanding on an earlier, more concise version I published in the *Seattle Stranger* on November 22, 2011.

398 Solidarity upsurge firsthand: See Weschler, *The Passion of Poland* (New York: Pantheon, 1984).

399 imagine its full eradication: See, in this context, the preface to *Revolutions in Reverse: Essays on Politics, Violence, Art and the Imagination* (New York and London: Minor Compositions/Autonomedia, 2011), a collection of essays from the 2004–2010 period by one of the principal theorists and tacticians behind what would become OWS, David Graeber.

How was it, then, that everything suddenly opened up once again, in terms of political possibility, early in the summer of 2011? The answer, of course, is that it didn't just suddenly open up. The opening was the result of thousands of hours of often seemingly

hopeless trenchwork by activists like Graeber, but they will be the
first to tell you (as Graeber himself *has* told me, as the Polish activists before him told me, and as have so many other such activists
around the world, across so many of my other similar reporting
stints) that they have no idea why, at this particular moment, things
finally clicked into focus when they hadn't before. As with any work
of the imagination, after all that preparation, there is something
else, something one is almost tempted to call *grace*. Its coming is one
of the recurrent and abiding mysteries at the heart of history.

404 Why not, say, on November 1, 2012: In this context, see Bill
Zimmerman, *Troublemaker* (New York: Doubleday, 2011).

405 sheer scale of individual indebtedness: "In the United States, student
debt has outstripped credit card debt, nervously edging toward the
one trillion dollar mark....Facing one of the highest rates of unemployment in recent times, an unprecedented two-thirds of 2010
graduates in the U.S. held debts above the $25,000 mark. Moreover,
the number of graduates carrying debt from the more draconian private loans schemes leapt from just over 930,000 in 2003–04 to
slightly under 3 million in 2007–08, and (leaving aside federal loans)
is currently estimated at around six billion dollars" (Angela Mitropoulos, "Trading Futures, Consolidating Student Debt," *Mute: Culture and Politics on the Web*, December 20, 2011).

405 precise terms of the respective demands: See Christopher Ketchem's
cover story, "Stop Payment! A Homeowner's Revolt Against the
Banks," in the January 2012 *Harper's* magazine. Ketchem anato-
mizes the notorious robo-signing scandal. At the height of the
housing bubble, with banks and mortgage firms locking in subprime loans like crazy and pushing said loans out the back door
almost as fast by slicing and dicing them into millions of little
bundled subpieces, the banks dispensed with normal due diligence
with regard to title, which in turn would have had them depositing
said titles, alongside the adjacent promissory notes, in the conventional time-honored way, with county clerks across the country.
Instead, they had recourse to their own brand-new for-profit corporation, the Mortgage Electronic Registration System (MERS),
founded in 1995, which rather quickly got into the habit of simply
stripping out the promissory note and dispensing with title altogether. As a result, it turns out that many, if not most, if not all, of
the underwater mortgages (and many that aren't underwater, and in
fact most any otherwise solid mortgages that have been refinanced
in the years since 1995, or even just changed their servicing bank—
any, that is, that have the acronym MERS feathered into the paper
trail of their oft-sliced-up promissory note, which is to say just
about all of them) are in fact illegal. The bank that one sends one's

mortgage payment to each month is in all likelihood just servicing the otherwise sliced-and-diced note (it doesn't have a clue where the title is). Some lawyers and former mortgage salespeople and other such entrepreneurs have begun setting up for-profit consultancies that will, for a fee, research any individual mortgage holder's situation and take the bank to court, demanding to see the title and, failing that, insisting that the mortgage holder no longer needs to pay any of his demonstrably unbacked loan: the house should simply be declared his. Many judges—by no means all, but enough to make things very interesting—have been going along with this gambit.

This is the unholy mess that a consortium of state attorneys general—led by those in Nevada, New York, and a few other states—have been pressing the banks over, seeking some sort of grand settlement that might also help force a fairer renegotiation of terms for those with underwater loans.

407 You mean…: See James Surowiecki, Financial Page, *The New Yorker*, December 19, 2011.

408 Were sufficient signatures to be gathered: The most disconcerting critique of this proposal that I have heard—apart from the sheer scale of the organizing effort involved, and the responsibility for people's lives and livelihoods that organizers would need to realize they were taking on—is the suggestion that bankers just might not care. As noted above, most banks don't actually own the mortgages they are currently servicing (though, on the other hand, as a group they are deeply invested in the wider paper the regular payments on those sliced-and-diced mortgages help sustain). Many of the mortgages are backed by Freddie Mac and Fannie Mae, which is to say the federal government, and bankers might be willing to just pass the massive headache on down the line (with no guarantee that the Obama administration would do anything to push back: indeed, we are far from having any such guarantee, alas). One lawyer even suggested to me that the banks might see any such developing movement as a further moneymaking opportunity, diving back into the Wall Street casino and betting against themselves by shorting their own stock, or at any rate, their portfolio of toxic mortgages.

410 collateral benefit of peeling off substantial portions of the Tea Party: It's worth recalling the first salvo in what would become the Tea Party wars, on February 19, 2009: CNBC's commentator Rick Santelli on the prospect of any federal government plan to bail out underwater mortgage holders. See http://www.pensitoreview.com/2011/10/11/the-true-tea-party-history-first-protests-were-over-a-govt-plan-to-help-underwater-homeownerster-homeo-febover-opposition-to-helping/.

It's difficult to get figures on how many Tea Party members are suffering under such underwater mortgages, though one suspects quite a good number, especially since the Tea Party's corporate sponsors (the Koch brothers, Donald Trump, Rupert Murdoch, Roger Ailes, etc.) specifically targeted lower-middle-class white voters in their various birther and other campaigns aimed at delegitimizing the black president. That is, they targeted the very people who'd likely face such mortgage problems in the ensuing months.

According to the Center for Responsible Lending's "Lost Ground, 2011" report, surveying only those mortgages originally taken out at the height of the bubble, between 2004 and 2008, African American borrowers had already lost almost 400,000 homes to foreclosure, and Latinos another 635,000 (1.5 million whites lost their homes during the same period). Furthermore, as of the publication of the report, 25 percent each of Latino and African American mortgage holders had homes either already lost or at serious risk of foreclosure, compared to "only" 12 percent among whites; not surprising since, earlier, African Americans had been 2.8 times more likely to be targeted for a predatory subprime loan than whites (Latinos were 2.2 times more likely to receive the same treatment). African Americans with good credit ratings had been 3 times more likely to be steered toward such predatory subprime loans than whites (Latinos, 1.7 times). Twenty percent of those living in high-risk neighborhoods have already been foreclosed upon or are at imminent risk of same. See http://www.responsiblelending.org/mortgage -lending/tools-resources/foreclosure-damage-index.html.

Similar figures could be marshaled for the student loan market. Mitropoulos notes, "The biggest increase in student debt has been in the subprime market. That is, private loans for smaller initial debts bearing more onerous conditions: over half of such loans are for attendance at institutions charging less than ten thousand dollars; they have few, if any, provisions for hardship; interest rates are not fixed, and they are almost impossible to discharge. That the expansion of student debt has been a lever for the increasing enrollment of poorer students is indicated by the rise in the numbers of African American undergraduates taking out private loans, quadrupling between 2003–04 and 2007–08. Some of this went to supplementing insufficient federal loans, a further index of rising costs and declining incomes."

410 the time to be doing so is now: On November 22, 2011, the New York chapter of OWS announced the launch of Occupy Student Debt (http://occupystudentdebt.com), which in turn announced the launch of a campaign to get student debtors to sign a pledge to the effect that once a million fellow debtors had signed on, they would

all stop paying their loans simultaneously. At least in the early phases of that effort, the going was slow, and only three thousand had signed the pledge by early January 2012.

Meanwhile, OWS and many of its far-flung allies (National People's Action, Right to the City, the New Bottom Line coalition, some of the successor organizations to what was once the ACORN coalition, etc.) were experimenting with a variety of responses to the home foreclosure crisis, among them eviction defense, in which dozens of similarly threatened homeowners set up phone trees and other social media networks to ensure that when any one of their homes is faced with an immediate threat, all the others will show up to defend it. Activists are also reoccupying empty foreclosed homes. In general, they are trying to find ways to gum up the gears of the foreclosure process, to make it more and more difficult for banks to foreclose (through neighborhood legislative initiatives to force banks to maintain abandoned foreclosed properties to an appropriate standard—or else by joining in on MERS title lawsuits and other legal challenges).

One hesitates to end on a note like this, but it's true: only time will tell.

Tyler Cowen and Veronique de Rugy / Reframing the Debate

411 Within that framework, protesters expressed unhappiness: OWS has not published a position paper, but a draft Statement of Non-Cooptation exists; see http://artsandculture.nycga.net/statement-of-non-cooptation-draft/. For an unsanctioned but seemingly representative journalistic treatment of some of the group's positions, see Alex Pareene, "A New Declaration of Independence," Salon.com, October 30, 2011, http://www.salon.com/2011/10/31/a_new_declaration_of_independence/singleton/.

412 except Norway and the Netherlands: Organisation for Economic Co-operation and Development, "OECD Health Data 2011: How Does the United States Compare," November 2011.

414 He finds that the number grew by 62.4 percent: Robert Frank, "Gauging the Pain of the Middle Class," *New York Times*, April 2, 2011.

415 Their average net worth has increased: Federal Interagency Forum on Aging-Related Statistics, *Older Americans 2010: Key Indicators of Well-Being* (updated January 14, 2011).

415 While official poverty numbers suggest: U.S. Census Bureau, Current Population Reports, *The Research Supplemental Poverty Measure: 2010* (issued November 2011).

415 those sixty-five and older have much lower poverty rates than most other demographic groups: Bruce D. Meyer and James X. Sullivan,

"Consumption and Income of the Poor Elderly Since 1960," September 20, 2010.

416 "it had ballooned to 47:1": Richard Fry, D'Vera Cohn, Gretchen Livingston, and Paul Taylor, "The Rising Age Gap in Economic Well-Being: The Old Prosper Relative to the Young," Pew Research Center, November 7, 2011, accessed December 30, 2011, http://www.pewsocialtrends.org/2011/11/07/the-rising-age-gap-in -economic-well-being/.

416 poverty has climbed: Jeffrey Thompson and Timothy Smeeding, "Inequality in the Great Recession—The Case of the United States," *FRDB International Income Inequality Project*, July 19, 2011.

417 the top 1 percent also comprises realtors, lawyers, doctors: Jon M. Bakija, Adam J. Cole, and Bradley T. Heim, "Jobs and Income Growth: Growth of Top Earners and the Causes of Changing Income Inequality: Evidence from U.S. Tax Return Data," November 2010.

418 hardly a story of villains: Matt Yglesias, "Blame Ikea and H&M for Inequality," Slate.com, December 14, 2011.

418 causes that are difficult to remedy: Scott Winship, from the Brookings Institution, explained on March 20, 2011, on his blog that once we correct for the permanent shift in reported income in the United States after the 1986 tax reform, the rising income share of the top 1 percent is similarly found in most developed economies. That means there are common factors at work across national boundaries. See his blog entry "What Would It Mean for Theories of U.S. Income Inequality Growth If the U.S Experience Has Been Similar to That Everywhere Else?," accessed December 30, 2011, http://www.scottwinship.com/1/post/2011/03/what-would-it-mean-for -theories-of-us-income-inequality-growth-if-the-us-experience -has-been-similar-to-that-everywhere-else.html.

418–19 the top 10 percent of households in the United States pays: Organisation for Economic Co-operation and Development, *Growing Unequal? Income Distribution and Poverty in OECD Countries* (October 2008).

419 reflects the greater role played in the tax system: Ibid., 104–6.

419 increase in marginal rates of taxation: Peter Diamond and Emmanuel Saez, "The Case for a Progressive Tax: From Basic Research to Policy Recommendations," *Journal of Economic Perspectives* 25, no. 4 (2011): 165–90. See also Thomas Piketty and Emmanuel Saez, "How Progressive Is the U.S. Federal Tax System? A Historical and International Perspective," *Journal of Economic Perspectives* 21, no. 1 (2007): 3–24.

419 "In a model that includes human capital": Michael P. Keane, "Labor Supply and Taxes: A Survey," *Journal of Economic Literature* 49, no. 4 (2011): 961–1075.

420 Another recommendation of many commentators: Diamond and Saez, "The Case for a Progressive Tax," 165–90.

421 less-well-educated groups have gained more leisure time: Mark Aguiar and Erik Hurst, "Measuring Trends in Leisure: The Allocation of Time over Five Decades" (Working Paper 06-2, January 2006, Federal Reserve Bank of Boston), accessed December 30, 2011, http://www.bos.frb.org/economic/wp/wp2006 /wp0602.pdf.

Jeff Madrick / Medicare for All

426 Democratic pollster Stan Greenberg: "Consider a [2010] survey... conducted by the Democratic pollster Stan Greenberg for the liberal Campaign for America's Future, which the group has cited to buttress its case that voters are prone to accept liberal arguments. Even in this poll, 76 percent of voters agreed that the top priority in Washington should be to 'reduce the size of government and the deficit.' And a plurality of voters (50 percent) said they were more worried about government spending and taxes than they were about government failing to invest in job creation" (Matt Bai, "Pat-Down Dispute Shows Mistrust of Government," November 23, 2010, *New York Times*, http://www.nytimes.com/2010/11/24/us/politics/24bai.html).

433 On a per capita basis, America spends 50 percent more: See http://www.kff.org/insurance/snapshot/oecd042111.cfm.

433 The Congressional Budget Office has estimated: See http://www.cbo.gov/ftpdocs/87xx/doc8758/maintext.3.1.shtml.

435 H.R. 676: See http://johnconyers.com/hr676text.

Michelle J. White and Wenli Li / How Bankruptcy Contributed to the Mortgage Crisis and How It Could Help the Economy Recover

456 Among mortgages that originated during the housing bubble: Debbie Bocian, Wei Li, Carolina Reid, and Roberto G. Quercia, "Lost Ground, 2011: Disparities in Mortgage Lending and Foreclosures," Center for Responsible Lending, November 2011.

457 still falling in fifteen of twenty metropolitan areas: Data from the S&P/Case-Shiller index of home values for the end of September 2011.

458 lenders rarely do so: The Home Affordable Refinance Program modified 390,000 mortgages between early 2009 and July 2010 but was expected to modify three to four million during that period ("Times Topics: Obama Housing Plan," *New York Times*, January 5, 2012).

459 Other hurdles were also put in place: Stephen R. Elias, *The New Bankruptcy: Will It Work for You?* (Berkeley, CA: Nolo Press, 2011).

459 The number of additional mortgage defaults was 225,000: Wenli Li, Michelle J. White, and Ning Zhu, "Did Bankruptcy Reform Cause Mortgage Defaults to Rise?" *American Economic Journal: Economic Policy* 3, no. 4 (2011): 123–47.

460 A version of this change: H.R. 200, 111th Congress, 1st Session (2009).

460 little difference between the availability and terms of mortgage loans: Adam J. Levitin, "Resolving the Foreclosure Crisis: Modification of Mortgages in Bankruptcy," *Wisconsin Law Review*, 2009, 565–655, http://papers.ssrn.com/sol3/papers.cfm?abstract_id=1071931.

461 lenders' losses are in fact smaller when mortgages in default are modified: Ibid.

Jeffrey D. Sachs / Occupy Global Capitalism

473 While there is no single platform: Some of the programmatic details for the specific case of the United States can be found in my book *The Price of Civilization.*

Michael Hudson / Debt Jubilee

475 edited and expanded upon: For a fuller version of these proposals, see http://michael-hudson.com/2011/11/reforming-the-u-s-financial-and-tax-system/, where the radio broadcast can also be accessed.

475 In Russia and Japan: The logic for a public banking option is the same as for governments providing free roads: the aim is to minimize the cost of living and doing business. Simon Patten, the first professor of economics at the Wharton Business School, spelled out the logic of public infrastructure as a "fourth" factor of production, alongside labor, capital, and land (see http://michael-hudson.com/2011/10/simon-patten-on-public-infrastructure-and-economic-rent-capture/). Its productivity is to be measured not by how much profit it makes but by how much it lowers the economy's price structure.

479 As part of the rules to define what constitutes "fraudulent" or irresponsible lending: The problem with debt write-downs, of course, is that when you cancel a debt, you also cancel some party's savings on the other side of the balance sheet. In this case, the banks would have to give up their claims.

Credits

Grateful acknowledgment is made to the following authors and to *The New Yorker*, *Tom Dispatch*, *Al Jazeera*, *Truthdig*, and *Bloomberg News*, where eight of the pieces in this collection originally appeared, most in slightly different form. John Cassidy, "What Good Is Wall Street?," originally published in *The New Yorker*, November 29, 2010: Copyright © 2010 by John Cassidy, used by permission of The Wylie Agency LLC. Barbara Ehrenreich and John Ehrenreich, "The Making of the American 99 Percent and the Collapse of the Middle Class," originally published in *Tom Dispatch*, December 15, 2011: Copyright © 2011 by Barbara Ehrenreich and John Ehrenreich, used by permission of the authors and International Creative Management. David Graeber, "Occupy Wall Street's Anarchist Roots," originally published in *Al Jazeera*, November 30, 2011: Copyright © 2012 by David Graeber, used by permission of the author and Trident Media Group. Chris Hedges, "A Master Class in Occupation," originally published in *Truthdig*, October 31, 2011: Copyright © 2011 by Chris Hedges, used by permission of the author, International Creative Management, and *Truthdig*. Michael Lewis, "Advice from the 1%: Lever Up, Drop Out," originally published by *Bloomberg News*, December 4, 2011: Copyright © 2011 by Michael Lewis, used by permission of the author. Rebecca Solnit, "Civil Society at

(*Brian Stanton*)

Janet Byrne is an editor who has worked with Nobel Prize–winning economists, Pulitzer Prize–winning writers, and leading political figures, financial journalists, academics, and bestselling authors. She is the author of *A Genius for Living: The Life of Frieda Lawrence*, a *New York Times* Notable Book, has served as a researcher for and as a contributor to numerous books, and has written for the *New York Times* and the *Wall Street Journal*. She lives in Bucks County, Pennsylvania.